# JOURNEY TO AVALON

## The Final Discovery of King Arthur

## Chris Barber
## & David Pykitt

SAMUEL WEISER, INC.

York Beach, Maine

First published in 1997 by
Samuel Weiser, Inc.
P.O. Box 612
York Beach, ME 03910-0612

Library of Congress Cataloging-in-Publication Data
Barber, Chris.
    Journey to Avalon: the final discovery of King Arthur / Chris Barber and David Pykitt.
        p.  cm.
    Includes bibliographical references (p.     ) and index.
    ISBN 1-57863-024-X (alk. paper)
        1. Arthur, King. 2. Christian saints—France—Brittany—Legends. 3. Brittany (France)—Antiquities, Celtic. 4. Britons—Kings and rulers—Folklore. 5. Great Britain—History—To 1066. 6. Wales—Antiquities, Celtic. 7. Armel, Saint, 482–552. 8. Britons—History. I. Pykitt, David. II. Title.
        [DA152.5.A7B35   1997]
        942.01′4—dc21                                                            97-17273
                                                                                      CIP

MG
Typeset in Sabon

Cover photograph: Bardsey Island, Britain's most romantic island, the true site of Avalon.
Back cover photograph is a stained glass window in the church of St. Armel-des-Boschaux, depicting the funeral of St. Armel (King Arthur).

Cover and interior photographs © 1997 Chris Barber FRGS

Printed in the United States of America

04  03  02  01  00  99  98  97
10  9  8  7  6  5  4  3  2  1

The paper used in this publication meets all the minimum requirements of the American National Standard for Permanence of Paper for Printed Library Materials Z39.48–1984.

This book is dedicated to the memory of the late Emrys George Bowen (1900–1983), Professor of Geography at the University College of Wales, Aberystwyth, whose work has inspired us to follow in the footsteps of the Celtic saints in our search for the true identity of King Arthur.

# CONTENTS

# iLLUSTRATiONS

# acknowledgments

We are grateful to numerous scholars whose considerable knowledge has been indispensable for our research and give particular thanks to the following:

Dr. Rachel Bromwich of Aberystwyth; Dr. Brynley F. Roberts, Librarian, National Library of Wales; Mr. D. B. Lloyd, Secretary of the National Library of Wales; Richard H. Lewis, Assistant Librarian, National Library of Wales; John Kenyon, Librarian, National Museum of Wales; Mrs. Enid Nixon, Assistant Librarian, Westminster Abbey; Mr. R. J. H. Hill, Reference Librarian, Hereford City Library; Mrs. Dowdle, Assistant Librarian, Gloucester City Library; Mr. P. J. Phillips and Mr. J. B. Jones, Cardiff Central Library; Ann Gallagher, University College of Wales Library, Swansea; Mrs. Barber, Truro County Reference Library; Mrs. Pauline Thomson, Assistant Librarian, The William Salt Library, Stafford; Mrs. Jennifer Smallman, Assistant Librarian, Ludlow Library; the staff of University of Birmingham Library, Birmingham City Library, Cambridge University Library, Cardiff City Library, Burton-on-Trent Library, Lichfield Library, Derby Local Studies; Mr. Walrond, Curator, Stroud Museum; Michael Williams, Bossiney Books, St. Teath, Bodmin, Cornwall; Chris Shepard of Needwood Bookshop, Burton-on-Trent; the staff of Byrkley Books, Burton-on-Trent, Bookstall Services, Derby, Fagin's Bookshop, Derby, Laura's Bookshop, Derby, Hornby's Bookshop, Birmingham, Dillon's Bookshop, Birmingham; John D. Austin of Arden House, Atherstone; Rev. A. Caldwell, Atherstone; Ray Tarr, St. David's Cathedral; Rev. Edwin Thomas Richards of Llangammarch Wells; Canon Raymond Lockwood Ravenscroft, Probus, Truro, Cornwall; Rev. Russen William Thomas, Stratton, Cornwall; Rev. Michael Mountney, Whitchurch, Herefordshire; Norman Stubbs of Alrewas; Chris Lovegrove, Kate Pollard, Eddie Tooke and Fred Stedman-Jones of the Pendragon Society; Charles Evans-Gunther of the Dragon Society; Elizabeth Leader, Patrick Graucob, Brian and Joyce Hargreaves of the Research into Lost Knowledge Organization; Arthur Stelfox, Robert Hardwick, Dave Pauley, George Perrell and our many friends and colleagues who have helped in various ways. Our gratitude is also extended to Dr. Ruth Williams, who made useful comments on the final draft of the manuscript.

*This Arthur of whom the idle tales of the Britons rave even to this day is a man worthy to be celebrated not in the foolish dreams of the deceitful fables, but in truthful histories. For long he sustained the declining fortunes of his native land, and roused the uncrushed spirit of the people to war . . .*

—William of Malmesbury[*]
*History of the Kings of England,* 1125

[*]William of Malmesbury: *The Kings Before the Norman Conquest,* translated from the Latin by Joseph Stephenson (Felinfach, Lampeter, Dyfed, Wales: Llanerch, 1989), p.11.

# INTRODUCTION

The quest for the truth about King Arthur is one of the most popular literary subjects in the world. New books are published about this sixth-century hero virtually every month and his name crops up on the radio, on television, and in the newspapers almost every day. However, the majority of writers continually go over the same old ground with the result that most people are firmly convinced that the long-sought solution to this mixture of legend and history is an impossible goal.

In this book, we have set out to reveal the truth about King Arthur by following a new approach to the mystery. Through an extensive program of prolonged and painstaking research, we have assembled a massive jigsaw puzzle of interconnecting identifications and information which throws new light on the history of Dark Age Britain.

Through the passing centuries, the so-called "Dark Ages" have become obscured, largely because manuscripts have been lost, destroyed, or censored and certain semi-historical records ridiculed. Some self-proclaimed experts have even gone so far as to declare that King Arthur did not exist. On the other hand, there are also numerous historians who are fairly certain that he was a real person whose identity has been confused because he has become a composite of several historical figures.

In order to set the scene, it is necessary to start by considering the legend of King Arthur. This means that we must first look at the work of Geoffrey of Monmouth, the 12th-century chronicler who wrote *The History of the Kings of Britain*. He was the first widely read writer to reveal to the world the story of the heroic King Arthur.

Beavering away at his manuscript probably in Oxford, Geoffrey provided us with a book of riddles. He produced a web of muddled clues, which for centuries have baffled scholars in many lands searching for a solution to the age-old mystery of King Arthur. *Historia Regum Britanniae*, to give the work its Latin name, was written between 1135 and 1148 by this cleric who was really a poet posing as a historian. In his first chapter, Geoffrey tells us how he obtained his source material:

Walter, Archdeacon of Oxford, a man learned in foreign histories, offered me a very ancient book in the Brittanic
tongue, which in a continued regular story and elegant style
related the actions of them all, from Brutus down to Cadwallader. At his request, therefore, I undertook the translation of that book into Latin.[1]

For the majority of readers, the section on King Arthur is the
most interesting part of the book. We follow Arthur's career
from his birth to his accession to the throne at the age of fifteen,
to his campaigns against the Saxons, Picts and Scots—in Ireland,
Iceland, the Orkneys, Norway, Denmark, and Gaul—to the final
Battle of Camlan. Here Arthur's rival, Mordred, is killed and
Arthur himself, mortally wounded, is carried from the battlefield
and taken to the Isle of Avalon to be healed.

Arthur's exploits in all these different countries obviously
suggest a series of major errors, or perhaps a case of deliberate
exaggeration intended to make him appear an even greater hero
than he actually was. For example, we are told that when Lucius,
Emperor of Rome, demanded Arthur's submission, the British
king marched across Europe to fight the Romans. This is probably a confused memory of Magnus Maximus (known in Welsh
tradition as Macsen Wledig). Maximus was a Celt from Spain
who had arrived in Britain in about 368 and held high office. On
being declared Emperor by his loyal Roman troops in Britain in
383, Maximus crossed the sea to Gaul. The Emperor Gratian was
assassinated and Maximus, pursuing even greater ambitions,
marched his legions into Italy in 387 and threatened Rome itself,
causing the Roman Emperor Valentinian II to flee to safety. However, Maximus was betrayed at Aquilla, captured, and put to
death on 28 July, 388. It would appear that Geoffrey, either by intention or in error, took this story and attributed it to Arthur.

There are numerous instances where Geoffrey seems to have
become very confused by his muddled source material, although
it is open to conjecture whether it was by intention or design that
he wove a series of entangled misidentifications into his story. We

---

[1]Geoffrey of Monmouth, *The History of the Kings of Britain*, Lewis Thorpe,
trans. (London: Penguin, 1966), p. 51.

examine the work of Geoffrey of Monmouth in more detail in the Appendices (see pages 291–297) and endeavor to show how some of these errors came about and how, by careful deduction, some truths can be revealed.

It can be said that Geoffrey of Monmouth's book had two results—one literary and the other political. In less than half a century, the romances of King Arthur gained an extraordinary popularity, for they were circulated in France, Germany, and Italy. For six centuries after it was written, Geoffrey's work was accepted by the majority of readers as accurate history, while the medieval poets found in its content a wealth of material for poetry.

Geoffrey of Monmouth identified Caerleon-upon-Usk in Gwent as the site of one of Arthur's courts, for like Giraldus Cambrensis, writing in the same period, he was much impressed by the Roman ruins that still existed there and found no difficulty in picturing Arthur holding court there after subduing all his enemies.

> When the feast of Whitsuntide began to draw near, Arthur, who was quite overjoyed by his great success, made up his mind to hold a plenary court at that season and place the crown of the kingdom on his head. He decided, too, to summon to this feast the leaders who owed him homage, so that he could celebrate Whitsun with greater reverence and renew the closest possible pacts of peace with his chieftains. He explained to the members of his court what he was proposing to do and accepted their advice that he should carry out his plans in the City of the Legions.
>
> Situated as it is in Morgannwg (now Gwent), on the River Usk, not being far from the Severn Sea, in a most pleasant position, and being richer in material wealth than other townships, this city was eminently suitable for such a ceremony. The river which I have named flowed by it on one side, which was flanked by meadows and wooded groves, they had adorned the city with royal palaces, and by the gold-painted gables of its roofs was a match for Rome.[2]

---

[2]Geoffrey of Monmouth, *The History of the Kings of Britain*, pp. 225–226.

In due course, we shall reveal that Caerwent (Venta Silurum) was the main center of Arthur's kingdom. It seems that Geoffrey either confused Caerwent with Caerleon or that he deliberately placed Arthur's court there because of its more impressive situation.

The poet Alfred Lord Tennyson, who had obviously read Geoffrey of Monmouth's *Historia*, came to Caerleon in 1856, seeking atmosphere and inspiration for his *Idylls of the King*. He stayed in the Hanbury Arms overlooking the river and wrote, "The Usk murmurs by the windows, and I sit here like King Arthur at Caerleon."[3]

Tennyson was, of course, following in the wake of other romantic writers such as Sir Thomas Malory, whose classic *Morte d'Arthur* insured that King Arthur was firmly placed in a legendary kingdom where he was surrounded by knights clad in medieval-style armor and where anything was possible, for Merlin the Magician was always on hand to work magic.

As a result, the story of King Arthur, for the majority of people, is represented by a romantic tale which concerns Uther Pendragon's illegitimate son who is born at Tintagel Castle in Cornwall. When he is a young man, he passes a supreme test by pulling a gleaming sword out of a stone and is consequently elected King of the Britons. He marries the beautiful Guinevere and they live in regal splendor at the magnificent court of Camelot. Here Arthur is surrounded by his followers, who all wear shining armor and are known as the "Knights of the Round Table." They ride off on dangerous missions to fight battles, kill giants and dragons, rescue maidens in distress, and search for the elusive Holy Grail. Arthur, after winning many battles, grows old and, while he is absent from his kingdom, his illegitimate son, Mordred, takes up arms and challenges his authority. On receiving news of the uprising, Arthur returns and fights Mordred and his army in a bloodthirsty battle at a place called Camlan. Wielding his mighty sword, Excalibur, Arthur kills Mordred, but is himself mortally wounded. He orders his faithful knight, Sir Bedivere, to take the magic sword and throw it into a lake. A slender

---

[3]Alfred, Lord Tennyson, *Idylls of the King* (New York: Airmont, 1969).

hand rises from the water to receive Excalibur and draws it down into the depths of the lake. Arthur is then taken away by boat to the mysterious island of Avalon to have his wounds tended. He is, of course, immortal, for he does not die, but merely sleeps in a secret cave with his band of knights, awaiting the call to come to the aid of his country in a time of great danger.

Based on this romantic drama, a whole series of false statements and misidentifications have been made. These have laid down a solid foundation of misconceptions and most people who have read or had cinema or television experience of the tale of King Arthur have had such imaginitive ideas firmly implanted in their minds. For centuries, writers, poets, and historians have been trying to place the various aspects of this traditional story in romantic, dramatic, and appropriate locations. In particular, Arthur's realm has been firmly located in the West Country of Somerset, Devon, and Cornwall. His reputed birthplace is at Tintagel Castle, perched high on sea-lashed cliffs and it attracts visitors from far and wide. Cadbury Castle, an extensive Iron Age hill-fort, is said to be the site of Camelot. At Slaughter Bridge, near Camelford, Arthur is supposed to have fought the Battle of Camlan and afterward been taken away by boat to Glastonbury, which, then surrounded by water, has mistakenly been identified as the Isle of Avalon. Here, in 1191, the monks of Glastonbury completed the falsification of the story by claiming to discover the grave of Arthur and his Queen, Guinevere.

It is important to understand that these long-established pictures of Arthur and his kingdom are meaningless. He was in reality a king of the Silurian Britons and his true location was in southeast Wales. His story has been taken from this area and planted in the West Country, where it has taken firm root and formed the basis of a very profitable tourist industry.

Unfortunately, the availability of source material for the history of the centuries between 400 and 600 is sadly inadequate to satisfy the requirements of today's academics, who shake their heads and say that it is not possible to solve the mystery of King Arthur. There are problems of corrupt and fragmentary material which has to be analyzed and compared with other questionable accounts. John Morris suitably summed up the nature of such problems in his book, *The Age of Arthur*:

... the historian looking at the fifth and sixth centuries has special problems. He has no main reliable witness, like Tacitus or Bede, to justify him in dismissing other evidence as unreliable or forged. He must borrow from the techniques of the archaeologist, and must uncover a mass of separate detail, most of it encrusted and corroded by the distortion of later ages. He must clean off as much of the distortion as he can, try to discover what the original sources said and then relate their statements to one another, and to the rest of the evidence.[4]

This is precisely the approach which we have taken. Over a period of many years, we have conducted an untiring and patient research program which has enabled us to gather together the pieces of a giant jigsaw puzzle which we have completed to provide a very convincing solution to one of the world's greatest mysteries.

To begin to understand the complex matter of King Arthur, one has to be familiar with the historical literature covering this period. This includes the writings of Gildas, Bede, Nennius, Geoffrey of Monmouth, the *Ancient Charters of Llandaff*, the *Lives of the Saints*, the *Welsh Triads*, the *Mabinogion*, etc. Anyone intent on becoming an Arthurian investigator will find that such a direction involves years of patient reading, strong commitment, considerable energy, and boundless enthusiasm. It is an addictive path which many have followed, but, disappointingly, the majority of writers have either come up with the same old material presented in a different form or with a new idea which on close examination is found to be so full of holes that it leaks like the proverbial sieve.

Others simply cry, "It cannot be done—there is insufficient contemporary source material to work from," or "Arthur is just a legend—a figure of medieval romance and as a historical figure he probably never existed."

---

[4]John Morris, *The Age of Arthur* (London: Weidenfeld & Nicholson, 1973), p. xiv.

One of the major problems which we experienced in writing this book was to find a way of presenting it in a readable style for English readers who may struggle to get their tongues around the names of personalities and places of ancient Britain. In matters concerning Wales, we were reluctant to anglicize the names, for then the vital truth remains hidden. The reader must understand that this is an account of ancient Britain at the time when the same tongue was spoken from Strathclyde to Cornwall and also in Brittany, which was then known as Armorica. The only written language of those times was Latin.

Names such as Arthur, Ambrosius, Guinevere, Merlin, Lancelot, and Bedivere are familiar to most people as essential components of the traditional story of King Arthur. However, these characters were not just figments of the imagination of such writers as Thomas Malory and Alfred Lord Tennyson. The majority of them really did exist and their true names are the British or Welsh versions, which also have Latin equivalents. It must be emphasized that the matter of Arthur has become confused and muddled largely because the original names of the personalities involved have through the centuries been anglicized and altered at the whim of the romantic writers.

In order to satisfy a wide audience and to make the book more readable to those unaccustomed to Welsh names, we have compromised by using a mixture of the familiar traditional names, certain Welsh names which are more readily pronounced, and Latin equivalents where appropriate.

You are about to begin a journey through Roman and Dark Age history in search of the truth about King Arthur, a sixth-century British hero who became a legend in his own lifetime and has captured peoples' imaginations ever since.

Chris Barber
and
David Pykitt

# 1

# BRITAIN IN ROMAN TIMES

THE ROMAN OCCUPATION of Britain lasted 350 years. During this period, the native Britons were first conquered and then gradually converted to the Roman way of life. Hundreds of forts were established and more than 6,000 miles of military highways constructed which transformed the prehistoric trackway system into a highly organized network of routes of a standard neither equaled nor surpassed until comparatively modern times.

Roman forts were always built at locations which were of strategic importance. Thus Chester, Wroxeter, and Gloucester were at positions from which Wales could be invaded, and at places where the plain could be defended from the incursion of the mountain tribes. Carlisle, York, and Lincoln all controlled important routes and were vital from a military point of view. London was the center of the military system which linked with all parts of Roman Britain, and from which supplies could be obtained in times of need. Beyond the Straits of Dover, the system of roads continued with the entire European network focused on Rome, giving rise to the old saying that "all roads lead to Rome."

One of the most important forts constructed by the Romans during their conquest of Wales was at Caerleon-upon-Usk in Gwent. In A.D. 75 they raised an earthen bank and surrounded it by a moat filled with water. By A.D. 110, a turreted stone wall measuring 540 meters by 450 meters had been built to enclose an area of 20 hectares. Gradually, a very impressive fortress town was constructed with considerable quantities of stone transported from Bath by barge down the Avon, across the Severn, and up the Usk.

*Figure 1. A view toward Caerleon-upon-Usk and the Wentwood escarpment in Gwent, an area which is the true land of King Arthur—the hereditary ruler of the Silurian Britons in the sixth century.*

*Figure 2. In the center of Caerleon is a museum founded in 1847 by the Caerleon Antiquarian Association. Its entrance has a classical appearance, incorporating genuine Roman pillars which were previously used in the old Market House. Here the story of Roman Caerleon is told in displays of inscribed stones, excavated artifacts, and artists' reconstructions.*

The Second Augustan Legion was stationed here with Julius Frontinus commanding the garrison, which in its heyday consisted of some 6,000 men. This particular legion was a highly trained force which had been brought here to deal with the difficult problem of subduing the Silures, who inhabited this area and were led in battle by the brave Celtic king, Caratacus.

Caer Wysg (Fortress on the Usk) is the ancient name for the settlement, which was a center of trade used by the Britons long before the Romans arrived. But when the Romans settled here, they abolished the old British name and their new fort became known as Isca Silurum. They named it Isca after the River Usk, near which it stands, and Silurum after the local tribe to whom they referred as Silures. This was one of three legionary

Figure 3. In the porch of Caerwent Church can be seen an inscribed stone which is of particular interest, for it bears a Latin inscription recording the setting up of a statue to Tiberius Claudius Paulinus by decree of the tribal senate, by the "commonwealth of the Silures." It dates from 220 and the reference to "the commonwealth of the Silures" confirms the importance of this Celtic tribe in this locality. The Romans never succeeded in fully subjugating the Silures and eventually a compromise had to be reached which resulted in the establishment of the Roman Republic of the Silures. Disarmed, the tribe was allowed to flourish and their territory expanded to Pencraig in the east and Moccas in the north, reaching within a few kilometers of Hereford. The Roman Republic of the Silures also included large parts of Gwent and extended west into Glamorgan and east into Gloucestershire.

fortresses established in Roman Britain and it was their chief city in South Wales.

The name Caerleon is a Welsh rendering of Castra Legionum and the abbreviated title of the Legion's name—LEG II AVG has been found stamped on countless bricks uncovered during many years of archaeological excavation. When Giraldus Cambrensis (Gerald of Wales) came here in 1190, the Roman remains were still very impressive and he described them as follows:

> [A]n ancient and authentic city, excellently and well built in olden times by the Romans. Many vestiges of its former splendour may yet be seen, mighty and huge palaces with gilded roofs in imitation of Roman magnificence . . . a town prodigious in size, wonderful bath buildings, the remains of temples and theatres, all enclosed within fine walls, which are yet partly standing. You will find on all sides, both within and without the circuit of the walls, subterraneous buildings, water-pipes, and underground passages, and, more remarkable than all, stoves contrived with wonderful art to transmit the heat insensibly through the narrow flues up the side of the walls.[1]

In sunshine, Caerleon certainly became a city of gold, for the many buildings were roofed with glazed brown tiles which caught and reflected the rays of the sun. Venta Silurum (Caerwent), just 13 kilometers away, must have been eclipsed by the rising splendor of Isca Silurum, which became the chief station of Britannia Secunda. It was here that the Praetor resided, the Roman eagle was deposited, and the principal courts of justice were located.

In A.D. 77, Julius Agricola arrived on the scene and subsequently became the most famous of the governors of Britain. He immediately turned his attention to the subjugation of the Ordovices and the Deceangli, who inhabited the area we know

---

[1]Giraldus Cambrensis, *Gerald of Wales—The Journey through Wales* and *The Description of Wales* (London: Penguin, 1978), pp. 114–115.

today as Clwyd. He went on to capture Anglesey. With the conquest of Wales thus consolidated, he was able to turn his attention to the north.[2]

He established a base at Chester, which was then known as Deva, after the River Dee, and in A.D. 79 he overcame the Brigante tribe. Next he moved on to make his headquarters at Eboracum (York). From here he conducted his northern campaigns and consolidated his position with the construction of roads and a chain of forts. Eboracum became the base of the Ninth Legion and in later years it developed into the chief military center of Roman Britain, known as "Altera Rome"—the other Rome.

The Romanized capital of the Brigantes was situated about sixteen miles northwest of York and was called Insurium Brigantium. Today, the site is occupied by the village of Aldborough, which stands on the road that still marks the route followed by Agricola on his advance into Scotland. He pushed on via Stirling and Perth to reach Inchtuthill, where another important base was established. In due course, a whole chain of forts was constructed from the Firth to the Clyde and this became the northern limit of the Roman Empire. It was decided not to proceed any farther north because of the harsh mountainous terrain and the problems already experienced with the fierce Pictish tribes.

In about A.D. 121, the Emperor Hadrian visited Britain and, after taking a hard look at the problems being caused by the troublesome Picts, decided that a permanent northern frontier for his province should be established. The location which he selected was much farther south than Agricola's chain of forts; it linked the Tyne Gap from Bowness on the Solway Firth, to Wallsend on the Tyne. Known as Hadrian's Wall, this mighty example of Roman engineering, stretching across the "neck" of Britain, was built within five years. Throughout its length of nearly 112 kilometers (70 miles) it was defended by a chain of forts. At each Roman mile stood a mile-castle which provided quarters for the man on sentry duty. Two turrets were located

---

[2]Julius Agricola was appointed Governor of Britain in A.D. 78 and Tacitus, the Roman historian, was his son-in-law. His *Annals* recording the early stages of the conquest of Britain are of particular importance.

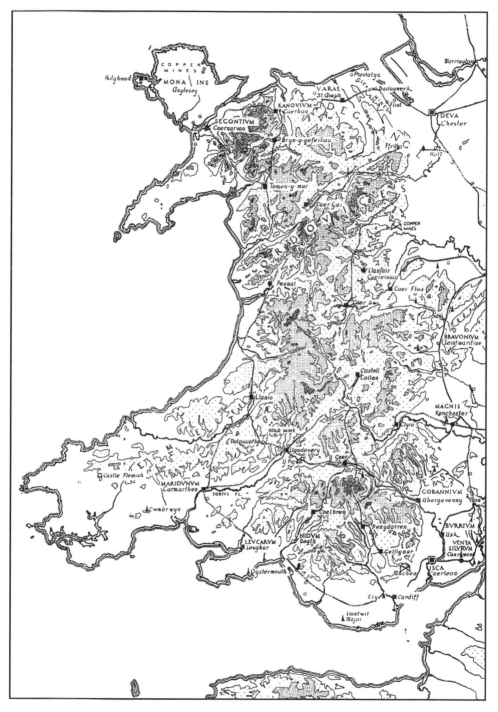

*Figure 4.  Wales in Roman times.*

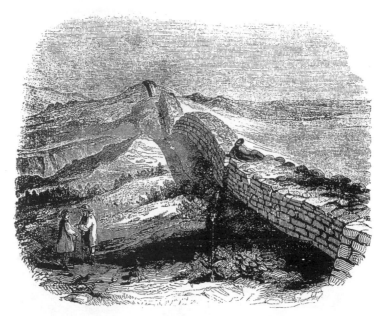

*Figure 5. Hadrian's Wall at Housteads, Northumber-
land is a 110 kilometer example of Roman engineering
which was constructed to defend the northern limits of
the Roman empire against a fierce tribe known as the
Scottis. The officer responsible for the defense of this
boundary was known as the Dux Britanniarum.*

between each mile-castle and these were used for signaling purposes. The wall was from 6 to 7 meters high and 2 to 4 meters
thick. It is one of the most impressive monuments in Britain and
perhaps the finest Roman military structure in the world.

When Antonius Pius acceded in A.D. 138, a decision was
made to establish another walled frontier farther north, along
the line of Agricola's chain of forts from the Firth to the Clyde.
This time, to speed up its construction, the defensive boundary
was built of turf instead of stone and, at 59 kilometers long, it
was half the length of Hadrian's Wall. It stretched from Old
Kirkpatrick on the Clyde to Bridgeness near Corriden on the
Forth and became known as the Antonine Wall. However, this

outer northern boundary of the Roman Empire was subsequently abandoned and left to the mercy of the threatening tribes and the destructive forces of the elements, while the legions retreated to the greater security of Hadrian's Wall.

Reinforcements were sometimes sent from Caerleon to this northern outpost. For the Second Legion this would have meant a march of nearly three hundred miles along the great Roman highways. A posting to Hadrian's Wall must have been regarded with dread, and in winter the men guarding the wall must often have felt homesick and lonely as they stared north over a bleak and mist-shrouded landscape.

The purpose of these great walls was to enable the legions to defend the northern limits of their extended empire against a fierce tribe known as the Scottis. It seems surprising today to realize that this name was originally given to the people of northern Ireland, and until the tenth century, Scotti meant Irishmen and Scotia was Ireland. The Scottis from Ulster crossed the sea in large numbers and moved into the territory which became known as Scotland. They settled along the west coast to the north of the Antonine Wall (in the area now known as Argyll) and created the kingdom of Dalriada. Settlers from Ireland also came to Wales and settled in Dyfed and South Wales, where they implanted the Irish language and founded a kingdom of their own. One band also penetrated the Welsh mountains and established a dynasty in the area which later became known as Brycheiniog (Breconshire). Evidence of the distribution of these early Irish settlers is today revealed by their Ogham inscriptions on the many memorial stones of the fifth/sixth century period which have been found in the old counties of Pembrokeshire, Carmarthenshire, and Breconshire.

In A.D. 197, the Emperor Septimus Severus divided Britain into two parts, which became known as Upper and Lower Britain. Lower Britain was in the north of the island and was divided into Britannia Secunda and Flavia Caesarentis. The south became Upper Britain and was reorganized into Britannia Prima and Maxima Caesarentis. In the north, the two new provinces had their capitals at York and Lincoln, as they are known today. Britannia Prima in the south had its capital at Cirencester and the administration center for Maxima Caesarentis was London.

It has been suggested that the Romans named the south of the country Upper Britain because this part of the island was nearest to Rome, while the territory farther away was regarded as Lower Britain.

The military command for Upper and Lower Britain was divided between three generals, who were given titles which are of particular significance, for this system of defense was continued by the Britons after the Romans departed. These titles were Comes Britanniae, Comes Litoris Saxonici, and Dux Britanniarum.

It was the Comes Britanniae (Count of Britain) who was the supreme military authority, with a roving commission to defend the country against foreign invasion. The other two were slightly subordinate officers under his command. For a long time after the departure of the Romans, the Britons kept intact the organization of defense which their conquerors had established during their years of occupation. It would seem that the position of Comes Britanniae as war leader was the same as Amherawdyr (Emperor), which is mentioned in early Welsh literature and is a title given to Arthur alone among British heroes.

When Saxon raiders began to harass the eastern shores of Britain, the Romans decided to erect a series of forts from the Wash to the Solent. These were placed under the control of an officer known as Comes Litoris Saxonici—the "Count of the Saxon Shore." He had the responsibility for guarding these coastal forts which had been erected as a bulwark against pirate raids. Saxon tribes from the Continent had plundered the British shores from the third century, but this chain of forts held them off at least until the middle of the fourth century.

The duty of the Dux Britanniarum was to guard Hadrian's Wall against the Picts and this must have been a daunting task for it was such a long frontier across the rugged Pennines. In 367, there was a particularly determined raid by the Picts and the Scots who succeeded in crossing Hadrian's Wall, while at the same time the Saxons landed on the east coast. This combined enemy force ravaged and destroyed as they advanced, causing the forces of the Count of Britain and the Count of the Saxon Shore to retreat.

Britain remained part of the Roman Empire until A.D. 410, when Rome fell into the hands of the Visigoths and the Roman legions were withdrawn from this island. The Emperor Honorius formally relinquished control of the province in a letter which informed the Britons that henceforth they would have to fend for themselves. This decision ended 367 years of Roman rule in Britain and put the island at the mercy of the Picts, Scots, Angles, Saxons, and Jutes. The Britons were beset by enemies on all sides and it was not long before Picts from the north began raiding British territory in earnest.

After nearly four centuries of Roman rule, the Britons had come to feel safe under the protection of their conquerors and it would have been quite natural for them to continue the same system of defense.

> The period which immediately succeeds the withdrawal of the Romans, and which includes the brief Celtic supremacy before the establishment of the Saxon kingdoms, is in many ways the most interesting period of our history. . . . It is the formative period which saw the birth of most of the languages, the ideals, and the traditions which still to-day predominate in the greater part of the British Isles.
>
> —Nora Chadwick[3]

[3]Nora Chadwick, *Studies in Early British History* (Cambridge: Cambridge University Press, 1954).

# 2

# IN THE WAKE OF THE
# RED DRAGON

ON A HILL OVERLOOKING Caernarfon in Gwynedd stand the ruins of Segontium, a fortress built by Agricola in A.D. 78, prior to his invasion of Anglesey. When Nennius, a priest from South Wales, compiled his *Historia Brittonum* in about 800, he included a list of twenty-eight cities; Cair Segeint (Segontium) was one of them. Evidently, the ruins of this fort must have been impressive, otherwise they would not have been worthy of a mention.

In the *Mabinogion* story titled "The Dream of Macsen Wledig," Magnus Maximus, who was known in Welsh tradition as Macsen Wledig, is explicitly associated with Segontium. This romantic tale relates how Maximus dreamed of making a journey across the sea to a land where he crossed a mountain range to reach the "fairest and most level region that any mortal had ever seen."[1] Near the mouth of a river, he came upon a castle where he observed a ceiling covered with gold and walls decorated with stones. In the great hall, he found a beautiful maiden, finely dressed and sitting in a golden chair. As in all fairy tales, he fell in love with her at first sight. Taking her in his arms, he sat down with her in the golden chair. At this point, just as the dream was getting interesting, Maximus woke up. But he could not get the beautiful girl out of his mind and he became obsessed with her memory. In due course, his quest to find her brought him to Aberseint, near the old Roman fort of Segontium in Gwynedd. Here he met the Princess Elen, who was exactly like

---

[1]Charlotte Guest, *The Mabinogion* (London: J. M. Dent & Sons, 1906).

*Figure 6. The Roman fort of Segontium was built under the governorship of Agricola in* A.D. *80 and occupied an area of 2 hectares. In the early 1920s, the site was excavated and it was revealed that, except for two long intervals, Segontium was garrisoned by Roman troops from* A.D. *80 until 383, when the last garrison was withdrawn by Magnus Maximus.*

the girl in his dreams, and they of course fell in love and married.[2]

Magnus Maximus was, in fact, a Spanish officer who came to Britain as an official in the household of Count Theodosius the Elder in 368. After the Count departed, the Picts were soon on the rampage again, but Maximus succeeded in driving them back from Hadrian's Wall and, within the new provinces of Strathclyde and Manau Guotodin, the Britons were able to live in peace. His son Antonius Donatus was made responsible for Strathclyde, while the province of Manau Guotodin was placed under the Romano-British Prince Paternus of the Red Tunic, who is remembered as the grandfather of Cunedda Wledig.

Maximus traveled south to Gwynedd to rebuild and garrison the abandoned fortress of Segontium, which became his new headquarters. While he was there, he met and married the Princess Elen. She belonged to the ruling British family whose seat was at Caer Seint yn Arfon, which is the old name for Caernarfon. Her father was Eudaf Hen, otherwise known as Octavius the Old,[3] who held the title of Dux Gewissei, i.e. Prince of Gwent, Erging, and Ewyas. The corresponding Welsh form of Gewissei is Iwys and this is preserved in Ewyas Harold and Ewyas Lacey in Herefordshire. In addition to Gwent, Eudaf's estate comprised that of the Hwiccas, a British and Christian people with whom the Anglo-Saxon settlers later intermingled. In later times, it was portioned out into the shires of Hereford, Gloucester, Worcester, part of Warwick, and the district between the Wye and the Severn, which included the Forest of Dean.

By marrying this British heiress, Magnus Maximus gained control of the Segontium-based troops, who were to form his personal bodyguard. Elen received as her dowry possessions in the areas of Caernarfon, Carmarthen, and Caerleon, which is an

---

[2]Macsen was the first to hold the title of Gwledig, which was later given to Cunedda, Ceredig, and Emrys. Taliesin the bard also gives it to Urien Rheged, hero of the Old North.

[3]Octavius dux Wisseoreum of Geoffrey of Monmouth's Latin *Brut* corresponds to Eudaf, Iarll Erging ac Euas in the Welsh *Brut*. His daughter is nameless in the Latin version, but she is called Elen in the Welsh. See *Brut Dingestow*, Henry Lewis, ed. (Cardiff, Wales: University of Wales Press, 1942), p. 133.

*Figure 7. On the outskirts of Caernarfon, close to the old Roman cemetery of Segontium, is the church of Llanbeblig which was founded by Peblig, a son of Maximus and Elen. It also became the burial place of their son Constantine the Blessed, who became Emperor of Britain. On his death, he was buried with due ceremonial pomp at Segontium, but about 840 years later, in 1283, on the orders of King Edward I of England, his tomb was transferred to Llanbeblig, the mother church of Caernarfon.*

*Nennius, writing in the ninth century, stated that the person commemorated in an inscription on a stone marking a tomb at Segontium was the Emperor Constantine, "son of the great, the very great." This statement gave rise to the belief that he was the son of Constantine the Great, but in Latin "the great the very great" is Magnus Maximus, so the tomb was obviously that of Constantine, the son of Magnus Maximus. Matthew of Westminster confirms that the body of the Emperor Constantine was found by digging and was, by the order of Edward I, honorably interred in the adjacent church of Llanbeblig.*

indication of the extent of this important British family's sovereignty, extending in an "L" shape around the coast of Wales.

There is a tradition that Elen caused highroads to be constructed from one fortified town to another, and the evidence for such an association is very clear, for in Wales, Roman roads and old mountain tracks are called Sarn Elen, Ffordd Elen, and Llwybr Elen, meaning respectively Elen's Causeway, Road, and Path. From Segontium, Roman roads led through the mountains, eastward to Chester and southward to Carmarthen and Caerleon, portions of which are known to this day as Sarn Elen, "Elen's Causeway."

Recorded in the *Mabinogion* story, *The Dream of Macsen Wledig,* are the travels of the Emperor Maximus. He came to Caerfyrddin (Carmarthen) to hunt and pitched his tents at a spot which is called Cadair Macsen to this day.

Up to the 18th century, the site of the hill-fortress of Pen-y-Gaer in Gwynedd was known as Pen Caer Elen and it has one of the rare examples of Chevaux-de-frise for defense. This consists of a belt of pointed stones set on end and close together to make approach difficult. Such an arrangement is identical to one which occurs in Spain and was presumably adopted for use in Britain by Elen's husband, Magnus Maximus, who was a Spaniard by birth.

In the last five years of his life, Magnus Maximus became one of the most celebrated personalities in Europe and at the same time one of the greatest influences on early Welsh tradition. His popularity with his troops resulted in a military usurpation, for in A.D. 383 he was elected as Emperor in opposition to Gratian, the legitimate Roman Emperor, who seemed to be more interested in hunting than in affairs of state. Maximus then promoted the garrison troops from Segontium to the palatine army and led them, under his personal ensign of the Red Dragon, from Britain to Gaul to challenge the authority of Gratian.[4]

---

[4]Gildas criticizes Magnus Maximus for taking all the British soldiers with him to the Continent, leaving the country denuded of its military resources. He left Britain "deprived of all her soldiery and her armed bands, of her cruel governors and of the flower of her youth, who went with Maximus but never again

It is evident that Maximus was an able and ambitious man and, before crossing the Channel, he must have been very much aware of the growing unpopularity of Gratian. On his arrival in Gaul, Maximus was warmly welcomed by both soldiers and civilians, while Gratian retreated southward to seek the protection of his younger brother, Valentinian II, who ruled Italy. Deserted by his troops and with just a few companions, Gratian escaped beyond the Alps, but was captured at Lyons and treacherously murdered by Maximus's commanding officer, Count Andragathius, on August 25, 383.

Elen and her brother Cynan accompanied Maximus in his conquest of Gaul and it was as a result of having marched with her husband's legions that Elen earned the epithet of Luyddog, meaning "of the Hosts."[5] Cynan's forces consisted of a large contingent of emigrants from Siluria (Gwent) and Gorwenydd (in Glamorgan). As a reward for his participation in the campaign, he received land, dominion, and authority in the area which included the old coastal command called the Armorican tract.

Maximus conquered Spain, but when he invaded Italy, the Eastern Roman Emperor Theodosius I sent his forces to deal with him. His navy slipped past Maximus' fleet, while his land armies defeated Maximus in Pannonia and finally caught and killed him at the third milestone from Aquileia on August 28, 388. In the same year, Maximus's eldest son Gwythyr (Victor), whom he had appointed Caesar, was hunted down and killed by Flavius Arbogastes who was Theodosius's general.

According to Nennius' *Historia Brittonum*, the armies which Maximus took to Gaul never returned to Britain, but settled in the area known as Armorica (Brittany). Elen, on the other hand, returned to Britain as the heiress of substantial estates.

---

returned." The country was abandoned "to be trodden underfoot by two very cruel and fierce foreign nations" (i.e. the Scots and the Picts—the Saxons were a later threat). Gildas obviously despised Maximus, for he goes on to relate how he "lost his accursed head in Aquilla." (See 13-1, p. 20.)

[5] According to the *Welsh Triads*, Elen Luyddog (Helen "of the Hosts") and her brother, Cynan Meiradog, led one of the "Three Silver Hosts of the Island of Britain" (Triad No. 35, pp. 77–78). Each of the hosts numbered twenty-one thousand men and was so called because the gold and silver of the island went with them.

The children of Maximus eventually succeeded to his domains. Owain, the son of Maximus by his first wife Ceindrech, became king of the area later known as Glywysing.[6] His residence was at Llanweryd (now St. Donat's in South Glamorgan) and he built a palace after the Roman style at nearby Caer Mead. It was probably reduced to ashes in the destruction of Cor Worgan (now Llantwit Major) by the Irish in 420. When news of the death of his father, Maximus, reached Britain, Owain was elevated by national convention to be Pendragon over the native princes, but he was subsequently slain fighting the Irish in 394, while defending Dinas Ffaraon Dandde ("Fortress of the Fiery Pharaoh") in Arfon. After the fall of Owain, the area around Segontium was subjected to constant attack by the Irish. Although the enemy did not succeed in breaking into the fortified town, Elen and her family found the situation intolerable and emigrated to Armorica. Here they remained in exile with her brother Cynan, who had been appointed Dux Armoricani by his brother-in-law Magnus Maximus.

Antonius Donatus, the son of Maximus and Ceindrech, was the ancestor of the Celtic kings of the Isle of Man. When Magnus departed for the Continent, Antonius set himself up as king of Strathclyde and Galloway and founded a dynasty. In later life, he retired to Man, where St. Garmon anointed him king.

Severa, daughter of Maximus and Elen, married Vortigern the Thin. This marriage brought considerable political advantage to Vortigern, for when Elen died, Severa, by rule of female succession, gained control of the territory belonging to the family of Eudaf Hen, who was Dux Gewissei, the Prince of Gwent, Erging, and Ewyas. Vortigern thus gained access to his wife's inheritance, thereby becoming Dux Gewissei himself and one of the most powerful rulers in southern Britain.

Constantine the Blessed, the son of Maximus and Elen, was just an infant when his father was killed in 388, and he spent

---

[6]In the earliest known draft of the cantrefs and commotes of Wales, Maximus is depicted as the father of Owain, King of Buellt, from whom sprang the kings of Glywysing, an extensive kingdom embracing Glamorgan in southeast Wales (*The Red Book of the Exchequer,* 12th century, F. 322d, ed. Rolls 17.760.2).

many years in exile in Armorica with his kinsman Aldwr, the ruler of the West Welsh settlements there. Some years later, when the Romano-Britons were being oppressed by inroads of Picts and Irish, they applied to Aldwr in Armorica for military assistance. Upon receiving their request, Aldwr dispatched his brother, St. Garmon, and Constantine with a large body of troops to deal with the problem. Constantine was no doubt keen to return from his long exile in Armorica and claim his patrimony in North Wales. However, this was not easily done, for when the last Roman garrison was withdrawn from Segontium by Magnus Maximus in 383, the region around the fortress was taken over by the local Goidelic (Irish) inhabitants. They took possession of Mona (Anglesey) and the greater part of North Wales.

## CUNEDDA WLEDIG

Cunedda Wledig was a chieftain of the Votadini tribe from the area northeast of Hadrian's Wall. He is credited with being the ruler of a wide district from Carlisle to Wearmouth, which he administered from his court at Carlisle. It would seem that he came from a powerful family, for his grandfather was called Paternus of the Red Tunic, which suggests that he held office under the Romans and wore the Roman purple. Cunedda was a post-Roman officer who filled the position of Dux Britanniarum in command of the forces on Hadrian's Wall. The name Cunedda is the equivalent of Kenneth in English and his epithet, Wledig (pronounced wul-ed-ig), was a military title indicating that he was the leader of an important army. According to Welsh tradition, Cunedda Wledig's retinue on the Wall consisted of 900 horses and it is said that he wore the badge of office of the "Dux Britanniarum." This item, as in the case of other Duces or Comes under the Empire, consisted of a gold belt, which a passage in a Welsh poem seems to allude to as Cunedda's girdle.[7]

---

[7]Cunedda is termed in all Welsh documents "Guledig." This title is derived from the word "Gulod," a country, and it means ruler. It is thus equivalent to the title and position of Imperator, which was conferred upon him by the troops in Britain.

On receiving a request from Constantine the Blessed to help expel the large numbers of Irish settlers who had taken possession of Mona (Anglesey) and the greater part of North Wales, Cunedda complied by dispatching his sons with their followers to deal with the problem. He had nine sons, who were named Tybion, Ysfael, Rhufon, Dunod, Ceredig, Afloeg, Einion Yrth, Dogfael, and Edern. The eldest son, Tybion, had died in their home province of Manau Guotodin, near the Firth of Forth, so he was represented in the war band by his son, Meirion.

This formidable band of warriors succeeded in expelling the Goidels and they were well rewarded by the princes of Gwynedd, who allowed them to take possession of the areas of land which they had won back from the Irish settlers. These new possessions of the sons and grandson of Cunedda Wledig lay on either side of a diagonal line from Rhuddlan on the Irish Sea to Cardigan on Cardigan Bay, forming a wedge through Wales from the northeast to the southwest. The remainder of Wales on either side of that wedge appertained to the family of Magnus Maximus. His son Constantine the Blessed ruled over Arfon in northwest Wales; another son, Antonius, ruled in the Isle of Man, while his son-in-law Vortigern the Thin, ruled from Powys to Gwent and southeastward to the Isle of Wight.[8]

When Cunedda's expeditionary force marched from Manau Guotodin to North Wales, it no doubt came with the sole purpose of giving aid to fellow Britons, but Cunedda was an opportunist and he decided to remain and conquer. He established his rule over Wales by inviting the Celtic tribes to the west of Britain to form a confederation under his leadership. Consequently, it was from Cunedda that all the subsequent reigning families of Gwynedd traced their descent. His power remained with his sons and continued through the line of their sons, with the result that

---

[8]Vortigern is a title which means "high king." Gildas (23-1, p. 26) described him as superbus tyrannus, which has been taken to mean "proud tyrant." His Welsh name was Gwrtheyrn Gwrtheneu (Vortigern "the Thin"). Triad 10 of the *Llyfr Goch Hergest* (The Red Book of Hergest) includes Gwrtheyrn Gwrtheneu among the "Three Dishonoured Men of the Island of Britain" (Triad No. 51, in Rachel Bromwich, *Troedd Ynys Prydein*, p. 132).

his great-grandson Maelgwyn Gwynedd, the "Island Dragon," was as powerful as Cunedda himself had been.

Once the Irish problem had been dealt with, Constantine the Blessed re-established himself at his old family seat at Caernarfon, which then became known as Caer Gystennin. It appears that the Britons were so grateful for the action taken by Constantine in dealing with the Goidels and Picts that they elected him Pendragon of the confederated states of Britain.[9]

The *Welsh Triads* refer to Constantine the Blessed as one of the "Three Foreign Princes of the Island of Britain." In his person, the office of Pendragon assumed once more the appearance of an imperial monarchy. He was referred to as "the Blessed" in consequence of having been considered a Saint of the British Church. In conjunction with Tewdrig, King of Garth Madryn, he founded Cor Tewdws (Choir of Theodosius) near the coast of the Severn Sea. They appointed Patrick Mac Lomman, a nephew of St. Patrick Mac Alpurn, Apostle of Ireland, as the first principal, but the monastic college was soon afterward destroyed by Irish pirates. Subsequently, the foundation was restored by St. Garmon who appointed St. Illtyd as principal and it became known as Llanilltyd Fawr, which was later anglicized as Llantwit Major.

Constantine the Blessed also founded Llangystennin (the Church of Constantine) in Gwynedd and Lann Custenhin Garth Benni (the Church and monastic enclosure of Constantine the Blessed), now Welsh Bicknor in Herefordshire.

## VORTIGERN, THE THIN

Constantine rewarded his brother-in-law Vortigern, who is known in Welsh as Gwrtheyrn Gwrtheneu, for his assistance in cleaning out the Irish, with the gift of Dinas Ffaraon Dandde, a

---

[9]Caernarfon was known as Caer Gystennin by A.D. 1100 and it is referred to by this name in *Hanes Gruffud ap Cynan* (Arthur Jones, ed.), p. 7.

hill-fort in Gwynedd.[10] But within a few years, Constantine the Blessed was dead. Whether he died of the plague of 443 or was assassinated on the instigation of Vortigern, we shall never know for sure. It would seem that the latter drew a discreet veil over the matter by taking the dead emperor's eldest son, Constantine the Younger, out of a monastery and temporarily elevating him to the imperial throne. At the time of his father's death, young Constantine was leading a monastic life and would have presented no immediate threat to Vortigern's plans for total supremacy. He no doubt trusted his uncle and his first action was to hand over the Council of Britain to Vortigern, whom he naturally understood to be very knowledgeable in such matters. This cunning old devil then began to plot how he might procure the crown of Britain for himself.

He treacherously assassinated young Constantine and forced the prince's younger brothers Ambrosius and Uthyr to seek exile in Armorica, just as their father had done years before. Vortigern then deceitfully took the crown and kingdom into his possession.

To preserve his realm from the intervention of the Romano-British faction, Vortigern then enlisted the assistance of Teutonic federates. His main fear was that the Romano-Britons might request reinforcements from the Romans under Aetius in Gaul. He also needed soldiers to help him repel the attacks of the Picts, who under their king, Drust Mac Erp, now threatened a full scale invasion and settlement of the British lowlands. Although the last frontier of the north still held, the Picts had started to

---

[10]The fortress of Dinas Ffaraon Dandde was identified by Edmund Gibson in his commentary on William Camden's *Britannia* (1695), with the ruins of a very strong fortification. It was protected by a triple wall and positioned on an eminence called Braich y Ddinas, "the ridge of the city," which forms part of the summit of Penmaen Mawr. "The greatness of the work," he says, "shows that it was a princely fortification, strengthened by nature and workmanship, seated on top of one of the highest mountains of that part of Snowdonia which lie toward the sea." The secret ambrosial city of Dinas Ffaraon Dandde subsequently became confused with Dinas Emrys (Fortress of Ambrosius). In their translation of the *Mabinogion*, T. P. Ellis and John Lloyd describe Dinas Ffaraon Dandde (Fortress of the Fiery Pharaoh) as the most exalted fortress in Arfon. See Lewis Spence, *The Mysteries of Britain* (Philadelphia: David McKay, 1946), pp. 80–81, 146, 158.

sail down the east coast of Britain, landing at will. Against this threat of seaborne invasion, Vortigern enlisted sufficient forces of the most experienced seafaring nation of the day—the Saxons.[11] However, after successfully accomplishing the task for which they were employed, a decisive section of the Romano-British faction refused to continue to finance these federates. Consequently, in opposition to the Romano-British party, Vortigern was driven to hire still larger numbers of the federates, who, unbeknownst to him, increased their numbers on their own initiative, until they were eventually strong enough to attack and defeat both parties.

An appeal by the Romano-British party against the settlement of the federates was made to Aetius during his third consulship in 446. The Romano-Britons had by now been driven to the borders of the Severn, and Caerleon-upon-Usk in Gwent became their capital. Following the failure of the appeal to Aetius for assistance, a large portion of the British aristocracy emigrated to Armorica. This considerable exodus of magnates with their bodyguards from southwest Britain must have greatly weakened the forces of resistance to the Saxons.

Vortigern's compliance toward the federates was obviously derived from the need that he felt to use them against the Romano-British party and the Picts, but in their united position the federates began to act independently. Vortigern was now in a situation where he was competing for the general command of Britain with the Romano-British families of Siluria and Armorica. At the same time, he was under imminent threat of rebellion by the federates whom he had recruited to protect his breakaway state.

After obtaining reinforcements for the troops of the Saxon brothers Hengist and Horsa, the alliance was further strengthened when Vortigern married Alis Ronwen, the daughter of

---

[11]According to Bede, the Britons "consulted how they might obtain help to reject the frequent attacks of their northern neighbours, and all agreed with the advice of their king Vortigern, to call on the assistance of the Saxon peoples across the sea." (See Bede's *Historia Ecclesiastica,* chapter 1, p. 18.) Obviously the intention was to use the Saxons as mercenaries, just as the Romans had done before them.

Hengist.[12] The marriage agreement was cemented by a gift of territory and it represented an effort to weld the Saxon federates under Hengist. However, Vortigern made a serious error. The fierce mercenaries were not so easily won over by rewards, for the lure of greater areas of land and loot was too strong. In 455, following the murder of Aetius, which removed the likelihood of assistance from Gaul, the federates revolted and conducted a sharp campaign against the Britons. Vortigern's two eldest sons, Vortimer the Blessed and Catigern, acted as his generals leading the British resistance against the Saxons.

The first battle of the British campaign under the leadership of Vortimer was fought in 455 at Aylesford, a crossing point on the River Medway. His brother Catigern and Horsa fell in mortal combat at the moment of victory by the invaders. Catigern was apparently buried at the ancient cromlech known as Kit's Coty, which stands near Aylesford in Kent. Horsa, his opponent, was entombed at the flint heap near Fort Horsted.[13]

A year later, the Britons under Vortimer prevailed at the battles of Darenth, Stonar, and Dartford, driving the federates temporarily back to their stronghold on the Isle of Thanet. However, in 457, at the decisive Battle of Crayford, in a quiet valley near Orpington, the Britons were defeated by the reinforced federates under Hengist and his son Oeric Oesc. Deserting Kent, they fled to London and, shortly after this disastrous defeat, Vortimer died from poison administered by his step-mother, Alis Ronwen.

Vortigern now realized that the Saxons were a very serious threat and that the only answer was to negotiate. Hengist then

---

[12]According to the Rev. Arthur Wade-Evans (*The Emergence of England and Wales*, p. 63), Hengist was merely a totemic name, meaning stallion, for Octha I, whose daughter, Alis Ronwen, married Gwrtheyrn Gwrtheneu (Vortigern the Thin) and had a son named Gotta or Octha II. The pedigree of the kings of Wessex, contained in the Anglian collection, tells us that Cerdic was the son of Elesa (Aluca), who was the son of Esla or Ebissa, who may be identified with Horsa, the brother of Hengist. Therefore, it looks very much as if Octha II (Osla) and Cerdic were cousins.

[13]The connection of Vortigern's son Catigern with the megalithic burial chamber of Kit's Coty House seems to have first been made by Lambard in his *Perambulation of Kent* (1570).

invited the British chiefs to a conference and banquet at Caer Caradoc, but before they arrived, he ordered his servants to kill the Britons when he gave the signal, "Saxons draw your knives!" Consequently, when Vortigern saw all three hundred of his followers being slain, he was forced to save his own life by agreeing that the Saxons could take possession of the areas known today as Essex, Sussex, and Middlesex, which were three of the wealthiest provinces of Britain. There is an account of this famous massacre in Nennius's *Historia Brittonum* and it is corroborated by the *Gesta Regum Anglorum.*

A positive result of this treacherous and tragic event was that Vortigern fell from favor and the Britons decided to support the enterprise of Ambrosius, a grandson of Magnus Maximus, who was in exile in Armorica and had been brought up in the royal house of the Emyr Llydaw. He now made preparations to lead a campaign to Britain to claim his inheritance.

## AMBROSIUS

Ambrosius Aurelianus, who is known in Welsh history as Emrys Wledig, was the eldest son of Constantine the Blessed and accordingly the grandson of Magnus Maximus, otherwise known as Macsen Wledig. Gildas described Ambrosius as the last of the Romans and the chief protagonist against the Saxons. He and his father, Constantine, were therefore connecting links between the Roman Empire and an independent Britain. It is obvious that Gildas had a high regard for Ambrosius, for he was the only one of his countrymen whom he did not set out to criticize in his writings. Instead, he referred to him as a "man of unassuming character, who alone of the Roman race chanced to survive the shock of such a storm as his parents, people undoubtedly clad in the purple, had been killed in it, whose offspring in our days have greatly degenerated from their ancestral nobleness."[14]

---

[14]Gildas ap Caw, *De Excidio et Conquesta Britanniae: Gildas—The Ruin of Britain and Other Works,* Michael Winterbottom, ed. and trans. (London & Chichester: Phillimore, 1978), passage 25.3, p. 28.

Nennius describes Ambrosius as a child living in Glywysing in a neighborhood called Campus Elleti, which means the Maes or Plain of Elletus. This name survives as Llanmaes and it is near Llantwit Major in South Glamorgan. Near the monastery of Llanilltyd Fawr (Llantwit Major) was also Palus Elleti, "the Marsh of Elletus," mentioned in the *Book of Llandaff*. It is interesting that the location of Campus Elleti has been confused by many Arthurian researchers with Bassaleg, near Newport in Gwent, which is mistakenly believed to be derived from Maes Elletus.

We are told by Nennius that Vortigern's emissaries found Ambrosius at "Campus Elleti" as a child and they took him to their leader who was residing at the time in a hill-fort called Dinas Ffaraon Dandde in North Wales. Geoffrey of Monmouth, no doubt having read the works of Nennius, repeats this story, but at the same time causes confusion. He has Vortigern asking the boy for his name and Ambrosius replying, "My name is Myrddin Emrys" (Merlin Ambrosius). Geoffrey thus translated Ambrosius Aurelianus into Merlinus Ambrosius and then shortened it to Merlin. This was the beginning of the legend of Merlin the Magician![15]

The young Ambrosius was forced to flee with his brother Uthyr when their eldest brother, named Constantine the Younger after his father, was murdered and his crown usurped by the evil Vortigern. The two brothers remained in exile for many years and were brought up as princes by their cousin Budic, Emperor of Armorica, whose name in Welsh is Emyr Llydaw.

In due course, Ambrosius, accompanied by Garmon, the soldier-saint, returned to Britain in a determined campaign to

---

[15]It becomes apparent that there were two Merlins—Myrddin Ambrosius and Myrddin Sylvester. The former appears in Nennius' work as Emrys Wledig (Ambrosius "the Imperator"). It is Geoffrey of Monmouth who first uses the name Merlin. Myrddin Sylvester lived in Arthur's time and he is supposed to have fled from the Battle of Arderydd, when Rhydderch of Strathclyde won a great victory against other Celtic rulers in 573. His chief bard, Myrddin, went mad and hid himself away in the Forest of Celyddon. He is reputed to have ended his days on the Isle of Bardsey guarding the thirteen treasures of Britain.

overthrow the usurper Vortigern, who by treachery had become the Pendragon or Chief Ruler. As a result of the massacre at Caer Caradoc, known as the "Treachery of the Long Knives," Vortigern had been branded a traitor and this meant that the Britons gave enthusiastic support to Ambrosius when he arrived with a strong force to claim his inheritance.

Pursued by Ambrosius and Garmon, Vortigern fled to Dinas Ffaraon Dandde in Arfon. After being forced to surrender it to Ambrosius, he fled to the Lleyn Peninsula and took refuge in the old Irish hill-fortress of Tre'r Ceiri, which is situated near Nant Gwrtheyrn (Vortigern's Valley). In this valley, he constructed a wooden fortress, but it was not long before his two pursuers and their army of supporters arrived on the scene. They surrounded the timber stockade and set it alight with fire-arrows. Inside at the time were Vortigern's granddaughter, Madrun, and her eldest son, Ceidio. She was allowed to pass out of the fire and fled with the child in her arms to seek shelter on a nearby solitary fortified hill crowned by rocks, which is called Carn Fadrun in her memory.

Apparently leading a charmed life, Vortigern once again eluded his pursuers and escaped to Craig Gwrtheyrn (Vortigern's Rock), which overlooks the River Teifi at Llanfihangel-ar-arth in Dyfed. Again he was pursued and besieged by Ambrosius and Garmon, who repeated their tactics by setting his stronghold alight with fire-arrows. Amazing as it may seem, this devious villain managed to escape a third time and sought refuge with his staunch ally, King Brychan, in the little mountain kingdom of Brycheiniog (later known as Breconshire) in south-central Wales.

With reinforcements, Vortigern crossed the border into Erging, where he reinforced an Iron Age fortress on Little Doward near Ganarew. But in due course, Ambrosius and Garmon located their adversary in his new hiding place and Little Doward Hill became the last refuge of Vortigern in Britain. This time they were convinced that he had perished in the flames, but had he? It would appear that Vortigern performed yet another "Houdini act" by escaping in a boat down the River Wye. He crossed the Severn Sea and made his way to Cornwall. From there he went on to Quimperle in Armorica, where he became associated directly with Grallon Mawr, King of Cornouaille, and his younger

*Figure 8. Little Doward Hill on the boundary of Gwent and Herefordshire was where Vortigern finally took refuge while being pursued by Ambrosius and St. Garmon. His followers died in the battle which ensued and a bend on the River Wye below the hill is significantly marked on the map as "The Slaughter." From a military point of view, this camp commanded not only the river below, but also the highway on its other side, which ran from Isca Silurum (Caerleon-upon-Usk) through Blestium (Monmouth) to Ariconium (beyond Ross-on-Wye).*

contemporary, Weroc I, Count of Vannes. Vortigern entered the church and, incredible as it may seem, he is celebrated in Brittany as St. Gurthiern.[16]

Following the expulsion of Vortigern in 465, Ambrosius became the first warlord of Britain and his special field of influence was in the lands adjoining the Severn Estuary, in the area of modern Gwent, Gloucestershire, and Somerset. This dominion appears to have been the same as that held by his great-grandfather, Eudaf Hen, which was later represented by the shires of Hereford, Worcester, part of Warwickshire, and the district between the Wye and Severn, including the Forest of Dean. However, in the case of Ambrosius, the area covered by Oxfordshire, Hampshire, and Wiltshire was also included. (We have used the old county names as a convenient way of indicating recognizable areas of country.)

Ambrosius provided strong leadership which the Britons desperately needed at this time, for the Saxons were becoming a serious threat. Early raiding parties seemed to have established a few short-lived settlements in the area now known as Berkshire, and Ambrosius probably feared that Hengist would move up from Kent to reinforce these advanced positions before swinging left into Wiltshire and Somerset, the heartland of British territory.[17]

To improve his defenses, Ambrosius ordered the construction of an extensive earthwork, which is known today as Wans-

---

[16]The 11th-century Life of St. Gurthiern (Vortigern), together with the inventory of his relics contained in the *Cartulaire de l'Abbaye de Saint-Croix de Quimperle* (p. 3ff), edited by Leon Maitre and Paul de Berthou (Paris, 1896), associate Gurthiern directly with the church of Quimperle in Cornouaille and Vannes in Bro-Weroc. Gurthiern's *Life*, which is the oldest Breton source for St. Gurthiern, occurs together with that of St. Ninnoc, also found in the Cartulary of Quimperle. The evidence afforded by the Lives of Saints Gurthiern and Ninnoc suggests that after his expulsion from Brycheiniog in 465 Gurthiern traveled to southern Brittany, where he became associated with King Grallon Mawr ("the Great") of Cornouaille and Count Weroc I of Bro-Weroc, who both flourished in the latter half of the fifth century.

[17]Nennius, in *Historia Brittonum*, relates that after the departure of Vortigern, "Ambrosius was king among all kings of the British nation" (passage 48, p. 33).

dyke. It is a remarkable fifth-century engineering achievement consisting of a ditch and rampart that stretches for 128 kilometers from Andover in Hampshire to Portishead in Avon. Undoubtedly, it was built to defend the kingdom of Domnonia (an area represented today by Devon and Cornwall) from an army marching up the Thames Valley. Certainly it seems to be orientated toward the Thames Valley and it was constructed at a time when the Saxons were pouring into and along the valley to settle in its upper regions. Such a mighty earthwork was not undertaken lightly and is in itself evidence that there were large reserves of manpower directed by decisive leadership. Today, this remarkable earthwork remains as a major monument to the British resistance. Its name, Wansdyke, comes from "Wodensdu" —Woden's Dyke, for the Saxons named it after their god.

However, the dreaded Saxon offensive did not immediately materialize and their Berkshire outposts presumably fell to the Britons in the 470s, but a later thrust from Kent along the Thames Valley would have been likely enough. By 473, the Teutonic settlers had established a large colony in Kent and a number of smaller ones elsewhere in eastern Britain. Parties of spoilers made raids in all directions, but Ambrosius put a stop to them and moved victoriously southeastward to seal off Kent. Henceforth, Hengist and his son Oeric Oesc confined their efforts to organizing a kingdom there and it became the first coherent political unit in Anglo-Saxondom.

Having lost Kent to Hengist, Ambrosius was also challenged by Vitalinus, who was a relative of Vortigern. A battle was fought at Guoloph in Hampshire, today known as Wallop, which is a name derived from Wiell-hop or Waell-hop, Valley of the Stream. If the name can be interpreted as the Empty or Dry River, then this Hampshire site is very likely the location of the battle, as streams would easily run dry in a chalky area. This battle was fought in 473 and it may well have been in defense of Ambresbyrig (Ambrose's Town), now Amesbury in Wiltshire, against a member of Vortigern's family who was trying to assert himself. It resulted in another victory for Ambrosius.

Ambrosius certainly led an exciting life, but as he grew old, his thoughts must have turned to the attractions of retirement and it seems that, like many great warriors who followed him, he chose to spend his remaining years in a monastery serving God. The location of the monastery in question has become very confused owing to Geoffrey of Monmouth's association of Ambrosius with Amesbury, to the east of Salisbury Plain. In order to find the true location of this monastery, it is necessary to examine the area where Ambrosius spent his childhood. Llanilltyd Fawr was a monastic training center and it is likely that Ambrosius used the knowledge taught there by St. Illtyd when he established his own monastery. Also, it would be more natural for him to situate it in the area where he spent his younger days than at Amesbury in Wiltshire.

The Welsh name for his monastery was Cor Emrys and in the *Welsh Triads* such a place is mentioned as one of the "Three Principal Choirs of the Island of Britain—Bangor Illtyd Farchog in Caer Worgan, Cor Emrys in Caer Caradoc and Bangor Wyrddin in the Isle of Afallach" (See Triad 80, First Series, and Triad 84, Third Series). In each of these three places, there were said to be 2,400 holy men, 100 of them in turn continuing each hour of the day and night in prayer and service to God without rest, acting as a perpetual choir. The word "cor" means circle or congregation. Bangor Illtyd we can identify as the location of St. Illtyd's Church at Llanilltyd Fawr, which is now known as Llantwit Major. Bangor Wyrddin we will identify in a later chapter dealing with the mysterious island of Avalon. The remaining religious center mentioned in this *Triad* is also in Wales and everything points to its being on a hilltop called Mynydd y Gaer in Mid Glamorgan, where the shell of a later church known as St. Peter-super-Montem still stands.

Geoffrey of Monmouth tells us that Bishop Eldad persuaded Ambrosius to visit the Cloister of Ambrius and its adjoining cemetery. While he was there, Ambrosius decided to build a national monument to commemorate the dead of the massacre of British noblemen which has become known as the "Treachery of the Long Knives." This monument was mentioned by Geoffrey of Monmouth, who called it the "Giant's Ring" and confused it with Stonehenge, which is not far from Amesbury in Wiltshire. Geoffrey identified Caer Caradawc with Salisbury, but it would seem far more likely that the Caer Caradoc situated on Mynydd-y-Gaer in the parish of Coychurch, Mid Glamorgan, is the place

*Figure 9. On Mynydd-y-Gaer (Mountain of the Fortress) in Mid Glamorgan is the site of a hill-fort marked on old maps as Caer Caradoc and a short distance away are the remains of an ancient church which stands on the site of the "Cloister of Ambrius." This monastic settlement was founded by Ambri or Ambrius, who is mentioned in the Book of Llandaff. Tref Meibion Ambrus (the Village of the Sons of Ambrus) was the property of the See of Llandaff and was probably in the same vicinity.*

*Ambrosius (Emrys Wledig) took over this site and established his monastery, which was known as Cor Emrys and was in later times confused by Geoffrey of Monmouth with Amesbury, to the east of Salisbury Plain. Today, the ruined Norman church of St. Peter-super-Montem stands on this windswept hill and it is a site of considerable historical importance.*

in question. Nennius includes Caer Caradawc (Caradoc) in his list of British cities, which again is an indication of its former importance.

We are also told by Geoffrey of Monmouth that, when Ambrosius died, he was buried in the Giant's Ring, subsequently followed by his brother Uthyr and Arthur's successor, Constantine. Unfortunately, the monumental circle set up to commemorate these heroic figures no longer exists, and it is feasible that in later years it was destroyed to provide stones for the construction of the Norman church of St. Peter-super-Montem.

We can determine the death of Emrys Wledig and the succession of his brother Uthyr Pendragon from a statement by Geoffrey of Monmouth that this event coincided with the appearance of a comet:

> There appeared a star of great magnitude and brilliance, with a single beam shining from it. At the end of this beam was a ball of fire, spread out in the shape of a dragon. From the dragon's mouth stretched forth two rays of light, one of which seemed to extend its length beyond the latitude of Gaul, while the second turned towards the Irish Sea and split into seven smaller shafts of light.
>
> This star appeared three times, and all who saw it were struck with fear and wonder. Uther, the king's brother, who was hunting for the enemy army, was just as terrified as the others. He summoned wise men, so that they might tell him what the star portended. He ordered Merlin (Myrddin Wyllt—Merlin the Wild, not to be confused with Myrddin Emrys) to be fetched with the others, for Merlin had come with the army so that the campaign could have the benefit of his advice. As he stood in the presence of the leader and was given the order to explain the significance of the star, he burst into tears, summoned up his familiar spirit, and prophesied aloud: "Our loss is irreparable," he said. "The people of Britain are orphaned. Our most illustrious king has passed away. Aurelius Ambrosius, the famous king of the Britons has died."[18]

The appearance of this comet is recorded in the Anglo Saxon Chronicle as taking place in 497, so therefore the exact year of the death of Ambrosius may be determined.

---

[18]Geoffrey of Monmouth, *The History of the Kings of Britain* (London: Penguin, 1966), pp. 200–201.

## UTHYR PENDRAGON, RULER OF BRITAIN (A.D. 497–512)

This brother of Ambrosius is a somewhat vague figure, for only scanty information about him seems to be available and the very fact that he is named Uthyr has itself resulted in considerable confusion. It is necessary to understand that Uthyr is a personal name and the word Uther is a title. An alternative name for Uthyr is Gwythyr and they both translate as Victor. Uther as a title, when linked with the word Pendragon, meant "Wonderful Head Dragon." The father of Arthur, as a commander of the British army, was given the title Uther Pendragon and this simple fact explains why Geoffrey of Monmouth stated that Arthur was the son of Uther Pendragon. This 12th-century writer seemed to be ignorant of the fact that the words were a title and not a personal name and this has made the identification of King Arthur even more difficult than it should have been.

The term Pendragon, which means Dragon's Head, is of ancient origin and it signifies an important war leader. Such a title stems from a tradition established in ancient Britain. The Welsh word "draig" for dragon, takes us back to the Latin "draco" and "draconis." These words relate to the Augustan era of the Roman Empire, when dragons began to figure in purple on the standards of some of the legions. Such a custom then extended itself to the emperors in times of peace and the Welsh word makes it highly probable that the practice was one of the Roman traditions which was cherished by the leaders or over-kings of the Britons,

It is significant that the purple dragon was the Roman Imperial Standard. Ammianus Marcellinus describes how Caesar was recognized in battle by the purple standard of the dragon which, ragged with age, fluttered from the top of a long spear. This symbol of Roman imperialism thus lived on in Wales in the sub-Roman age, and survives today as Y Ddraig Goch, "the Red Dragon."

It would appear that, although Ambrosius nominated Arthur as his successor, the older and more experienced leaders held sway for a time. They were Uthyr, the brother of Ambrosius, and Geraint, the son of Erbin, who was subsequently killed at the Battle of Llongborth in 508. Any sons of Ambrosius himself must have perished in battle or died of natural causes, for otherwise he would surely have been succeeded by one of his offspring.

Uthyr displayed considerable bravery in opposing the Saxons, but his reign only lasted fifteen years. An entry in the *Anglo Saxon Chronicle* tells us that Cerdic of the Gewissei defeated and slew a British Pendragon with five thousand of his men on Dragon Hill near Uffington Camp in Berkshire. The name of this hill commemorates this famous battle and the death of Uthyr Pendragon in 512. His body was brought from Dragon Hill back to South Wales, for according to Geoffrey of Monmouth, Uthyr was buried beside his brother Ambrosius Aurelianus in the "Giant's Ring" at Caer Caradawg, which has been located in Mid-Glamorgan.

•  •  •

It is time now for Arthur to enter the arena. We have been a long time coming to him, but it has been necessary to set the scene to give an understanding of the historical background to the age in which he lived. He was preceded by a series of great war leaders who were all of noble stock, some holding the military title of Gwledig. This indicated that they were powerful enough to lead several tribes or armies instead of just one. In their time, these men were regarded as saviors of the nation and, when Arthur was elected Pendragon, he inherited their power and the overall responsibility for the defense of his country.

# 3

# The Historical King Arthur

ONE OF THE MAIN REASONS why the identification of King Arthur has proven so difficult is the fact that history has been blended with romance, causing utter confusion. The early bards first mentioned the name of Arthur in their epic war poems, which were composed in the area of Britain now known as Cumberland. These verses celebrated the military prowess of Arthur and it seems that, in the beginning, he was more famous in the north than he was in the south. This has led some writers to place him in the border region of Scotland. On the other hand, there are others who firmly believe that his realm was in the West Country. This book, however, reveals why such confusion has arisen and locates Arthur in his authentic kingdom.

First of all, it is necessary to understand that the name Arthur is derived from a number of similar sources which, over the passing centuries, have become very confused. Basically, the name is an anglicized version of a Celtic title which has been used by, or given to, several important war leaders. They have become fused together into one powerful personality, whose life seems so incredible and unlikely that he has come to be regarded as a figure of fiction and fantasy.

In the Welsh language, Arth Fawr means the "Great Bear." In ancient times this was the name given to the polar god who symbolized all the forces which come to us from the region of the seven main stars of the constellation called Ursa Major, which is Latin for Great Bear. The word Arctus comes from the two celestial constellations which are commonly called Ursa Major and Minor. Arcturus is a star near the tail of the Great Bear. Accordingly, Arcturus seems a more likely Latin root-name for Arthur than Artorius, for it dates back to pre-Roman times and is derived from the early Celtic form—Artorix meaning "Bear King."

According to the historians Gildas and Bede, the word Arthwyr was a title rather than a name. Any man given such a title was thus believed to be strong and powerful just like a bear. It was bestowed by the Cymry upon Ambrosius, who displayed considerable bravery in his conflicts against Vortigern and the Saxons. This is most significant, for Ambrosius has become confused with Arthur and some of his battles have been mistakenly attributed to him. It would seem that Ambrosius was known to the Britons as Arthwyr, for in times of national crisis they elected a leader to whom they gave this title as a token of respect. It meant "the Bear Exalted," a reference to the Celtic bear deity.

Arviragus, the 73rd king in Geoffrey of Monmouth's list, was also known as Arthwyr and he lived in the first century at the time of the Roman invasion. Significantly, his area of operation was in the West Country in the vicinity of Cadbury Castle and Glastonbury, which are both strongly associated with the later King Arthur.

In the last quarter of the fifth century, the victorious leader of the northern Britons who fought off the Picts was Arthwys, who also bore the title Arthwyr. He was the grandson of Coel Hen, the founder-father of a tribe known as the "Men of the North." Arthwys fought an ongoing border war against the Pictish Goidels until his death, when he was succeeded by his son, Pabo Post Prydain, who continued the campaign until he was eventually driven from his kingdom to settle in Wales. This Arthwys was in due course confused with Athrwys or Athruis, the son of Meurig, King of Gwent, who also assumed the appellation of Arthwyr. In 506, this Arthwyr was elected by the states of Britain to exercise sovereign authority, just as other princes before him had been chosen as leaders in times of national danger. He was none other than the historical King Arthur, who undoubtedly became a legend in his own lifetime.

Further confusion has been caused by the existence of a soldier-saint called Arthmael ("Bear Prince"), who lived at the same time as Athrwys, the son of Meurig. He is remembered for the part that he played in liberating the Bretons from the tyranny of

Marcus Conomorus (otherwise known as King March) in the sixth century, and he established a persistent legend of a King Arthur operating in Brittany which is remembered to this day. In Breton, a bear is "arz" and Arth (Arz) mael, means bear prince. The key to the real identity of King Arthur is to understand that Athrwys ap Meurig and Arthmael were in fact the same person, as we shall demonstrate in due course.

Albert Le Grand, who compiled the *Life of St. Arthmael* in 1636, states that Arthmael was born in 482 at the Roman station of Caput Bovium, which in later times became known as Boverton. It is situated to the southeast of Llanilltyd Fawr (now anglicized to Llantwit Major) in the old cantref of Penychen, which in modern terms is in the county of South Glamorgan.

The name of Arthmael's parents is not given in this account, but they may be determined from the genealogy of the kings of Morgannwg and Gwent contained in the ancient register of the cathedral church of Llandaff in Cardiff. This manuscript is generally referred to as the *Book of Llandaff* and Athrwys is named as the son of Meurig and Onbrawst, the daughter of Gwrgant Mawr ("the Great"), King of Erging.

In our search for proof that Arthmael, Athruis, and Athrwys are alternative names for the same person, we found a very significant statement (page 31) in the *Life of St. Cadoc,* compiled in the 11th century by Lifris or Lifricus, son of Bishop Herewald, Archdeacon of Glamorgan. He mentions that a grant of land, now known as Cadoxton-juxta-Neath, was made to St. Cadoc by a certain King Arthmael. This was where our identification really started to make sense, for, according to the genealogy contained in the *Book of Llandaff,* the king reigning over Morgannwg and Gwent at this time was Athruis ap Meurig. (See also pedigree prepared by S. Baring-Gould and J. Fisher, *Lives of the British Saints,* vol. 2, p. 375.)

It also became possible for us to sort out the Brittany connection after finding an interesting statement in a book titled *Early History of the Cymry or Ancient Britons from 700 B.C. to A.D. 500,* written by the Rev. Peter Roberts and published in 1803. He referred to Arthur as an Armorican prince. Such a prince can be none other than Arthmael, the national messiah of Brittany. This great soldier-saint was known to the Bretons as

Armel. During his life, he founded churches in Brittany at Plouarzel, St. Armel-des-Boschaux, and Ploermel. The name of Arthmael, like all Celtic names of that period, has taken many variants: Armel, Ermel, Ermin, Armail, Arzel, Armahel, Hermel, and Thiamail. In Latin, it is written as Armagillus.

Dr. John Morris, in *The Age of Arthur,* makes a very significant statement: "The most important of the sixth-century immigrant leaders was probably Arthmael but little is known of him."[1] It seems that Dr. Morris failed to look at the writings of Albert Le Grand. The lack of interest by other Arthurian scholars in the *Life of St. Arthmael* (pp. 383–387) has resulted in the true identity of the historical King Arthur remaining a mystery.

It is most unlikely that there would have been two leaders with the same name flourishing at exactly the same period. The Arthmael who reigned over Glamorgan and Gwent in the time of St. Cadoc must have been the same man who liberated Domnonia in Brittany from the tyranny of Marcus Conomorus in 555. We shall deal with this important incident in a later chapter.

We found further relevant statements in the *Life of St. Efflam,* the text of which is contained in Arthur de la Borderie's *Annales de Bretagne* (pp. 279–311), written in 1892. It has been ignored by the majority of Arthurian students and it is of interest that here Arthur is referred to as Arturus Fortissimus ("Arthur the Mighty").

It is significant that in Nennius' *Historia Brittonum* (passage 73, p.83), Arthur is called Arturus Miles, ("Arthur the Warrior"). Turning to the *Breviary of Léon* (1516) and the *Rennes Prose* (1492), we found that the legend of St. Arthmael is mentioned and he is referred to as Miles Fortissimus "Mighty Warrior").[2] He is invoked as "the armigere against the enemies of

---

[1] John Morris, *The Age of Arthur* (London: Weidenfeld & Nicholson, 1973), pp. 251–254 notes.

[2] In the legend of St. Arthmael, as given in the *Rennes Prose* (1492) and the *Breviary of Léon* (1516), he is invoked as the armigere against the enemies of our salvation. This would seem to indicate that the great soldier-saint Arthmael (Bear Prince) was the national messiah who delivered his people from tyranny and that he was identical with King Arthur. Mael (prince) enters into the composition of many Welsh names, e.g. Maelgwyn, Maelog, Maelrhys, etc.

our salvation." The Latin version of Arthmael's name is Armag-illus and this appears to have been derived from armigere, mean-ing armor-bearer or squire. In some writings Arthur is referred to as "The Hammer of the Saxons" and it is interesting that other warrior-kings have also been given this nickname. For example, Edward I was known as "The Hammer of the Scots."

The fact that Arthmael was not only a religious leader but also a military commander ties in extremely well with Nennius's description of one of Arthur's victories "in which he carried the portrait of Saint Mary, ever virgin, on his shoulders, and the pa-gans were routed on that day, and there was great slaughter of them through the power of our Lord Jesus Christ and the strength of the Holy Virgin Mary, his mother."[3]

By combining the evidence from the *Life of St. Arthmael* with that from the lives of St. Paul Aurelian and St. Samson, who were respectively Arthmael's cousin and nephew, we were able to construct the following information:[4]

Arthmael was the cousin of St. Paul Aurelian, and they were educated together at St. Illtyd's famous monastic college at

---

[3]Nennius, *Historia Brittonum* in *Nennius—British History and the Welsh Annals,* John Morris, ed. (London & Chichester: Phillimore, 1980), passage 56, p. 35.

[4]Wrmonoc's *Life of St. Pol de Léon*, written in 884, but compiled from an ear-lier Breton Life of the Saint, confirms that the Count of Léon at this period was Withur, which is clearly the same name as Uthyr (Victor). He is described as a pious Christian who ruled his principality of Léon in Armorica from his strong-hold on the Ile de Batz, north of Roscoff, by the authority of the Frankish King Childebert, who reigned from 511 to 558. A relevant statement is made by W. A. S. Hewins in his book, *The Royal Saints of Britain from the Latter Days of the Roman Empire* (1929): "At this period, the Count of Léon, according to the *Life of St. Pol de Léon,* and other authorities, was Withur. He is also called Ider, the son of Yvain, clearly the same as Uther or Withur (Victor). We may compare also Yetr or Uther in the pedigrees of the Welsh princes. It simply means a ruler or director, and seems to be the same as Arthur with which we may compare the Basque words Arthega = right, and Artegari or Arthegari, which means Director or Ruler. This Withur was related to St. Paul Aurelian and was ruler when the latter arrived. St. Paul Aurelian received from him the Ile de Batz and founded a monastery there in about 530." See also "La Vie de Saint Paul," in Albert Le Grand, *Les Vies de Saints de la Bretagne Armorique,* pp. 98–115.

Llanilltyd Fawr (Llantwit Major). The two cousins crossed the Severn Sea to Cornwall and while Paul traveled further south to administer the religious affairs in the petty realm of Marcus Conomorus, the exiled son of the Glamorgan prince Meirchion Vesanus ("Marcianus the Mad"), Arthmael continued his education as a secular priest under an abbot named Carentmael, who was apparently another cousin. This took place at Bodmin which lay within the principality of Gelliwig (Callington), under the jurisdiction of Count Gwythian, the son of Count Gwythyr of Léon. During his stay in Cornwall, Arthmael must have been on very good terms with Gwythian's family, for he married Gwythian's sister Gwenhwyfar (Guinevere).

Also in Cornwall at this time was Arthmael's nephew, St. Samson, who must have been a great inspiration to him. After founding his own church (now called St. Erme) in the deanery of Powder, Arthmael decided to visit Armorica (Brittany). He went to his cousin Carentmael and told him of his decision. The abbot agreed to accompany him and they both returned to Gwent, where they gathered a large body of men from Caerleon-upon-Usk for the purpose of a mission to Léon in Armorica.

With his band of missionaries, Arthmael landed in the mouth of Aber Benoit or Benniguel ("The Blessed River") in Finistere in the principality of Léon. This territory was named Léon or Lyonesse by Count Gwythyr after Caerleon in Gwent, from where he and his band of colonists came.[5]

---

[5]According to the Charter of Alan Fyrgan ("White Ankle"), the founder of the House of Léon was Yvain, the son of Urbgennius, who was the Consul de Badon of Geoffrey's *Historia* (p. 227), and the Rev. Arthur W. Wade-Evans (*The Emergence of England and Wales,* p. 111) identifies him with Gwrgant Mawr ("the Great"), King of Erging. Yvain married Alienor, the sister of Riwal Mawr ("the Great"), and became the father of Count Gwythyr. Chretien de Troyes depicts Yvain as the Knight of the Lion. He probably saw in his material that Yvain was from Lyonesse but substituted "lion" for Léon. In her Breton poem "Yonec," which was composed some forty years after Geoffrey's *Historia,* Marie de France mentions a ruler named Muldumarec, whose kingdom lay between Caerwent and Caerleon. Muldumarec is widely known in Arthurian literature as King Urien of Gorre. Urien was buried in the coronation chapel of St. Aaron at Caerleon-upon-Usk.

Arthmael and his party traveled inland from Aber Benoit and formed a religious settlement at Plouarzel. Also in Armorica at the time of Arthmael's arrival were his cousin Riwal Mawr ("the Great"), the son of Emyr Llydaw ("the Armorican") and King of Breton Domnonia (509–524), and Arthur's father-in-law Gwythyr, Count of Léon (510–530), whose daughter Gwenhwyfar Arthmael had married.[6]

This is a brief account of the early years of Arthmael and an indication of his connections with Brittany. However, he is not only remembered for founding monasteries there but also for his military achievements, which we will come to in a later chapter.

## ARTHUR, KING OF THE SILURES

During the 18th century, a number of writers actually stated that Arthur was the hereditary king of the Silures in South Wales, but such an idea seems to have been ignored by the vast majority of present-day historians. This is largely due to an academic error which has placed Athrwys ap Meurig in the wrong century. Consequently, the true identity of King Arthur has been obscured and shrouded in mystery.

The Silures were a branch of the Veneti of Armorica who established themselves in South Wales, Cornwall, and the Scilly Islands. It is not just a coincidence that the main field of influence of the royal princes from Glamorgan and Gwent was in Cornwall, the Scilly Islands, and Brittany. It is interesting also to observe that Caerleon, Cernyw, and Gelliwig in Gwent have their counterparts in both Cornwall and Brittany. If the Léon or Lyonesse in Brittany was so named after Caerleon-upon-Usk in

---

[6]According to Wrmonoc's *Life of St. Pol de Léon,* St. Paul Aurelian and Count Gwythyr were cousins. It therefore follows that they had the same grandfather—the mighty Gwrgant Mawr. A copy of the Gospels made by Count Gwythyr was kept in the Cathedral of St. Pol de Léon until the French Revolution, when it was destroyed. See Albert le Grand, *Les Vies des Saints de la Bretagne Armorique,* pp. 98–115.

Gwent, then so must have been its counterparts in Cornwall and the Scilly Islands. It thus becomes obvious that King Arthur's greatest achievement was to recreate the empire of the Silures, which was threatened internally, first by the Gewissei (Irish confederates), and second by a dynastic revolution led by Arthur's treacherous nephew which resulted in the long-remembered Battle of Camlan.

David Williams, in his *History of Monmouthshire* (now called Gwent), published in 1796, appeared to have no doubts about the identification of King Arthur and he was also aware that Arthwyr was a title. He wrote:

> Athrwys or Athruis, the son of Meurig ap Tewdrig, King of Gwent, assumed the appellation of Arthwyr, or the Bear Exalted. In 506 Arthwyr was elected by the states of Britain to exercise sovereign authority, as eminence in consequence of superior abilities and bravery; having been until then only a chieftain of the Silurian Britons.[7]

Seven years later, William Owen Pughe, in his *Cambrian Biography*, published in 1803, made a similar statement, but disagreed slightly with the date of Arthur's election:

> About the year 517, Arthur was elected by the states of Britain to exercise sovereign authority . . . having been from 510 till then, only a chieftain of the Silurian Britons, being the son of Meurig ap Tewdrig.[8]

The area generally supposed to be Arthur's main sphere of activity is Wales, Somerset, Devon, Cornwall, and the Welsh Marches. This territory fitted neatly within the boundaries of Britannia Secunda. Its capital, Isca Silurum, otherwise known as Caerleon-upon-Usk, is where Arthur, in the tradition established

---

[7]David Williams, *The History of Monmouthshire* (Monmouthshire, Tudor & Hall, 1796), p. 75.
[8]William Owen Pughe, *The Cambrian Biography* (London: Edward Williams, 1803), pp. 13–18.

by Geoffrey of Monmouth, is supposed to have held court. Undoubtedly, the key to the identity of King Arthur is the fact that the Glamorgan and Gwentian princes held territory in South Wales, Cornwall, and Brittany, for these lands became the main field of his influence.

## THE LATIN NAME OF ARTHUR

In Latin chronicles, the name of Arthur appears as Arturus (or Arthurus) and it is generally considered that this rendering is derived from the Roman name of Artorius. This was quite a common name during the period of Roman occupation of Britain and it continued to be quite commonly used in subsequent years. One Artorius in particular was Lucius Artorius Castus, who led the VIth Legion on an expedition to Armorica in the middle of the second century. The name Artorius is mentioned by Tacitus and it was certainly a very common name in Rome. In the latter part of the sixth century, there were at least four or five people called Artorius who lived in the Celtic areas of the British Isles.

However, the idea that the name Arthur comes from the Latin Artorius is not very satisfactory and it is our belief that its origin was much more straightforward. As we have already stated, the Celtic word for bear was Arth and the name of Arthur is more likely to be derived from Arthwyr, which was a title or a descriptive term implying a person of high renown or of undaunted fierceness. The name Arthur is merely another form of Arthwyr and the Latin version of the name is more likely to be Athruis, as given in the ancient *Book of Llandaff*. In this instance, the name Athruis is more likely derived from Arturus, which is in fact the name given by Nennius in *Historia Brittonum*, and it may be found in the earliest of the manuscripts dating from the 10th or 11th century.

## THE BRETON ARTHUR

The earliest record of King Arthur originated in Brittany and in a later chapter we shall reveal that this was the country where he spent his last days, so it is quite naturally the place where legends concerning his life are particularly strong. As far as we have been able to ascertain, the earliest record of Arthur being a "king" is in the Breton legend of St. Goeznovius (ca. 1019). By the 12th century, the legend of Arthur, which had included a belief in his "return," had taken firm root in Brittany, and we can thus assume that it was from the Bretons rather than the Welsh that the Normans derived their knowledge of Arthur. From the stories connected with him, they constructed the romantic cycle known as *Matière de Bretagne*.

Wales, Cornwall, and Brittany all claim to be associated with the legends of King Arthur and his knights, and in this book we have set out to show how each claim is justified. Through his "life" and the lives of his kinsmen, St. Samson and St. Paul Aurelian, it is possible to follow the activities of King Arthur from Glamorgan and Gwent, across Cornwall, to Brittany. In Wales, he is the celebrated Arthwyr, King of the Silures; in Cornwall, he is appears to have been confused with his brother-in-law, Count Gwythian of Gelliwig (now Callington); in Brittany, he is remembered as the great soldier-saint Arthmael, or Armel.

## THE CROWNING OF ARTHUR

According to the *Life of St. Dyfrig*, contained in the *Book of Llandaff*, Arthur was crowned emperor when he was 15 years old. Today, it seems almost unbelievable that a boy of 15 could be made ruler of his country. However, there are many other examples in later history of young people who were crowned rulers at an early age. For example, Richard II was crowned at the tender age of 10 and Queen Victoria was a young lady of 18 when she became Queen of England.

We know that Arthmael was born in 482, so this means that he was crowned in 497, which was the year that Ambrosius died. According to Geoffrey of Monmouth, the ceremony took place at Silchester, but when we consulted the *Brut Tysilio* (p. 138) we found an interesting statement to the effect that Arthur was crowned by St. Dyfrig (Dubricius) at Caer Vudei—"the camp in the wood." Geoffrey's misidentification of this ancient fort helped to push it into obscurity. It is, in fact, the old name for Woodchester and this site, protected by the Minchinhampton complex of earthworks, was used by Ambrosius as the headquarters of his armed forces to prevent inroads by the Saxons into his domain.

Ambrosius's campaign against the Saxons culminated in a victorious battle fought in 493 at Bown Hill, overlooking the Severn Valley, close to Woodchester. When he took control of the territory east of the Severn, he established a base at Caer Vudei, which was formerly the residence of a Roman governor. The names in this locality indicate that this fortified place was the city or seat of authority of Ambrosius, whom the Welsh knew as Emrys Wledig. His court was called Ambrosii Aula and was situated at Amberlys in Rodborough, near Woodchester. It seems appropriate that Arthur, nominated by Emrys himself as the new leader of the British resistance, should be crowned at Woodchester. It is an interesting fact that Henry II was crowned just a few miles away at Gloucester in 1216.

## KING ARTHUR'S FAMILY BACKGROUND

Following the departure of the legions, the Roman republic of the Silures was displaced by a monarchy and Teithfallt became the ruler of this area. It appears that he was a wise and heroic king, who fought valiantly against the Saxons. He ended his days as a monk, having abdicated in favor of his son, Tewdrig.

Tewdrig has been described as an eminently good king, who drove the infidel Saxons and Goidels (Irish) out of his kingdom and founded many churches and colleges, endowing them with possessions. In conjunction with the Romano-British Emperor Constantine the Blessed, he is credited with having reestablished the college of Cor Worgan, which was named after Eurgain, the sister of Eudaf Hen. It was later called Llanilltyd Fawr (now corrupted to Llantwit Major), after its principal, St. Illtyd.

After the demise of Constantine the Blessed in 443, Tewdrig preserved a shaky alliance with Vortigern, as a result of the marriage of Ynyr I (a sub-king of Gwent) to Vortigern's granddaughter Madryn. Tewdrig had surrendered the rule of Garth Madryn (Talgarth in Powys) to the Irish chieftain Anlach Mac Cormac, who had married his daughter Marchell. It is very important for us to mention these marriage alliances in order to give a full picture of the interconnecting families who are essential parts of Dark Age history.

In his old age, just as his father had done before him, Tewdrig abdicated and the government of his kingdom passed into the hands of his son Meurig. He then went into retirement to lead a monastic life in the solitude of the Wye Valley at a place which is now called Tintern. This name has originated from Din Teyrn, which simply means the fort of the king. There have been settlements in the lower Wye Valley since prehistoric times and excavations have revealed the site of a small Roman building

*Figure 10. Tintern Abbey is beautifully situated in the Wye Valley on the east side of Gwent. It was near here that King Tewdrig settled in retirement during the latter part of the fifth century.*

within the foundations of Tintern Abbey. This may have been occupied by Tewdrig, but there is also a tradition that he lived as a
hermit "among the rocks at Tintern."

However, he was not able to enjoy the peace of his beautiful
surroundings for very long. It came to an abrupt end one day
when the Saxons crossed the Wye and entered Gwent. The old
king, who had been victorious in all his battles, bravely took up
arms and, mounted on horseback, led his household troops to
deal with the enemy. It is likely that the battle took place in the
nearby Angidy Valley, where a stone bridge bears the name Pont
y Saeson—"Bridge of the Saxons." The invaders were put to
flight, but one of them hurled a lance which struck the old king,
who fell to the ground. By now, his son Meurig had arrived on
the scene, and the mortally wounded Tewdrig was taken from
the battlefield in a cart drawn by two stags toward the Severn Estuary. The intention was probably to bury him on the island of
Flat Holm on the Severn Sea, but he died at a spot on the Gwent
side of the estuary, where a clear and strong spring started to
flow from the ground.

This spring is in the village of Mathern and since the Dark
Ages it has been used as a well. It was once of stone construction
but has sadly in recent years been encased in concrete. A metal
plaque on the wall confirms that it is the site of Tewdrig's Well.
"By tradition at this spring King Tewdrig's wounds were washed
after the battle near Tintern about 470 A.D. against the pagan
Saxons. He died a short way off and by his wishes a church was
built over his grave."[9]

We know that this is indeed an ancient site, for Nennius,
writing in about 822, mentions the well and refers to it as one of
the *Marvels* of Britain. "There is another wonder in the region
that is Gwent. There is there a spring near the valley of the Well
of Meurig." The Well of Meurig is a reference to the nearby village of Pwllmeurig, which means Meurig's Pool and provides a
link with the son of Tewdrig, who was of course the father of
Arthur. Just around the corner from Tewdrig's Well is the grand

---

[9]Nennius, *Historia Brittonum*, passage 72, p. 42.

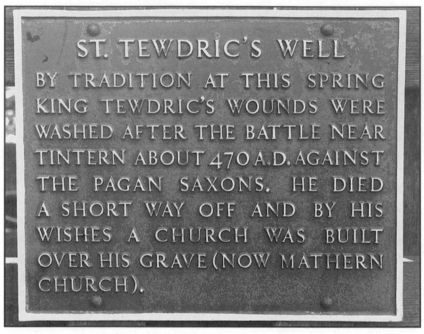

*Figure 11. St. Tewdrig's Well is situated near Mathern Church, Gwent, and it is mentioned by Nennius, writing in about 822, as one of the marvels of Britain.*

old church of Mathern, which provides the next connection in this fascinating story.

It seems that Tewdrig had requested that a church be raised on the spot where he died, and his son, Meurig, obeyed his last wishes by having an oratory erected over the grave. In due course, it was blessed by St. Oudoceus (whose church is at Llandogo in the Wye Valley), and it became known as Merthyr Teyrn (the church of the martyred king). Mathern is the anglicized version of this name. The land around the church was made over to St. Oudoceus for the monastery of Llandaff and, in later times, the bishops established a palace there.

Inside Mathern Church, on the north wall of the chancel, is a large stone tablet which tells the story of the last days of King Tewdrig:

*Figure 12. The first church at Mathern in Gwent was built over the grave of King Tewdrig and it became known as Merthyr Teyrn ("the church of the martyred king"). Over the years this name has been anglicized to Mathern.*

Here lyeth entombed the body of Theoderick, King of Mor-
ganuck, or Glamorgan, commonly called St. Tewdrick, and
accounted a martyr because he was slain in battle against
the Saxons, being then pagans, and in defence of the Christian religion. The battle was fought at Tintern, where he obtained a great victory. He died here, being on his way home-
ward, three days after the battle, having taken order with
Maurice, his son who succeeded him in his kingdom, that in
the same place he should happen to decease a church should
be built and his body buried in ye same, which was accordingly performed in the year 600.

This tablet was erected by Bishop Godwin in the early years of
the 17th century. He had been intrigued by the story of Tewdrig
contained in the ancient *Book of Llandaff* and excavated the site
of the tomb to check its authenticity. To his undoubted satifac-
tion, he found a fifth-century style stone coffin containing a
skeleton with a badly fractured skull. Godwin was over one hundred years out in his dating of the event, but the wording of his
inscription is based on the account given in the *Book of
Llandaff*. It is of interest that the Book also records three separate grants of land and rights given by Meurig and Brochmael—
son and grandson of Tewdrig respectively—in honor of the late
king. There is a pool in the River Wye, near Tintern, named after
Brochmael, which again helps to confirm the family connection
with this locality.

Several Llandaff bishops are buried in Mathern Church
and one of them is Miles Sally, who left instructions in his will
that his heart should be buried before the high altar near the
grave of "King Theoderick." When Bishop Godwin opened the
grave in the 17th century, he found an urn beside Tewdrig's
stone coffin and this most certainly contained the heart of
Bishop Sally.

Meurig succeeded his father, Tewdrig Fendigaid, as King of
Morgannwg and Gwent and he would have held paramount
authority over a tract forming the principal part of Glamorgan,
the whole of Gwent, and the portion of Herefordshire which lies
to the southwest of the River Wye. He married Onbrawst,

daughter of Gwrgant Mawr, King of Erging.[10] They had four
sons, Athruis, Idnerth, Frioc, and Comereg. Their daughters
were Anna, who married Amwn Ddu, Gwenonwy, who married
Gwyndaf Hen, and Afrella, who married Umbrafael. In fact, all
three of Meurig's daughters married sons of Emyr Llydaw
(Budic, Emperor of Armorica) and thus achieved an important
alliance between the two royal families. We did not realize it at
first, but these family connections were going to be of enormous
significance when we came to identify the locations of the Battle
of Camlan and the mysterious island of Avalon.

It is of interest that Meurig's daughter Gwenonwy can be
tied in with Pwll Meurig, for a document dated 1311 mentioned
a place called Tref Elenni, which was subsequently shortened to
Trelenny. It has been suggested that this location was originally
the site of the village of Gwenonwy, named after the daughter of
Meurig and the sister of Arthur. A chapel dedicated to her stood
in a brake between Pwll Meurig village and Mounton and, at the
time of the dissolution of the monasteries in 1534, it belonged to
Chepstow Priory. In the *Book of Llandaff*, there are two documents recording the grant of the villa of Guennoe or Guinnonui
(Gwenonwy) to the Church of Llandaff in the time of Bishop
Berthwyn. It was described as being situated "juxta paludem

---

[10]Gwrgant Mawr ("the Great"), king of Erging, has been identified with Urien
of Gorre (Gower) by both Dr. John Morris and the Rev. Arthur Wade-Evans.
This is a plausible hypothesis, for further research reveals that Gwrgant was
ousted from Erging by the usurper Gwrtheyrn and established himself in the
Gower Peninsula, which he liberated from the Irish. Iolo Morganwg maintained that, whereas Cunedda Wledig was responsible for expelling the Irish
settlers from North Wales, it was Urien of Gorre who expelled them from
Gower. Emrys Wledig reinstated Gwrgant as king of Erging, but he still retained Gower with his court at Aber Llychwr (Leucarum). It is also interesting
to note that the famous son of Urien of Gorre was Yvain, the Knight of Léon,
and he was the father of Count Gwythyr of Léon, whose daughter, Gwenhwyfar, Arthur married. The relationship between these two important families of
Gwent is an integral part of the story of King Arthur and the colonization of
Brittany. See Morris, *The Age of Arthur*, p. 229, and Wade-Evans, *The Emergence of England and Wales*, p. 111.

Mourici," which again helps to link Gwenonwy with this locality named after her father, Meurig.

An interesting question which needs to be answered is why the King Arthur of tradition is supposed to have been the son of Uthyr Pendragon, while we have in fact identified him as the son of Meurig. The simple explanation is that Meurig bore the title Uther Pendragon which means "Wonderful Head Dragon," indicating that he was a leader of the British army. Geoffrey of Monmouth was the first writer to refer to Arthur as the son of Uther Pendragon and he obviously confused the title with the personal name of Uthyr, the brother of Emrys (Ambrosius). Geoffrey may also have misinterpreted the writings of Nennius, who described Arthur as *mab uter, id est filius horribilis*, a name which the Britons gave him because of his love of war. The fact that *uter* means marvelous, and, as *mab uter,* Arthur becomes "marvelous son" may have led to Geoffrey's confused statement that Arthur was the son of Uthyr Pendragon.

Confusion may have also been caused because Arthur (Arthmael) married the daughter of Count Gwythyr. This is the same name as Uthyr, which in Latin is Victor. In other words, Uthyr was the father-in-law of Arthur and not his father, as stated by Geoffrey of Monmouth. These may seem complicated explanations, but they all provide sound reasons why such a puzzling statement was made.

We have already mentioned that the paternal grandfather of Arthur was Tewdrig, but it is particularly relevant to identify his grandfather on his mother's side of the family. King Arthur's mother was Onbrawst, the daughter of Gwrgant Mawr, King of Erging. Gwrgant had been expelled from his kingdom by the usurper Vortigern, but was later reinstated by Ambrosius. It is this complex web of family connections which, after careful scrutiny, provides the essential elements in the sequence of events which ultimately lead to King Arthur's downfall. One of the sons of Gwrgant Mawr was Caradog Freichfras, who took over the reins of government while Arthur was away fighting battles. It was Caradog's grandson Medraut who tried to seize power while Arthur was absent; the outcome was the Battle of Camlan. We shall deal with this incident in a later chapter.

## LLACHEU, THE SON OF KING ARTHUR

In the *Welsh Triads*, Llacheu, a son of King Arthur, is mentioned with Gwalchmai, son of Gwyar, and Peredur, son of Earl Efrog, as one of the "Three Fearless Men of the Island of Britain," and also, with Gwalchmai and Rhiwallawn Wallt Banhadlen ("of the Broom Blossom Hair") as one of the "Three Learned Ones of the Island of Britain." It is also stated that Llacheu ("the Gleaming or Glittering One") wore a circle of gold to distinguish him as the son of the Amherawdyr (Emperor). He was a man of most accomplished character, and was no less renowned for his war-like prowess than for his deep knowledge.

During our search for information relating to King Arthur's long lost son, Llacheu, we soon came to realize that it was first necessary to establish the connections of King Arthur himself with the Welsh Border country in the county of Herefordshire.

One of the most ancient tales in the Welsh language is the story of "Culhwch and Olwen" contained in the *Mabinogion*. Culhwch was said to be the cousin of King Arthur and an episode in the story relates how Llwydawg Govynnyad ("the Hewer") went to Ystrad Yw, where he met the men of Llydaw. There he slew Hirpeissawc ("of the Long Tunic"), King of Llydaw, Llygatrudd ("the Red-Eyed Emys"), and Gwrfoddw Hen ("the Old"), who were Arthur's uncles (his mother's brothers). Thus, Arthur, through his mother, is incidentally associated with the border country near Hereford.

Ystrad Yw was a district in south Brecon separated from the kingdom of Erging (between the rivers Monnow and Wye in Herefordshire) by the cantref of Ewyas. Gwrfoddw Hen was doubtless the Gwyndaf Hen mentioned in the *Liber Landavensis* (the "Ancient Register of the Cathedral Church of Llandaff") as ruling Erging, only one district removed from Ystrad Yw. He was the son of Emyr Llydaw ("the Armorican") and he married Gwenonwy, the daughter of Meurig ap Tewdrig Fendigaid ("the Blessed"), King of Morgannwg and Gwent. The Emys in Llygatrudd Emys may be, as Sir John Rhys suggested in his *Studies in the Arthurian Legend* (1891), a scribal error for Emyr. If this is the case, then the person intended is none other than Emyr

Llydaw, the ruler of the British settlements in Armorica, whose sons married daughters of Meurig ap Tewdrig, King of Morgannwg and Gwent.

The *Liber Landavensis* was translated from the Latin by the Rev. William Jenkins Rees in 1839, who informed us that Cernyw was a district in Erging over which reigned Custennin Fendigaid (Constantine "the Blessed"), the son of Macsen Wledig (Maximus "the Imperator") and the father-in-law of Pepiau Clavorauc ("the Dravellor"), also king of Erging. Pepiau was the father of Efrddyl, the mother of St. Dyfrig (Dubricius). There is a district in Gwent also called Cernyw in which King Arthur's court of Gelliwig was situated (see page 65). The *Book of Llandaff* records the grant of Lann Custenhin Garth Benni (the Church and Monastic Enclosure of Constantine "the Blessed") made by King Pepiau to his grandson, St. Dyfrig. Lann Custenhin Garth Benni has been identified with Welsh Bicknor in the county of Hereford and is called Ecclesia Sancti Custenhin de Biconovria in a St. Florent charter of 1144. The *Life of St. Dubricius*, contained in the *Book of Llandaff*, records how St. Dubricius, Archbishop of Llandaff, crowned the celebrated King Arthur in the 15th year of his age.

Also recorded in the *Book of Llandaff* is a grant made by King Athrwys (Arthur) of Gwent to his brother Comereg, abbot of Mochros (Moccas in Herefordshire). Included in this grant is Campus Malochu which can be none other than Mais Mail Lochou or Llecheu ("the Plain or Field of Prince Llacheu"), also known as Ynys Efrddyl after the mother of St. Dyfrig. Mochros was the site of a palace of fifth/sixth-century kings and may well have been the residence of Prince Llacheu, son of King Arthur, for Mochros was situated in Mais Mail Lochou.

The *Life of St. Dubricius* informs us that the Saint, after leaving his monastery at Henlann (Hentland), spent a further period of time in Ynys Efrddyl. King Pepiau Clavorauc of Erging had made the young Dyfrig heir to the whole of the island, which was called Ynys Efrddyl after his mother. It is not an island, as suggested, but a wooded tongue of land, bounded by the Wye, the Worm, and the hills which divide the plain from the Dore. This wide district contained Matle (Madley), which owed its name of "the good place" to the fact that "the blessed man"

was born there, and Mochros, which means Swine Moor, is derived from St. Dyfrig's encounter with a white sow and her litter
when he was looking for a suitable place for his new monastery.
He accepted this as a good omen and there he planted his
monastery. Close by is Madley, which was also dedicated to
St. Dyfrig. The name Campus Malochu seems to have survived
in that of Mawfield Farm in the parish of Allensmore, the church
of which is about three-and-a-half miles southeast of Madley
Church. It is observed that Arclestone, now Arkstone Court,
close to Allensmore, belonged to the Bishops of Llandaff
all through the Middle Ages, the sole remnant of all the St.
Dubricius land grants in Herefordshire claimed by the *Liber
Landavensis.*

The majority of his dedications are found in the country between the rivers Wye and Monnow, reaching westward to the
Golden Valley and including Hentland, Whitchurch, Ballingham,
and St. Devereux. They must mark the territory where St. Dyfrig
preached and founded his churches, an area which was the essential core of the Romano-British kingdom of Erging.

St. Dyfrig widened his field of activity and moved to South
Wales, where, according to the *Achau y Saint*, he was consecrated Bishop of Llandaff by St. Garmon in about 470. According to Archbishop Ussher, he was raised by Emyrs Wledig (Ambrosius the Imperator), to the Archbishopric of Caerleon. Dyfrig
still retained the Bishopric of Llandaff, where he mostly resided.
His connection with Caerleon is confirmed by his possession of
the Church of the Martyr-Saints Julius and Aaron. In the capacity of Archbishop of Caerleon, he crowned Arthur king-emperor
at Caer Vudei (Woodchester), the former court and military
headquarters of the Romano-British Emperor Emrys Wledig (see
page 46). St. Dyfrig's association with Gloucestershire may be
confirmed by Doverow Hill, in Stroud, which is derived from his
other name, St. Devereux. In his later years, St. Dyfrig resigned
the primacy of Llandaff to his successor St. Teilo, and then credited the honors of the Archbishopric of Caerleon to St. David,
who removed the archepiscopal see from Caerleon to Menevia.

In the *Black Book of Carmarthen*, there is a reference to a
battle between Cai Wyn and Llacheu, and Gwyddno Garanhir
claims that he was present at the place where Llacheu was killed.

According to Bleddyn Fardd, he was killed below Llech Ysgar. The story of Culhwch and Olwen tells us how a feud developed between Arthur and his seneschel, Cai. This feud attains its climax in the episode narrated in *Perlesvaus,* in which Cai is said to have treacherously slain Arthur's son Llacheu.

Nennius, in his *Historia Brittonum,* records a "Wonder" of Britain which he describes as a tomb by a spring called Llygad Amir (the Eye of the Emperor). He suggests that the man whose body lies buried in the tomb was the son of Arthur the Amherawdyr (Emperor). Llygad Amir has been identified with Gamber Head, the source of the River Gamber near Wormelow Tump in Herefordshire. It appears that King Arthur considered himself responsible for the tragic death of his son Llacheu and built a magnificent tomb in his memory. The alternative solution is that Llygad Amir is derived from Llygatrudd Emys (the Red-Eyed Emys), in which case, the man who is buried there would be none other than Arthur's uncle, Emyr Llydaw. Unfortunately, whatever the truth of the matter, the tomb has long since been destroyed.

> Arthur was, at an early period of life, entrusted with a pre-eminent military command, and owing, we may reasonably conclude, to the experience his countrymen already possessed of his talents and courage. From the time that Arthur was thus raised to the chief dominion over his countrymen, it is reasonable to presume, that the distracted state of the times may have involved him in much war and bloodshed. His whole life, indeed, from the period alluded to, was, in all probability, a continued series of martial achievements. For, in the north of England, in Wales, and in Cornwall, the Britons, or Cymry, were still in sufficient force to resist, as they often did with signal advantage, the incursions of their Saxon invaders. Nennius, who in his "Historia Brittonum" has given a brief outline of the exploits of Arthur, enumerates twelve battles, in which he commanded against the Saxons, and in all of which he ascribes the victory to the British chief.[11]

---

[11]John H. Parry, *The Cambrian Plutarch* (London: W. Simpkin & R. Marshall, 1824), p. 7.

# 4

# The Land of the Silures

THE SILURES WERE A BRANCH of the Veneti tribe of Armorica who established themselves in South Wales and Cornwall early in the second century B.C. Their first landings were on the shore of the River Severn, at Sudbrook and Caldicot. They settled in this area and, as their numbers grew, they spread out over the coastal areas of Glamorgan and Gwent to the valleys of the Black Mountains in the north. The River Wye formed an approximate eastern boundary separating the Silures from the Dobunni tribe.

It would seem that the Silures of Britain maintained close diplomatic relations with their associates, the Armorican tribe called the Veneti, who controlled the cross-channel trade. The Silures were responsible for the design and construction of the multivallated hill-fortresses which are still impressive even today. Successive lines of defense enabled the defenders to utilize the greatest possible distance between themselves within the fort and the attacking enemy outside. This use of multiple ramparts was first introduced at the cliff-top fortresses which the Veneti tribe established on the rocky coast of Armorica. Along the coasts of Cornwall are similar cliff-top defensive positions which appear to be either the work of the same Veneti or their British associates, the Silures.

This principle of multiple ramparts was particularly suitable for defense by men armed with slings. With the aid of a simple leather loop, a man could hurl a smooth pebble or a baked clay bullet with considerable force over a range of several hundred yards to maim or kill his enemy. A well-organized company of slingers could wreak havoc among their foes advancing from below. The establishment of these ring-forts and hill-top fortresses of larger size continued inland and it was from Devon and Cornwall along the coast of the Bristol Channel that this new art of war developed.

Llanmelin hill-fort to the north of Caerwent was once a key fortress of the Silures in this area, but until now its significance has not really been understood. It is an elaborate example of a multiple-ramparted fort and dates back to the latter part of the early Iron Age. The summit plateau is about 110 meters above sea level and the defenses closely follow the 100 meter contour line. The main camp is contained within a roughly elliptical enclosure measuring 250 meters by 170 meters and covers an area of about 2 hectares. There is also an oblong "annex" to the main camp, measuring 134 meters long by 73 meters wide and covering an area of about 0.5 hectares. Both sections of the fort were defended by multiple banks and ditches and the inner rampart was 6 meters wide and faced with stone.

This was once the site of a busy Silurian town whose inhabitants lived in simple huts constructed of wattles plastered with mud or clay. They were farming folk who kept oxen, pigs, sheep, and red deer for food, as revealed by a partial excavation carried out in 1930–1932.

At the time of the Roman invasion, the Silures were the most powerful tribe in Britain. Their reputation as fighters attracted to them the defeated Celtic chieftain Caractacus, who became their leader in a series of battles against the Romans. He was finally beaten and taken to Rome as a prisoner, but the Silures still continued to fight bravely and they won yet another battle against the Second Legion in A.D. 52. These Silurian warriors of Gwent and Glamorgan were certainly no easy prey, nor were they amenable to negotiation or threat. The Roman historian, Tacitus, paid them a worthy compliment when he wrote: ". . . the Silures were turned neither by brutality or clemency from pursuing war and required the encampment of legions to keep them down."[1]

When the Romans finally managed to subdue the area, which today is known as Gwent, they converted the name Syllwg

[1]Tacitus, *The Annals of Imperial Rome*, Michael Grant, trans. (New York: Dorset, 1984), p. 266–269.

*Figure 13. The outer walls of Venta Silurum, a Roman fortress constructed as the administrative center of Britannia Secunda. On the southern side of the fort, the wall is 500 meters long and still stands in places to a height of 6 meters. Constructed of limestone, sandstone, and grit with pebble fillings held together by an extremely durable cement, the Roman walled fort of Caerwent is surely one of the wonders of Wales.*

to Siluria and referred to the natives as Silures. Gwent was then known as Venta and a short distance from their landing point on the Severn Estuary they constructed a military station which they named Venta Silurum. Today, it is better known as Caerwent. Here the remains of a fascinating Roman fortress town can be seen. It covers a rectangular area of about 20 hectares and is surrounded by an impressive stonewall constructed in about A.D. 200. At the base it is nearly 4 meters wide and at one time it must have been more than 6 meters high, tapering to a width of 2 meters at the top. There were four gates placed centrally in the four sides and the main road to South Wales passed through the east and west entrances. With the exception of Hadrian's Wall, the stone defensive perimeter of Caerwent is one of the most impressive above-ground Roman remains to be seen in Britain. It also has the distinction of being the only Romano-British town in Wales and was once the center of the Silurian tribal government. The Silures were persuaded by the Romans to leave their hill-top fort at Llanmelin, just to the north, and come to Venta Silurum to sample the Roman way of life. By the third century, about two or three thousand people were living here.

Venta Silurum, with its shops and business premises, became a profitable center of trade and its merchants lived in luxury. Buildings included a market place, a basilica (town hall), large public baths, shops, inns, houses, and an amphitheater which provided entertainment. This fortress town was ideally situated, for, being close to the Severn Estuary, it was possible for goods to be brought from various parts of the Roman Empire and unloaded at Caldicot Pill or Sudbrook harbor. From there, they were conveyed on smaller boats along the Nedern waterway to reach their final destination.

It is of significance that the fort stood on the route of the Via Julia Strata, an important Roman highway which ran from Aquae Sulis (Bath) to the harbor of Abonae (Avonmouth). From here, a ferry crossed the Severn to Sudbrook and the road continued through the center of Venta Silurum, to cross the Wentwood ridge and descend into the garrison fortress of Isca Silurum, which is now known as Caerleon-upon-Usk.

The Romans governed Siluria for a period of 365 years and, on their departure in about 407, the native princes resumed the government of this area. Venta Silurum itself fell largely into decline, although there is a tradition that, during the time of Arthur, the fort was occupied by King Ynyr II of Gwent-is-Coed (below the wood), who ruled this locality as a sub-king.

Under the patronage of King Ynyr, a church was built within the walls of the old Roman fort by St. Tathan, who settled here. He was the son of an Armorican king and the tradition is that Tathan set sail from his homeland accompanied by eight disciples. They reached the Severn Estuary and came up the River Nedern to Caerwent. Here they were warmly received by King Ynyr, whose father Caradog Freichfras, an uncle of Arthur, was probably in residence at Llanmelin fort. Caradog, who acted as Arthur's Chief Elder, sent for Tathan and asked him to found a church at Caerwent. In due course, the saint founded a college here to provide instruction in the arts and sciences. It was said to rival the college of Dyfrig at Caerleon. Tathan's most famous pupil was Cadoc, the son of Gwynllyw, who will come into our story later.

From the walls of Caerwent, Llanmelin hill-fort can be seen a couple of miles away to the north. When the Romans departed, the Silures, concerned by the threat of Saxon invaders, no doubt made the decision to return to the way of life of their ancestors and the security of this fortified hilltop.

The annex to the fort is an unusual feature, and its existence may be explained by the fact that, when some of the old Iron Age hill-forts were refortified in the Dark Ages, they were in some instances extended as well. Obviously, they became an essential part of the Romano-British system of defense and much of this improvement work was probably undertaken during the time of Ambrosius, to whom the building of Wansdyke is credited.

The question that concerns us is whether Llanmelin was occupied in Arthurian times. Having been an important headquarters of the Silures at the time of the Roman invasion, it seems only natural that in later years Arthur, as King of the Silures, would also have made it his main base. It was also close to Caerwent which had been the British capital in Roman times.

There is evidence that a number of similar forts which had fallen into disuse were restored in the Dark Ages and reoccupied. Excavations at Castle Dore in Cornwall, Dinas Powys and Deganwy in Wales, Cadbury in Somerset, and Maiden Castle in Dorset, have shown that these forts were certainly occupied during the time of Arthur. It is important for the reader to come to terms with the fact that the type of fortress used by King Arthur was nothing like the medieval castle depicted by the romance writers of the Middle Ages, who saw Arthur and his men as knights in shining armor relevant to their own times.

Unfortunately, the brief excavation of 1930–1932 failed to show evidence of sixth-century occupation at Llanmelin, but with such a small excavation, it cannot be accepted as conclusive proof that the fort was *not* occupied during this period. Only a

*Figure 14. Llanmelin hill-fort, near Caerwent in Gwent, was the headquarters of the Silures at the time of the Roman invasion, so it seems only natural that in later years, Arthur, as King of the Silures, should also make it his main base. The fort is situated 110 meters above sea level and, with difficult access, would have been easily defended. The oval camp is surrounded by a double foss with each ditch 3 to 4 meters deep.*

more extensive excavation would decide this one way or the other.

Llanmelin was certainly used in medieval times, when it was incorporated into the Lordship of Shirenewton and apparently rented by the Lord of the Manor to his farmer-tenants, who established their huts within the old earthworks. They used it until the 13th century, when the site was finally abandoned. It is possible that finds relating to the Dark Ages were made by the people living here at this time.

## THE SEARCH FOR ARTHUR'S COURT OF GELLIWIG

In the *Welsh Triads*, Gelliwig in Cernyw is mentioned as one of Arthur's "Three Principal Courts in the Island of Britain." Before trying to pinpoint the location of Gelliwig, it is necessary to identify the area once known as Cernyw, for this in itself is an essential key to the mystery of King Arthur. The main problem is that its real location has been obscured by medieval writers who have firmly identified Cernyw as Cornwall. However, they completely missed the point that Cernyw was once part of southeast Wales.[2] Cornwall did not become known as Cernyw until the 10th century and this simple fact has resulted in the story of King Arthur being wrongly located in the West Country.

Cernyw was the name given to the coastal area between Chepstow and Cardiff and it survives on the present day Ordnance Survey map in Coed Kernew, which lies just to the west of Newport. Here a church was founded in the sixth century by Glywys Cernyw, a son of Gwynllyw Filwr ("the Warrior"). The present church only dates back to 1853, but it stands on an ancient site.

The *Welsh Triads* mention Gelliwig (small wood or grove) as one of the "Three National Thrones of the Island of Britain,"

---

[2]In his book *Celtic Folklore* (Oxford: Clarendon Press, 1891), Sir John Rhys suggests that Aust Cliff in Gloucestershire is the location of Penrhyn Austin yn Kernyw. He also makes the point that this implies the use of the name Kernyw in its ancient sense to denote the whole of the Domnonian Peninsula. (See vol. II, p. 506.)

and one of Arthur's chief seats of the empire, in which he used to celebrate the high festivals of Christmas, Easter, and Whitsuntide. One of the *Triads* states that, when Arthur was supreme ruler, Bedwin was the chief bishop, and Caradoc Freichfras was the chief elder of Gelliwig. This court was one of the "Three Archbishoprics of Britain" and Bedwin Sands in the Severn Estuary appears to have been named after Bishop Bedwin.

We gradually came to the conclusion that the Gelliwig in question can be no other place but Llanmelin hill-fort and the evidence is substantial. Close to this Silurian base is Cuhere Wood, a small grove or Gelliwig, and Llanmelin is also situated in Gwent-is-Coed, i.e., Gwent below the wood (now known as Wentwood). During Arthur's campaigns abroad, his chief elder, Caradoc Freichfras, ruled both Gwent-is-Coed and Gwent-uth-Coed (above the wood) from his headquarters near Caerwent. It seems that Arthur shared power with Caradoc and they jointly ruled from Gelliwig, i.e. Llanmelin or Caer Melin, as it was formerly known.

The name Llanmelin means "the church of the mill" and it has obviously become associated with the old mill which is situated below the fort beside the Troggy Brook. However, the previous name for this location was Llan y Gelli, i.e. "the church of the gelli" (grove). This was corrupted into Llangethyn. The name of the mill would therefore be Melin Llan Gelli, which was later abbreviated into Llan y Gelli. The actual site of this early church has not been determined but it may have occupied the site of the present Llanmelin Farm or perhaps stood within the hill-fort itself. It is interesting that the name of the parish church and the manor of Shirenewton is in Welsh "Dre Newydd Gelli Farch," i.e. "the new town of the Earl's Grove." Thus Llan y Gelli may well be the site of the older church of the Gelli.

Geoffrey of Monmouth was convinced that King Arthur's court was at Caerleon-upon-Usk, but this was probably one of his many errors—deliberate or otherwise. It is feasible that he in fact substituted Caerleon-upon-Usk for Gelliwig as the site of the main court of Arthur, because, with its extensive Roman remains, it was a more impressive location. Furthermore, it may be conjectured that, because Arthur was King of Gwent, his court was more likely to have been at or near Venta Silurum

(Caerwent), which after all was the British capital. Isca Silurum (Caerleon-upon-Usk), on the other hand, was the old Roman capital of the province and would have been a less likely place for him to choose as his headquarters.

We found further confirmation of our theory in the *Mabinogion* story which tells of the pursuit of the Twrch Trwyth (Irish Boar) by Arthur's men:

> The Twrch Trwyth went from Ystrad Yw to between Towy and Ewyas and Arthur summoned the men of Devon and Cornwall unto him to the estuary of the Severn and he said to the warriors of this island, "Twrch Trwyth has slain many of my men, but by the valour of my warriors, while I live he shall not go into Cernyw. I will not follow him any longer, but I will oppose him life to life. Do as you will." Arthur then resolved that he would send a body of knights, together with the war dogs of the island, as far as Ewyas, that they should return thence to the Severn, and that tried warriors should traverse the island and force the Twrch Trwyth into the Severn.
>
> Then Arthur, together with all the champions of Britain, fell upon the boar betwixt Llyn Lliwan and the Aber Gwy, plunged him into the Severn and overwhelmed him in Cernyw. Then he was hunted from Cernyw and driven straight forward into the deep sea. Arthur then went to Gelliwig in Cernyw to anoint himself and rest from his fatigues.[3]

This ancient story can be deciphered like a riddle. It tells how the hunting of the Twrch Trwyth ranged from the west of Ireland, across the Irish Channel to West Wales, and then on to South Wales as far as the River Severn, threatening Gelliwig in Cernyw—the very seat of Arthur's government. Obviously Arthur feared that the "boar," a symbolic representation of the Gewissei, his Irish enemies, might penetrate Cernyw and reach

---

[3]Lady Charlotte Guest, trans., the *Mabinogion* (London: J. M. Dent, 1906), pp. 133–134.

Gelliwig, so he reacted violently. However, despite Arthur's efforts, the boar does succeed in penetrating Cernyw and a desperate battle takes place. After the boar is successfully overwhelmed, Arthur retires to his court at Gelliwig to bathe and rest. These events were a prelude to the battle of Badon and we shall deal with them in more detail in chapter 12.

The land of the Silures is undoubtedly the realm of King Arthur. In the fifth century, the old Roman Republic was displaced and the Silurian Commonwealth was re-established when the small kingdom of Glywysing, named after its founder, King Glywys, became united with Gwent. The first ruler of this new kingdom was Tewdrig Fendigaid, an eminently good king who founded many churches and colleges. During the reign of his son Meurig, the area today known as Glamorgan became united with Gwent and Erging. Subsequently, his son Athrwys succeeded in recreating the ancient empire of the Silures. He was the King Arthur of legend and history whose story has become so confused and obscured during the passing centuries. It is only by establishing him in his correct dynastic setting that the truth of the matter can finally be revealed.

> Arthur was the son of Meurig ap Tewdrig, a prince of the Silurian Britons at the commencement of the sixth century, and who is, in all probability, to be identified with our hero's reputed sire, Uthyr, or Uther, of legendary celebrity. For the custom of adopting assumed appellations was by no means unusual with the Britons of that age; and hence the epithet of Uthyr, or Wonderful, may naturally have been appropriated to Meurig, whose exploits, in his wars with the Saxons, appear to have given him a claim to such a distinction.[4]

---

[4]John H. Parry, *The Cambrian Plutarch* (London: W. Simpkin & R. Marshall, 1824), p. 3.

# 5

# CORNISH CONNECTIONS

KING ARTHUR HAS BECOME so firmly identified with the West Country that, for most people, it is probably very difficult to come to terms with the idea that this was not the area of his domain after all. The truth of the matter is that the story of King Arthur has been removed from Wales, converted into legend, and firmly planted in the West Country, where it has become an important part of the tourist industry. In order to unravel the background to Dark Age connections in Cornwall, it is necessary to look closely at the area and the lives of the native Britons and Celtic saints who came here from other parts of the British Isles.

The name Cornwall is derived from Corn, Cornu, or Kerneu, which in turn probably originated from the name of the Cornovii tribe which once occupied this area. There is no history of Roman occupation in Cornwall, for once they realized that the tribes in this area offered no threat, the Romans left them alone. The territory, today known as Devon and Cornwall, was then inhabited by a mixture of Celts and Invernions, but ruled by the Brythonic tribe of Dumnonii. Later they became known by the Saxons as the Deofnas and the name of that tribe is preserved in the county name of Devon. The Celts of Cornwall were known as the Cornovii, which meant "promontory people," and the Saxons referred to them as Cornwealas, meaning "Foreigners of the promontory." From this term is derived the name Cornwall.

When many of the Celts migrated from Cornwall to Brittany, they took the name of their homeland in its ancient form. Consequently there was a Breton Cornouaille as well as a British one. The same applies to British and Breton Domnonia.

One of the most exciting and best-known places which has been linked with the legend of King Arthur is Tintagel Castle on the north coast of Cornwall. This connection was entirely due to Geoffrey of Monmouth, who identified this romantic fortress as the castle of Gorlois, Duke of Cornwall, and claimed that Arthur was born here. He tells that the Duke's wife, Ygraine, was seduced by Uther Pendragon and that Arthur was the result of their union.

Perhaps it is a relevant fact that, when Geoffrey was writing his history, the castle on this site was under construction by the Normans, so as a location it was obviously of topical interest to the men of the day who mattered. It was Reginald de Dunstanville, an illegitimate son of Henry I, who had the castle built after being created Earl of Cornwall in 1141. He needed an impressive citadel in that area and the Anglo-French name of Tintagel dates from that time.

Today, Tintagel takes full advantage of its supposed connection with King Arthur, and the associated tourist trappings in its one long narrow street include such venues as the "Excalibur Restaurant," "King Arthur's Hall," "King Arthur's Hotel" "King Arthur's Café" and even "King Arthur's Car Park." Undoubtedly, the writings of Geoffrey of Monmouth have enabled this little town to reap considerable benefit from its reputed Arthurian associations and a lucrative tourist trade has been established as a result.

Originally, the name Tintagel just referred to the castle, for the settlement which grew up nearby used to be known as Trevena. This was changed to Tintagel following the opening in 1893 of the North Cornwall Railway to Camelford, which had obvious tourism implications for the area. The most interesting building in the town is the old post office, which is owned by the National Trust. This curiously built stone cottage with its undulating stone roof was built in the 14th century as a small manor house. It is of special interest now, for it was the first post office established in Great Britain.

One needs a good head for heights to make the ascent to the ruins of Tintagel Castle, for it is perched on the summit of a headland 270 feet above the Atlantic Ocean. Several flights of stone steps lead up to a bridge spanning the gap between the

*Figure 15. Tintagel Castle is traditionally held to be the birthplace of King Arthur and this idea, established by Geoffrey of Monmouth eight centuries ago, has been a misleading clue in the quest for the real identity of Arthur and his realm. There was certainly no castle standing here in the sixth century, but it is of interest that a monastery was founded on the same headland by St. Juliot, who came from Wales in about A.D. 500.*

mainland and the "island" where the castle is positioned. Overhead, the swooping and weaving seagulls add to the atmosphere of the place with their plaintive cries. It is difficult not to be impressed by such an awe-inspiring and dramatic situation, and it really does seem the perfect setting for the birthplace of the legendary King Arthur.

Once you get there, the actual ruins of the castle are rather disappointing, for they are quite insignificant. Of the original 12th-century fortress, only the chapel nave and the remains of the Great Hall have survived. During the period 1236 to 1272, it was extended considerably by the younger brother of Henry II and much of the stonework which can be seen today dates from that time.[1]

Of greater interest to the Dark Age historian is the site of a Celtic monastery, which has been excavated on the area of headland adjoining the castle. It was probably established in the fifth century by St. Julian or Juliot, one of the sons of Brychan from Brycheiniog in South Wales. Here he built his cell and probably a simple church around which a monastic community was gradually established. This was certainly here in Arthur's time, but it is unlikely that he had any connection with it. However, it is interesting to consider that, when the Normans were extending their castle, they probably uncovered the remains of the Celtic monastery. Remembering the writings of Geoffrey of Monmouth, they no doubt proclaimed these ruins to be the site of the palace of Gorlois where Arthur was said to be born.

Directly opposite Tintagel Castle on Barras Head is a massive castellated building called King Arthur's Castle Hotel. It was opened in 1899, following the growth and realization of the tourist potential of Tintagel, for by this time visitors had begun to flock here in search of the domain of King Arthur.

Today, however, the official guidebook, written by the eminent historian and archaeologist, C. A. Raleigh Radford, puts the

---

[1]King Henry II was granted possession of Tintagel Castle in 1155. A grandson was born to him in 1187, and he was named Arthur in the expectation that he would accede to the throne as King Arthur II. However, his uncle, King John, removed him, and tradition has it that the infant Arthur was murdered during a visit to France. In 1337, King Edward III made his eldest son (also named Edward) the Duke of Cornwall, and Tintagel Castle, together with all the other possessions of the Duchy of Cornwall, passed into his hands. He became known as the Black Prince because he went to war in black armor. It was the Black Prince who was responsible for carrying out extensive repairs to the wooden drawbridge connecting the castle with the mainland.

matter straight, so that the visitor to Tintagel Castle has no illusions. "No evidence whatsoever has been found to support the legendary connection of the castle with King Arthur. The earliest reference to this connection is in the works of Geoffrey of Monmouth, who wrote when the first Norman castle was being built."[2]

The name of Tintagel is derived from the Cornish Tyn-tagell and this can be explained in the following way. Tyn, or dyn, means fort, and tagell means constriction, which obviously relates to the neck of rock connecting the mainland with the "island." In Norman times, a bridge would have spanned the gap between one part of the castle and the other, but, over the years, the cliffs collapsed on either side to form a mound of debris. The rift is now spanned at a much lower point by the present bridge. An alternative explanation for the origin of the name Tintagel is that the fortress was once known as Tente d'Agel, from the Norman-French meaning, "stronghold of the Devil."

Guidebooks to the locality give details of numerous Arthurian curiosities which have been identified in this area over the years. Obviously, the aim has been to lengthen the list of possible visits which the eager tourists might include during their relentless search for the legendary King Arthur.

Hollows in boulders near the castle are said to be Arthur's cups and saucers and at Killmor his bed can be seen shaped in the rocks. Near Tintagel is Porth-iern, which is either the Iron Port or named after Igerna, Arthur's legendary mother. At Boscastle is Pentargon ("Arthur's Head") and his spirit is said to haunt Tintagel Castle in the form of a white gull which flies backward and forward wailing over the past glories of Britain.

Trebarwith Strand, near Tintagel, is one of the finest stretches of coastline in Cornwall and this beautiful beach has been suggested as a possible location of one of Arthur's battles. According to the ninth-century historian, Nennius, the tenth battle he fought was on the shore of the river called Tribruit. This name can be translated as "the broken strand" and it is certainly

---

[2]C. A. Raleigh Radford, *The Pillar of Eliseg* (Edinburgh: H. M. Stationery Office, 1980).

appropriate, for here a river flows down the valley to enter the sea and divides the beach into two parts.

In Bossiney, a little hamlet which was once a place of great importance, a large mound can be seen near the Methodist Chapel. It is an ancient earthwork which was once the site of an early castle, but local legend has linked it with King Arthur. They say that his golden Round Table lies buried beneath the mound and on Midsummer Night makes a magical appearance.

Just six miles away from Tintagel, near Camelford, is the reputed site of the Battle of Camlan, which was Arthur's last battle on British soil. The name of this town is supposed to be derived from Camlan and the battlefield is traditionally near a stone bridge, about a mile away to the north. Appropriately named Slaughter Bridge, it spans the infant River Camel and tourists come here in large numbers to see the place where the fateful battle was fought. It resulted in the death of his adversary Mordred, and Arthur himself received terrible wounds.

*Figure 16. Slaughter Bridge on the River Camel, about one mile north of Camelford, is the traditional site of the Battle of Camlan which resulted in the downfall of King Arthur.*

*Figure 17. On the bank of the River Camel, just upstream from Slaughter Bridge, lies this hefty oblong chunk of granite which bears a bold but now largely illegible Latin inscription. At one time it was mistakenly believed that one of the words depicted was Artorius (Arthur), but it actually reads "LATINUS THE SON OF MAGO."*

A few hundred yards upstream is an inscribed stone which, due to a misreading, has for centuries been believed to bear Arthur's name and mark his burial place. It is in fact a memorial stone to Latinus, the son of Magorus, and at one time it served as a footbridge on the estate of Lord Falmouth at Worthyvale. At that time, it was known as Slaughter Bridge and, when it was removed in the mid-18th century and brought to its present position, the name was transferred to the nearby bridge which carries the road over the River Camel.

This location has been identified as the site of the Battle of Camlan purely because of the similarity of the names Camel and Camlan. There are, in fact, several Rivers Camel in Britain, but this one was thought to be the place in question because of its close proximity to Tintagel Castle.

Leland, writing in the 16th century, did his best to encourage the belief that this was the site of Camlan and he related how local farmers had ploughed up bones and a harness from the spot where "Arture fowght his last feld." However, it would appear that, in 823, a battle was fought near here between the Cornish Britons and the Saxon King Edgar. Over the course of time, this battle has become mistakenly linked with King Arthur.

Camelford has been suggested as the site of Arthur's court of Camelot and an ancient British camp about five miles away to the southeast is sometimes referred to as Arthur's Hall. He is also said to have had a hunting lodge at Castle-an-Dinas, near St. Colomb Major, which he used as a base from which to hunt the wild deer of Tregoss Moors. Another site of interest is Castle Killibury (or Kelly Rounds), an Iron Age fort, standing in a commanding position above the River Allen. This has been identified as a possible candidate for Arthur's court of Gelliwig.

Yet another challenge for the Arthurian sleuth is to find the site of the castle of Gorlois which was mentioned by Geoffrey of Monmouth. He referred to it as Castle Damelioc and claimed that Gorlois, Duke of Cornwall, was attacked there by Uther Pendragon, while his wife, Igerne (the supposed mother of Arthur), was in residence at Tintagel Castle. There is in fact a Domellick situated north-northwest of St. Dennis, which is a few miles to the northwest of St. Austell. The church of St. Dennis is built on an ancient fortified site which was once part of the manor of Dimelihoc. To the west of the church, about one mile away, is a building known as Domellick. The walls of the churchyard follow the shape of the ancient fort and it is certainly possible that this was the place referred to by Geoffrey.

Beside the road leading from St. Neot to the A30 is Dozmary Pool, where tradition claims that Sir Bedivere returned the sword Excalibur to its keeper, the Lady of the Lake. According to the highly imaginitive Sir Thomas Malory, when this noble knight cast the sword toward the pool, the waters parted and a slender hand rose up to catch it and then drew it down into the depths of the lake.

These are just some of the Arthurian sites which have been located in Cornwall over the years, with the result that this part of Britain has become firmly established as King Arthur Country.

In the late 12th century, the West Country connection was strengthened even further when an incredible "discovery" was made at Glastonbury Abbey in Somerset. Following the destruction of this great abbey in a fire, the monks desperately needed an attraction which would entice pilgrims in large numbers. These visitors could then be asked to make donations which would help to finance a rebuilding program. An excavation in the grounds of the ruined abbey conveniently revealed the grave of Arthur and his Queen, Guinevere, and Glastonbury was thus identified with the Isle of Avalon.

## SIGNIFICANT DARK AGE CONNECTIONS IN CORNWALL

While it is easy to pour scorn on the legendary accounts of Arthur's life, it is, on the other hand, particularly fascinating to examine places which really do have authentic connections with personalities who lived at the same time as Arthur and came into contact with him. Many of these people were related to Arthur, King of the Silures, and the places named after them all provide pieces of a massive jigsaw puzzle which, when fitted together, makes a great deal of sense.

During the Dark Ages, an important royal family ruled Domnonia, the area we know today as Devon and Cornwall, and Athrwys (Arthur), King of the Silures, was related to them. It is necessary to remember the story of Constantine the Blessed, who was a son of Magnus Maximus. When Constantine was an infant, his father was killed in 388. After spending many years in exile in Armorica with his kinsman Aldwr, he returned to Britain with St. Garmon and expelled the Irish settlers from Gwynedd. Constantine was then elected Pendragon of the Confederated States of Britain. He ruled until 443, when he either died of the plague or was assassinated by Vortigern. Constantine's son, Erbin, then fled from North Wales in fear of his life and settled in Cornwall, where he raised a family and died in about 480.

The most important son of Erbin was Geraint, who gave his name to Gerrans in Roseland. His palace of Dingerrin was situated near the church which he founded, and he lived there with his wife, Gwyar. Their children included Cadwy, Iestyn, and Selyf.

Cadwy played an important part in the life of King Arthur, for he ruled the area corresponding to northwest Somerset jointly with Arthur after the death of Geraint. The various Cadbury hill-forts in Somerset are possibly named after him, for the name simply means Cado's town. In due course, we shall describe how Cadwy fought with Arthur at the important Battle of Mount Badon and had the satisfaction of avenging his father's death at the Battle of Llongborth by slaying Cerdic, the leader of the Gewissei.

Just to the west of Gerrans, hidden among trees in the beautiful Restranguet Creek, is a church called St. Just-in-Roseland. It was founded by Iestyn, otherwise known as Justin, who was the brother of Cadwy. It is also possible that he founded St. Just-in-Penwith, seven miles west of Penzance. In Goran parish is Porthest ("Iestyn's Port"), now called Goran Haven, with a chapel dedicated to St. Just. A dynastic conflict later caused Iestyn to leave Cornwall and settle in Armorica (Brittany) for a while. He later returned to found Llaniestyn Church on the Isle of Anglesey, where he lies buried.

Selyf, the third son of Geraint, was a prince of Domnonia and he ruled the land between the Rivers Tamar and Lynher in the old principality of Gelliwig, named after Arthur's principal court in Cernyw. He resided with his wife, Gwen, at Callington and their son Cuby was born there. This town is believed to occupy the site of the royal residence of the kings of Domnonia and it was known as Gelliwig, which confusingly had its equivalent both in Gwent and Brittany. It was here that Arthur also had one of his courts, where Caradoc Freichfras ruled on his behalf and occasionally resided with his wife, Tegau, described in the *Welsh Triads* as the most honest woman in Arthur's Court. Callington is a corruption of Gelliwick-ton and it is possible that nearby Caradon may have taken its name from Caradoc Freichfras. It is plausible that it was once known as Dun Caradoc and it may also be assumed that Craddock Moor is also named after him.

The death of Selyf occurred in about 550 and a stone which may possibly be a memorial to him, can be seen in St. Just-in-Penwith Church. On one side of the stone is a Christian monogram (Chi-Rho) and on the other face is a vertical inscription which reads:

SELUS IC IACIT
(Selus lies here)

Gwen (St.), the wife of Selyf, was the sister of St. Non and it was probably due to this family connection that Non and her son, Dewi (St. David), came to Cornwall and founded Altarnon, which is derived from Allt-ar-Non and means "the cliff of St. Non." They also founded Pelynt and Davidstowe Churches.

Cybi (Kebius) was the son of Selyf and Gwen, and his aunt was Non. This means that he was a cousin of St. David, who became the patron saint of Wales. He spent a good part of his life in Wales and his name is preserved at Llangybi in Gwent and in Caercybi on Anglesey.

On a headland above the Helford River to the southwest of Falmouth stands the church of Constantine. It is set in a hollow and has massive granite walls and an impressive tower. Dedicated to St. Constantine, the son of Cadwy, it provides yet another link with the time of Arthur. Geoffrey of Monmouth tells us that it was Constantine who took over from King Arthur when he abdicated after the Battle of Camlan. Constantine was the son of Arthur's cousin and ally, Cadwy, and he became King of Domnonia following his father's death.

At age 79, toward the close of the sixth century, Constantine was converted to Christianity by St. Petrock, and he built a simple church on an oval-shaped mound. It became known as Langostenyn, which is the old name for Constantine; the Cornish Lan denotes a monastery or holy place. Immediately opposite is Glebe Land, which has belonged to the church for over a thousand years and the Glebe Lands of Constantine were mentioned in the Domesday Book. They would have been cultivated by the monastic community who resided there.

This present-day church is mainly a 15th-century structure and its tall tower is a landmark seen from afar. Inside the church at the east end of the Lady Chapel is a fairly recent stained glass window depicting the figures of Mary, the mother of Christ, and the Archangel Gabriel. In the bottom right-hand corner is the regal figure of St. Constantine, holding high a cross. His sword is significantly shown abandoned.

In the vicinity of St. Ives' Bay are a number of locations which feature in the story of a band of Irish missionaries who were attacked in the fifth century by Tewdrig Mawr ("the Great"), the local ruler. This incident is of particular interest, for it may explain a confused statement by Geoffrey of Monmouth concerning Uther Pendragon fighting a battle against Gorlois, Duke of Cornwall, who was waiting for assistance from the Irish. The Cornish Tewdrig Mawr ("the Great"), son of Emyr Llydaw, may have been confused with the Gwentian Tewdrig Fendigaid ("the Blessed"), who bore the title Uthyr Pendragon and was the grandfather of Arthur. Geoffrey probably managed to muddle the title and the two Tewdrigs together.

Gwithian, near Hayle, embodies the name of St. Gwythian (or Gothian), who was a member of the party of Irish missionaries led by Gwinear or Fingar (a name which has been Latinized into Wynnerus). They landed at the Hayle Estuary and proceeded to a settlement called Conetconia (now Lelant), where they were brutally murdered by Tewdrig of Cornwall.

Gwinear, the leader of the party, had brought with him his sister Kiora, whose name became Piala, or Phillack in Cornish. It is said that the party consisted of over seven hundred emigrants who made their way from Hayle to Connerton. Here they spent the night and then pushed south to where the church of Gwinear now stands. Here the leader left his party and went ahead to reconnoiter. He reached Tregotha, where there is a fine spring of fresh water, and paused to drink. On hearing shouts and screams, he hurried back to find that King Tewdrig, who lived at Riviere, on a creek of the River Hayle, had descended on the party of colonists and massacred them. When Gwinear arrived on the scene, Tewdrig savagely killed him as well. Piala, his sister, was not harmed and subsequently settled near Riviere, where she founded the church of Phillack.

Ia (Ives), a daughter of an Irish chieftain, was another member of Gwinear's party. She managed to escape from Tewdrig and was given protection by a local chieftain named Dinan. Her name is now remembered at the popular holiday resort of St. Ives, where she founded a simple church.

While Tewdrig was fighting the Irish, he fell from his horse and was killed. According to local legend, he was buried beneath a large tree-covered barrow near his fortress at Goodern near Blancheland, where an impressive rectangular earthwork can be seen.

His successor was King Mark, who is said to have used the Goodern fortress as his hunting lodge. King Mark is of particular interest to us, for he was the exiled son of King Meirchion of South Wales and was also known as Marcus Conomorus.

King Mark's main court was at Castle Dore, which is an impressive circular fort of Iron Age construction just outside Fowey. It was abandoned in Roman times but excavations carried out by Raleigh Radford in 1936 proved that the site was reoccupied during the fifth and sixth centuries. His well-organized dig revealed a set of postholes, indicating that, some fourteen centuries ago, a great timber hall had stood here. It measured 33 meters long and 13 meters wide. Such a building would have been occupied by someone of considerable importance and the most likely candidate was King Mark. His palace was named Lancien by a medieval French writer and it is surely more than coincidence that in the Domesday Book the word is written as Lantien. Such a name appears to be retained by a farm called Lantyan, which is just two miles from this ancient site.

Another indication that Castle Dore may be the site of King Mark's palace is provided by an inscribed stone which used to stand in a small enclosure beside an ancient road which led to the great earthworks. In recent years, the stone was removed to a more prominent position and it can now be seen about a mile outside Fowey, near the junction of the A3082 and the B269. It is known as the Tristan Stone and is roughly square in shape and over 2 meters high. Carved on it is an early Christian Tau Cross and a Latin inscription in two vertical lines:

DRUSTANUS HIC IACIT FILIUS CUNOMORI
(Here lies Drustanus son of Cunomorus.)

The lettering on the stone is now so badly weathered that it is very hard to see, but the persons mentioned can both be identified with some degree of certainty. In Cornish, the D becomes T

*Figure 18. The Tristan Stone used to stand beside a trackway leading to Castle Dore, but it has been moved to a more prominent position just outside Fowey. Carved on it in two vertical lines is a Latin inscription which commemorates Tristan, the son of Marcus Conomorus.*

so Drustanus is the same as Tristan. In the *Welsh Triads*, Tristan is mentioned under the title of one of "The Three Mighty Swineherds" and in the romance stories he is called Tristan of Lyonesse. It seems very significant that within a short distance of Castle Dore is the hamlet of Leyonne.[3]

Cunomorus is the Latin form for the British Cynvawr and there was certainly a West Country ruler of that name in the first half of the sixth century. He was a contemporary of Arthur and held sway over old Domnonia, which included Cornwall, and his power extended as far as Brittany.

*The Life of St. Paul Aurelian*, written by a Breton monk named Wrmonoc who spent time in Cornwall, states that Cynfawr was also called Mark. One of the *Welsh Triads* informs us that Mark, or March, was the father of Tristan. Looking at the medieval romance stories of the Arthurian period, we found that Drustanus was turned into Tristan and then Tristram (Sir Tristram). Conomorus was Marcus Conomorus who was referred to as King Mark of Cornwall in the love story of Tristan and Iseult. Turning once more to Wrmonoc's biography of St. Paul Aurelian, we learned that Drustanus had a quarrel with a king of Cornwall named Quonomorius. In this manuscript, the monk also refers to this person as Marcus dictus Quonomorius, which translates as "Mark called Conomorus."

John Leland, the 16th-century antiquary, came to Castle Dore to examine the stone and he was able to read a third vertical line of inscription. It stated "CUM DOMINA CLUSILLA," which could have meant "with the Lady Clusilla." This is an Irish name and if, as Leland claimed, the inscription really was on the stone, then it could have been the equivalent of the Cornish name of Eselt (Iseult). It is quite likely that, since Leland's visit in the 16th century, a fragment bearing the missing inscription has broken off the stone.

---

[3]The 12th-century Anglo-Norman poet Béroul sets the story of Tristan near St. Samson-in-Golant and says that King Mark's palace was at "Lancien." Lantyan or Lantyne is now a farm about a mile south of Lostwithiel. The manor of Lantyan-in-Golant in the Middle Ages significantly included Castle Dore.

*Figure 19. St. Samson's Church at Golant, near Fowey, is a 15th-century building that stands on the site of a simple church founded in the sixth century. Samson was a soldier-saint of Arthur's time and his story is one of the earliest of the Celtic saints to be recorded.*

A few miles to the north of Castle Dore is the little church of Golant, which was founded by St. Samson, who came to Cornwall from South Wales. His father was Amwn Ddu ("the Black"), Prince of Graweg, the country around Vannes in Armorica which had earlier been colonized by British settlers. Following a family feud, Amwn fled to South Wales where he married Anna, the daughter of Meurig ap Tewdrig. This makes Samson the nephew of King Arthur and he was one of the so-called knights of Arthur's court. In a later chapter, we shall reveal how he and Arthur fought a battle in Brittany to overthrow the usurper, Marcus Conomorus.

A few miles north of Truro is the church of St. Erme, which is dedicated to St. Erme or Ermel. Latin ecclesiastics have corrupted the name into Hermes, but St. Erme is in fact St. Arthmael, who was none other than King Arthur and here is a church in Cornwall dedicated to him.

# 6 ❧

# IN SEARCH OF CAMELOT

ONE OF THE MOST ELUSIVE LOCATIONS in the story of King Arthur is his main court[1] which, owing to a 12th-century French writer, Chrétien de Troyes, has become known as Camelot. He may have had some information which is no longer available, but, on the other hand, it is possible that in his poem, *Lancelot,* he just invented Camelot, for it is certainly a name which falls off the tongue easily. Thomas Malory in his book, *Le Morte d'Arthur,* obviously liked the idea, for he also established Arthur in this fairy-tale city. However, he was more positive in his approach and stated that it was located at Winchester.

The common practice for Arthurian sleuths trying to identfy Camelot is to attempt to tie it in with placenames which contain an element of the word cam or camel. The name Camelot may be nothing more than an Anglo-French invention, but, on the other hand, it is perhaps significant that Camulos was the Celtic god of war. Arthurian research is full of amazing coincidences and red herrings!

John Leland, who served as King Henry VIII's antiquary, was a well-traveled man who claimed to identify the site of Arthur's Camelot during a visit to Somerset in 1532.

---

[1] There is a tradition that Arthur maintained three principal courts so that Britain should remain united. According to Triad No. 85 (first series) "there were three principal festivals, Christmas, Easter and Whitsunday which were all celebrated with joy, particularly at the three courts of Arthur, at Caerleon on Usk in Cymru, at Gelliwig in Cerniw and Penrhyn Rhionedd in the North." See Triad No. 85 in Rachel Bromwich, *Troedd Ynys Prydein* [The Welsh Triads](Cardiff, Wales: University of Wales Press, 1978), p. 211.

> At the very south end of the church of South Cadbury standeth Camelot, sometimes a very famous town or castle.

He added "The people can tell nothing there but they have heard say that Arture much resorted to Camelot." No doubt, Leland, like William Camden in later years, was impressed by the fact that at the foot of the hill is the River Cam or Camel and nearby are the villages of Queen's Camel and West Camel. Camden mentioned that local people referred to the fort as "Arthur's Palace," whereas in the 18th century, the more astute antiquary, William Stukely, pointed out that local people had no knowledge of that particular name.

The idea of a Somerset Camelot took firm root and, by the 19th century, many stories of Arthur being associated with the Iron Age hill-fort known as Cadbury Castle had been created. During the years 1966–1970, an excavation was carried out on the summit plateau of the fort, which covers an impressive area of 18 acres. It was a well-organized investigation which resulted in a remarkable discovery. Postholes indicating the site of a great hall measuring 21 meters long and 11 meters wide were revealed in a central position. It was also found that, during the fifth and sixth centuries, the fort had been defended by a massive drystone wall some 7 meters thick and, on the evidence of pottery discovered, the hall was dated to the time of Arthur. The very size of the structure indicated that it must have been the base of an important sixth-century chieftain. Such a person must have been a military leader of some status who commanded a large army, a "dux bellorum," and the most likely candidate to suit that time period was King Arthur. If he was not Arthur himself, then he must have been someone of similar standing. The fort was certainly well-placed as a base from which to organize campaigns against the West Saxon advance into the Upper Thames basin. One of the artifacts discovered on the site was a silver ring displaying a Germanic animal which had been fashioned in the sixth century. It was probably brought here as an item of loot or dropped by a hostage taken at some time.

Originally constructed during the Iron Age, the fort was strongly defended by four lines of banks and ditches. Excavations at other selected hill-forts, particularly in Wales, have also confirmed that many of them were refortified during the days of Arthur, after long periods of disuse following the Roman conquest.

It is puzzling that the name Cadbury is also attached to other West Country hill-forts, e.g. Cadbury Hill (Congresbury, Avon) and Cadbury Camp (Tickenham, Avon). The word seems to be a blend of Celtic and Saxon terms, for Cad is a Celtic word meaning either army or battle, while bury is from the Saxon burb, meaning a settlement. So on this basis, the name suggests that it was a headquarters for an army.

However, the name may also be derived from a Celtic personality who lived at the time of Arthur. Such a person was Cadwy, the son of Geraint Llyngesog ("the Fleet Owner"). Not only was Cadwy related to Arthur, he was also his ally and they would have ruled this area of Domnonia jointly. It would therefore seem likely that the site of the timber hall, excavated on the summit of Cadbury hill-fort, was the headquarters of Cadwy, from whose name Cadbury is derived.

Cadbury Castle can also be shown to be connected with the first-century British king Arviragus, the son of Cunobelinus. From the Kentish Chronicles, we can learn that, upon the landing of Roman reinforcements at Portus Lemanis (Lympne) under Vespasian and Titus, the British king Arviragus abandoned Dover. It is interesting to note at this point that there is a King Arthur's Tower at Dover Castle which suggests that two personalities have become confused. Arviragus subsequently took refuge in the hill-fort of Cadbury Castle in Somerset. When Vespasian landed at Totnes and took the place now called Exeter, it was Arviragus who led the British resistance against him.

The existence of a British king named Arviragus is proved by the Roman satirist Juvenal, who makes one of his characters ask a pale nervous-looking man, "What is the matter with you? Have you seen the chariot-driven British king Arviragus? A mighty omen this you have received of some great and noble triumph. Some captive king you'll take, or Arviragus will be hurled from his British chariot. For the monster is a foreign one. Do you see the sharp fins bristling on his back like spears?"[2]

---

[2]Juvenal 4, 127. *The Satires of Juvenal,* Rev. Lewis Evans, trans. Bohn's Classical Library (London: George Bell & Sons, 1880), Satire IV, p. 32.

*Figure 20. Cadbury Castle Iron Age hill-fort at South Cadbury in Somerset is popularly known as King Arthur's Castle. It was excavated during the years 1966–1970 and the site of a great hall measuring 21 meters long and 11 meters wide was discovered. Undoubtedly, it was used by an important British chieftain of King Arthur's time, but this chief is more likely to have been Cadwy or Cado, who gave the hill-fort its name of Cado's Town or Cadbury.*

Hector Boece, in his *History and Chronicles of Scotland,* informs us that Vespasian, who was laying siege to South Cadbury, captured a royal crown and a magnificent sword which he used for the rest of his life. It is recorded elsewhere that the Emperor Claudius received the submission of Arviragus at Cadbury Castle. The Romans began to introduce law officers and erected a stone temple at Cadbury with two statues in it. One was for victory and the other represented the Emperor Claudius.

Arviragus allied himself with the Roman invaders by marrying Claudius's daughter Gennissa, and he emerged as a client-ruler, holding sway from his hill-fortress at South Cadbury. He held out defiantly in the area of hill-forts and the stretches of marshes, lakes, and islands which then lay between South Cadbury and the Bristol Channel. As a leader of the Britons and bearing the title Arthwyr he has thus become confused with the King Arthur of legend who lived four hundred years later.

We took up the challenge of trying to find a more convincing identification for Arthur's Camelot and to explain the origin of its name. Surprisingly, it was in Thomas Malory's *Le Morte d'Arthur* that we found a statement which pointed us in the right direction.[3] He had identified Camelot as Winchester, but in the introduction to the book, the editor obviously disagreed with him, for he commented that the ruins of Camelot were still visible in Wales. This part of Britain was a much more likely location, for it is extremely doubtful that Arthur would have been able to maintain a court in Winchester, which during most of the sixth century was in the possession of the Gewissei, who were his enemies. Winchester, the old Roman city of Venta Belgarum, was undoubtedly a very important place where several kings were crowned. It became the capital of Wessex under Alfred the Great (whose statue can be seen in High Street) and it was the chief city in England until after the Norman Conquest.

Malory must have confused Winchester with a place in Wales which had a similar name and this error was written into his book, with the result that Camelot was mislocated. The following equation provides in simple terms a very satisfactory solution to the mystery:

Venta Belgarum = Caer Wynt = Winchester
Venta Silurum = Caerwent = Camelot

On consulting the book of Nennius, we found that his list of "Cities in Britain" included Caer Calemion—the fortress of Calemion—and by changing letters around in the second word we get Camelion. This sounds and looks very much like the origin of the name Camelot. Suddenly everything falls into place.

---

[3]See William Caxton's preface to Thomas Malory's *Le Morte d'Arthur*, 1485 (London: J. M. Dent & Sons, 1909), p. xxix.

The name Caer Calemion is surely derived from Caer Melin, which today is called Llanmelin, the former Silurian hill-fort just north of Caerwent, described in the last chapter.

These arguments for identifying Camelot with this hill-fort at Llanmelin are new and certainly more convincing than anything which has ever been written on the subject before.

Leslie Alcock, who excavated Cadbury Castle hill-fort and found the site of the ancient hall, observed in his book, *Arthur's Britain*, "The truth is, however, that attempts to identify Camelot are pointless. The name, and the very concept of Camelot, are the inventions of the French medieval poets."[4] He may well be right, but we believe that we have come as close as anyone will ever get to identifying the true site of Camelot.

## THE CAERLEON CONNECTION

According to Geoffrey of Monmouth, Arthur's main court was at Caerleon-upon-Usk, where Isca Silurum was abandoned by the Romans during the last quarter of the third century. Archaeology, however, has not provided any evidence of Dark Age occupation here, so if Arthur did in fact hold court in this location, then it is more likely to have been on the outskirts of the old Roman city. Overlooking a curve of the River Usk is a large hill-fort on the summit of Lodge Hill and it was certainly used by the Silures at the time of the Roman invasion. Situated 100 meters above sea level, it consists of a main enclosure, oval in form, with defenses covering an impressive 7.2 hectares. Three massive ramparts protect the main enclosure and the ditches are in places about 10 meters deep. A tumulus 12 meters high protects the site of the western entrance and is placed on the inner rampart. The whole camp measures 110 meters long and is on average 60 meters wide.

At one time the fort was known as "Belinstok," a name which probably originated from the writings of Geoffrey of Monmouth, who connected it with King Belinus. The name "Be-

---

[4]Leslie Alcock, *Arthur's Britain* (London: Penguin, 1971), p. 163.

*Figure 21. High above a curve of the River Usk is a large hill-fort on Lodge Hill which was probably used by King Arviragus (known to his people as Arthwyr) during the time of the Roman invasion. This well-fortified and extensive site has never been excavated, but perhaps a dig may one day be undertaken here to reveal evidence of Dark Age occupation. It is as important a site as Cadbury Castle, but unfortunately the Roman fort of Caerleon continues to claim the archaeologists' attention and the meager financial resources which are available to them.*

linstok" signifies the stockade of Belinus who is said to have ruled over this area jointly with his brother Bran. The poet Churchyard may have been Coxe's source, for in the 16th century, he described the fortress as "on a very high hill of marvellous strength," and added, "Bellinus Bagnus made this called Belinstocke."[5]

Turning to the *Brut Breninoedd*, we found an entry under the date 406 B.C. which reads: "Beli, son of Dyfnwal Moelmud,

---

[5]William Coxe, *Coxe's Tours of Monmouthshire* (1801). T. Cadell Juriar & W. Davis, eds. (Reprint: Cardiff, Wales: Merton Press, 1995).

was king of the whole Isle of Britain. This Beli founded a city on the side of the river Wysg (Usk) and he called it Caer Leon or Wysg."[6]

Geoffrey of Monmouth is in agreement here, for he tells us that: "Belinus returned to Britain (from Italy) which he governed during the remainder of his life in peace; he repaired the cities that were falling to ruin and built many new ones. Among the rest he built one city or fortress upon the River Usk, near the Sea of the Severn, which was for a long time called Caerosc."[7]

It is possible that the fort of King Beli has become identified with King Arthur through confusion with Arviragus, the son of Cunobelinus, who, like Arthur himself, bore the title Arthwyr.

Arviragus was the brother of the warrior-king Caradoc (Caractacus) who led the Silures in battle against the Romans. A true prince of the Silures, Arviragus ruled over the area which today is known as the West Country. His brother, Guiderius, was slain in a battle with the Romans and Arviragus then succeeded his elder brother to the kingdom of the Silures. But Caradoc had arrived on the scene with a proven reputation as a military expert and was elected Pendragon to conduct the war against the invading Romans.

For nine years, Caradoc and Arviragus fought valiantly against the Roman generals, winning battle after battle. In the hope of making peace, the Emperor Claudius offered his daughter, Gennissa, to Arviragus in marriage and in A.D. 45 they were married in Rome during a period of peace when a six-month truce had been declared. Caradoc and Arviragus, accompanied by his Roman wife, Gennissa, in due course returned to Britain, declaring the peace terms unsatisfacory. Ostorius Scapula was sent over to replace Aulus Plautius and the war continued for another seven years.

Caradoc was eventually defeated at an unidentified hill-fort site in Mid Wales in A.D. 52, while besieged by a massive Roman

---

[6]*Brut Breninoedd* [The Chronicle of the Kings], a 13th-century Welsh manuscript.
[7]Geoffrey of Monmouth, *The History of the Kings of Britain* (London: Penguin, 1966), p. 99.

army. He managed to escape, but was taken prisoner, following an act of treachery by Queen Cartimandua of the Brigantes. With his entire family, he was then taken as hostage to Rome. His daughter Gwladys adopted the name Claudia Britannica and married the Roman senator Rufus Pudens. Their marriage is referred to by the Roman commentator Martial, a close friend of Pudens. In his *Epigrams* (Martial 13 B.XI 53), he speaks of "Claudia peregrina et edita Britannis" (Foreign Claudia, native of Britain).Their children were raised as Christians and in the grounds of the Palace of Pudens can be seen the church of St. Pudenziana, dedicated to Pudentiana, one of the martyred daughters of Claudia and Pudens.

Meanwhile, Arviragus took over as Pendragon and continued to lead the British forces against the Romans. Juvenal, the Roman writer, obviously in awe of Arviragus, asked: "Hath our great enemy Arviragus, the car (chariot) borne British king, dropped from his battle throne?"[8]

Tacitus wrote: "In Britain, after the captivity of Caradoc, the Romans were repeatedly defeated and put to rout by the single state of the Silures alone." He described the Silures as "a fierce and obstinate people."[9]

In A.D. 53, Ostorius Scapula suffered a massive defeat at Caervelin (Caermelin), against a force led by Arviragus. He wrote to Nero, who had succeeded Claudius as Emperor that year, asking to be relieved of his command due to ill health. Nero accepted his resignation and immediately replaced him with Aulus Didius (Didius Gallus), who founded Caer Dydd, "the Castle of Didius" which is now known as Cardiff.

Arviragus, as King of the Silures, was certainly a very worthy predecessor of Arthur and he was known by the Romans as Taurus Negri—"the Black Bull." His presence as Pendragon in Gwent, and the fact that he was given the title Arthwyr has certainly added confusion to those following the trail in search of the truth about King Arthur.

---

[8]Juvenal, 4, v. 127.
[9]Tacitus, *The Annals of Imperial Rome* A.D. 14–66, Michael Grant, trans. (New York: Dorset, 1986), pp. 266–269.

# 7 ❧

# Tbe ROUNd TABLE ANd
# ARTbUR'S KNIGbTS

I T WAS ROBERT WACE OF JERSEY who first brought the Round
Table into the story of King Arthur, when in his *Li Romans
de Brut* (1155), he told us that:

> This Round Table was ordained that when his [Arthur's] fair
> fellowship sat to meet, their chairs should be high alike,
> their service equal, and none before or after his comrade.
> Thus, no man could boast that he was exalted above his fel-
> low . . .[1]

As the first Arthurian writer to mention this circular piece of fur-
niture, Wace was ensured literary celebrity. He intimates that he
gained his knowledge from the Bretons, who he says, "tell many
a fable of the Round Table." Unfortunately, Wace does not explain just where the fables came from, or where he had heard
them told.

Layamon's account of the Round Table is much more detailed, however, and it is based upon popular legends of wiz-
ardry. He informs us that in Cornwall, when there was once a
quarrel among his knights, Arthur met a stranger from beyond
the sea, who offered "to make him a board, wondrous fair." Although it was very large, and took four weeks to make, the table
could, by some magical means, be carried by Arthur as he rode,
and be placed by him wherever he chose. Layamon had evidently
heard more about the Round Table, "of which the Britons

---

[1]Robert Wace, *Li Romans de Brut* (1155) in *Wace and Layamon—Arthurian
Chronicles*, Eugene Mason, trans. (London: J. M. Dent & Sons, 1912).

boast," than he cared to disclose in his poem; but "the Britons," he tells us, "say many leasings of King Arthur and attribute to him things that never happened in the kingdom of this world."[2]

Thomas Malory, in his story, gives another version of the table's origin. He says that, when Arthur married Guinevere, her father presented him with a Round Table which had once belonged to Uther. It was large enough to seat 150 knights and Arthur had it taken to Camelot. In alternative versions of the legend, the Round Table was originally made by Merlin for Uther Pendragon, Arthur's father. When Uther died, Merlin gave it to Arthur and his knights.

An obvious, but nevertheless fascinating, fake is the Round Table which hangs on the wall in the Guild Hall near Westgate at Winchester. This building is all that survives of a castle built by William the Conqueror. Winchester was mistaken by Malory for Camelot and the association persisted, resulting in the introduction of a Round Table claimed to be used by King Arthur and his knights.

It is believed that the table was made for Edward III, who was undoubtedly an admirer of King Arthur. In 1344, he swore an oath in the chapel of St. George at Windsor that he would, like King Arthur, create a Round Table for his knights. His example was followed by Phillip de Valois, King of France, who made a similar table in his dominions; and several instances may be cited of prominent persons holding round tables at this period in imitation of King Arthur and his companions. Among others, Roger Mortimer, Earl of March, is said to have held round tables of knights at Kenilworth, Bedford, and in Wales; and by the Patent Rolls of 1344 and 1345, it appears that the king granted leave to certain knights to establish a similar association at Lincoln for encouraging "hastiludes or jousts."

The institution of the Round Table revived by King Edward III was superseded by that of the Garter. On his return from fighting battles at Crecy and Calais, Edward established on St. George's Day in 1348 the Order of the Garter. It was ordained that "this Order would be a society, Fellowship, College of

---

[2] *Wace and Layamon—Arthurian Chronicles.*

*Figure 22. Hanging on a wall inside the Guild Hall at Winchester is an oak table measuring 6 meters across which is known as King Arthur's Round Table. It was made for Edward III, who in 1344 swore an oath in the chapel of St. George at Windsor that he would, like King Arthur, create a Round Table for his knights. The surface of the table is divided into 24 segments which are painted green and white and indicate the named places of the knights who are supposed to have sat around its rim. Arthur's place is at the top, where the picture of a king is shown.*

Knights in which all were equal to represent how they ought to be united in all Chances and various Turns of Fortune; co-partners both in Peace and War, assistant to one another in all serious and dangerous exploits, and through the course of their lives to show Fidelity and Friendliness, the one towards the other."[3] Twenty-six knights were appointed by King Edward to form the new order. The Order of the Garter, conceived by King Edward III in 1344 in imitation of King Arthur's Round Table, was the first of many honorary secular orders of knighthood, some short-lived, some lasting for centuries, designed to reward valor and glorify knighthood, and to create a bond between the patron of the order and those on whom he had bestowed membership.[4]

Constructed of oak and measuring 1.5 meters across, the table at Winchester has twelve mortice holes cut into it which indicate that it once had as many legs. Weighing one ton, it is fixed to the wall, giving the appearance of a giant dartboard. It is divided into 24 segments, which are painted green and white and bear names indicating the places of the knights who are supposed to have sat around its rim. Arthur's place is at the top, where the picture of a king is shown.

King Henry VII also firmly believed that Winchester was the site of Camelot and he insured that his first son was born there. The infant prince was christened Arthur—Arthurus Secundus (Arthur the Second)—at Winchester on 19 September 1486. In

---

[3]E.O. Gordon, *Prehistoric London* (London: The Covenant Publishing Co., 1946), p. 62.

[4]Edward III and his young queen, Philippa, made a pilgrimage to King Arthur's supposed tomb at Glastonbury and subsequently decided to refound the British Order, revive the Round Table Assemblies, and make Windsor Castle the center of European chivalry. Edward instructed his young secretary, William of Wykeham, to enclose an artificial mound, 30 meters in diameter, with a round tower. Within the walls of this unroofed enclosure, the knights of the Order of St. George and the Garter, from the day of the inauguration, St. George's Day, April 23, 1351, to the time of Charles II, celebrated the annual festival of the Garter. Wykeham's inquiries into the traditions of the Order showed that the British Church of the first five centuries had been entirely free of papal control, and that one of the first acts of Arthur's reign had been to refuse the tribute demanded by special emissaries sent from Rome. King Edward accordingly determined to obtain a Bull from Pope Clement VI (1348) declaring the Chapel of St. George a chapel free of papal jurisdiction. The royal chapel of St. George, Windsor, may therefore claim to be the keystone of the Reformation. The visit of King Francis I of France in 1520 was made spectacular by a pageant of the Nine Worthies and the declaration by King Henry VIII of England that the Order of the Garter was the badge and First Order of King Arthur.

*Figure 23. King Arthur, depicted at the top of the Winchester Round Table, bears a striking resemblance to King Henry VIII who had designs painted on the table to impress Charles V, a visiting emperor, in 1522.*

due course, the youngster was created Prince of Wales and a treaty was drawn up with Spain involving a contract for Arthur to marry Catherine, the daughter of Ferdinand, King of Aragon, and Isabella, Queen of Castille. However, before the marriage could be consummated, the sixteen-year old prince was taken ill and suddenly died at Ludlow Castle. Thus, the return of Arthur as king was not to be and it was his younger brother who later ruled England as Henry VIII.

It was Henry VIII who had the designs painted on the table in 1522 to impress Charles V, a visiting emperor.[5] In the foreign accounts of Henry VIII, it appears that a sum of £66. 16s. 11d. was expended in the repair of the *Aula regis infra Castrum de Wynchestre et le Round Tabyll Ibidem.*

The colors, white and green, are those of the Tudor Dynasty, indicating that to be the period of its painting; the same style and color appear to have been copied each time that it has been repainted. King Arthur, seated at the head of the table, wears a beard and bears a remarkable resemblance to Henry VIII; in the center is a Tudor Rose.

When the table was taken down in 1874, it was found that the original framing was in the form of a wheel with twelve radiating spokes, in each of which is a mortice hole to receive a tenon, with two stout pins partly left in it; this proves beyond all doubt that the table originally had legs, and that it was not always suspended as at present. In addition to these legs, there is evidence of some central support, probably either a sturdy leg or perhaps a large block of timber. The table is a most interesting piece of early carpentry, showing in its framing two distinct dates of carpenters' work, and the use of tools of two different periods.

The twenty-four knights around the rim of the Round Table remind one of the twenty-four elders in Revelation 14:4 and the table also seems to have a symbolic link with the Last Supper. Accordingly, Arthur can be likened to Christ sitting there with his disciples.

A significant statement in T. W. Stone's *History of Hampshire* (1892) suggests that the Winchester Round Table "was probably placed there by King Henry III, who ordered a Rota Fortuna or Wheel of Fortune to be built for this building." This statement provides a different slant on the origin and purpose of the Round Table which is worthy of consideration.[6]

---

[5]The Emperor Maximilian, "Der Letzte Ritter"—the "Last of the Knights," as he is called in Germany—honored the traditions of Arthur and his Round Table by a visit to Winchester Castle to see the table relic on his return journey following his installation as a knight of St. George at Windsor Castle.

[6]T. W. Stone, *History of Hampshire* (London: Elliot Stock, 1892; republished Wakefield: E. P. Publishing, 1976), p. 174.

Oracular Wheels of Fortune, worked by ropes, are still found in a few churches on the Continent. There is also a history of them in Ireland, for the celebrated Druid Mogh Ruith of Kerry derived his name, which signifies Magus Rotarum, the wizard of the wheels, from the wheels of fortune by which he used to make his magical observations. In O'Grady's *Silva Gadelica,* there is an account of Mogh Ruith's daughter who went with him to the East to learn magic, and there made a "rowing wheel."

In Geoffrey of Monmouth's *Vita Merlini* (Life of Merlin), Morgan is named as "the chief of nine sisters who presided over the insula pomorum que fortunata (Island of Apples which is called Fortunate), to which the wounded King Arthur was brought to be healed after the battle of Camlan."[7] The name Fortunate is derived from Fortuna, the Roman goddess of fate and chance, who carried a wheel in her hand to show that she was the goddess of the turning year. According to the 15th-century Middle English prose romance called the *Alliterative Morte Arthure,* Arthur meets Morgan as the goddess Fortuna herself, upon whose wheel he has often been praised and derided. Arthur's enmity with Morgan is very significant, for it resulted in the demise of the Round Table Fellowship, which is nothing less than the re-ordering of the land of Britain under a new regime. As the Lady of the Wheel, Fortuna herself, Morgan turns the Wheel of the Pendragons inexorably so that there is always a king, but on the occasion of her quarrel with Arthur she whirled the wheel so violently that the result was his overthrow, so ending the rule of the Pendragons.[8]

Arthur was indeed the Son of Prophecy. His coming was foretold by Merlin and his overthrow predicted by Morgan, the

---

[7]Geoffrey of Monmouth, *Vita Merlini* [Life of Merlin]. See J. J. Parry, *The Vita Merlini* (Chicago: University of Illinois, 1925).

[8]The Zodiacal Wheel is the archetype for the Round Table. The knights gathered around the table in devotion to the Blessed Virgin. The role of Arthur as the culture-hero of the Round Table stands in the same relation to Arthur as the Teacher of Righteousness stands in relation to Jesus, the Christ. Arthur certainly lends himself to the role of a Celtic Messiah. The prophesied second coming of Arthur in many respects represents the "second coming of Christ."

Lady of the Wheel. In her notes appended to *The Mabinogion*, Lady Charlotte Guest informs us that Myrddin (Merlin) was one of the "Three Baptismal Bards" who presided over the Round Table. The other two were Madog and Taliesin and the real meaning behind their priviliged positions is that they were Guardians of the Totems or Lords of the Wheel.

King Arthur appears on the Winchester Round Table on top, as it were, of a Wheel of Fortune, while in Malory's *Morte d'Arthur,* we see Arthur himself in the richest cloth-of-gold sitting upon a chafflet in a chair and the chair is fastened to a wheel.

The "Wheel of Fortune" seems to have been a very common symbol in the 13th century. San Zeno at Verona, Saint Martin at Basle, and Saint Stephen at Beauvais, all of the Romanesque period, exhibit the wheel as the origin of the Rose windows. It is equally found in the marble pavement of the Duomo of Siena, and among the half-obliterated frescoes of Catfield in Norfolk, giving a remarkable example of conformity in different countries in the aesthetic symbolism of the middle ages.

The Roman amphitheater at Caerleon in Gwent is one of several places identified as the site of King Arthur's Round Table and indeed it would have made a very fine council chamber in the land of the Silures where Arthur was king. Other Round Table sites in Wales which are known to local people as Bwrdd Arthur are located near Llansannan in Clwyd and close to Beaumaris in Gwynedd. There are also Round Table sites to the south of Penrith in Cumbria and at Stirling Castle in Scotland, where an octagonal earthwork surrounds a flat-topped mound set in a formal garden.

It is interesting how the symbol of the Round Table can be examined in a variety of ways, but the simplest concept of its place in Arthurian literature may have just evolved from a folk memory of an age-old custom whereby a chief sat with his men in a circle to hold a meeting while they dined.

## THE KNIGHTS OF THE ROUND TABLE

For most people, an essential part of the story of King Arthur is the famous band of loyal knights whose names have become al-

*Figure 24. Before it was excavated in 1926, Caerleon amphithe-*
*ater in Gwent was a grass-covered hollow in a field known as*
*King Arthur's Mead and the depression itself was referred to as*
*his Round Table. It is open to conjecture that in the sixth cen-*
*tury this abandoned arena was used by Arthur as a council*
*chamber which became known as his "Round Table." When the*
*site was excavated by Sir Mortimer Wheeler, the remains of an*
*impressive Roman amphitheater were revealed. It is oval in plan*
*with stone walls, vaulted passages, and entrances. The entire gar-*
*rison of 6,000 men could be accommodated as spectators who*
*sat above the arena to watch the gladiatorial entertainment. It*
*also served as a training school for sword exercises and regimen-*
*tal drill.*

most as well known as that of Arthur himself. However, it is important to understand that the names of these characters have
been anglicized and their true Welsh identities obscured. The tradition is that Arthur had twenty-four knights in his court and,

with his numerous warriors, they are all mentioned in the *Mabinogion* stories.

Writers in medieval times brought Arthur into their own period so that he could be more easily identified and, between 1250 and 1450, stories of this hero king and his knights of the Round Table appeared in almost every western-European language. These imaginitive poets contrived a fairy-tale kingdom and accounts of daring deeds which were told and retold by bards in Cumbria, Wales, Cornwall, and Brittany. Today, we are faced with the problem of deciphering the names of Arthur's followers in order to relate them to personalities and places which really did exist, but have become obscured by distortion and exaggeration through the passing centuries.

Sir Lancelot was in fact a character based on Llwch Wyddel, who was also known as Llwch Llawinawg, Lord of the Lakes. His Latin name was Lucius Hibernus and, in the romance stories, he became Lancelot of the Lake. He was slain by Arthur in a battle beyond the mountain of Mynneu in Ireland, after which Arthur returned to Britain to fight the Battle of Camlan.

Sir Tristram can be identified with Drustanus, who was the son of Marcus Conomorus, a Glamorgan prince who held sway in Cornwall and Brittany. In the Romance stories, Tristram is called Tristan of Lyonesse. He is commemorated on a sixth century inscribed stone which can be seen beside the road just outside Fowey in Cornwall (see pages 81–83). It is of some significance that a short distance away is the hamlet of Lyonne.

Sir Bedivere was Bedwyr ap Bedrawc who, according to the *Mabinogion,* was the Chief Butler at King Arthur's Court. He was also one of the most valiant of his knights. His name is often coupled with that of the knight Cai, and their fortunes appear to have been very similar. They were the two knights whom Arthur selected as his sole companions in the expedition to Mont-Saint-Michel to avenge the death of Lady Helena, the niece of Riwal Mawr (the Great). The place of Bedwyr's sepulchre is recorded in the *Stanzas of the Graves* as being on a hill bearing the name of Tryfan, which is derived from Tryvaen. Dunraven Castle in Glamorgan is mentioned in ancient writings as Dindryvan and this may be the place referred to in the *Stanzas.*

Sir Kay was Cei ap Cynyr Ceinfarfog and his traditional name has been derived from the Latin Caius. He may have been of Irish origin and it is significant that there was a legendary Irish figure named Cai Cainbrethach. Cai and Bedwyr were Arthur's two first lieutenants and, like Arthur, they have passed into the realm of myth. In the *Black Book of Carmarthen* is a poem relating how Kei fought at the battle of Traeth Trevroit, called here Traethau Trevrwyd. Some writers have mistakenly identified Cai with St. Kew, who is really Docwin—otherwise called Cyngar, the founder of Congresbury in Somersetshire. He was a son of Gildas, the historian.[9]

Sir Howell can be identified with Howel (Riwal) Mawr the son of Emyr Llydaw. This prince of Erging (Archenfield) was a nephew of Arthur, for he married Arthur's half-sister Gwyar. In several battles, he was Arthur's principal ally and he took command of the king's army at the memorable Battle of Langres, in which he fought alongside Lords Jagus, Ichomarch, and Bodloi against Llwch Wyddel, who was none other than Lancelot, Lord of the Lakes. The *Welsh Triads* refer to Riwal as one of "The Three Royal Knights of the Court of King Arthur." Riwal left his kingdom in southeastern Wales with a large number of colonists to establish the Breton Kingdom of Domnonia. He set up his court at Lishelion and here he continued to rule as Dux Britanniarum on both sides of the sea until his death in 524. It is said that he was buried at Llanilltyd Fawr in South Glamorgan.

Sir Craddock's identity is easily sorted out, for he was none other than Caradog Freichfras ("of the Strong Arm"). He was

---

[9]One of the earliest references to Cai is possibly on the Porta della Pescheriu of the Cathedral of Modena, where "Che" is one of the horsemen represented as attacking a castle with "Artus de Bretania." These 12th-century sculptures are made by the well-known sculptor Nicolaus, whose works are found in many places in north Italy. In Brittany Sir Kay is known as St. Ke, and he is the patron saint of at least three Breton parishes: Saint Quai Portrieux, Saint-Quai-Perros, and Plogoff. In the *Black Book of Carmarthen* is a poem which tells how Kei fought at the battle of Traeth Troit, called here Traethau Trevrwyd. Kei was probably a Romano-Briton of the name Caius, like Ambrosius, Gerontius, etc. His father, Cynyr, is the Welsh form of Cunorix. It was Geoffrey of Monmouth who developed the habit of Latinizing Welsh names.

the son of Gwrgant Mawr ("the Great"), King of Erging. Gwr-
gant was also the father of Onbrawst, who married Meurig,
King of Gwent. This makes Caradog Freichfras the uncle of
Arthur.

Following the fall of Arthur at the Battle of Camlan,
Caradog led a band of British immigrants who established themselves at Vannes in Brittany. This is confirmed in the *Life of St.
Padarn,* which associates Caradog Freichfras with the colonization of Brittany. It is significant that he is depicted as a king ruling in Vannes in the 13th century *Livre de Carados*, contained in
the first continuation of Chretien de Troye's *Percival.* Caradog is
celebrated in Brittany as St. Caradec and he is the patron of St.
Caradec Tregomel near Guemene and St. Caradec Hennebont,
which are both in the diocese of Vannes.

Gawain, who is identical with Gwalchmai ("Hawk of
May"), was a son of Lleu ap Cynfarch and Gwyar, a half-sister
of Arthur. He was one of Arthur's most prominent warriors and
had a reputation for courtesy and eloquence. He reigned in Wal-
weithia, now part of Dyfed; near Haverfordwest is Castell
Gwalchmai (Walwyn's Castle). Gwalchmai was expelled from
his kingdom by the Saxons under Octa II, but not until he had
compensated for his exile by killing many of his enemies. He was
wounded by the followers of Medraut and cast out in a shipwreck. His supposed tomb was discovered during the reign of
William I, the Conqueror, in 1086, upon the seashore in the
cantref of Rhos in modern Dyfed.

Galahad is identical to Gwalchaved ("Hawk of Summer"),
the alter-ego of Gwalchmai, as is Yvain, the Knight of Léon, to
Owain, the son of Urien of Gorre and Modron. Yvain married
Alienor, the daughter of Emyr Llydaw and founded the House of
Léon in Brittany. Their son was Count Gwythyr, whose daughter
Gwenhwyfar married Arthmael (Arthur).[10]

It seems that Count Gwythyr, the son of Yvain, the Knight
of Léon, sailed with a large army of immigrants from Caerleon-
upon-Usk in Gwent and landed on the northwest coast of Ar-

---

[10]It was Sir Thomas Malory who anglicized the name of Gwenhwyfar to
Guinevere.

morica. He took possession of the land from Aber Ildut to Morlaix, founded two religious settlements, and formed an organized
state which he called Léon, or Lyonesse, after Caerleon, and governed from Ile de Batz. To make quite sure that he should not be
dispossessed or assailed by the natives, he entered into an agreement with the Frankish King Childebert at his court in Paris and
secured a promise of support.

Gwenhwyfar, the daughter of Count Gwythyr, became the
wife of Arthmael (King Arthur) and, on the death of her brother
Count Gwythian she became the principal heir to the family estates. When Count Gwythyr died in about 530, King Arthur
gained access to her inheritance and overall control of the principality of Léon. Subsequently, Léon was absorbed into the Breton
Kingdom of Domnonia, which Arthur ruled jointly with his
cousin Deroch, son of Riwal Mawr.

# 8 🍀

## SOLÒ1ER-SAINTS

THE FIFTH AND SIXTH CENTURIES are regarded as the
"Golden Age of Saints," for this was the period when the
greatest of these pioneers of the Celtic Church flourished.
It is important to understand that these holy men and women
were not formally canonized saints, but they were so called because they devoted their lives, or their remaining years, to the
service of God. The word saint is derived from the Latin *sanctus,*
which means holy, and the word holy itself comes from the old
English hal, meaning whole or healthy. In the Latin church, the
term saint was a distinctive title of honor, but to the Celts it
merely indicated that the person to whom it applied was a Christian or a member of an ecclesiastical tribe who was generally regarded as a saint of a particular district.

Saints were chosen by the Romans and the Saxons for their
merits, but many of the Celtic saints inherited the title. However,
it did not necessarily indicate that they were honorable characters or that they had led entirely holy lives. Such a saint was born
of a saintly family and belonged to a tribal church which allowed
little scope for individuality. For this reason, it is constantly
found that the saints whose names are scattered in such confusion around Wales were closely related to one another and the
positions of abbot and bishop belonged by inheritance to select
families. For example, Dubricius, the first Bishop of Llandaff,
was cousin to Teilo, his successor, who in turn was followed by
his nephew Oudoceus.

Many of the names of these Celtic saints are familiar today
from the innumerable commemorative names of towns, villages,
and church dedications in Wales, Cornwall, and Brittany. The
ancient churches and chapels which still bear the names of these

saints owe their foundation to the fact that the saints actually went there to establish a monastic community on the site where the present-day church stands.

The chiefs or kings who ruled the petty kingdoms no doubt felt obliged to be hospitable to these missionaries who traveled through their territory, and generally went out of their way to provide them with protection and land on which to establish a simple church. Having been granted such a site, the saint would mark out the boundary of the intended sanctuary in a circle or oval, about 30 meters across, and erect stones to mark the limits. This would then serve as a burial ground; such enclosures are known as llans in Wales and vlans in Cornwall. Both these words mean a "clearing" or a "flat space." Within or close to this burial ground the missionary saint would then build a hut or cell. In due course, a village would often grow up around the llan and this would usually take its name from the saint who first settled there. When the founder died, he or she would be buried by the local community of Christians and an inscribed memorial stone would be erected nearby. Burial close to the tomb of the much-respected saint would then become very desirable for local persons of importance.

During our research, we came to realize that, in many instances, there was another side to the lives of these holy men, for at times they found it necessary to exchange their priestly apparel for armor and swords in order to overthrow oppressive tyrants. Such men of God were known as "Soldier-Saints" and many of King Arthur's followers can be included in this illustrious company.

## St. Garmon

One of the first of these great crusaders was St. Garmon, the brother of Aldwr, who was the father of Emyr Llydaw and the ruler of the Welsh settlements in Armorica. St. Garmon, the Bishop of Aleth, came to Wales with Ambrosius and participated in the overthrow of Vortigern, thus helping to re-instate the Romano-British dynasty. Garmon also led the insurrection which

deposed Benlli Gawr ("the Giant"), King of Ial, and installed
Cadell Ddyrnllug ("of the Gleaming Hilt") in his place.

Having accomplished his work in toppling the two tyrants,
Vortigern and Benlli, from their thrones and blessing the succes-
sions of Ambrosius and Cadell, St. Garmon then concentrated on
the establishment of new monasteries, one of which was Deerhurst in Gloucestershire, which was modeled on the church type
which originated in Tours, then a member of the Armorican
Federation.

St. Garmon had been instrumental in setting up Constantine
the Blessed's brother Anhun Dunawd (Antonius Donatus) as
King of Man and he now decided to settle on the island himself.
Here he spent the remainder of his life as Bishop of Man, evan-
gelizing the inhabitants, among whom St. Patrick had already
preached. Garmon set up his headquarters on the island near the
place now called Castletown. Among the churches he founded
was Kirk Garmon, near Peel, where he was buried after his death
in 474. The medieval cathedral which stands within the walls of
Peel Castle, on St. Patrick's Island, was dedicated to the honor of
St. Germain, the first Bishop of Man. The village of St. Ger-
mains, which stands halfway between Douglas and Ramsey, is
also named after him.

## St. Illtyd Farchog

Probably the most important soldier-saint of Arthur's time was
Illtyd Farchog ("The Golden Chained Knight"). He was the son
of Bicanys, a nobleman of Armorica who was married to Gweryla, a daughter of King Tewdrig, the grandfather of Arthur.
Therefore, Illtyd and Arthur were first cousins.

Illtyd left his home in Armorica and studied in Paris. He became a disciple of St. Garmon, Bishop of Aleth, and then trained
as a soldier in Britain. Here he married Trynihid[1] and entered the

---

[1]There can be little doubt that the name of Illtyd's wife, Trynihid, survives in
Llantryddid and in another form in Llanrhidian in Gower, Llanrhidian in St.
Davids, and another Llanrhidian in Tremarchog near Fishguard.

service of Paul of Penychen, who was one of the sons of Glywys, King of Glywysing. After being made captain of the guard, he eventually rose to the position of Magister Militum (Military Magistrate).

In consequence, he was known thereafter as Illtyd Farchog ("the Knight"). However, he decided that his true vocation lay in the service of God. St. Cadoc, the nephew of Paul Penychen, advised him to become a monk and he accordingly resigned his military position to withdraw from the prince's service. His great-uncle, St. Garmon, ordained him as a priest and for a while Illtyd lived in a reed hut beside the River Nadafan in Glamorgan. Having separated from his wife, he spent time as a hermit in the wooded valley of the Hodnant to the west of the River Thaw. Trynihid, who was also a devout Christian, went to a solitary place in the mountains, where she founded an oratory.

The ruler of South Glamorgan and the Gower Peninsula at this time was Meirchion Vesanus (Marcianus the Mad), who was another son of Glywys. At first he resented Illtyd's intrusion into his domain, but he later relented and granted Illtyd the Hodnant valley. Without hindrance, Illtyd then began to cultivate the land surrounding his settlement. Before long he had a hundred followers in his household and as many workmen. Together, they rebuilt the monastery of Cor Tewdws (Choir of Theodosius) and Illtyd was appointed principal by St. Garmon. From that time the place was called Llanilltyd Fawr (the Great Church of St. Illtyd), but today this name has been anglicized to Llantwit Major.

Under Illtyd's direction, his monastic school rapidly earned a considerable reputation and attracted large numbers of scholars from important families over a wide area. His students included Gildas the historian, Taliesin the poet, Maelgwyn Hir ("the Tall"), Prince of Gwynedd, Samson, who became Bishop of Dol in Brittany, Paul Aurelian, who was appointed Bishop of Léon, and Arthmael.

This monastic college was undoubtedly one of the most famous places in Wales. It was a sort of Oxford and Cambridge rolled into one. Saints, abbots, and bishops of the old British Church lectured here and it was visited by the kings and princes of western Britain. In the *Life of St. Samson* of Dol in Brittany, we are told that "Illtyd was the most learned of all the Britons

*Figure 25. Llanilltyd Fawr, now known as Llantwit Major, in South Glamorgan, was founded in the sixth century by St. Illtyd. He established a monastic college here which became the first university in Britain and the greatest in Europe. Among Illtyd's most famous pupils were Gildas the historian, Taliesin the poet, Maelgwyn, who became King of Gwynedd, and Samson, who became Bishop of Dol.*

in his knowledge of the scriptures, both Old and New Testaments. In every branch of philosophy, and rhetoric, grammar and arithmetic he was most sagacious and gifted with the power of foretelling future events." Some writers have called Llanilltyd Fawr the "Pompeii of the Saints," for more saints were sent out from here during the fifth and sixth centuries than from any other similar monastic establishment. However, the stewards of King Meirchion, who were jealous of Illtyd's success, began to persecute him, making his life so unbearable that he was forced to retire to a secret cave on the River Ewenny. After due consideration, St. Illtyd was obliged to resort to the military experience which he he had gained as Magister Militum and the threat to his existence rapidly diminished.

Even after the death of Illtyd, the college continued to operate with a good reputation right up to the 11th century when the Normans arrived on the scene. Robert Fitzhamon then took away most of its property, giving much of it to the monks of Tewkesbury Abbey. From that time, the college went into decline, with its importance sadly diminished until, during the reign of Henry VIII, it finally ceased to exist.

## ST. PAUL AURELIAN

According to Wrmonoc's *Life of St. Pol de Léon*,[2] which was written in 884, but compiled from an earlier *Life* of the saint, St. Paul Aurelian was born in 487 at the Roman Station of Caput Bovium (Boverton), near Llanilltyd Fawr (Llantwit Major) in the center of Penychen, Glywysing (southeast Glamorgan).

He was the son of Porphyrius Aurelianus, who was descended from the family of Ambrosius Aurelianus (Emrys Wledig) and married a daughter of Meurig, King of Glamorgan and Gwent. Wrmonoc informs us that St. Paul Aurelian's father, Count Porphyrius Aurelianus, was a landowner in Domnonia who served as a military companion to the local king in Glywysing. His Christian name may well be derived from Porphyrion, the Red Dragon, which he used as his personal emblem.[3]

Paul, at a very early age and against his father's wishes, went to study under St. Illtyd at his monastic school of Llanilltyd

---

[2]Before the destruction of the Breton monasteries by the Northmen in the tenth century, Wrmonoc's *Life of St. Pol de Léon* was taken to the great Abbey of Fleury, a few miles from Orleans. It is in the hand-writing of the ninth century and is now preserved in the public library at Orleans. See Albert Le Grand, *Les Vies des Saints de la Bretagne Armorique* (Quimper, 1901), pp. 98–115.

[3]Wrmonoc identifies St. Paul Aurelian with Paul of Penychen, but this is difficult to reconcile with the known facts, for Paul of Penychen is recorded in *The Genealogies of the Welsh Saints* (in *Lives of the British Saints*, Rev. Sabine

Fawr. In due course, Illtyd arranged for Paul to go to Caldey Island (Ynys Pyr) where he made the acquaintance of Saints David, Samson, and Gildas. They were all subsequently transferred to Llanilltyd Fawr, where Illtyd employed them in building an embankment along the edge of the Severn to reclaim areas of alluvial soil for agricultural purposes. In the course of time, Paul was ordained priest, possibly by St. Dubricius (Dyfrig).

The next few years of his life he spent in Cornwall, having been summoned by Marcus Conomorus, the exiled son of the Glamorgan prince Meirchion Vesanus, to direct the spiritual affairs in his petty realm. Paul's memory in this area is preserved in the place-names with the prefix Pol in the vicinity of the Fowey Estuary. After spending two years in Cornwall and having no desire to become a bishop to Marcus Conomorus, Paul sailed to Armorica to seek a wider field for his energies. He landed on the island of Ouessant at the port of Porz Ejenned (Port of the Oxen). Here he erected a church at the place which is still called Lampaul and is the principal village there. However, the limitations of Ouessant proved inadequate for Paul's ardent spirit, so he crossed to the mainland where he founded another church which today is called Lampaul Ploudalmézau.

Within two years Paul had itchy feet again, so he moved on along the coast in an easterly direction until he reached Plou-Meinin, a rocky island colonized by some of the clansmen of his cousin Count Gwythyr. This Gwentian prince had arrived with a large party of emigrants from Caerleon-upon-Usk and taken possession of an area of land from the Aber Ildut to the River Morlaix. He set up an organized state which he named Léon, or

Baring-Gould and John Fisher, eds., 1907–1913) as being the son of Glywys of Glywysing. On the death of Glywys, his domain was divided up among his ten children and the third son, called Paul, received as his share the province of Penychen. Dr. John Morris in *The Age of Arthur* (London: Weidenfeld & Nicholson, 1973) p. 363, informs us that Paul Aurelian's father, Perphirius Aurelianus, was a landowner in Domnonia (Devon), who served as a military companion to a local king in Glywysing. This fits the pattern well for the Glamorgan princes held estates in both Cornwall and Brittany.

Lyonesse, after Caerleon in Gwent. He established his headquarters on the Ile de Batz and from here he governed the entire tribe.

It seems that Paul decided to visit his cousin Count Gwythyr, partly because he was a relative, but also because he could not settle in the district without his cousin's consent. A short boat journey brought him to the Ile de Batz, where Gwythyr made him welcome, no doubt because he was delighted to see his cousin from South Wales. Paul must have heard of the death of Gwythyr's only son, Count Gwythian, in Cornwall and, knowing that his cousin was now without a male heir, he demanded his right to a slice of Gwythyr's principality of Léon. The Count consented to his request, but bade him first obtain the permission of the Frankish King Childebert.

Arthmael, who was also in Armorica at this time, interceded, for, having recently married Gwythyr's daughter Gwenhwyfar, he had a vested interest in the negotiations. Acting as a delegate, he went on a mission to discuss with King Childebert the religious administration of Léon. He thus paved the way for Paul's visit to the court of the Frankish king at Paris. Childebert expressed his willingness to ratify the negotiations on the condition that Paul be made Bishop of Léon. With reluctance Paul agreed to his request.

On his return to Léon, the new bishop undertook missionary work throughout the diocese with great energy and established a monastic center in the ruined town of Ocismor. Count Gwythyr then made over the site of the old Roman fort on the Ile de Batz to Paul and went to reside in one of his mansions. Paul continued to build chapels and establish monasteries throughout the principality, but he eventually settled in the place now called St. Pol de Léon.

When Count Gwythyr died in 530, his daughter Gwenhwyfar inherited his estates, and her husband, Arthmael, gained access to her inheritance, thus obtaining overall control of the principality of Léon. In due course, Léon was absorbed into the Armorican kingdom of Domnonia under the joint rule of Arthmael and his second cousin Deroch, the son of Riwal Mawr. Deroch, following the death of his father, was King of Domnonia from 524 to 535. Meanwhile, Paul Aurelian ruled as a true saint-prince over the portion which he had claimed and received by the right of his kinship to Count Gwythyr. His inheritance consisted of one ecclesiastical principality conterminous in later times with the diocese of Léon. St. Paul Aurelian died after a long career as first Bishop of Léon at the ripe old age of 86 years in 573.

## ST. SAMSON OF DOL

The story of this soldier-saint is of particular interest, for it is described in detail in the *Vita Sancti Samsonis*, which was compiled between 610 and 615 by Tigernomail, Bishop of Léon and nephew of St. Paul Aurelian.[4]

St. Samson was born in Glamorgan in 486. He was the son of Amwn Ddu (Annun "the Black"), son of Emyr Llydaw and his wife, Anna, daughter of Meurig ap Tewdrig, King of Glamorgan and Gwent. At age 5, Samson was taken by his parents to the monastic school of St. Illtyd. Here he remained for many years and was taught the Old and New Testaments, together with philosophy, rhetoric, grammar, geometry, arithmetic, and all the arts known in Britain at that time. St. Illtyd, in due course, procured Samson's ordination to the deaconate and to the priesthood. Samson then left Llanilltyd Fawr and joined the monastery of Piro on Caldey Island (Ynys Pyr).

On the death of Abbot Piro, St. Illtyd sent a message to the island monks to come to his monastery at Llanilltyd Fawr to elect Samson as their new abbot. It seems that Samson only lasted eighteen months in this position, for he became tired of the monks' opposition to his authority. He made the decision to

---

[4]Bishop Tigernomail states that his sources for the *Life of St. Samson* (See Thomas Taylor, *The Life of Samson of Dol,* London: SPCK, 1926) included a life of the saint written by the deacon Henoc, a nephew of St. Samson. Henoc himself handed it to Tigernomail, who described him as an old man, eighty years of age. He also made use of information which was communicated verbally to him by the elderly Henoc and by monks of the monastery of Llanilltyd Fawr. This early "Life" of St. Samson is of exceptional interest since it can be shown to be very old and to be based on information derived from intimate friends of St. Samson himself.

accompany a band of Irish monks who were returning from a visit to Rome, on their journey to Ireland.

When Samson returned from his visit to the Irish monasteries, he refused to resume his position as abbot on Caldey Island and decided to go into retreat with his father Amwn Ddu and two other holy men at St. Garmon's monastery at Deerhurst in Gloucestershire. Within a short time, he was summoned by the Synod and appointed by the elders to be abbot of that monastery. At a congregation of the bishop's counselors, it was unanimously resolved that St. Samson should be made bishop and he was consecrated by St. Dubricius on February 22, 521.

Shortly after his consecration, Samson decided to visit Cornwall. He sailed across the Severn Sea and landed at Padstow, where he met St. Petroc. After founding a chapel on the hill near Place House, he continued his mission across the Cornish Peninsula. Passing through the district of Trigg or Tricorium (now Tregeare), Samson came across a group of people performing idolatrous rites around a standing stone, with the apparent approval of their ruler, Count Gwythian of Gelliwig. Samson Christianized the stone by carving a Chi-Rho cross upon it and it is of interest that such an ancient stone was discovered when St. Samson's Well at South Hill was being renovated. It can now be seen in the rectory grounds near the site of a monastery which he founded. Standing nine feet high, it bears a Latin inscription commemorating Cumregnus, son of Maucus, as well as the Chi-Rho cross.

According to Count Nikolai Tolstoy, in *The Quest for Merlin* (see p. 92), it is clear that St. Samson's encounter with Gwythian and his fellow worshippers was a factual account of the celebration of the "Feast of the god Lugh at the Festival of Lughnasa," which took place on the first of August. It is particularly significant that the place called Gwithian is just a dozen miles from Morvah, which was the scene of the last great Lughnasa Festival surviving into the last century. So it appears that the ritual encountered by St. Samson was a British version of the Irish Festival of Lughnasa, when the god Lugh brought fertility to the land and prosperity to the kingdom. Evidence suggests that at Lughnasa Festivals there was a custom of bringing a stone head from a nearby sanctuary and placing it on top of the hill during the celebrations.

*Figure 26. St. Samson, presiding at the Council of Prelates. From the Cathedral at Dol: 13th-century window.*

St. Samson, during his stay in the district of Trigg, made the acquaintance of Count Gwythian and rendered him some service by helping his son, who had been stunned by a fall from his horse. As a result, the grateful Count accepted St. Samson as patron, abandoned his estate of Gelliwig to Caradog Freichfras, and subsequently followed Samson to Armorica.

Leaving South Hill, Samson traveled overland to the south coast of Cornwall and arrived at Golant on the estuary of the River Fowey. Here he established a church which is still dedicated to him. He remained here until the arrival of his cousin, St. Maglorius, who brought news of the usurpation of Count Marcus Conomorus (King March) in Armorican Domnonia in 549. Entrusting his church at Golant to a disciple, Samson crossed the sea to Armorica and settled at Dol, where he founded a monastery.

In chapter 16, we shall relate in detail how Samson raised an army to depose Conomorus and restore the rightful heir to the throne of Breton Domnonia. He trained his band of men on the Channel Islands and, while there, found time to introduce

Christianity into Guernsey. Near the South Quay of St. Samson's Harbor, he founded a monastery and it is interesting that his cousin St. Maglorius established a monastery on the Island of Sark soon afterward.

Returning to Armorica, Samson and his army fought three battles and defeated the tyrant Marcus Conomorus in 555. His mission accomplished, Samson then lay down his arms and returned to Church matters. He attended the third Council of Paris in 557 and signed his name among the bishops. Following his death in 565, his cult immediately became very popular, with large numbers of pilgrimages being made to his sarcophagus at Dol in Armorica.

## St. Gwynllyw

In southeast Wales, there were four important kingdoms known as Brycheiniog, Glywysing, Gwynllywg, and Gwent. The ruler of Brycheiniog was Brychan, whose father, Anlach, was married to Marchell, the daughter of King Tewdrig of Garth Madryn. Brychan's kingdom included the area around Brecon, Talgarth, and the northern part of the Usk Valley.

Glywysing was named after Glywys and it extended westward from the Usk to the River Neath. Like Ambrosius, Glywys was a direct descendant of the Roman Emperor Magnus Maximus. On his death, the nine sons of Glywys divided the kingdom of Glywysing up among themselves. The portion that fell to Gwynllyw Filwr ("the Warrior") was the marshy cantref of Gwynllywg, now called the Wentloog Level. It lies between Newport and Cardiff and extends north to the foot of the Brecon Beacons. The Caldicot and Wentloog Levels had been reclaimed from the Severn by the Second Augustan Legion, stationed at Caerleon-upon-Usk, but, following their withdrawal, the land no doubt reverted to swamp.

A well-known story describes how Gwynllyw fell in love with Gwladys, the beautiful daughter of Brychan Brycheiniog ("of the Speckled Tartan"), and he sent messengers to request her hand in marriage. But King Brychan treated the messengers with insolence. Gwynllyw, highly incensed, armed three hundred men and left his fort near Newport in Gwent to ride north. They crossed the Black Mountains and descended to the court of Brychan Brycheiniog, near the town now called Talgarth. Brychan reacted with anger and refused to hand over his daughter, so Gwynllyw decided to use force. He snatched Gwladys from the door of her own chamber in Brychan's court and headed back to his own territory.

Brychan set off in hot pursuit, accompanied by a strong force, to rescue his daughter and caught up with Gwynllyw and his party at Rhiw Carn, to the north of Gelligaer, which was just within the boundary of Gwynllyw's territory. It was a fierce and bloody encounter in which two hundred of Gwynllyw's men perished. However, according to the more popular version of the story, the fight was stopped by the timely intervention of King Arthur, who happened to be in the vicinity with his two followers, Cei and Bedwyr. As a result, Gwynllyw succeeded in escaping with his intended bride and they completed their journey back to his fort on Allt Gwynllyw, which is now known as Stow Hill and overlooks Newport in Gwent.

A son was born to the couple and they named him Cathmael or, in Welsh, Cadfael (Battle Prince), and no doubt Gwynllyw intended that his firstborn son should become a brave soldier. However, he subsequently chose to spend his life in the service of God and has since been known as Cadoc or Cattwg.[5]

## St. Cadoc

The young Cadoc was entrusted to the care of St. Tathan, who was the principal of a monastic college at Caerwent. When he

---

[5] In the *Life of St. Finian*, Cadoc is referred to as Cathmael or Cadfael (Battle Prince), and Lifris gives him three names: Cadoc in Wales, Cadfael in Ireland, and Cadfoddw in Brittany. Lifris wrote the *Vita St. Cadoci* [Life of St. Cadoc] between c. 1073 and 1086. His name appears in the witness lists in the *Book of Llandaff*, and he was the son of Bishop Herewald. He was born c. 1050–1055 and became Archdeacon of Glamorgan and Master at St. Cadoc's Monastery at Llancarfan.

was about eighteen, Cadoc returned to his father Gwynllyw, who tried to persuade him to help make war on a neighboring king. But Cadoc had no desire for a military life and went back to St. Tathan's monastery. On completing his education, Cadoc deserted his father's kingdom and traveled to the territory of his uncle Paul in Penychen, a cantref of an area later known as Morgannwg. Paul granted Cadoc a marshy valley which he gladly accepted and where he set about building a monastery on a dry piece of ground. Soon he was joined by other young men who had been his fellow students at Caerwent and who also had no desire to become soldiers.

After about five years, Cadoc left his monastic college at Llancarfan and traveled to Ireland to study under St. Carthagh, a disciple of St. Ciaran, at Saighir. He remained at this monastic school for about three years and then returned to Britain with a large company of Irish and British clergy. Seeking new pastures, Cadoc then traveled to the land of his grandfather and placed himself under a scholarly monk who was known as Bachan of Brycheiniog. Here at Llanspyddid, near the Romano-British town of Bannium (Y Gaer), he was taught Latin after the Roman method.

Cadoc then moved on to found another monastery at Llangadog, which is pleasantly situated between the Rivers Bran and Sawdde, above their junction with the Towi. To the east rise the majestic Brecon Beacons and to the south is the purple ridge of the Black Mountain, otherwise known as the Carmarthen Fan. Below this latter range of hills is an outcrop which is crowned by the stone fort of Garn Goch, established in prehistoric times to command the basin of the Towi. Nearby is the site of Llys Brychan (the Court of Brychan), and it is probable that the extensive stone fort also bore his name at one time, but this was discarded for the more descriptive term of Garn Goch (Red Cairn).

While at Llangadog, St. Cadoc was harassed by Sawyl Beneuchel, the son of Pabo Post Prydain, who had established himself in the pleasant mountain basin of Cynwyl Gaio. Here he commanded the area from his fort which bears the significant name of Pen-y-Ddinas. This was an eminently suitable position from which a British chief could harry the neighborhood, especially the Irish of Brycheiniog. Below it stands Llansawl, which was founded by Sawyl. It was not long before Cadoc became

*Figure 27. St. Cadoc, from his statue at Lampaul-Guimilau, Brittany.*

weary of the problems caused by his troublesome neighbor and he abandoned the construction of his new monastery and returned to his earlier foundation at Llancarfan. To his dismay, he found it deserted and in ruins. However, undaunted, he ordered all his monks, clerics, and workmen to go to the woods and cut timber for repairing the structure.

It was about this time, in 527, that Gwynllyw, his father, fell sick. The old king had given a great deal of trouble in his time, but in later years he had been converted by his son and persuaded to lead a Christian life. When he realized that he was dying, he sent for Cadoc and Bishop Dubricius, who gave him penance and deliverance.

When Gwynllyw died, Rhain, the son of Brychan Brycheiniog, quickly took advantage of the situation. He invaded the province of Gwynllywg to plunder and lay it waste right down to the shore of the Severn Sea. But the men of Gwynllywg organized themselves and pursued Rhain and his marauding army. They defeated him in one battle after another and eventually captured him. However, they did not dare put him to death, for he was related to St. Cadoc. On hearing of his uncle's situation, Cadoc went to see him and obtained his liberation.

At this time, there was no king in Gwynllywg. Cadoc, not wishing to reign himself, made Meurig, the son of Caradog Freichfras (not to be confused with Meurig ap Tewdrig), ruler and gave him his aunt Dibunn, in marriage. According to the *Book of Llandaff*, Meurig then confirmed the privileges granted by Arthur and Maelgwyn. The recorded witnesses were Saints David, Cynidr, Teilo, Illtyd, Maidoc, and Cannou.

In 528, St. Gildas passed through Penychen and visited St. Cadoc, who seized the opportunity to ask Gildas to take charge of his monastery at Llancarfan while he himself went to Alba. Gildas consented, but fell out with St. David before Cadoc left. David and Gildas argued over who should be the head of the ecclesiastics in Dyfed, and Gildas made strenuous efforts to turn David out and occupy his position. Cadoc was called in to settle the argument and, this being a delicate matter, he little relished the prospect of displeasing either of the rivals. So he delegated the thankless task to St. Finian, his friend and companion, who gave his judgment in favor of St. David.

Cadoc departed for Alba in about 529 and there he built a stone monastery. Camuslang is dedicated to him. Through the adjoining parish of Carmunnock runs a range of hills called the Cathkin Hills which separate Strathclyde from Ayrshire to terminate in Strathgryf, Renfrewshire. Apparently at the request of Gildas, Cadoc, while he was in this area, located the grave of Gildas's father, Caw Prydein of Cwm Cawlwyd, who had lost his territory in a conflict with the Pictish Goidels. As a token of his friendship with Gildas, Cadoc erected a church over the tomb of Caw Prydein.

On his return to Llancarfan, Cadoc resumed his position at the head of his monastery. Before Gildas moved on to Glastonbury, the two saints spent Lent in simple retreats on the adjoining islands of Flat Holm and Steep Holm in the Severn Estuary. Their period of prayer and meditation was only broken by visits to one another on their respective islands. These two island retreats later became unsafe due to the threat of pirates who infested the Severn Sea, and Cadoc was obliged to look for another place where he could peacefully withdraw from the world. He found one on the banks of the River Neath and sent gifts to King Arthmael (Arthur), who thereupon made a grant of this location, which became known as Cadoc-juxta-Neath.

Soon afterward, Cadoc fell out with Arthur. He gave refuge to a man named Ligessauc Lawhir ("the Long-Handed"), who had killed three of Arthur's soldiers. Cadoc sheltered this fugitive in Gwynllywg for seven years before Arthur discovered where he was concealed. This period exceeded the time limit for sanctuary and Arthur was incensed. He demanded that Cadoc send a deputation to him to settle terms. Cadoc's commissioners proceeded to the banks of the Usk, and Arthur held communication with them by shouting across the river. At last it was proposed that Cadoc should pay to the king a blood fine of three of the best quality oxen for each man slain, but this proposal was rejected by Arthur and it was then decided that Cadoc should instead pay three hundred cows. However, when the cattle were collected and driven to the river bank, Arthur refused to receive them unless they were all of uniform color. He required that the forepart should be red and the rear part white. Cadoc found it impossible to comply with such a request. Arthur then sent Cei and Bedwyr into the muddy water to meet Cadoc's men in the middle of the river, and finally he consented to receive the cattle. This incident, from the *Life of St. Cadoc,* serves to illustrate that Arthur was an all-powerful monarch ruling over Glamorgan and Gwent and that Cadoc was his subject. He certainly drove a hard bargain.

In 534, St. Gildas returned to his monastic settlement at Rhuys in Armorica and Cadoc undertook a pilgrimage to Jerusalem and Rome. On his return from Rome, he visited his friend Gildas at Rhuys and was told of a potential site for a monastery on an island in a lagoon called the Sea of Belz. The two men visited the location together and Gildas did his best to persuade Cadoc to settle there, but Cadoc decided to return to Britain.

When he arrived at Llancarfan, Cadoc learned that the Synod of Llandewi Brefi had been held to pass penitential canons. He was furious that such a meeting should be held without his either being consulted or invited to be present. His resentment was specifically directed against St. David, who had taken a leading role in the matter. In his wrath, Cadoc proceeded to fast in protest and was only persuaded to stop when it was pointed out to him that his conduct was contrary to the principles of Christian charity.

In 547, the bubonic plague broke out and caused panic throughout the land. Cadoc decided to return to Armorica and, on his way through Cornwall, he broke his journey to found a chapel, the ruins of which can be seen near St. Minver, Padstow.

On reaching Armorica, Cadoc remembered his visit to the land-locked Sea of Belz and, with a body of monks, he established a community on the island which is now called Ile de St. Cadou. The present day chapel contains a statue of St. Cadoc which represents him as a young ecclesiastic, with mitre and pastoral staff. The right hand is extended and is kept continually supplied with bunches of flowers by the children who live in the little fishing hamlet on the mainland. Access to the island is by a causeway, originally built by St. Cadoc, using massive blocks of granite brought from the neighboring moors. According to Albert Le Grand, St. Cadoc remained on this island for three years. He then placed a disciple named Cadwaladr in charge and returned to Llancarfan.

In 564, King Ainmire summoned Gildas to give assistance in reviving the Christian religion in Ireland, and his invitation was also extended to Cadoc, who accepted and subsequently established a new monastery on lands granted to him on the banks of the Liffey.

A year later, Cadoc returned to Llancarfan. By then he was starting to feel his age, for the management of such a large monastic establishment was becoming too much for him. So he decided to relinquish his position in favor of a young disciple named Elli. When Cadoc departed, he left with the brethren of Llancarfan a Book of the Gospels which had been translated by Gildas, and he gave instructions to the monks that all trials and settlements of disputes should take place under a hazel tree which he had planted.

From Llancarfan, Cadoc traveled to Beneventum where, according to his instructions, Elli was to pay him annual visits to report on the conditions and affairs at Llancarfan. At Beneventum, Cadoc was elected abbot over a large community of monks who had recently lost their superior. The walls of the monastery, constructed of mud and wattle, were in a very poor state, being full of holes. It was not long before Cadoc gave instructions for repairs to be undertaken.

After such a long and busy life, Cadoc was no doubt ready for a peaceful existence, but this was abruptly brought to a close in 577. A hostile Saxon raiding party attacked the settlement, intent on plundering and slaughtering everyone in sight. A soldier entered the church and killed Cadoc with a spear as the old man was celebrating the Holy Mysteries. For a while his body remained at Beneventum and a new church was later erected over it.[6]

## ST. DAVID

David or Dewi, to use his Welsh name, is ranked with Teilo and Cadoc as one of the three  canonized saints of the Island of Britain. As the patron Saint of Wales, he is by far the most celebrated. According to tradition, David was born at Llan Non, the church of St. Non in Pembrokeshire. It seems that Sandde

---

[6]De Keranet, in his edition of Albert Le Grand's *Les Vies des Saints de la Bretagne Armorique,* identifies Beneventum with Caerwent, as does Professor Bury in his edition of Muirchu's *Life of St. Patrick.* Alternatively, it is possible that Beneventum is a misreading of Lan bent nant auan, which means Nant Nadauan, the Valley of the Thaw, and the monastery in question was at Llan Synnwyr, now Llansannor, which is about 6 miles northwest of Llancarfan. This may have been where St. Cadoc was buried in a silver coffin.

(Sant—son of Ceredig, son of Cunedda), King of Ceredigion, was visiting Menevia and violated a nun named Non (Nonnita), who subsequently gave birth to a son who was christened Dewi. Both the parents were of noble stock, for Sandde was the great-grandson of Cunedda Wledig and Non was the great-granddaughter of Vortigern.

By all accounts, David was educated at a place called Henfynyw, situated near the west coast of Wales just to the south of Aberaeron. This was a small Celtic monastery which had a good reputation as an educational establishment. It was directed by a bishop named Guistianus, who was the brother of St. Non and accordingly David's uncle. Afterward, young David was sent to further his education under the instruction of St. Paulinus at Tygwyn-Daf (Whitland) in Dyfed. He then traveled into Gwent and made his way up into the Black Mountains, where he built a simple cell and chapel on the site now occupied by St. David's Church, which adjoins Llanthony Priory. After spending a few years here in prayer and meditation, he returned to his homeland in Menevia.

Accompanied by three disciples, Aedan, Eiludd, and Ysvael, David approached Valle Rosina, where they were met by a hostile Irish Druidic chieftain named Boia, who ruled this locality from an Iron Age hill-fort. It can be seen on a prominent outcrop of rock overlooking the present-day farm of Clegyr Boia, about a mile from the city of St. David.

After several skirmishes, David managed to persuade Boia to allow him to build a monastery in Valle Rosina which was situated in a very secluded position and later became known as Mynyw. (In David's time, this locality was known as the "Vale of Roses" from the wild Burnet rose which grew in rich profusion on the cliffs and is pictured in the diocesan arms.) Leading a very strict and spartan life consisting of simple food, hard work and devotion, David set an example which had to be followed by all who joined him. He drank no wine, ate no meat, and never used oxen to till the ground, preferring to yoke his fellow monks to the plough.

From this monastery, David sent his missionaries on journeys far and wide to convert the pagans. His influence went out to people all over South and West Wales, Ireland, Scotland,

Cornwall, and Brittany. Villages named Llandewi mark locations where the original churches were founded by St. David or his disciples and they are to be found in many parts of Wales.

In 529, David convened a synod which exterminated the Pelagian heresy and was in consequence named "The Synod of Victory." It ratified the canons and decrees of Llandewi Brefi, as well as a code of rules which he had drawn up for the regulation of the British Church, a copy of which remained in the Cathedral of St. David until it was lost during an attack by pirates.

According to the computation of Archbishop Ussher, St. David died in 544, aged 82, in his monastery at Mynyw (Menevia) and was honorably buried there by order of Maelgwyn Hir of Gwynedd. Preserved in a casket in St. David's Cathedral are some human bones, which were discovered in 1866 in a recess at the bottom of the high altar. They have long been thought to be those of St. David and his confessor, St. Justinian.[7] Recent carbon dating, however, has proved that they are of the 12th-century period and may well be the bones of St. Caradoc.

In the poem "Armes Prydein Vawr" (ca. 930), St. David is portrayed as a soldier-saint leading the Britons to victory against the invading Saxons. He is thus shown as a typical figure of the British Heroic Age, comparable with Arthur himself. It would appear that David dominated the military as well as the religious scene in southern and western Dyfed and greatly contributed to the completion of the Cuneddan conquests in Wales. In later years, it was this image of David as a patriotic leader which helped to ensure his recognition as Patron Saint of Wales. Sometimes the actual relics of St. David were even carried into battle in the belief that they would ensure a great victory. He was undoubtedly a soldier-saint of the same mold as St. Arthmael.

---

[7]The earliest "Life" of St. David dates from the latter part of the 11th century and was written by Rhigyfarch, who was the son of Sulien of Llanbadarn Fawr. He was himself twice bishop of St. David's and wrote this document in 1086 in an attempt to boost the fame of St. David's shrine and to promote the establishment of the diocese of St. David.

*Figure 28. This casket in St. David's Cathedral contains some human bones which were discovered in 1866 in a recess at the bottom of the high altar. They were thought to be those of St. David and his confessor, St. Justinian, but recent carbon dating indicates that they are more likely to be those of the 12-century St. Caradoc.*

## St. Efflam

The story of this saint, composed in the 12th century, has been pieced together out of vague traditions which have come to us in a corrupt form. Nevertheless, there is a substructure of truth in the tale, which until now has been largely ignored by Arthurian students.

We found that the name Efflam is derived from the Welsh ef-flan, meaning splendid or bright. The name in Irish is Felim and he was the son of the Irish king of Dyfed, who was engaged in continuous wars with another Irish ruler. Eventually, peace was obtained by the agreement of a marriage between Efflam and Elenora, the daughter of the rival king.

Efflam, however, had set his mind on becoming a monk, so it was not long before he sailed away to Armorica and landed in the estuary near Pléstin-les-Greves. He had been preceded by Iestin, another immigrant, who had taken possession of land between Toul Efflam and Loc-mikel, below a great rock known as Querlaz. However, Iestyn, who was generous by nature, gave up some of his land to Efflam so that he could build a monastery.

In Albert Le Grand's *Life of St. Efflam*, we found an interesting story which concerns St. Efflam and King Arthur:

At this time Riwal Mawr was king of Armorican Domnonia. He was akin to the great Arthur, who occasionally visited him and hunted on his preserves. Now there lived in a cave in the rock called Querlaz a hideous dragon which infested the land. Arthur, who was king in those days, heard of this dragon and went in quest of the monster. The dragon, however, was particularly crafty, and always walked backwards when going to its cave, so as to delude visitors into thinking he was abroad. Arthur fought with the dragon for a whole day but could not overcome it. When Arthur had failed abjectly, Efflam asked the king to allow him to do battle with the dragon. Arthur gave his consent and Efflam made the sign of the cross, whereupon the monstrous reptile, spouting blood and venom, plunged off the rock into the waves below and perished. The cliff which was stained with the dragon's

blood is called Red Rock to this day. Riwal Mawr, in gratitude to the Saint for having rid his country of this creature,
gave him lands surrounding the cell.[8]

This legend is written in riddle form and it represents the combined efforts of Saints Arthmael and Efflam to destroy a huge
"serpent temple" of upright stones, like those of Carnac. They
represented the old pagan religion and Christianity required their
removal.

## St. Derfel Gadarn (The Mighty)

Derfel (or Derfael) was the son of Riwal Mawr, the son of Emyr
Llydaw. He is usually given the epithet Gadarn ("the Mighty"),
because in his early life he was a warrior, and his might and
prowess in war are constantly alluded to by medieval Welsh
bards. It would appear that he greatly distinguished himself at
the Battle of Camlan, which was fought in 537.

Derfel is patron of Llanderfel in Gwynedd, where his
wooden effigy used to be held in high reverence. It depicted him
mounted on a horse and holding a staff. However, only remnants
of the wooden horse and staff have survived and they can be
seen in the church porch.

In 1538, Dr. Ellis Price, who was Thomas Cromwell's agent
for the diocese of St. Asaph, wrote to Cromwell requesting special instructions regarding this effigy. The problem was that local
people had so much faith in Derfel that they came daily in pilgrimage to the church, with cows, horses, or money. On 5 April,
which is St. Derfel's Day, as many as five or six hundred people
came to worship his effigy and they obviously believed the tradition that any person who offered anything to Derfel on his day
would be delivered out of hell by the saint.

It is recorded that Thomas Cromwell gave an instruction to
Dr. Price to send this wooden effigy to London, and despite a

---

[8]Albert Le Grand, "Life of St. Efflam," in *Les Vies des Saints de la Bretagne Armorique* (Quimper, 1901), pp. 582–589.

£40 bribe by the local people, this order was obeyed. Subsequently, a Franciscan Observant friar from Greenwich named Forest was burned at Smithfield Market on 22 May 1538 for denying King Henry VIII's claim to be the supreme head of the Church of England. Just before the friar's execution, the wooden effigy of Derfel was thrown onto the pyre. It is a remarkable coincidence that the Welsh had a prophecy that one day this wooden figure would set a whole forest on fire and it can be said that this was fulfilled, for it indeed set Friar Forest ablaze and reduced him to ashes.

Near Blaenau Ffestiniog in Gwynedd is a place called Llys Dorfill and it has been surmised that this was once the site of a residence used by Derfel Gadarn during his military days. This location is quite relevant to our placing of the Battle of Camlan (see chapter 13). Some sources state that, in his latter days, Derfel retired to Bardsey Island, where he became a monk in the monastery of St. Cadfan, and when he died he was buried there.

• • •

It is important to understand that the soldier-saints were all royal princes and many of them can be shown to belong to the same family. The following summary should help to make these connections much easier to comprehend:

Elen Luyddog (Helen "of the Hosts,") the wife of Magnus Maximus, was given an epithet which indicated that she marched with the legions of her husband. After his death, she returned to Wales and married St. Rhedyw (Ridicus), who was the son of Ithel Hael ("the Generous") of Llydaw. He may be identified with the great veteran fighter Riothamus and was the father of Aldwr (Aldroen), the ruler of the West Welsh settlements in Armorica, and St. Garmon (Germain), Bishop of Aleth (St. Servan in Brittany) and later first Bishop of Man.

It is significant that St. Garmon was the great-uncle of St. Illtyd Farchog ("the Knight"), whom he appointed principal of Cor Tewdws (Choir of Theodosius), which later became Llanilltyd Fawr (the Great Church of St. Illtyd). St. Illtyd was the son of Bicanys, the son of Aldwr, who was the brother of St. Garmon. Bicanys was a nobleman and a soldier from Llydaw

*Figure 29. This unusual stone can be seen in the north wall of Eglwysilan Church, near Caerphilly, Mid Glamorgan. It was found some years ago in the graveyard and depicts a Celtic warrior who was perhaps a soldier-saint of Arthur's time. The figure appears to be wearing a long tunic and is holding a sword and shield.*

(Brittany) and he married Gweryla, the daughter of Tewdrig Fendigaid ("the Blessed"), King of Morgannwg and Gwent. This makes his son Illtyd the first cousin of Athrwys ap Meurig ap Tewdrig, the King Arthur of history and legend.

Meurig brought about an important alliance by marrying his daughters to the sons of Emyr Llydaw, the brother of Bicanys. One of Emyr's sons, Amwn Ddu ("the Black"), married Anna, the daughter of Meurig and sister of Athrwys, and their son was none other than the great soldier-saint, Samson, the nephew of King Arthur. Another son of Emyr Llydaw was Riwal Mawr ("the Great"), who was the staunch ally of King Arthur. Riwal's sons included St. Derfel Gadarn ("the Mighty"), who fought with King Arthur at the Battle of Camlan, and St. Arthmael II, the prodigy of King Arthur who gained fame in his own right as the son of the Duke of Little Britain (Brittany). He may also have fought at Camlan and was buried on Bardsey Island.

St. Paul Aurelian was of the House of Ambrosius Aurelianus and St. Cadoc was of the House of Macsen Wledig (Magnus Maximus). They were both cousins of King Arthur and were trained as soldiers, but obviously preferred to use their administrative abilities in preference to their military expertise. St. Gwynllyw Filwr ("Soldier"), the father of Cadoc, is represented at his church in Newport by an effigy of a man in armor with a crown on his head. His abdication as ruler coincided with his conversion to Christianity.

St. David was of the House of Cunedda Wledig and he completed the Cuneddan conquests in Wales on behalf of his great-grandfather before devoting his life to the Celtic Church and becoming bishop to his kinsman King Arthur.

In the 12th century, the tradition of the soldier-saints was rekindled by St. Bernard of Clairvaux, who, in 1118, founded the Order of Templar Knights. They too were a band of warrior-monks, just like the men of Arthur's time. Their main aim was to protect, by force of arms, all pilgrims traveling to the Holy Land and they undertook many military campaigns against the enemies of Christ, particularly in the Holy Land. St. Bernard wrote of them:

> They are milder than lambs and fewer than lions. They combine the meekness of monks with the fighting courage of knights so completely I do not know whether to call them knights or contemplatives.[9]

---

[9]St. Bernard of Clairvaux, "In Praise of the New Chivalry," contained in Frances Gies, *The Knight in History* (New York: HarperCollins, 1984), pp. 108–109.

# 9 ❧

## STORIES IN STONE

TWO HUNDRED YEARS AFTER the legions departed from this
land, the Britons were still doing their best to retain certain Roman customs. In particular, they adopted the
practice of erecting memorial stones bearing Latin inscriptions.
These stones provide contemporary records of the arrival of
Christianity in Wales and there is a surprising total of about 440
inscribed stones of the fifth/sixth century period throughout the
principality. Many of the names recorded on the stones can be
shown to interrelate, thus providing additional clues and confirmation of the existence of certain Dark Age personalities.

These ancient memorial stones of Wales are of considerable
importance, for they represent the only remaining manuscripts of
the Dark Ages. Unfortunately, over the passing centuries, vast
numbers of them have been destroyed or utilized as building materials, but occasionally they come to light during restoration
work in ancient churches.

Wales is one of few places where bilingual inscriptions
(Latin and Ogham) on Dark Age memorial stones can be found.
There are, of course, many stones in Ireland, on the Isle of Man,
and in Scotland which are inscribed in Ogham alone. This form
of writing was made by cutting notches along the edges of stones
and it probably originated in southern Ireland during the fourth
century. It is in areas of Wales, where the Goidelic invaders from
Ireland settled, that the greatest number of Ogham stones are to
be found. In Dyfed, there are 21 such stones. There are nine in
Powys and two in Glamorgan. Twenty-six of the Ogham stones
in Wales have Latin inscriptions which make them bilingual.

In Powys, within the ancient kingdom of Brycheiniog
(the Land of Brychan), there are seven stones with Ogham

*Figure 30. The Carbalengus Stone stands in the middle of a field near Penbryn in Dyfed. It bears a Latin inscription commemorating Balencus, the Ordovician.*

inscriptions and this confirms the strong Irish connections with this area. Brychan's father, Anlach, came from Ireland. His son Brychan married Meneduc, the daughter of Custennin Fendigaid, and their offspring founded many churches in this area.

During our investigations, we inspected a considerable number of these ancient memorial stones and the ones mentioned in this account are those which proved of particular relevance to our quest for the truth about King Arthur.

The earliest inscribed stones were set up by the Romans and they provide fascinating information about Roman Britain, for they often record the name, age, birthplace, and even the profession of the departed person. Sometimes these Roman stones were later re-used as memorial stones by the Britons who added another Latin inscription. A good example can be seen in the little museum of ancient stones near Margam Abbey in West Glamorgan. The original Roman inscription on the stone informs us that it was set up in the reign of the Emperor Caesar Flavius Valerius Maximianus, the unconquerable Augustus. It also bears a later inscription:

HIC IACIT CANTVSVS PATER PAVLINVS
(Here lies Cantusus the father of Paulinus)

In North Wales we found a stone commemorating an Irishman with Roman connections. The inscription translates:

Carausius lies here in this heap of stones.

It is open to conjecture, but this may well have been Carausius, an Irishman of distinguished ability from Menapia, who was appointed commander in Gaul and was in charge of the maritime ports. Eventually, he broke off relations with the Roman government and proclaimed himself emperor in Britain in opposition to the Romans. He was an able statesman and a fine fighter who reigned over Britain for seven years (287–293). At the same time, his brother Cabri Lifeacher was a ruler in Ireland.

Carausius established a dynasty, the members of which in the course of time rivaled the descendants of Maximus. It is also quite feasible that the stone marks the grave of the son of Carausius, who is referred to as Carausius II. He reigned in the middle

*Figure 31. The Carausius Stone, Penmachno Church, Gwynedd.*

of the fourth century, about the time of the revolt of Magnentius in Gaul (350–353) and would have been a contemporary of Eudaf Hen (Octavius the Old), the all-powerful prince of Arfon whose daughter, Elen Luyddog, married Macsen Wledig (Maximus the Imperator).

At Llanhaelhearn in Gwynedd, we examined an inscription which might be termed a tribal commemoration. It states that "Aliotus the Elmetian lies here." This brief statement is of particular interest, for it indicates that Aliotus must have migrated from the northern kingdom of Elmet to North Wales where he subsequently died. A similar example can be seen on a stone at Penbryn near the Cardigan coast in Dyfed. It reads:

(the stone) of Carbalengus; (here) he lies, an Ordovicium.

In Roman times, the Ordovices were a tribe in north-central Wales, and Carbalengus must have traveled down to this area and died here, where he was buried under his Latin name. The fact that he is described as an "Ordovicium" shows that the tribal divisions survived the Roman occupation.

Inside Penmachno Church in Gwynedd is a stone that informs us:

> Cantorix lies here;
> he was a citizen of Venedos,
> cousin of Maglos, the magistrate.

Venedos is the Celtic form of the old name for northwest Wales (the area of Caernarvonshire and Anglesey). The wording implies that an administrative center had been formed which was based on Segontium, the old Roman fort linked with Magnus Maximus (Macsen Wledig—see chapter 1). The name "Maglos" on the stone may well be an abbreviated reference to Maglonocus, which is the Latin for Maelgwyn Gwynedd.

At Nevern Church in Dyfed can be seen an inscribed stone which has been utilized as a window sill. Fortunately, the inscription is on the upper surface and it reads:

MAGLOCVNI FILI CLVTORIS

It has been suggested that this might be a memorial to Maelgwyn Gwynedd, the son of Cadwallon Lawhir (the Longhanded).

Outside in the churchyard is a stone set in the ground which is known as the Vitalianus Stone. Bearing Latin and Ogham inscriptions, it commemorates Vitalianus, which is the name of Gwrtheyrn Gwrtheneu's (Vortigern's) grandfather. The word Emereto indicates that he served in the army.

*Figure 32. The Maglonocus Stone, Nevern, Dyfed.*

VITALIANI EMERETO
(The tomb) of Vitalianus

We have tried hard to find a memorial stone to Gwrtheyrn Gwrtheneu (Vortigern the Thin), but the best that we could come up with was a stone at Penmachno in Gwynedd, which bears no inscription, but is traditionally known as Llech Gwrtheyrn. It is possible that it was at one time inscribed with his name, but the lettering has been eroded away by the elements. It must be emphasized that the existence of an inscribed memorial stone does not necesssarily mean that the named person is buried at that location, for such stones were often erected merely to commemorate the name of the deceased. In modern times, we put up statues for the same purpose.

On a hill two miles to the north of Margam Abbey in West Glamorgan there used to stand an inscribed stone which was known as Maen Llythrog (the Lettered Stone). Some years ago, it was removed to Margam Museum, where it is now referred to as the Bodvoc Stone. It displays the following inscription:

BODVOC—HIC IACIT / FILIVS
CATOTIGIRNI / PRONEPVS
ETERNALI (S) / VEDOMAV
(The Stone) of Bodvoc. Here he lies, son of
Catotigirnus (and) great-grandson of Eternalis Vedomavum.

It is possible that this dedication refers to Bodvoc, a son of Catigirn and a grandson of Vortigern. Catigirn fell in a battle against

*Figure 33. The Bodvocus Stone, Margam Museum, near Port Talbol, West Glamorgan.*

the Saxons, who were led by Hengist and Horsa. Bodvoc, his son, reigned in Buellt (Builth Wells) after the death of Pascent, the third son of Gwrtheyrn Gwrtheneu. Catigirn is traditionally said to be buried at Kit's Coty, a prehistoric dolmen in Kent.

At the National Museum of Wales in Cardiff, we examined the Tegernacus Stone. It is 3 meters tall and used to stand on the ridge of Cefn y Brithdir near Tirphil in Mid Glamorgan. The inscription on it reads:

TEGERNACVS FILIVS MARTI HIC IACIT
Tegernacus son of Martius lies here.

Translated into Welsh, this inscription seems to signify that Teyrnoc, the son of Mar, lies here. Mar was the son of Glywys of Glywysing. The name Mar also appears in Marstow (Herefordshire), Margam (West Glamorgan), and Marcross (South Glamorgan). Margam (West Glamorgan) was originally Mar-gan, which meant literally "Mar's Chant;" hence Margam would denote Mar's choir. This is also the form given to the name in the *Annales de Margam.*

The name Tegernacus also appears on a stone at Cwmdu in Powys, where it refers to Catacus, the son of Tegernacus. The stone is built into a buttress on the south side of the church and it measures 2 meters high. A Latin inscription in two lines reads vertically:

CATACVS HIC IACIT FILIVS TEGERNACVS
Catacus lies here, son (of) Tegernacus

Previously, the stone stood in a field called Tir Gwenlli, about a mile southwest of the church and this valley was once known as Cwm Cattwg. The Catacus mentioned on this stone is not the well-known St. Cadoc, who founded many churches in Wales and Brittany, but his nephew of the same name. It is possible that a memorial stone to Cadoc, the son of Gwynlliw, at one time used to stand on the threshold of Llandefaelog Fach Church in Powys. Unfortunately, it was either destroyed or lost some years ago, but was apparently inscribed with the name CATVC.

*Figure 34. The Catacus Stone, Llantihangel, Cwmdu, north of Cmckhowell, Powys.*

There are in fact numerous stones bearing the names of well-known Dark Age saints and their relations. We inspected, for example, a stone built into the external south wall of the nave at Llandysilio West Church in Dyfed. It bears an inscription which, translated from Latin, reads:

(The Stone) of Clutorix, son of Paulinus Marinus of Latium.

This is probably a memorial stone to the son of St. Pol de Léon. The place named Latium is the same as the Welsh Llydaw for Brittany. Paulinus was, of course, a very popular name and at Cynwy Caeo in Dyfed can be seen a fragment of a slab bearing an inscription which, translated, reads:

He serveth the faith and his homeland ever loved
Here lies Paulinus, devoted to Justice he lived.

In this instance, the inscription most likely refers to St. Paulinus, who was the teacher of St. David and died in about 550.

Another important saint is remembered at St. Sadwrn's Church at Llansadwrn, Anglesey, Gwynedd. Inside this church is the memorial stone of St. Sadwrn, the founder. It was discovered under the wall of the chancel and reads:

HIC BEATV (S) SATVRNINVS (PVLTIS I) ACIT
ET SVA SA (NCTA) CONIX P(AX)
Here lies buried blessed . . . Saturninus and his saintly wife.
Peace be with you both.

The word Beatus or Beatissimus is fairly common in early Christian epitaphs, particularly for martyrs, confessors, and bishops. Santa Caniux often occurs in pagan epitaphs and accordingly has no Christian meaning, but in this instance a saintly reference is no doubt intended. Saturninus is most likely Sadwrn Farchog, who was an Armorican prince and the brother of St. Illtyd, the founder of the great college at Llanilltyd Fawr (Llantwit Major) in South Wales. Sadwrn's wife was Canna, his cousin. A few miles from Llansadwrn, at Beaumaris, is a tomb decorated with delicately carved representations of Anglesey saints. Two of them

*Figure 35. St. Sadwrn's Stone, Llansadwrn Church, Anglesey, Gwynedd.*

depict Sadwrn and Canna. He is shown wearing armor, his sword in a sheath, and holding a pilgrim's staff in his left hand. With his right hand he appears to be giving a benediction. Canna was the daughter of Tewdwr Mawr ("the Great"), son of Emyr Llydaw. She founded Llangan in South Glamorgan, which is an area where many of the family of Emyr Llydaw settled.

One of the most important memorial stones to a saint can be seen at St. Cadfan's Church, Tywyn in Gwynedd. When this stone was discovered in 1761, it was being used as a gatepost, but fortunately someone recognized its importance and it has been preserved. The inscription on the stone is in archaic Welsh and it is probably one of the earliest records of the Welsh language. Not only is it a memorial stone, it also records the burial place of St. Cadfan and tells us that his great patron, Cyngen of Powys, lies beside him.

> Beneath the mound of Cynfael lies Cadfan where the earth extols his praise, let him rest without a blemish. The body of Cyngen and between them will be the marks.

Cadfan was the son of Eneas Lydewig by Gwen Teirbron, a daughter of Emyr Llydaw. In the sixth century, Cadfan came to Wales and founded a church at Tywyn. He also founded a

*Figure 36. The Cadfan Stone, St. Cadfan's Church, Tywyn, Gwynedd.*

monastery on Bardsey Island, which we shall mention in chapter 15 in more detail. In addition, he founded a church at Llangadfan in Powys and here his patron was Cyngen, the son of Cadell. Cyngen succeeded his father in the principality of Powys and was distinguished for his patronage of the saints and liberal

endowments to the church. His son Brocmail Ysgythrog was defeated at the battle of Chester in 613.

The memorial stone of Brocmail (Brochwel or Brochfael)
Ysgythrog was found buried inside his grave at Pentrefoelas in
Gwynedd. It also commemorated his wife and formed the cover
slab to a stone cist which was found to contain a six-foot skeleton. On the stone is inscribed the name Brohomagli, which is the
equivalent of Brochmail in old Welsh and Brocmailus in the oldest manuscript of Bede. He was styled *Ysgythrog* ("of the
Tusks") because he probably had very prominent teeth. His wife
was Arddun Benasgell, a daughter of Pabo Post Prydain, who
had received lands from Brochwel's father, Cyngen. The children
of Brochwel and Arddun were Tyssilio and Cynan Garwyn.
Brochwel died soon after the battle of Chester, in which he acted
as an escort to a large body of British priests and monks. They
were mainly from the monastery of Bangor-on-Dee and they had
come to pray for the success of the Britons against the Saxons led

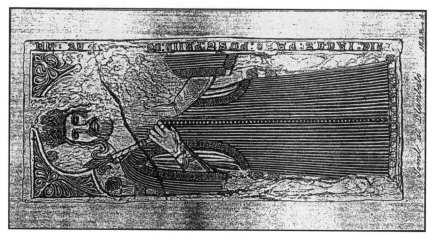

*Figure 37. At Llanbabo Church on Anglesey in Gwynedd can be
seen this memorial to Pabo Post Prydain. He flourished in the
middle of the fifth century and was known as the Pillar of
Britain. One of his sons was St. Dunawd, who gave his name to
St. Donat's in Glamorgan and was the father of St. Deiniol of
Bangor Fawr in North Wales.*

by Ethelfrith. Only fifty of the one thousand two hundred and fifty monks are said to have survived.

In St. Cenydd's Church at Llangenydd, Gower, in West Glamorgan, an ancient stone was found some years ago in the center of the chancel floor. It is an incised coffin lid and it is believed that it marked the grave of the patron saint. According to the Penrice and Margam Abbey documents, St. Cenydd's skull used to be kept in the church and, in the second half of the 15th century, it was used for swearing upon. An indenture of 1472 mentions that a certain man had to swear in the church "*upon Seiunt Keynthis Hedde.*"

Memorial stones to Dark Age kings are of particular interest and in Wales several identifications are possible. One interesting example is at Merthyr Mawr Church in West Glamorgan. Here a fragment of a sixth-century inscribed stone was found on the site of St. Teilo's Church during its restoration in 1849–1851. It is inscribed with the name PAUL . . . , but unfortunately the name is not complete, for the stone is broken. However, it is fairly safe to assume that it belongs to a certain Paulinus and, as this territory was once ruled by Paul of Penychen, the son of Glywys, we can tentatively suggest that it is his memorial stone.

Merthyr Mawr Church was rebuilt in Victorian times, but the site is undoubtedly an ancient one, for this building replaced a church "in a ruinous condition." The foundations of the earlier church can be seen on the south side of the present structure. Other memorial stones dating back to the sixth century have also been found on this site and these provide strong evidence that here stood a very early and important church.

One of the most important of all the memorial stones in South Wales is one commemorating a king of the sixth century who can be positively identified. It must be emphasized that there is no comparable memorial stone to an English king of this period in existence. Known as the Vortiporix Stone, it can be seen in Carmarthen Museum, Dyfed. On this stone is inscribed a bilingual inscription in Latin and Ogham:

MEMORIA / VOTEPORIGIS / PROTICTORIS
In memory of Vortiporix the Protector

*Figure 38. The Vortiporix Stone, Carmarthen Museum, Dyfed.*

Gildas, writing in about 540, named and criticized five contemporary kings and one of them was Vortiporix. He described him as being "like a panther in manners and wickedness of various colours . . . the worthless son of a good king."[1] Vortiporix was the son of Aircol Lawhir (Agricola "the Long-handed"), who was a good patron of the church. He reigned in the area equivalent to Pembrokeshire during the time of St. Teilo.

---

[1]*Gildas—The Ruin of Britain and Other Documents*, Michael Winterbottom, trans. (London & Chichester: Phillimore, 1978), see "De Excidio Britonum," p. 31.

The British name of Vortiporix in the inscription takes an Irish form, which is appropriate, for he belonged to a line of Irish kings who were officially recognized by the Romans. He is given the title PROTICTORIS (Protector or Defender) and this is significant, for Protector was the term which the Romans gave to the ruler of a treaty kingdom. The fact that the term is inscribed on this sixth-century stone is an indication that the title of "Protector" was still in use over 100 years after the Romans departed.

A Welsh king is also mentioned on a stone discovered in the sands on the coast near Barmouth, about one hundred yards below the water mark. The inscription reads:

HIC JACIT CALIXTVS MONEDD REGI
Here lies the boatman to King Gwynddo

The stone was later used as a footbridge and has since disappeared.

We visited Llangadwaladr Church on Anglesey to examine the stone of another Dark Age king who can be easily identified. This little church is dedicated to St. Cadwaladr and it is situated near Aberffraw, where the kings of Gwynedd once had their principal court. Set in the north wall of the chancel is an ancient stone commemorating Cadfan (not to be confused with St.

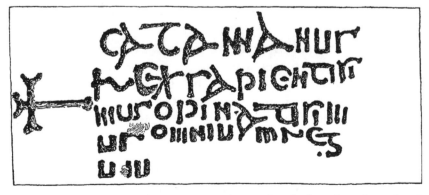

*Figure 39. The Cadfan Stone, Llangadwaladr Church, Aberffraw, Anglesey.*

Cadfan), a seventh century king of Gwynedd. The inscription is cut in manuscript half-unicals, and it is one of the later Dark Age memorial stones known to exist. It reads:

CATAMANVS REX SAPIENTISMVS OPINATISMVS,
OMNIVM REGVM
Cadfan the king, wisest and most splendid of all kings.

It was probably erected to Cadfan's memory by his grandson Cadwaladr, who founded the original church on this site in about 650. King Cadfan died in 625 and was succeeded by his son Cadwallon, who nine years later was killed in a battle near Hexham (in the vicinity of Hadrian's Wall) against King Oswald of Northumbria. Cadwaladr (Cadfan's grandson) ruled until 664, when, according to the *Annales of Wales,* "the crown of the Isle of Britain came to an end," for Cadwaladr fell victim to a terrible plague. He is depicted in one of the stained glass windows of the church wearing royal attire and holding his scepter and orb.

To find an inscribed stone bearing the name of King Arthur in its Latin or Welsh form was obviously our final aim. By this time, we knew that his final years were spent in Brittany, as we shall reveal in due course, but it seemed likely that such an important person would be remembered in his homeland by a Latin inscription on at least one surviving stone, perhaps in association with a contemporary personality.

There are, in fact, two stones in South Wales which commemorate the name of Arthmael, who is, of course, none other than King Arthur.

In the National Museum of Wales is exhibited a memorial stone which was discovered during restoration work at Ogmore Castle in West Glamorgan. It was being used as a doorstep and, when it was removed, an inscription was noticed on its bottom face. A replica of the stone stands on a plinth inside the castle ruins. The inscription reads:

(SCIENDVM) EST OMNIB(VS) QUOD DED ARTHMAIL DO
ET GLIGWS ET NERTART ET FILI EPI
Be it known to all that Arthmail has given this field to God and to Glywys and to Nertat and to Bishop Fili.

*Figure 40. The Arthmael Stone from Ogmore Castle can now be seen in the National Museum of Wales, at Cardiff, Glamorgan.*

This appears to be a record of a land grant made by Arthmael (King Arthur) to the church of Glywys, at Merthyr Mawr, which is situated a short distance away on the other side of the River Ogmore.

The particular usage of "Sciendum est quod" is rare elsewhere and it is extremely significant that it can also be found in the charters attached to the "Vita Cadoci" from Llancarfan, in which King Arthmael makes a grant of Cadoxton-juxta-Neath to St. Cadoc circa 530.

Arthmael, Glywys, Nertat and Fili were all contemporaries in the sixth century. St. Glywys Cernyw was the son of Gwynllyw Filwr ("the warrior"), king of Gwynllywg (Wentlooge). St. Nertat was the daughter of Brychan Brycheiniog ("of the Speckled Tartan"), king of Brycheiniog (Brecknock), and Bishop Fili was the son of St. Cenydd and grandson of St. Gildas.

Glywys, in association with Nertat, is also mentioned on a stone pillar-cross which used to stand in a field near the ruins of St. Roque's Chapel in the grounds of Merthyr Mawr House. When translated, the inscription on it reads:

Conbelan placed this cross for his (own) soul (and for) the
soul of Saint Glywys, of Nertat, and of his brother and
father prepared by me, Sciloc.

The cross was obviously carved by Sciloc.

About ten miles away, inside St. Illtyd's Church at Llantwit
Major, can be seen another stone which features the name of
Arthmael. It is known as the pillar of Abbot Samson and is a
quadrangular cross shaft bearing decorated panels of carving and
a Latin inscription:

> IN NOM / INE DI SV / MMI INCI /
> PIT CRV / X SALVATO / RIS QVA /
> E PREPA / RAVIT / SAMSO / NI APA /
> TI PRO / AMIMA / SVA & P / RO ANI /
> MA IV / THAHE / LO REX
> & ART/MALI / TECANI

The strokes indicate the end of each line and this fascinating inscription has been translated to mean:

> In the name of the MOST HIGH GOD
> was begun the cross of the Savior which
> Samson the Abbot prepared for his soul
> and for the soul of King Iuthahel,
> and for Artmal the dean.

Historians have dated this stone to the ninth century, basing
their assumption on the fact that there was a king of Gwent
named Ithael who, according to the *Annales Cambriae* and *Brut
Twysogion,* was killed in 848. The style of lettering indicates that
it was carved in the ninth century, but it must be emphasized that
it mentions Abbot Samson who was a contemporary relative of
Arthmael(Arthur). This suggests that its message relates to the
sixth-century. There was in fact a royal person by the name of
Judwal, who was a Breton ruler of the sixth century and he was
also related to Samson, the Abbot of Dol. An alternative version
of his name is Ithael.

*Figure 41. The Samson Pillar, in St. Illtyd's Church, Llantwit Major, Vale of Glamorgan.*

If the stone was carved in the ninth century, it seems that these three important persons, who were all contemporaries living nearly three hundred years previously, were still remembered with high regard. But most important of all, this stone can be regarded as a memorial to Arthmael, who is none other than King Arthur himself. In chapter 16 (see page 235), following further research, we re-examine the Pillar of Samson and reveal the true meaning behind its fascinating inscription.

# 10

# ENEMIES OF THE BRITONS

BRITAIN REMAINED PART of the Roman Empire until 410, when Rome fell into the hands of the Visigoths and it became obvious that the Roman legions, who had been withdrawn in 407, would never return to this island. The Emperor Honorius formally relinquished control of the province in a letter which informed the Britons in no uncertain terms that henceforth they would have to fend for themselves. This decision ended 400 years of Roman rule in Britain and put the island at the mercy of the Irish, Picts, Scots, Angles, Saxons, and Jutes.

At first, the Britons considered the Picts and the Scots to be their main enemies. They failed to anticipate that the most serious threat was to come from the more distant Anglo-Saxon invaders, who first came as pirates in search of loot, but gradually began to settle in corners of Britain and take possession of substantial areas of land.

These new invaders came from three different Germanic nations: the Jutes, the Saxons, and the Angles. Originally, the Jutes resided in Jutland, but they migrated south to the area around the mouth of the Rhine and from there made raids on Britain. The Saxons came from the lands north of the River Elbe, which is now called Holstein, and from that district between the Rivers Elbe and Elms which became Hanover. The Angles lived in the territory between Jutland and Holstein which today is known as Schleswig. They also inhabited the adjacent islands which are now the property of Denmark.

A Gaulish chronicle tells us that in 449, "the Britons were devastated by an incursion of the Saxons," and that thirty two years later, "the Britons up to this time torn by the various slaughters and disasters are brought under the dominion of the

Saxons." This last statement obviously refers to the southeastern part of Britain where the Saxons settled in large numbers after the "Treachery of the Long Knives" incident, when Vortigern had been forced at knife-point to cede territory to the Saxons in return for his freedom. The area corresponding to Essex, Middlesex, and Sussex was thus lost by the Britons to hordes of Teutonic invaders.

The Jutes settled in Kent, while the most important Saxon settlements were made in the south. Meanwhile, the Angles worked their way inland along river routes by following the Wash, the Trent, and the Yorkshire Ouse. They must have been forced to leave their countries of origin for some definite reason. Possibly, their numbers had increased so rapidly that many of them were compelled to seek new homes, but in addition they would have been feeling pressure from other tribes who were moving westward. There is a tradition that the Huns carried their terrible ravages as far as Germany and that the fear that they inspired led to this migration. Obviously, the fertile plains of Britain were a considerable attraction.

Gradually, the eastern part of Britain was permanently occupied by these people who introduced their own customs, different forms of government, and dialects of a new language, which eventually became the English language. From them, we inherited such Anglo-Saxon words as ton (an enclosure), as in Brighton and Stockton; field (a clearing), as in Sheffield; weald (a wood), as in the Weald; shaw (a road), as in Crawshaw; and ford (a ford), as in Ilford.

The superstitious Saxons allowed the Roman towns which they captured to fall into decay, for, rather than occupying the elegant and deserted buildings, they preferred to establish their own settlements behind earthen ramparts. Such a collection of dwellings was known as a "ton" and the central building of a Saxon chieftain's "ham" (home) was the "heal" (hall). The head of the community was the king and the title "Bretwalda" was claimed by the more powerful of the eight monarchs of the Saxon Heptarchy into which England was subsequently divided. This title seems to have been the reward for suppressing hostile forces rather than denoting an overlordship of the whole country. For example, Ethelfrith the Fierce became Bretwalda for defeating the Britons at Chester. Raedwald of East Anglia seized the title when he slew Ethelfrith and placed Edwin on the throne of Northumbria. These were unstable and tempestuous times, when the Saxon domains were constantly torn apart by warfare between the various kingdoms.

Wales, being a mountainous country, has traditionally been a place of retreat and any invaders, whether they were Roman, Saxon, or Norman, required considerable courage and the employment of special tactics to achieve any degree of penetration. Following the withdrawal of the Romans, this wild and rugged corner of Britain was the only part of the western Roman Empire which managed to retain its identity and fight off the menace of the Saxon invaders. They never succeeded in making progress beyond the border subsequently defined by Offa's Dyke.

It proved of considerable importance in our research to establish that the Saxons, who allied themselves with the Picts and the Scots, were not the only enemies of the Britons during this period when our island was the scene of a mighty struggle for domination. The other foes who had to be dealt with were a tribe known as the Gewissei, who can only be described as "the enemy within."[1]

---

[1]The Gewissei were Irish federates whose leaders claimed descent from Casnar Wledig and Carawn (Carausius). It is significant that, in "The Death Song of Uther Pendragon," by Taliesin (*The Book of Taliesin*, p. 71), the enemies of Uther are referred to as the "Sons of Casnar." It is probable that the Gewissei were a branch of the Gwyddel Ffichti (Goidelic Picts). This would seem a very plausible hypothesis when one considers that Gwrtheyrn (Vortigern) hired the Gwyddel Ffichti to dispose of the Romano-British Emperor Custennin Vychan (Constantine or Constans the Younger) in 446. It is also significant that Gwrtheyrn's great-grandfather was Gloui Gwalltir, whose epithet ("of the Long Hair") seems to indicate that he was a Goidel, not a Romano-Briton. His descendants were called the Gwyddel Ffichti and may have been named after Guitol, his grandson, to distinguish them from the Picts of the north. Guitol's son was none other than the infamous Gwrtheyrn (Vortigern). In the *Brut*, Gwrtheyrn is called Gwrtheneu, which Williams ap Ithel translates as "of the Repulsive Lips." Sir John Rhys explains the epithet by suggesting that Vortigern spoke a language which was unfamiliar to his subjects. He was in fact a Goidelic king ruling over the Brythons of Wales. See *Historia Brittonum*, HB 49 (ca. 830).

To understand fully the identity of the Gewissei, it is first necessary to give further consideration to the life of Vortigern. This powerful king of Irish descent was the son of Vitalis, the son of Vitalinus, the son of Gloiu Gwalltir, who hailed from Gloucester. Therefore, Vortigern's father, grandfather, and great-grandfather bore Romano-British names and the family belonged to the area around the mouth of the Severn.

The Gewissei (Confederates) were Irish federate troops employed by the Roman Empire to police the republic of the Silures and they were associated with the city of Gloiu, which is now called Gloucester. Gloiu was given the epithet Gwalltir ("of the Long Hair") and this probably stemmed from a hair plume which he wore in his helmet to signify his position as commander of the Gewissei.

The epithet of Gloiu Gwalltir ("of the Long Hair") seems to indicate that he was a Goidel, not a Romano-Briton. His descendants were called the Gwyddel Ffichti (Goidelic Picts), and may have been named after Guitol (Vitalis), his grandson, to distinguish them from the Picts of the north. In the *Brut*, his son Gwrtheyrn is called Gwrtheneu, which translates as "of the Repulsive Lips." It has been suggested by Sir John Rhys that this means that Vortigern spoke a language which was unfamiliar to his subjects. He was, in fact, a Goidelic king ruling over the Brythons of Wales. Confirmation can be found in the early Welsh genealogies that Gloui Gwalltir was of the same pedigree as Casanauth (Casnar Wledig) and Carawn (Carausius):

> Carawn (Carausius)
> Casanauth (Casnar) Wledig
> Gloui Gwalltir (Long Hair)
> Guoitolin (Vitalinus)
> Guoitaul (Vitalis)
> Gwrtheyrn Gwrtheneu (Vortigern "the Thin")

Let us now recall the story of Magnus Maximus who took over the rule of Britain by marrying Elen, the daughter of Octavius the Old (Eudaf Hen), prince of Arfon. Geoffrey of Monmouth gives Elen's father the title Dux Gewissei and significantly also attaches the same title to Vortigern, whom he clearly regarded as the subsequent ruler of the same territory.

On studying the ancient inscription displayed on the ninth-century Pillar of Eliseg at Valle Crucis in the Vale of Llangollen, we found confirmation of the association between Vortigern and Sevira, the daughter of Magnus and Elen. The statements made by Geoffrey of Monmouth and the Pillar of Eliseg may be reconciled by the fact that Vortigern derived his ostensible claim to the territory of the Gewissei through his wife, who was the heiress of Magnus Maximus.

It is possible that the pillar was originally a Roman column which Cyngen re-used as a memorial stone. It is also very similar to the Mercian crosses which can be seen in the Peak District. Cyngen was the last king of Powys of the old line and he died while on a pilgrimage to Rome in 854. His ancestor, Brochmail Ysgythrog, fell in the battle of Bangor-is-Coed in 613 when the Welsh army was defeated by the Angles under Aethelfrith. There is a memorial stone to Aethelfrith at Bewcastle, a little Cumberland village north of Hadrian's Wall. Here an ancient cross bears an inscription recording that it was erected by Hwaefred and Worthgaer in honor of Aethelfrith, son of Aethelric.

There is a long Latin inscription inscribed on the Pillar of Eliseg, but it has weathered so badly that it is now impossible to read. Fortunately, it was written down in 1696 by the antiquary, Edward Llwyd. There are 31 horizontal lines (only seven can be seen now), divided into paragraphs, each introduced by a cross. Translated into English this fascinating inscription reads as follows:

- Concenn son of Cadell, Cadell son of Brochmail, Brochmail son of Eliseg, Eliseg son of Guaillauc.

- And so Concenn, great-grandson of Eliseg, erected this stone for his great-grandfather Eliseg.

- This is that Eliseg, who joined together the inheritance of Powys . . . out of the power of the Angles with his sword of fire.

- Whosoever repeats this writing, let him give a blessing on the soul of Eliseg.

*Figure 42. The Pillar of Eliseg, near the ruins of Valle Crucis Abbey, Clwyd, was once part of a tall cross erected here, in the Vale of Llangollen, by Cyngen in honor of his great-grandfather Eliseg who regained the kingdom of Powys from the Saxons. The valley became known as the Valley of the Cross, "Valle Crucis," and the field where it stands used to be called Llwyn y Groes, "The Grove of the Cross." Long before the Cistercian Abbey was founded, the first church here was called Llan Egwestl after its founder Gwestl or Egwest who lived here at the end of the fifth century.*

- This is that Concenn who captured with his hand eleven hundred acres which used to belong to his kingdom of Powys.

[The next two paragraphs were illegible.]

Maximus . . . of Britain . . .

Concenn, Pascent . . . Maun, Annan.

- Britu, moreover (was) the son of Guorthigirn (Vortigern)
  Whom Germanus blessed and whom
  Sevira bore to him, daughter of Maximus the king, who
  killed the king of the Romans.

- Conmarch painted this writing at the request of King Concenn

- The blessing of the Lord upon Concenn and upon his entire household and upon all the region of Powys until the day of doom. Amen.

Eliseg was the tenth generation of this Powys dynasty and he lived in the middle of the eighth century. His grandson Cadell died in 808 and was succeeded by Concenn, or Cyngen, who erected this pillar cross in memory of his great-grandfather. This suggests that the cross was erected during the first half of the ninth century, for Concenn died about 854 during a pilgrimage to Rome, and he was the last of the line.

Vortigern and his son Britu are given special mention in the inscription, and also Pascent, who was Vortigern's third son. It is of interest that Nennius, writing in the early ninth century, records that the later kings of Buellt (now Builth Wells) and Gwrtheyrnion, subkingdoms of Powys, were descended from Pascent. It is possible that Pascent's memorial stone was found at Tywyn in the 18th century. It was inscribed with the name Pascentius, but this was quite a common Romano-Christian name and may not necessarily have applied to him. Unfortunately, the stone was subsequently lost or destroyed.

It is important to understand that the inscription on this pillar shows that Eliseg traced his ancestry to both Vortigern and Magnus Maximus. It is also significant that the writings of Nennius indicate that all the princes of Powys descended from Gwrtheyrn (Vortigern), who is mentioned on the pillar with his wife Severa, a daughter of Magnus Maximus (otherwise known as Macsen Wledig).

Our next step was to consider the background of Cerdic, the Ealdorman of the Gewissei, for he was the son of Elesa, the son of Esla, the son of Gewis, who was the eponym of the Gewissei. Cerdic had a British name which was a variation of Ceredig. Geoffrey of Monmouth relates how the Saxons arrived in the days of Careticus, who is none other than Cerdic of the Gewissei. His name, as Ceretic, also crept into Nennius's tale of Vortigern, in which he is an interpreter for Hengist.[2]

By now it had become evident to us that Cerdic was not a Saxon transmarine invader, but a man of insular stock. His pedigree both upward and downward contains British names. Not only is there a striking similarity between Elesa and the Eliseg of the ninth-century Pillar of Eliseg in the Vale of Llangollen, but the two names Elesa and Esla, the father and grandfather of Cerdic, compare with the Eliseg and Elise of the Powysian pedigree. Consequently, Elafius (Elasius), who welcomed St. Germanus, Bishop of Auxerre, on his second visit to Britain in 447, can hardly be anyone else but Elesa, the father of Cerdic. This would serve to explain the admittedly strong claim which Cerdic held as legitimate ruler and the subsequent anxiety of the kings of Wessex to trace their descent from him.

---

[2] The Harleian Pedigree No. 4181 (see MP3 in P. C. Bartram, *Early Welsh Genealogical Tracts*, Cardiff, Wales: University of Wales Press, 1966, p. 122) gives Edric, king of Glamorgan, as having married Henwen, the daughter of Kynmarch ap Meirchion, and Geoffrey of Monmouth gives Henwinus the title of Dux Cornubiae (*Historia Regum Britanniae*). As no Edric is mentioned in the Welsh genealogies as reigning over Morgannwg and Gwent at this time, then perhaps Cerdic of the Gewissei is intended here. If this is the case then Cerdic, by right of marriage, could lay claims to territories in Glamorgan and Gwent, and these same territories would have been sought after by his descendants. According to the Welsh Triads (Triad 26 W p. 48), it was prophesied that the Island of Britain would be worse for the womb-burden of Henwen. The subsequent hunting of Henwen (White Sow) by Arthur is the symbolic interpretation of the expulsion of the Gewissei. In the Annals of Cambria, King Alfred is called rex Giuoys, "king of the Gewissei."

Octavius the Old (Eudaf Hen) was a prince of Arfon who married the daughter of Carausius II and thus gained control of the territory of the Gewissei, which gave him the right to hold the title of Dux. The corresponding Welsh form of Gewissei is *Iwys* and this is preserved in Ewyas Harold and Ewyas Lacey in Herefordshire. Besides Gwent, Octavius's estate comprised that of the Hwiccas, a British and Christian people with whom the Anglo-Saxon settlers later intermingled. It was portioned out into the area equivalent to the shires of Hereford, Gloucester, Worcester, part of Warwick, and the district between the Wye and Severn, which included the Forest of Dean. Octavius's daughter Elen married Magnus Maximus whose sons Owain and Constantine, were clearly British Pendragons, from whom the rulers who governed the Hwiccas (the country between the Wye and the Severn) were descended.

The title Dux Gewissei, i.e. Prince of Gwent, Erging, and Ewyas, was also held by Vortigern, who derived his claim to rule this territory through his marriage to Sevira, the daughter of Magnus Maximus and Elen. This marriage was undoubtedly calculated to gain political advantage and to pacify the border, for when Elen died, Sevira, by rule of female succession, was heiress. She succeeded her mother and gained control of the territory belonging to the family. Vortigern had access to his wife's inheritance and thereby became one of the most powerful rulers in southern Britain.

After the expulsion of his father, Elesa, which coincided with the overthrow of Vortigern by Ambrosius in 465, Cerdic was regarded with suspicion and dispossessed of his inheritance. He sought refuge on the Continent and came to the mouth of the Loire, which was the territory of a Saxon chief named Odovacer. It became Cerdic's recruiting ground and, in 494, he returned to Britain to claim his inheritance, accompanied by a mongrel contingent of Saxon federates.

Cerdic, his son Creoda, and their followers, landed at a place which thereafter became known as Cerdicesora. It lies between Calshot and the River Beaulieu on the shore of Southampton Water. Here Cerdic carved out a principality for himself by asserting his rights and fighting all comers. At first his followers were small in number, for the future showed little promise and the Britons kept the Gewissei in this area firmly in check. However, Cerdic succeeded in subjugating the Teutonic settlers who passed through his neighborhood and his followers grew significantly in number.

It was Cerdic's heirs who eventually succeeded in reaching the Thames Valley where they imposed their authority on the unorganized peasants, who formed the major West Saxon body. In the course of political rearrangements, Cerdic was probably made overlord of the various Jutish and Saxon colonies under British domination. He sided with the Saxons in the long wars and started a lineage which was at once Celtic and Teutonic. His descendants finally emerged as the kings of Wessex.

Accordingly, it can be established that the Gewissei were now living in the territory of Venta Belgarum (Winchester) in the canton of the Belgae, which stretched from Portsmouth Harbor, including the Isle of Wight, across southern Hampshire and Wiltshire into Somerset. Under their leader Cerdic, they spread eastward as far as Cerdicesora on the Solent and Cerdicesleaga (Netley).

In 501, a band of Jutes from Kent, under their leaders Bieda and Maegla, landed at Portsmouth Harbor (which has been mistakenly identified as Llongborth). They pillaged Portus Adurni (Portchester) and Clausentum (Bitterne) and then formed an alliance with the Gewissei. By 508, the two factions had made themselves masters of the district between the mouth of the Itchen and Portsmouth Harbor. From here, they made a piratical raid up the Severn Estuary, but their advance was halted by the western Britons led by Geraint Llyngesog ("the Fleet-owner") and a battle was fought at a place remembered as Llongborth, which we shall investigate in the next chapter.

Nennius, in his *Historia Brittonum*, implies that the chief opponent of Arthur and the Britons was Octha, but he persists in confusing him with Hengist's son Oeric Oesc. The Venerable Bede, in his *Historia Ecclesiastica*, however, makes him the grandson of Hengist and this is confirmed by the Kentish king-list cited by the same author.

It was just prior to the emergence of Kent as a powerful kingdom in the southeast, in the now rapidly fading twilight of Roman Britain, that Arthur and Octha II emerge. While Arthur has achieved worldwide renown, Octha has barely escaped oblivion. At first, the enemies of the Britons were not the Saxons, but Picts and Scots, and together Arthur and Octha II took on the role of defenders of Britain against the northern tribes. Their victories were followed by a period of comparative calm and prosperity. Arthur was appointed Comes Britanniarum (Count of Britain), while Octha, passing into Kent, filled the post of Comes Litoris Saxonici (Count of the Saxon Shore) protecting the southeast coast from invaders. Arthur, with assistance from the kings of the Britons, guarded the west and the north, while Octha was commissioned to guard the Saxon shore in Kent.

Octha II was the son of the union of Vortigern and Alis Ronwen, the daughter of Hengist (Octha I) and he features in the *Mabinogion* story titled "The Dream of Rhonabwy," where his name is written in the earlier Welsh form of Osla. Under this name, he also appears in the *Mabinogion* tale of "Culhwch and Olwen," where his prowess in the hunt of the Twrch Trwyth or Porcus Troit, resulted in the loss of his marvelous knife. He was known as Osla Gyllellfawr ("of the Great or Long Knife"), which associates him with the Saxon short sword. This weapon featured in the massacre of the British nobles at Caer Caradoc which became known as "The Treachery of the Long Knives."

We shall discuss Osla Gyllellfawr (Octha II) again in due course, but we must at this point stress the importance of revealing the background to a long-sustained struggle for power between two rival dynasties. During Arthur's time, the majority of alliances were achieved by marriages, and most dynastic wars were fought over disputed territorial claims. It is only when one fully realizes this situation that one can fully comprehend the results of Arthur's expansionist policies.

As already stated, Gwrthefyr Fendigaid (Vortimer the Blessed) was the eldest son of Gwrtheyrn Gwrtheneu (Vortigern the Thin) by his wife Sevira, the daughter of Macsen Wledig (Maximus the Imperator). Gwrthefyr was the father of a saintly daughter Madryn, that is Matriona, the foundress of Trawsfynydd, Gwynedd, who married Ynyr I of Gwent and left her name at Garth Madryn (Matriona's Enclosure), now Talgarth, and also Garth Fadrun (Madryn's Cairn) in the Lleyn Peninsula. Gwrthefyr himself was long remembered at

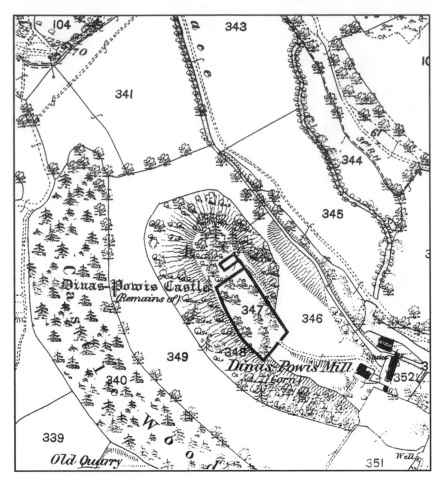

Figure 43. This extract from the 1881 Ordnance Survey Map shows Dinas Powys near Cardiff in South Glamorgan, which is the site of the largest Dark Age dwelling yet found in Wales. Excavation by Leslie Alcock, the eminent archaeologist, also revealed Mediterranean amphorae, fine tableware and bronze brooches with ornamental settings of enamel and glass indicating trade and cultural connections across the Irish Sea, the Atlantic sea routes, and via the coasts of Brittany and Iberia to the Mediterranean. Relics were discovered which demonstrate the possibility of a settlement of Teutonic and Irish federates in Glamorgan. They were most likely led by Osla Gyllellfawr ("of the Long Knife").

It is generally accepted that there was no Saxon settlement as far west of the Bristol Channel until after the battle of Dyrham and the capture of Gloucester, Cirencester, and Bath in 577, but it is certainly not impossible that Saxon settlers could have crossed the Severn as early as the fifth century. There may well have been a band of military adventurers set on carving out territory for themselves under a noble leader, who then established a dynasty. It is of interest that, in the 12th century, Iestyn ap Gwrgan, a direct descendant of King Arthur and the last prince of Glamorgan, also established a fortress on this site.

Gwrthefyrig (Vortimer's Town), the ancient name of Wonastow in Gwent. The Forest of Dean was sometimes known as Llwyn Danet and it is therefore possible that Nennius's story of Gwrthefyr's three blockades of the Isle of Thanet is based upon battles fought against the Gewissei about the lower reaches of the River Wye in Gwent and western Gloucestershire.

After his disastrous defeat, Gwrthefyr died from poison administered by his stepmother, Alis Ronwen. His bones formed one of "The three Precious Concealments in the Island of Britain," for, as long as they remained concealed in the chief ports of the island, no invasion would take place. They were, however, reputedly revealed by Gwrtheyrn (Vortigern) for the love of Alis Ronwen, the daughter of Octha I (Hengist). Alis Ronwen became the mother of Octha II who, after the death of his stepbrother, Gwrthefyr, in 457 and his father, Gwrtheyrn, in 465, could lay claim to their territories. This he did with the help of the Gewissei.

Octha II, the Osla Gyllelfawr of Welsh tradition, laid claim to the former territory of his stepbrother Gwrthefyr Fendigaid (Vortimer the Blessed), and Cerdic, Ealdorman of the Gewissei, laid claim to the territory of March ap Merchion through his marriage to March's daughter Henwen. It is of the utmost significance that March (Marcus Conomorus) bore a lifetime grudge against Arthur, who had expelled him from his territory in Gwent. Thus, it all becomes very clear why Octha, Cerdic, and Marcus Conomorus were the principal enemies of King Arthur.

### The Kings of Kent

| | |
|---|---|
| Ebissa (Horsa) | 455 |
| Octha I (Hengist) | 455–488 |
| Oeric Oesc | 488–512 |
| Octha II | 512–534 |
| Eomenric | 534–560 |
| Ethelbert I | 560–616 |
| Ealdbald | 616–640 |
| Earconberht | 640–664 |
| Egbert I | 664–673 |
| Hlothere | 673–685 |
| Eadric | 685–686 |

There is acceptable evidence that Arthur was a genuine historical figure, not a mere figment of myth or romance. He achieved fame as a great soldier, who fought battles in various parts of Britain in the late fifth and early sixth centuries.[3]

[3]Leslie Alcock, *Arthur's Britain* (London: Penguin, 1971), p. xv.

# 11

# THE BATTLE OF
# LLONGBORTH

UNDOUBTEDLY THE TWO most important rivers in Britain are the Thames and the Severn, for they have both played a major role in the shaping of this country's history. During our research, we quickly came to the conclusion that the Severn Estuary is of enormous significance in the story of King Arthur, for this coastline provides the key to the location of his domain and also some of the battles which took place during his time.

As we have already demonstrated, on the Gwent side of the Severn Estuary was the land of Cernyw, where the site of Gelliwig, Arthur's main court, can be found. His birthplace was at Boverton, near Llantwit Major in South Glamorgan, which was the location of the monastic school of St. Illtyd, where Gildas and many other sixth-century celebrities had their schooling. Previously, we have mentioned how Arthur's grandfather, King Tewdrig, was buried close to the Severn at Mathern, near Chepstow. Further important Arthurian connections and battle sites will be revealed in this area in due course.

The River Severn has the second highest tidal range in the world, with a difference in height between high and low water which sometimes exceeds 17 meters and is only surpassed by that of the Bay of Fundy. At a particularly high tide, the in-rush of the water from the sea stops the flow of the river water and forces it back upstream, forming a moving wave, or bore, which occurs on about one hundred and thirty-five days of the year. It is particularly impressive on twenty-five days and the best place to observe the spectacle is at Newnham, where the A48 runs alongside the Severn. Perhaps it is more than coincidence that the Severn phenomenon is called the bore, for in this area there is a folk memory of the boar hunt of Twrch Twryth, described in *The Mabinogion*.

It is important to remember that this estuary has altered considerably over the passing centuries and, since the Dark Ages, the river has become very silted. For every century which has passed since Arthurian times, the sea has risen approximately one quarter of a meter. This means that, in the fifth century, the high-water level would have been 4 meters lower than it is today.

Encroachment of land by the sea is evident from the reduced size of Sudbrook Camp, which originally would have been circular, but is now a semi-circle. At Goldcliff, the foundations of the old priory were eroded away by high tides until it collapsed and eventually disappeared completely. In 1758, a witness at a trial held in Monmouth swore that, when he was a young man, he used to mow the grass on Charston Rock, which was then a meadow united to the mainland, but is now just a tiny islet several hundred yards from the coast.

In ancient times, there were several natural harbors along the Gwent side of the estuary and they were located at inlets which are now referred to as "pills." Today these seem no more than mere indentations in the coastline, but at one time they provided safe anchorages. The word pill is Celtic for creek or harbor.

There has been traffic across the Severn since Roman times and these little harbors were once of great importance, for they had considerable influence on the development of this southern part of Gwent. For example, three large houses—Moynes Court, St. Pierre, and the Bishop's Palace at Mathern—stand in close proximity to one another and are sited for easy access to the harbor at St. Pierre Pill. The stream to this pill, and also to the one at Sudbrook further along the coast, were once substantial rivers, but they are now heavily silted and much diminished.

According to the *Welsh Triads*, the three great ports of the Isle of Britain in ancient times were Porth-is-Coed (on the Severn Estuary in Gwent), Porth Wygar (at Cemaes near Llanbadrig, Anglesey) and Porth Wyddno (Borth in old Cardiganshire).[1]

---

[1]Porth Wyddno is named after Gwyddno Garanhir ("long-Shanks"), who was a chieftain mentioned in the *Mabinogion*. See Sir John Rhys, *Studies in the Arthurian Legend* (Oxford: Clarendon Press, 1891), p. 263.

*Figure 44. St. Pierre Pill, near Mathern, although heavily silted, is used today as an anchorage for pleasure craft, but in the Dark Ages it would have been one of several important harbors along this coastline between Newport and Chepstow.*

The exact location of the Gwent port of Porth-is-Coed is difficult to ascertain, for there are several sites where it may be have been located. In old manuscripts, the name is written as Porth Yshewydd or Porth Kiwedd and Porth Yskiwed, which probably translates as the "Harbor of the Elder Wood." In later times, it was written as Porthscueth and subsequently this became Portscuett and Portscuit, from which the present day village of Portskewett takes its name, but this is not necessarily the site of the ancient harbor of Porth-is-Coed.

In the *Welsh Triads*, we found that this ancient harbor is also referred to as Abertwggi and, as the Troggy Brook enters the River Nedern at Llanfair Discoed Village (The Church of St. Mary below the Wood), there is an obvious connection between the two names. The Troggy Brook rises on the edge of Wentwood, passes Maesgwyneth (mentioned in the *Mabinogion*), rounds Caerwent, and, before reaching Caldicot, changes its name to Nedern. At Deepweir in Caldicot, the brook divides, with the main stream entering the Severn at Sudbrook Pill. In fairly recent years, a new cut was made to improve the drainage. As a result, the Nedern was turned directly into Caldicot Pill and Sudbrook Pill became silted up. The Latin name of the harbor was Portus Tarogi and, in the Domesday Survey, this became Porteschuiet, which by medieval times was altered to Porth-is-Coed. The strong tides of the Severn and centuries of coastal erosion have obscured the site and it no longer resembles a port or harbor.

Sudbrook Pill is to the west of the village of Portskewett and it was obviously once a harbor of considerable importance. This is confirmed by the fact that a Silurian fort, later used by the Romans, was established here for defensive purposes. Adjoining it is a ruined Norman chapel, which stands on the site of an earlier church which was known as the Church of the Castle of Conscuit. This is not a reference to nearby Caldicot Castle, but relates to another name associated with the fort. This was Castell Twyn Iscoed—"Fortress Mound below the Wood"—which suggests that the part of the camp eroded away by the sea once contained a fortified mound.

On consulting the *Book of Llandaff*, we found that a relevant grant was made by the kings of Gwent to the Bishops of Llandaff at the beginning of the tenth century. It recorded the gift of the Church of Castle Conscuit and lands with free approach for ships at the mouth of the Taroci (Troggy or Nedern Brook) and all its weirs and fisheries. One of the boundaries mentioned was the junction of the Taroci with the Severn Sea.

Our examination of these ancient harbor sites was undertaken in order to establish the location of the sixth-century Battle of Llongborth. When we eventually pieced together the evidence which led to the solution of this particular problem, it seemed astonishing to us that no other Arthurian sleuth had realized that the Battle was fought in this part of Britain.

However, we soon came to realize that three battles have been confused and this has resulted in the popular misconception that Llongborth was either Portsmouth[2] in Hampshire (where Bieda and Maegla landed in 501 (see page 168) or Langport in Somerset. The latter used to be an important river crossing and, at one time, navigation from the sea would have been possible. It would appear that a certain Prince Geraint of Devon was killed while fighting the Saxons here at some time in the eighth century. But we were investigating a battle which occurred in the early years of the sixth century, when a Geraint of Arthur's time lost his life. It would seem that these two incidents have been confused, with the result that Langport has been wrongly identified as the location of the battle of Llongborth.

We first examined the name itself and found that in the old British language, the words Llongu Borth meant a "Port of Boats" or "Haven of Ships." According to the well-known Arthurian scholar Geoffrey Ashe, in *A Guidebook to Arthurian Britain*, it means "Warship Port." The word "Llong" when translated from Welsh suggests ships of all types, but this word originally comes from the Latin Longa Navis—"A Port of Warships"—in other words, a naval base.

From the *Welsh Triads,* we learned that Geraint was a naval commander who possessed not only an army, but also a fleet of ships. He was known as Geraint Llyngesog (Gerontius "the Fleet-owner") and he kept a fleet of six score ships moored in a harbor in the Severn Estuary, with six score men on board each one.[3] Their purpose was to patrol the coast against the Saxon

---

[2]*The Anglo-Saxon Chronicle* tells us that, in 501, an indecisive battle was fought against the invading Saxons under the leadership of Port and his two sons Bieda and Maegla. They came with two ships to a place called Portsa (Portchester?) where they seized land and "slew a young Briton, a very noble man." It has been suggested that this noble man was Geraint. See *The Anglo-Saxon Chronicle*, G. N. Garmondsway, trans. (London: J. M. Dent & Sons, 1972), p. 15.

[3]Geraint ap Erbin is described in Triad 25 Series II (*Y Cymmrodor*, vol. III, p. 127), as one of the "Three Fleet Owners of the Island of Britain"; the other two being March ap Meirchion (Marcus son of Marcianus) and Gwenwynyn ap Naw. Geraint and March were both rulers in southwestern Britain and, as fleet owners, they maintained contact by sea with Brittany. Traditions of Geraint and March were certainly known in Brittany as early as the ninth century and both were rulers in Domnonia, which may be assumed to have maintained

pirates, who in conjunction with the Irish, infested the coast of the Severn Sea. Some readers may find this idea somewhat hard to accept, for many of us tend to have preconceived ideas of the ancient Britons having limited resources and construction abilities. However, it is important to remember that many of the Roman methods of defense were continued by the British, and the presence of Geraint's fleet would have had a precedent, for there are indications that the Romans, just like Geraint in Arthur's time, kept a fleet moored in the Severn Estuary. An interesting piece of evidence which supports this idea has been uncovered at Lydney Park. On a hilltop overlooking the Severn a few miles beyond Chepstow are the remains of a Roman temple dedicated to the god Nodens. Excavations here have revealed a fourth-century mosaic bearing the inscription PR.REL, which quite conceivably stands for Praefectus Reliquationis Classis. He was the supply officer for the western fleet, which was probably moored in the Bristol Channel for defensive purposes.

Geraint Llyngesog was the son of Erbin[4] and he was a West Country prince who lived at the end of the fifth century. He was a grandson of Constantine the Blessed and according to the

---

some kind of connection with the Breton kingdom of the same name during the early period. The *Iolo Manuscripts* mention Geraint as Lord of Gereinwg (Geraint's Land), by which Erging is meant, and the same documents further state that Geraint was a patron of a church at Caerffawydd or Henffordd (Hereford), but it seems more likely that Gerascen, king of Erging, is intended here.

[4]As the son of Custennin Fendigaid, Erbin became king of Domnonia. His brother was St. Digain, who founded Llangernyw (the Church of the Cornishman) in Clwyd. Two of Erbin's sons were Dywel and Erinid, who are mentioned as warriors at the court of King Arthur. But his most important son was Geraint Llyngesog ("the Fleet Owner"), who became king of Domnonia after him. In his old age, Erbin sent messengers to King Arthur asking him to allow Geraint to return to Cornwall to take over the sovereignty. Erbin formerly had one church dedicated to him in Wales, that of Erbistock (Erbin's Stockade), a parish in Clwyd. In Cornwall he is probably the founder of St. Ervan and Marazion. According to the early Welsh traditions, utilized by the authors of the *Mabinogion* and the *Bonedd y Saint* [Pedigrees of the Saints], ambassadors from Cornwall representing Erbin, the son of Custennin, appeared at Arthur's court at Caerleon-upon-Usk. In the *Bonedd y Saint* No. 30, Geraint is given as the son of Erbin, son of Custennin Gorneu (the Cornishman). He is described in the Welsh and Breton *Lives of the Saints* and the *Exeter Martyrology*, not as a saint, but as a monarch at whose court saints were welcome.

*Peniarth Manuscript* (No. 27, Pt. II), he married Gwyar, the daughter of the Romano-British Prince Amlawdd Wledig. Their children were named Selyf, Cyngar, Iestyn, Caw, and Cadwy. Geraint's second wife was Enid, the daughter of Ynywl, Lord of Caerleon, whom Geraint delivered from great distress when he was deprived of his lands and position by a usurping kinsman. Geraint took Enid home to Cornwall, where his father, Erbin, exhausted by old age, resigned the kingdom of Domnonia to him.

In addition, Geraint also held territory in Armorica. He had a palace in Belle Ille and portions of newly acquired land in the Blavet, in Morbihan, and near Martignon, in Côtes-du-Nord. Dedications to him include St. Gerran, Pontivy, which was the center of his plou, and another St. Geran in the deanery of Porhoet, while the bishopric of Vannes has him as patron. There was a chapel of St. Geran in Dol Cathedral and between Loudeac and Pontivy is a parish of St. Gerand.

Geraint was chosen as Pendragon to head the confederacy of British kingdoms upon the death of his uncle Ambrosius and he carried on the struggle against the Saxons. In consequence of this appointment, we find traces of his name in Wales, Herefordshire, Somerset, and Cornwall. He had the honor of being canonized and four of his sons, Selyf, Cyngen, Iestin, and Cadwy, are also included in the list of saints.

The death of Geraint Llyngesog at the Battle of Llongborth is described in an elegy which is reputed to have been written by Llywarch Hen ("the Aged").

> In Llongborth I saw a rage of slaughter,
> and biers beyond all count,
> and red-stained men from the assault of Geraint.

> In Llongborth I saw the edges of blades meet
> Men in terror, with blood on the pate,
> Before Geraint, the great son of his father.

> In Llongborth Geraint was slain,
> A brave man from the region of Dyfnaint,
> And before they were overpowered, they
> commited slaughter.

*Figure 45. Saxon ships, from an engraving in Strutt's* Chronicle of England.

The invaders' ships entered the warship port of Llongborth and probably succeeded in landing. They then had to face the Britons of Domnonia and the soldiers of Arthur led by Geraint. A land battle ensued and Geraint was slain during the conflict.

Having located the approximate site of the Battle of Llongborth, our next task was to seek the burial site of Geraint, which we decided could well be in the vicinity of the Severn Estuary. Such an important royal commander would have been given a hero's burial and he would have long been remembered as a martyr who died defending his countrymen. The discovery of his burial site would help to confirm the general location of the Battle of Llongborth and thus provide yet another piece in the jigsaw puzzle.

We turned once more to the *Book of Llandaff* and found a very significant clue. In one of the ancient charters, mention is made of an ecclesiastical site called Merthyr Gerein. This name appears on old maps, but the present-day Ordnance Survey map shows it as Chapel Tump, near Magor. Here on a low mound once stood a little chapel overlooking the ancient port of Abergwaitha, which became deserted after the Black Death. Originally a simple building known as Merthyr Gerein was erected on this site and it seems highly probable that it was a martyrium raised to the honor of Geraint, who fell at the Battle of Llongborth.

## CONFUSION OVER SEVERAL GERAINTS

In the Dark Ages, Geraint was a very popular name and this simple fact has caused considerable confusion and led to the Battle of Llongborth being wrongly placed and misdated. Many Arthurian writers have tended to follow the same old standard theories and failed to study the genealogies properly. It would seem that Geraint Llyngesog, who died at Llongborth, has been confused with his grandson, who bore the same name.[5]

On examining the Life of St. Teilo, contained in the *Book of Llandaff,* we found that mention is made of a certain Gerennius, King of Cornwall. We are told that, when St. Teilo fled from the Yellow Plague to Armorica in 547, he passed through Cornwall and paid a visit to King Gerennius. The king was getting on in years, and Teilo promised him that when his death was near he would be sure to visit him. On his return from Armorica in about 555, Teilo brought a stone sarcophagus as a present for the elderly king. Landing at Dingerrin, the round fort in the parish of St. Gerrans, Teilo set off to visit the king. He found him alive, but very ill. Shortly after receiving the communion, Gerennius passed away and was laid in the sarcophagus provided by Teilo.

There is a local tradition that his body was rowed in a golden boat with silver oars across Gerran's Bay to his reputed burial place, a barrow called Carn Beacon. There, it is said, he was laid to rest, in full regalia, with his sword clasped in his hand and the golden boat beside him, so that it would be available for him to use on the day he rose again to reclaim his kingdom. The tumulus was opened in 1858 by treasure hunters who hoped to find the golden vessel, but all they found was a kistfaen

---

[5]Another Geraint was the son of Carannog, of the family of Cadell Deyrnllwg, who was prince of Erging or Archenfield, in Herefordshire. The *Welsh Pedigrees* make him the father of St. Eldad or Aldate, Bishop of Gloucester, who was slain by the Saxons following the Battle of Dyrham in 577. The *Life of St. Meven* states that St. Eldad was a son of Gerascennus King of Orcheus, a district in Gwent. It appears that Orcheus is a misprint for Erchens, meaning Erging, and that Gerascen is an affected form of Geraint (the son of Carannog).

*Figure 46. The remnants of the Cross of Irbic can be seen in Llandough Churchyard, near Cardiff in South Glamorgan. Llandough-juxta-Cardiff has been variously called Bangor Cyngar and Bangor Dochau. Its founder was Cyngar, who was also called Docwin and Dochau. His father was Geraint, who fell at Llongborth, and his brothers were Iestyn, Selyf, Caw, and Cadwy. Their grandfather was Erbin and it is probably to his memory that this splendid cross of Irbic was erected.*

*Cyngar also founded a monastery at Congresbury in Somerset and, in later life, he went to North Wales to join his nephew Cybi. Foundations there are attributed to him under his name Cyngar.*

containing bones. A later Geraint appears in Aneurin's epic poem "Y Gododdin," which tells the story of the Battle of Catraeth, fought in the Scottish Lowlands between 586 and 603. This Geraint was a Strathclyde chieftain. The name appears yet again in the West Country when, in 705, St. Aldhelm wrote a letter to King Geraint, urging him to abandon certain Celtic religious customs in his realm and to conform to the ways of Rome. This Geraint fought against Ina, King of the West Saxons, at Taunton in 710.

Llwyarch Hen's elegy (on page 179) represents Geraint, the martyr of Llongborth, and Arthur as contemporaries, while the episode relating to "Geraint ap Erbin," contained in the *Mabinogion*, tells us that Arthur was a cousin of Geraint and the nephew of Erbin. During the wars, the Domnonian forces obviously accepted Arthur as emperor and superior ruler over their own leader Geraint. Following the death of Geraint at Llongborth, it seems that Arthur continued to be accepted as a joint ruler with Cadwy, the son of Geraint.

# 12

# The King Goes to War

I N HIS *HISTORIA BRITTONUM*, Nennius tells us that Arthur fought no less than twelve important battles. The location of these sites has always been one of the great challenges facing Arthurian scholars. Countless historians have tried to place them on the map and an incredible assortment of guesses have been made, with little more reasoning behind them than the similarity of place names. Henry of Huntingdon, writing in the 12th century, could not identify the battle sites even in his day, but perhaps he was expecting to find them all in England.

Nennius makes a brief statement on the matter which is lacking in detail to say the least:

> The first battle was at the mouth of the river called Glein; the second, third, fourth and fifth on another river, which is called Dubglas in the region of Linnuis, the sixth battle on the river called Bassas. The seventh battle was in the forest of Celidon, that is the battle of Coed Celidon. The eighth battle was at Castellum Guinnion, where Arthur carried the portrait of Saint Mary, ever Virgin, on his shoulders; and the pagans were routed that day, and there was a great slaughter of them through the power of our Lord Jesus Christ and the strength of the Holy Virgin Mary, His mother. The ninth battle was fought in Urbs Legionis. The tenth battle was fought on the shore of the river called Tribruit. The eleventh battle was fought on the mountain called Agned. The twelfth battle was on Mons Badonis, where in one day nine hundred and sixty men were killed by one attack of Arthur,

and no one save himself laid them low, and he appeared as victor in all the battles.[1]

This campaign list has provided a fascinating topic for speculation, investigation, and debate among Arthurian scholars for many centuries. Today, the ancient British names are very difficult to identify from the map and, over the years, many unlikely sites have been suggested. Professor Kenneth Jackson even went so far as to comment, "Only two can be regarded as fairly certainly identifiable . . . The rest are all conjectural and unknown."

For most people, it is difficult to accept that twelve battles could have been fought by one man, for they clearly refer to struggles covering a length of time which appears to be much longer than the life span of any one individual. The question has been posed time and time again: if there really was a historical King Arthur, and assuming that all the battles said to be fought by him actually took place, should in fact *all* of them be attributed to him? Some cynics also suspect the number of battles credited to Arthur, for a round dozen seems too neat to be true. However, this may, of course, just be a coincidence, for it is a fact that in later times there were twelve battles involved in the Wars of the Roses.

### Battle I: At the Mouth of the River Called Glein.

There is a River Glen in Northumberland and also one in Lincolnshire. The latter River Glen flows through the area between Grantham and Stamford, near the B1176. It is quite probable that this battle was fought at a ford and Nennius tells us that it happened at the mouth of a river. This suggests that the location was at the point where the Glen converges with the River Welland, about 4 miles north of Spalding.

---

[1]*Nennius' British History and the Welsh Annals*, John Morris, ed. and trans. (London: Phillimore, 1980), p. 35.

*Figure 47. King Arthur's twelve battles.*

**Battles 2, 3, 4, and 5: Supereliud flumen quod dictur Dubglas et est regionis Linnuis.**

This statement indicates a River Douglas in the area of Linnius. The most likely interpretation is that Linnius is in the Lindsey district of Lincolnshire, which at that time was an Angle kingdom.

We can safely assume that Arthur's enemies at these battles were the Angles of Lindsey and that he probably based his forces at Lincoln, which at that time was the abandoned Roman fort of Lindum Colonia. It had four gates, four main streets, and a public bath. The Romans linked it to the sea via rivers and canals— the longest canal being Car Dykes, which was nearly 48 kilometers long and built during the reign of Nero.[2]

Arthur's cavalry would have ridden to Lincoln along the great Roman highways which led from the south via the city of Uriconium (Wroxeter) in Shropshire. The purpose of his expedition would have been to deal with the Anglo-Saxon settlers who had arrived in their boats along the Wash and the Humber and advanced inland. Arthur probably fought them initially on the banks of the Lincolnshire Glen, which flows toward the Wash. He then fought a further battle beside the River Douglas (also in Lincolnshire, just a few miles from an area called Lennox, which is probably Nennius' Linnuis), before finally defeating the enemy after two long gruesome battles fought in Lindsey, which is in the northern part of Lincolnshire, close to the Humber.

According to *The Chronicle of the Kings of Britain* (page 140), Arthur's principal ally in his campaign against the Angles of Lindsey was Riwal Mawr. Their combined forces rode to Lincoln along the Roman road which later became known as the Ermine Way. It is possible that this name is derived from the name Erme or Ermin, which are both variants of Armel or Ermel. In

---

[2]Geoffrey of Monmouth tells us that, after the Saxons had helped Vortigern defeat the Picts "beyond Humber," Vortigern "gave their general Hengist, large possessions of land in Lindesia" (see p. 157). This is probably the same location as Lindsey, where a battle was fought by Arthur.

other words the road was named after Arthur himself in memory of this sixth-century expedition.[3]

The *Welsh Triads* tell us that Riwal Mawr, the son of Emyr Llydaw (the Armorican), was one of "The Three Royal Knights of the Court of King Arthur." It would seem that the combined forces of Arthur, Riwal, and Cadwy set out from Caerleon-upon-Usk to follow the Ermine Way via the military base at Cirencester and then on to Lincoln, where in four battles they conquered the small Angle Kingdom of Lindsey.

Arthur's task force of fast-moving cavalry was modeled on the earlier mounted cohorts of the Romans and their mobility was certainly impressive. In those times, it was quite normal for such a war band to be called upon by the ruler of a petty kingdom to give assistance when threatened.[4]

It is important to realize that, during the sixth century, it would have been far easier to travel long distances in Britain than it would have been, for example, in Norman times, for the intricate network of Roman highways was still intact and in relatively good condition. These well-engineered routes were the equivalent of today's motorways and they enabled considerable distances to be covered easily and relatively quickly, particularly by men on horseback. The roads could, of course, be utilized by the Saxons as routes of penetration, but they also enabled Arthur and his war bands to travel quickly and directly to places where they were urgently needed.

---

[3]It is interesting to note that Riwal Mawr held the title of Dux Britanniarum and that he was subordinate to Arthur. This is an indication that Arthur held the higher office of Comes Britanniae. The last person to have held the title before Arthur was Magnus Maximus, as he was the successor of Count Theodosius the Elder. Arthur went one step further, however, and achieved the supreme title of Amherawdyr, meaning Emperor. The Roman name of Riwal Mawr was Pompeius Regalis.

[4]It is likely that the medieval romances of Arthur's knights of the Round Table represent a genuine folk memory of a mounted war-band led by Arthur. The Romans had certainly made use of cavalry and two units served in Britain during the fourth century. It would appear that Arthur established a similar mobile force a century later. The best description we have of a sixth-century war-band riding to battle is contained in Aneurin's epic poem "Gododdin."

A marching army would have only covered ten Roman miles in a day. If it was a forced march, then the distance might be doubled, but a cavalry unit or war-band would have ridden 40 to 50 miles in a day. By comparison, in the sixth century, it would have been easier to travel, for example, from London to York along the Roman highways than it would have been to cover the same distance 1200 years later, in the 18th century, when Britain's roads were in a deplorable state. When one takes this into consideration, it makes it easier to discard any preconceived notions that it would not have been feasible for Arthur to have fought so many battles spread over such a wide area of Britain.

It is easy to picture Arthur's war bands riding out along the Roman roads to battle and it is significant that, in later times, they were used for exactly the same purpose. King Harold, in 1066, rode south toward his fateful battle at Hastings along Roman roads from London to Rochester and Maidstone to the coast. In 1485, Henry Tudor and King Richard III fought the Battle of Bosworth beside a Roman road leading out of Leicester.

The Roman occupation of Britain lasted for nearly four hundred years and, during that time, the legions constructed more than 6,000 miles of major highways, as well as many miles of minor roads and trackways. Initially, their purpose was to assist the Romans in the conquest of Britain and these military routes are the Romans' most enduring monument to their invasion and occupation of this country.

When the British chieftains and nobles went to war, they would have been as magnificently dressed as the Romans had been years before. Arthur himself probably dressed in Roman-style armor but carried a long-bladed sword known as a spatha instead of the shorter type of sword used by the Romans.

Cavalrymen wore protective helmets consisting of iron-framed leather caps with neck and cheek guards. Their shields would have been round and made of iron or iron-covered wood. Gold ornaments such as arm bracelets and brooches to fasten their cloaks would have been worn with pride. Posidonius, in the second century, described Celtic warriors in Europe as wearing "ornaments of gold, torcs on their necks and bracelets on their arms and wrists, while people of high rank wear dyed garments be-sprinkled with gold."[5] In Arthur's day similar customs no doubt prevailed but only noblemen would have been entitled to wear the gold torque, which was believed to have magical properties which would protect the warrior from danger.

### Battle 6: On the river called Bassas.

This location presented a very difficult problem, although we felt that it was also in Lincolnshire, for "bass" is a very common prefix in this part of Britain. For example, there is Bassingthorpe on Ermine Street and Bassingham to the northwest of Leadenham.

However, our research revealed that, in 510, Glast, a great-grandson of Cunedda Wledig, was defending an important strategic intersection of two Roman roads. At Luitcoyt, which is near Lichfield, Watling Street, the road leading from London to Chester, was crossed by the Icknield Way. Luitcoyt was the Roman fort of Letocetum, which is situated about two miles west of the present city of Lichfield. The fort was being besieged by an army of Middle Angles and Arthur came to Glast's assistance and routed the enemy in a battle which took place on the banks of the River Bassas, now known as Hammerwich Water. This runs southwest of Lichfield and has left traces of its former name in the three Staffordshire Basfords.

The present-day village of Wall-by-Lichfield takes its name from the remains of a Roman fortress, once known as Letocetum. This name is derived from Caer Llwyd Coed, which is Celtic for "the camp in the Grey Wood." Nearby was a very important Celtic religious site where a Druidic sacred grove was set in dense woodland. It contained a great pagan temple to Minerva, the Romanized form of the Celtic goddess Brigit, whose name can be found in other parts of Britain. This was a pagan temple of the Cornovii tribe and their name means "worshippers of the horned one." A number of carved stones with human horned heads have been found built into the walls of the Roman settlement just below the Church of St. John. It seems that the

---

[5]Posidonius' History of the Period 146–88 B.C. (in 52 volumes).

*Figure 48. Letocetum, at Wall-by-Lichfield, was a Roman post-ing station and a small town situated on Watling Street, covering an area of about 12 hectares. Today, the remains consist of a bath house with various rooms, a furnace, and a hypocaust. The intinerary of Antoninus informs us that Letocetum is the next station after Manduessedum, which is Mancetter near Ather-stone, and this, in Nennius' catalogue of Britain's 28 cities, is Caer Mancegued.*

Romans destroyed the ancient shrine, but re-used the stones, which they turned upside down as a small gesture to the Celtic gods.

It is significant that Julius Caesar recorded that "the Gauls all assert their descent from Dis Pater and say that this is the Druidic belief." Cernunnos, "the horned one," fits the description of the father-god who was the ultimate ancestor of the Celtic tribes. Julius Caesar also recorded that the Gallic Druids came to Britain for religious instruction, so it is evident that the principal seat of the cult of Dis Pater was in Britain. The capture of this shrine by a continental tribe (i.e the Saxons) would have been an event of considerable concern to the Britons, for it is clear from Caesar's account that the Druidic Dis Pater was the transcendental god of the Hyperboreans who took precedence over all other gods.

It is also stated by Julius Caesar that the Druids held their great festival "at a consecrated place in the territory of the Carnutes, whose country is supposed to be in the middle of Gaul." As the institution is said to have originally come from Britain, there must have been a corresponding holy place in the center of this island. In Christian times, the omphalos (navel) of England is believed to have been in Lichfield. The village of Wall is situated on Watling Street, which was constructed by the Romans along an ancient Celtic route which was marked by holy places, thus indicating a highway of Druidic influence. It runs through the Trent-Severn passage to the Vale of Clwyd and then on across the Menai Straits to the Island of Anglesey, which became the last stronghold of the Druids.

The name Lichfield is derived from "death's field," lych meaning death. It is likely that this is a reference to the legend that the Christians were slaughtered here by the Romans on an order of the Emperor Diocletian.[6] It was undoubtedly an area of considerable importance to the Britons and one which must be defended at all costs.

Another battle was fought here in 665 when a local prince called Morfael of Luitcoyt joined the Welsh Prince Cynddylan of Powys and won a victory over the invading Angles of Mercia at Caer Luitcoet, which is Wall-by-Lichfield.

### Battle 7: Cat Coit Celidon.

This battle is one which can be more readily identified, for it is fairly certain that the name refers to Coed Celyddon (the

---

[6]Tradition states that there was a massacre of holy men at Llywyd Coed during the reign of the Roman Emperor Diocletian. It is more than coincidence that there is a St. Helena at Polesworth, east of Glascote, and a Thorpe Constantine to the north. These dedications must have been made when the new wave of Christianity sponsored by Constantine the Great swept these areas in the wake of the Diocletian persecutions.

Forest of Celyddon), near Hart Fell in the western lowlands of Scotland. It was once an extensive forest covering the area of Dumfries and Selkirk. The *Welsh Triads* contain a statement to the effect that Myrddin ap Morvryn became insane as a result of the Battle of Arferydd (Arthuret) in 573 and subsequently lived a wild life in the Forest of Celyddon.

This appears to be the Caledonian Forest, which once covered most of Strathclyde to the north of the Solway Firth. It was known to the Welsh as Coed Celyddon and Arthur's enemies here would have been the Picts, or the Irish, or both. It is possible that Arthur's main purpose in fighting this battle was to deal with a British nobleman who was in league with the Picts. He was Hueil, the son of Caw, and Arthur subsequently beheaded him in Ruthin, Clwyd, where a block of stone in the center of the town is still known as Maen Huail.

## Battle 8: Castellum Guinnion.

This location was obviously a fort. It has been suggested that the name is a reference to Caerwent, but this does not really seem very likely. For once, Nennius gives a more detailed description of this battle, telling us that "Arthur carried the image of the Holy Mary, the everlasting Virgin, on his shoulder [meaning shield] and the pagans were put to flight that day and there was a great slaughter upon them, through the power of our Lord Jesus and the power of the Holy Mary, His mother."

Folk memories of events which occurred long ago have very often been found to be based on an element of truth. Our research led us to the Church of St. Mary at Stow-in-Wedale, southwest of Lauder in the Borderlands. Here the fragments of an ancient shield are preserved and, according to a local legend, it is the very one carried by Arthur in the battle of Castellum Guinnion. Significantly, the name Wedale, means "the dale of Woe" and it was given to this valley by the Saxons, with the obvious implication that they experienced a great disaster here. Surely it is more than coincidence that the church is dedicated to St. Mary and not far away is the site of a Roman Castellum which may well have been the fort of Guinnion mentioned by Nennius as the scene of Arthur's eighth battle.

## Battle 9: Fought in the Urbs Legionis.

Nennius refers here to the City of the Legions, which could be either Chester or Caerleon-upon-Usk. However, important clues contained in the *Mabinogion* indicate that it is much more likely to have been at Caerleon. It would appear that Arthur won a battle in the vicinity of this legionary fort and chased his enemies, who were led by Osla Gyllelfawr ("of the Long Knife"), eastward in the direction of the Severn Estuary.

The actual site of the Battle of Urbs Legionis is difficult to determine. It may have been at the old Roman fort, as the name suggests, but it is also possible that it may have taken place on a ridge above Caerleon. Bearing in mind that Osla was being pursued by Arthur toward the Severn Estuary, it is reasonable to suppose that he followed the Via Julia, which left Caerleon by the South Gate, crossed the Usk on a trestle bridge, passed through Ultra Pontem and ascended to cross the Wentwood ridge at a pass known today as Cat's Ash. This is a significant name, for the word Cat is generally derived from cad meaning battle, so it is quite feasible that Cat's Ash, which in itself is a meaningless name, originated from Cad Aesc and represented the Battle of Aesc or Oesc, who was the son of Hengist. No doubt he was killed in this battle and his corrupted name is a folk memory of that event. Remnants of an ancient chapel at Cat's Ash can be seen and the fact that it is dedicated to St. Curig, who was known to the bards as both Curig Llwyd ("the Blessed") and Curig Farchog ("the Knight"), may be of some significance. The truth of the matter will most certainly never be known, but this scenario is a plausible and interesting conjecture.

## Battle 10: On the shore of the river called Tribruit.

Various unlikely suggestions, including the Scottish Lowlands, have been made for the site of Arthur's tenth battle. However, if one bears in mind that it occurred after a battle fought at the City of the Legions, it would seem logical to suppose that the enemy force was chased by Arthur to the Gwent shore of the Severn Estuary which is a close and significant location.

We found a useful clue in Tennyson's *Idylls of the King*. In the poem concerning Lancelot and Elaine, he describes Arthur's

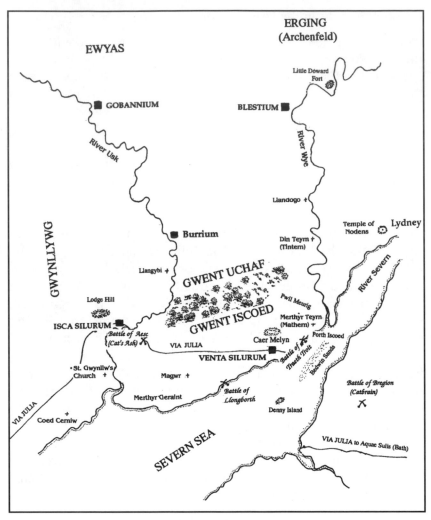

*Figure 49. Arthurian locations in Gwent.*

tenth battle as follows: "and down the waste sand-shores of
Traeth Troit, where many a heathen fell."[7] Alfred Lord Tennyson spent a great deal of time in Gwent researching the story
of King Arthur and he obviously based his account of Arthur's

---

[7]Alfred, Lord Tennyson, *Idylls of the King* (New York: Airmont, 1969), p. 179.

exploits on local traditions, many of which are no longer remembered. The original Cymric form of Traeth Troit can be found in two of the poems contained in the *Black Book of Carmarthen*. It features in one as Trywruid and in the other as Traetheu Trywrid, which implies a sandy shore, and in this instance can only be applicable to a river having an estuary.

We looked for further clues and examined the story of Arthur's hunt of the Porcus Troit, which is first recorded in the *Mirabilia* appended to Nennius' *Historia Brittonum* (passage 73, page 42). However, it is told with greater elaboration in his hunt for the Twrch Trwyth (Irish Boar) in the story of Kilhwch and Olwen, contained in the *Mabinogion* (page 133). Here we learn that the course taken by the Twrch Trwyth was across Carn Cavall (near Rhyader in Mid Wales) and the Brecon Beacons to Aber Gwy, where the Wye falls into the Severn below Chepstow. The princely monster then dashed into a flood, to appear for a short time in Cernyw, before he vanished entirely from view. This riddle story is undoubtedly a folk memory of the expulsion of the Gewissei from Gwent. It becomes apparent that the Gewissei were collectively known by the Welsh as the Twrch Trwyth, or Irish pig.[8]

Whether the immersion of the Trwyth in the Severn near Llyn Lliwan, or Llinlivan, as it is generally called, has any reference to the wonders which characterize this remarkable locality does not appear. However, it seems reasonable to suppose that something more than a natural cause must have led to the marvelous results which are related in the tract titled "De Mirabilibus Brittonum," contained in Nennius' *Historia Brittonum*:

> There is another wonder, which is Aber Llyn Lliwan, the mouth of which river opens into the Severn, the sea in the like manner flows into the mouth of the above-named river,

---

[8]To the Celt, the boar represented strength and ferocity and boar images were often displayed on shields. The River Troggy, which flows through the area once known as Cerniw, was originally called the Twrc. The Romans knew it as Tarocus and today the name has become anglicized to Trogy and Troggy. It seems significant that Twrc means "boar," and in the early charters its source is mentioned as Pen Tyrch "the Head of the Boar."

and is received into a pool at its mouth, as into a gulf, and does not proceed higher up. There is a beach near the river, and when the tide is in the Severn, that beach is not covered; and when the sea and the Severn recede, then the pool Lliwan disgorges all that it had swallowed from the sea and that beach is covered therewith, and it discharges and pours it out in one wave, in sight like a mountain. If there should be a whole army of all that country there, and they should turn their faces towards the wave, it would draw the army to it by force, their clothes being full of moisture, and their horses would be drawn in like manner. But should the army turn their backs towards the wave, it will not injure them. When the sea has receded, then the whole beach which the wave had covered is left bare again, and the sea retires from it.[9]

The *Brut Tyssilio* mentions Arthur and Riwal viewing a lake near the Severn, called Llyn Lliwan, "which ebbs as the tide fills, and does not rise to the surface, not withstanding the influx of fresh water, from which those who face them scarcely escape with life, whereas those whose backs are to them, escape however near they be."[10]

From the evidence contained in Nennius' *De Mirabilibus Britanniae* (page 40), the *Brut Tyssilio* (page 145), and the story of Kilhwch and Olwen featured in the *Mabinogion* (page 133), it may be conjectured that Arthur utilized the natural phenomena called the Severn Bore as part of his strategy in defeating the Gewissei at the battle of Traeth Troit.

## Battle 11: Fought on the mountain called Agned.

This battle has always defied attempts at guessing its location. The brief description suggests a hill named after a person called Agned and many an Arthurian sleuth must have spent long hours

---

[9]Nennius, *Historia Brittonum*, passage 69, p. 40.
[10]*Brut Tyssilio*, in Peter Roberts, trans. *The Chronicle of the Kings of Britain* (London: Edward Williams, 1811), p. 145.

*Figure 50. Catbrain Lane, leading to Catbrain Hill, which was probably the site of the Battle of Cath Bregion. It is situated near Bristol in Avon and this was Arthur's eleventh battle, which he fought prior to Mount Badon.*

scanning old maps in search of anything remotely resembling this name. However, there is an alternative name for this battle, for in some versions of the Nennius manuscript it is referred to as Cath Breguoin. Quite by chance, we came across a clue to its location in a book written by Joseph Ritson in 1825, titled *The Life of King Arthur from Ancient Historians and Authentic Documents*. Ritson had examined the Cotton Nennius manuscript and noticed in the margin opposite this particular battle someone had written, "In Somersetshire, quem nos Cath bregion."

On examining the Ordnance Survey maps covering the West Country, we discovered the name Catbrain just north of Bristol. Quite close to it is the site of a hill-fort. As previously stated, the word Cat or Cad generally seems to indicate an old battle site and "brain" may well be derived from Bregion. The location of this place is now in the county of Avon, but prior to local government reorganization (1974), it would have been in the old county of Somersetshire, which of course agrees with the comment on the manuscript.

It is certainly a feasible location for Arthur's eleventh battle, for geographically it makes sense if one accepts that the Battle of Badon which followed was fought at Bath, as stated by Geoffrey of Monmouth. This most important twelfth battle will be dealt with in the next chapter.

> There is acceptable evidence that Arthur was a genuine historical figure, not a mere figment of myth or romance. He achieved fame as a great soldier, who fought battles in various parts of Britain in the late fifth and early sixth centuries.[11]

---

[11]Leslie Alcock, *Arthur's Britain* (London: Penguin, 1971), p. xv.

# 13 &

# VICTORY AT BADON HILL

ARTHUR'S SERIES OF BATTLES culminated in the Battle of Badon. This was his finest victory, in which the enemy force suffered a crushing defeat. Gildas, the sixth-century historian, tells us that the Battle of Mons Badonicus was a siege where the Saxons were defeated and there followed a fifty-year period of peace. But unfortunately, Gildas gives us neither an exact date for the battle or its location, nor does he say who was actually besieged. Was it the Saxons or the Britons? Also, we are not told the name of the commander of the British army. Over the years, historians have argued whether it was Arthur or Ambrosius and have endeavored to place the date of the battle in one or another of their respective time periods.

Because Gildas does not mention Arthur, some historians have even suggested that he did not exist as a historical person. However, it is significant that, in reference to battles, with the exception of Ambrosius, Gildas does not mention by name a single British chieftain. Yet the fact that he fails to provide the name of a leader in connection with such an important event as the Battle of Mount Badon is most surprising. We can only surmise that it did not suit his purpose to celebrate the names and virtues of the British princes.

However, the *Annales Cambriae* confirm that Arthur was at least involved in this battle:

> 517: The Battle of Badon, in which Arthur wore the cross of our Lord Jesus Christ on his shoulders for three full days and in which the Britons were victorious.[1]

[1]Annales Cambriae, in *Nennius' British History and the Welsh Annals*, John Morris, ed. and trans. (London: Phillimore, 1980), p. 45.

Nennius, on the other hand, is more explicit about the part played by Arthur, for he tells us that: "The Twelfth battle was on Mons Badonis, where in one day nine hundred and sixty men were killed by one attack of Arthur and no one save himself laid them low."[2]

Various locations have been suggested as the site of the first Battle of Mount Badon and they include Liddington Castle, near Swindon; Badbury Hill, near Faringdon; Badbury Rings, near Wimborne Minster; and three possible sites at Bath.

Bath is the strongest contender for the location and the evidence in its favor is quite considerable. Badon was the only major battle mentioned by Gildas, who is our sole independent authority on the matter. He speaks of it as *obessio Montes Badonis*—"the siege of Mount Badon"—and places it near to the mouth of the Severn, *prope Sabrinae ostium*. Bath was the Caer Baddon of the Britons and "dd" has in Welsh the sound of "th,"as in though; thus we have Caer Baddon, pronounced Bathon.

William Camden, writing in the 17th century, identified Bannerdown near Bath as the site of the battle.[3] Apparently at one time, local people used to gather cupsful of teeth from this hillside. It is also relevant that Bede describes the Battle of Badon as "the siege of Baddesdown-hill" and, without stretching the imagination too far, this appears to be a reference to Bannerdown Hill.[4] The fact that it was referred to as a siege can be explained by the possibility that Arthur and his men came here to attack an enemy who were besieging a British force occupying a hill-fort.

John Aubrey, writing his *Monuments Britannica* in about 1680, suggests that the Battle of Badon was connected with a siege of Bath and that it took place on Banner-Down at Batheaston. The Roman city of Aquae Sulis, which later became known as Bath, would of course have been abandoned and ruined, but

---

[2]*Nennius' British History and the Welsh Annals*, p. 35.
[3]See p. 345 of notes appended to the *Mabinogion*, Lady Charlotte Guest, trans. and ed. (London: J. M. Dent & Sons, 1906).
[4]Bede, *A History of the English Church and People* (London: Penguin, 1968).

*Figure 51. Black Rock, just below the Severn Bridge on the Gwent side of the estuary, is most probably the location where Arthur gathered his army prior to crossing the Severn to fight the Battle of Badon at Bath. This incident and location is described in the* Mabinogion *story titled "The Dream of Rhonabwy."*

*Figure 52. The city of Bath takes its name from its famous Roman Baths but it was once known as Aquae Sulis. In the writings of Nennius, mention is made of the "baths of Badon" and this simple statement provides confirmation of the location of the Battle of Badon in an area occupied by the Gewissei, who were enemies of the Britons.*

as a sacred site, it would still have been of great importance to the sixth-century Britons. Consequently, it was most desirable that it should be defended and not allowed to fall into the hands of the enemy. This was no doubt the main reason why the Battle of Badon was fought.

The Romans had been attracted to this ancient place by the presence of natural springs which supply gushing water at a temperature of 170° F (49° C) and they named their city Aquae Sulis after the British Goddess of The Springs—Sul or Sulis. It became an important center for medicinal bathing where offerings were made to Sulis-Minerva, who was a combination of Minerva, the

*Figure 53. The ramparts of an Iron Age hill-fort can be seen on Solsbury Hill above Batheaston. This hill is probably named after the Celtic goddess Sul or Sulis. Arthur's enemies were pursued from the neighboring hill of Bannerdown during the Battle of Badon in 517 and they took refuge on the summit of this citadel.*

Roman goddess of healing, and Sulis, her native counterpart. To the Celts, this extraordinary spring of hot water must have been a source of wonder and they would have set up a shrine here to the goddess of the hot water. It is certain that a sacred shrine to Sul or Sulis was established here before the Romans arrived. Generally, they took care not to suppress the native deities when they conquered an area and preferred to combine them with their own gods. In this instance, the sacred site of Sulis, with its Druidic associations, was incorporated into a new Roman temple.

Nennius, writing in the ninth century, describes these hot springs as one of the "Marvels of Britain." We are told that: "There is the Hot Lake, where the baths of Badon [note the use of the word Badon] are in the country of the Hwicce [a reference to the Gewissei people]. It is surrounded by a wall made of brick and stone and men go there to bathe at any time, and every man can have the kind of bath he likes. If he wants it will be a cold bath, and if he wants a hot bath it will be hot."[5]

This statement in the book of Nennius is of considerable significance, for it not only mentions the name Badon, but also confirms that the area had been occupied by the Gewissei. This is of interest because, in recent times, historians have tended to dismiss Bath as a possible site for the Battle of Mount Badon, their main reason being that, by 518, the Saxon invaders had not penetrated this far into the southwest. However, this argument does not stand up when we substitute the Gewissei for the Saxons, for it is important to realize that Arthur's protracted campaign against the Gewissei culminated in his victory at Caer Badon and resulted in their expulsion from South Wales and Somerset.

When one considers that the center of the Gewissei activity was just two miles east of Bath at Bradford-on-Avon, formerly known as Wirtgernesburg (Vortigern's Town), after Vortigern, Dux Gewissei, it all becomes clear. Arthur's victory at Mount Badon prevented a permanent linkup between the Gewissei of South Wales and Wiltshire.

Arthur's opponents at the Battle of Badon can be identified as Osla Gyllelfawr and Cerdic of the Gewissei, with their Jutish and South Saxon allies, who made an abortive break-out and joined forces with the Saxon invaders from the Upper Thames Valley. At this battle, the entire future of Britain was at stake. It was a "last-ditch" attempt—a final throw by the Saxons, who had been frustrated by a lack of success in previous encounters. Arthur was the hero of Badon just as fourteen and a quarter centuries later, Montgomery was the hero at the Battle of Alamein in World War II.

Geoffrey of Monmouth, who, despite his muddled and embroidered statements, was often correct, tells us that the battle was fought at Bath and he describes it as follows:

> Then they (the Saxons) proceeded by a forced march to the neighbourhood of Bath and besieged the town . . . Arthur

---

[5]Nennius' *British History and the Welsh Annals*, p. 40.

put on a leather jerkin worthy of so great a king. On his head he placed a golden helmet, with a crest carved in the shape of a dragon; and across his shoulders a circular shield called Pridwen, on which there was painted a likeness of the Blessed Mary, Mother of God, which forced him to be thinking perpetually of her. He girded on his peerless sword called Caliburn, which was forged in the Isle of Avalon. A spear called Ron graced his right hand: long, broad in the blade and thirsty for slaughter. Arthur drew up his men in companies and then bravely attacked the Saxons, who as usual were arrayed in wedges. All that day they resisted the Britons bravely, although the latter launched attack upon attack. Finally, towards sunset, the Saxons occupied a neighbouring hill, on which they proposed to camp. Relying on their vast numbers, they considered that the hill in itself offered sufficient protection. However, when the next day dawned, Arthur climbed to the top of the peak with his army, losing many of his men on the way. Naturally enough, the Saxons, rushing down from their high position, could inflict wounds more easily, for the impetus of their descent gave them more speed than the others who were toiling up. For all that the Britons reached the summit by a superlative effort and immediately engaged the enemy in hand-to-hand conflict. The Saxons stood shoulder to shoulder and strove their utmost to resist.

When the greater part of the day had passed in this way, Arthur went beserk, for he realised that things were still going well for the enemy and that victory for his own side was not yet in sight. He drew his sword Caliburn, called upon the Blessed Virgin and rushed forward at full speed into the thickest ranks of the enemy. Every man whom he struck, calling upon God as he did so, he killed at a single blow. He did not slacken his onslaught until he had dispatched four hundred and seventy men with his sword Caliburn. When the Britons saw this they poured after him in close formation, dealing death on every side. In this battle fell Colgrin with his brother Baldulf and many thousands of others with them. Cheldric, on the contrary, when he saw the danger threatening his men, immediately turned in flight with what troops were left to him. As soon as Arthur had gained the upper hand, he ordered Cador, the Duke of Cornwall, to pursue the Saxons . . .[6]

In order to accept the *Annales Cambriae* date of 518 for the Battle of Badon, it is necessary to sort out a confusing statement made by Gildas. He gives the impression that the battle was a siege fought at Mons Badonicus in the year of his own birth— forty-four years before he wrote his *De Excidio*. However, this would mean that, if the battle took place in 518, *De Excidio* was written in 562. But this would not make sense, for in his book Gildas verbally attacks Maelgwyn, King of Gwynedd, who died at the outbreak of yellow plague in 547. This was the date given in the *Annales Cambriae* for Maelgwyn's death and Gildas in his work gives the impression that Maelgwyn is still alive. Further examination of the words of Gildas is thus necessary:

> That they might not be utterly destroyed, they (the Britons) take up arms and challenge their victors to battle under Ambrosius Aurelianus . . . To these men there came victory. From that time, the citizens were sometimes victorious, sometimes the enemy . . . This continued up to the year of the siege of Mount Badon and of almost the last great slaughter inflicted upon the rascally crew. And this commences as the forty-fourth year, with one month now elapsed.[7]

This statement gives us two undated events, the victory of Ambrosius and the victory at Mount Badon, between which there was a period of success and defeat. It is highly probable that Gildas was referring to this period between the two battles as 44

---

[6]Geoffrey of Monmouth, *The History of the Kings of Britain*, Lewis Thorp, trans. (London: Penguin, 1966), pp. 217–218.

[7]Gildas ap Caw, *De Excidio. et Conquesta Brittania*. See *Gildas—The Ruin of Britain and Other Documents*, Michael Winterbottom, ed. and trans. (London & Chichester: Phillimore , 1978), p. 28.

years duration "less a month." So, if the Battle of Mount Badon took place in 517, then the battle fought by Ambrosius and the start of the aforementioned period of 44 years was in 473.

Furthermore, the passage "It is also the year of my birth," refers, not to the year of Mount Badon, but to that of the victory of Ambrosius. Such an explanation provides a practical solution to the frequently discussed problem of the dating of Badon which has been caused by the strange literary style of Gildas. Thus, the victory of Ambrosius and the birth of Gildas occurred in 473, which means that he was about seventy years of age, if he wrote *De Excidio* after the battle of Camlan and Arthur's abdication.

Matters have been further confused by a statement in the *Annales Cambriae* that a second Battle of Mount Badon was fought in the year 665. It appears that there were approximately one hundred and fifty years between these two battles and in the second one, Morcantius was slain. The most likely site for this battle is on Mynydd Baedon in Mid Glamorgan, where a number of entrenchments can be seen. The victim mentioned was Morgan, the great-grandson of Arthur, whose court was, significantly, just a few miles away at Margam.

Nennius makes a strange statement concerning the first Battle of Mount Badon. He tells us

> ". . . on that day—there fell in one onslaught of Arthur's, nine hundred and sixty men; and none of them but he alone, and in all the battles he remained victor."[8]

Not surprisingly, this seemingly exaggerated claim has been treated with ridicule and suspicion, for it gives a dramatic impression of Arthur standing alone slaying hundreds of men completely unaided. However, it must be compared with earlier words of Nennius to make sense, for he informs us that, in another battle, Arthur "was fighting with all the kings of Britain."[9]

---

[8]Nennius' *Historia Brittonum*, p. 35.
[9]Nennius' *Historia Brittonum*, p. 35.

It is therefore reasonable to conclude that at Badon, it was just Arthur's army who were fighting the enemy. The other kings of Britain and their armies were not present.

In the *Mabinogion* story titled "The Dream of Rhonabwy," additional clues to the true location of the Battle of Badon can be found and also the site of Arthur's fort of Gelliwig. In the story, Arthur is gathering his army together on the banks of the Severn prior to fighting the Battle of Badon. He is described as sitting on a flat island just below a fording point on the river and he is accompanied by Bishop Bedwin.[10]

The mention of this bishop is of particular interest for he also appears in the *Mabinogion* story of Culhwch and Olwen, where we are told that he was the "one who blessed Arthur's meat and drink."[11] One of the *Welsh Triads* states that Bedwini presided as archbishop over Arthur's court at Gelliwig, which we have already shown to be at Llanmelin just to the north of Caerwent. The description of Arthur sitting with Bedwini on an island in the Severn is significant because, on the Ordinance Survey map, at a point just below the ancient crossing point, is a strip of land called the Bedwin Sands. This connects with Denny Island, which may well have been the island in question. The *Mabinogion* story tells that Arthur's great army is gathering here to fight the Battle of Badon at noon and it is again significant that Caer Badon (Bath) would have been just a few hours ride from here.

Historians, examining this *Mabinogion* story in the past, have pondered on these possible clues to the site of the Battle of

---

[10]There are references to Bishop Bedwini in Welsh literature and he is associated with King Arthur and the area known as Cerniw, where he was chief bishop. Caradog Freichfras was chief elder at Arthur's court of Gelliwig. One of the Welsh Triads (Triad No. 1) makes Gelliwig one of the three archbishoprics of Britain over which Bedwini presided as archbishop. We also find Bedwini's name in two of the *Mabinogian* tales, in "Culhwch and Olwen" he is mentioned as the one "who blessed Arthur's meat and drink," and, in "The Dream of Rhonabwy," as we have already described (*Mabinogion,* pp. 95–150). Unfortunately, there are no churches dedicated to St. Bedwini, nor is he celebrated in a saintly festival.

[11]*Mabinogion,* pp. 95–135.

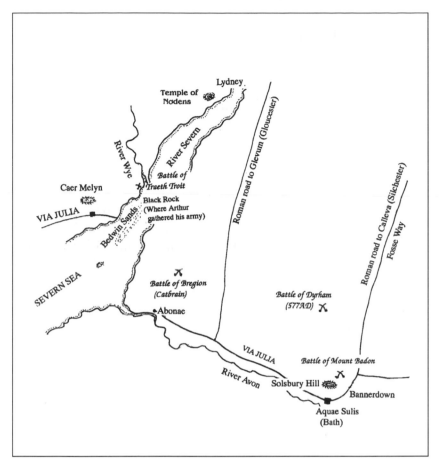

*Figure 54. The Battle of Mount Badon.*

Badon and have come up with the idea that the ford on the Severn was near Welshpool. Arthur's army crosses the river and then
heads toward "Cefn Digoll" to later dismount "below Caer Fad-
don." It appears that Cadwallon of the seventh century has been
confused with Arthur, for he fought on Caer Digoll against the
Angles of Northumbria. The spur of this long hill is also known
as Buttington Ridge and it is feasible that its earlier name of Bot-
inum gave rise to the mistaken idea that this was the location of
Badon.

Some writers, without any foundation, have placed the scene of this battle in the north; but we would rather agree with Camden, who says, it was fought near the hill now called "Bannesdown, hanging over the little village of Bathstone, and shewing in his day," as he tells us, "its bulwarks and rampire." And it is no small proof of this being the Badon alluded to, that the adjacent vale on the Avon bears still among the Welsh the name of Nant Badon, or the Valley of Badon.[12]

This last of twelve battles fought by Arthur resulted in a fifty-year period of peace for the Britons and enabled them to become a united nation. It may be said that this was Arthur's greatest achievement, but sadly, on his abdication in 537, the unity quickly disintegrated.

---

[12]John H. Parry, *The Cambrian Plutarch* (London: W. Simpkin & R. Marshall, 1824), p. 8.

## 14 ❧

# Tbe Battle of Camlan

FOR CENTURIES, HISTORIANS have endeavored to identify the true location of Arthur's thirteenth battle, which was fought at the place known as Camlan and resulted in his downfall. A multitude of unlikely theories have been produced, but most of them can be disregarded with very little hesitation.

Geoffrey of Monmouth's embroidered description in his *History of the Kings of Britain* provides very few clues to the site of the battle. It obviously took place near the River Camlan and Arthur's adversary was called Mordred, who was branded as a traitor. This indicates that he was a Briton and previously a follower of Arthur. Mordred and his men appeared to be in a fixed position and Arthur and his army were advancing toward them. This strongly suggests that Mordred was waiting for Arthur.

Mordred was killed but Arthur, although mortally wounded, did not die at the battle. He was taken away to the Isle of Avalon, which must be a comparatively short distance away, and there he received medical attention. The event occurred in 542 and, after the battle, Arthur abdicated. His cousin, Constantine, the son of Cador, the Duke of Cornwall, took over from him.[1]

These few statements are really all that one can glean from Geoffrey's account of the battle, so obviously it is necessary to look elsewhere for additional clues.

It is first necessary to consider the identity of Arthur's adversary, Mordred, and to establish him in his correct dynastic set-

---

[1]Geoffrey of Monmouth (p. 261) says that the Battle of Camlan took place in 542, but the *Annales Cambriae* (p. 45) give the date as 537.

ting. Geoffrey of Monmouth confused matters by changing the Welsh name of Medraut to the Cornish Mordred (or Modred). Identification is further complicated by the fact that there were two British princes of this name in the sixth century. They were Medraut ap Llew ap Cynfarch and Medraut ap Cawrdaf ap Caradog Freichfras. The former Medraut was the nephew of Urien of Rheged, who died in 580 and would have lived too late to have fought Arthur at the Battle of Camlan, which according to the *Welsh Annals* was fought in 537. The more likely candidate to be Arthur's adversary is therefore his contemporary, Medraut, the son of Cawrdaf ap Caradog Freichfras.

Medraut's father, Cawrdaf, is recorded in the *Welsh Triads* (Triad No. 13) as one of the "Chief Officers of the Island of Britain." It seems that he was the prime minister and chief adviser to King Arthur. The *Welsh Triads* (Triad No. 1) also record that Cawrdaf's father, Caradog Freichfras, was Arthur's Chief Elder at his court of Gelliwig in Cernyw, which we have located in Gwent. During Arthur's absence, he ruled the two Gwents, above and below Wentwood, from Llanmelin hill-fort near Caerwent.

According to the *Lives of the Saints* (pages 95–97), Cawrdaf was not only an influential politician but also a leading light in the Welsh Church. He established a religious house for three hundred monks at Cor Cawrdaf, above Miskin in Mid Glamorgan. In addition, he also became patron of Abererch in the Lleyn Peninsula (North Wales). It therefore becomes apparent from the evidence of the *Welsh Triads* and the *Lives of the British Saints* that Medraut was the member of a very powerful family who held sway in Gwent and the Lleyn Peninsula. This may be the principal reason why Arthur appointed him as his regent.

From the evidence of early Welsh tradition, contained in the *Mabinogion* and the *Welsh Triads,* it appears that Arthur's expansionist policies left a power vacuum which resulted in a dynastic revolution. The preliminary weaving of a plot is referred to in the *Mabinogion* story of Kilhwch and Olwen. This story names Gwenhwyfach as the sister of Gwenhwyfar, (Guinevere in English), Arthur's queen. This is of considerable interest, for, according to the early Welsh genealogies, Gwenhwyfach was the wife of Medraut ap Cawrdaf, Arthur's adversary. Furthermore, according to the *Welsh Triads* (Triad No. 53), it was she who contributed to the cause of the Battle of Camlan by inflicting a blow on her sister, Gwenhwyfar.

The *Welsh Triads* (Triad No. 54) also state that the first of "Three Unrestrained Ravagings of the Island of Britain" occurred when Medraut came to Arthur's court at Gelliwig in Cernyw (Gwent) and dragged Gwenhwyfar from her throne and struck her. The second one occurred when Arthur made a retaliatory assault on Medraut's court. This was obviously the prelude to the Battle of Camlan.[2]

It would appear that Arthur left the government of Britain in the hands of Medraut while he made a journey to Ireland to deal with the Irish warlord, Llwch Wyddel (Lucius Hibernus), who was also known as Llwch Llawinawg, Lord of the Lakes. He, in the Arthurian romance stories, became Lancelot of the Lake and was made out to be one of Arthur's noble knights. Llwch had dispatched messengers to Arthur to demand payment of tribute to him and the men of Ireland. Arthur's reply to Llwch's messengers was that the men of Ireland had no greater claim to tribute from Britain than this island had from them.

Without delay, Arthur mustered the most select warriors of his kingdom and led them across the sea against Llwch and his army. The two forces met beyond the mountain of Mynneu and an untold number were slain on each side. Finally, Arthur encountered Llwch and slew him. When Medraut heard that Arthur's army was dispersed, he decided to seize the reins of power. On receiving news of this uprising, Arthur returned with all that remained of his army and succeeded in landing a force in opposition to Medraut. In the resulting Battle of Camlan, many brave warriors died, but the uprising was quelled. The end of the fighting no doubt came when Arthur slew Medraut in mortal combat, but was himself badly wounded.

---

[2]"The Dream of Rhonabwy" (p. 138) mentions that Iddawc Cord Prydein (the Hammer or Agitator of Britain) betrayed Arthur by divulging his plans to Medraut. The meeting between Iddawc and Medraut took place in Nant Gwynant in Gwynedd, before the Battle of Camlan, and it is spoken of in the Welsh Triads (No. 51, Peniarth 51) as one of the "Three Traitorous Meetings of the Island of Britain."

A verse from "Yr Afallenau Myrddin," which is attributed to Myrddin Sylvester, also mentions the Battle of Camlan:

> Of Medraut and Arthur, leader of hosts;
> Again shall they rush to the Battle of Camlan,
> And only seven escape from the two days' conflict,
> Let Gwenhwyfar remember her crimes,
> When Arthur resumes possession of his throne,
> And the religious hero leads his armies.[3]

So where did the Battle of Camlan take place? Well, it was certainly not Camelford in Cornwall, nor was it Camelon on the River Falkirk in Stirlingshire, as some writers have suggested. The popular interpretation has been to tie it in with any locality which contains an element of the word Camlan in the present-day place-name. In the *Annales Cambriae*, the word is spelled "Camlann" and it was known to the Welsh bards as a terrible slaughter, with the word cadgamlan coming to mean "a rout." There is even a place marked on the present-day Ordnance Survey map as Camlan, where a mountain pass to the north of Dinas Mawddwy provides an ideal site for an ambush. Local tradition suggests that this was indeed the site of Arthur's ill-fated battle, but there is no evidence of any consequence to convince the historian that this really was the place where Arthur's reign came to an abrupt end.

For a number of reasons, which will in due course become apparent, we came to the conclusion that the Battle of Camlan was fought on the Lleyn Peninsula, for this was an area where Medraut's family had strong associations. Scouring maps, both old and recent, of the Lleyn Peninsula, we looked in vain for the name Camlan. Then, just to the east of Aberdaron, near the tip of the Peninsula, which is known as the "Land's End of Wales," we spotted the name Porth Cadlan, which significantly translates as "Battle Place Harbor." Adjoining this little inlet is a detached rock named Maen Gwenonwy. This name rang a bell and in due

---

[3]Myrddin Sylvester, "Yr Afallenau Myrrdin" in Thomas Stephens, *The Literature of the Kymry* (1849), p. 215.

course we recalled that Gwenonwy was the daughter of Meurig ap Tewdrig. In other words, she was the sister of King Arthur and the rock was named after her, probably through folk memory of the Arthurian battle which took place here in the sixth century.

Gwenonwy married Gwyndaf Hen, the son of Emyr Llydaw, and one of their children was St. Henwyn, who established a church on the edge of the sea at Aberdaron, about two miles away, so it is quite feasible that she was a witness to the battle while visiting her son.

It is easy to imagine the scene, as Arthur's boats, laden with warriors, landed in this little harbor, while Medraut waited with his army on the sloping fields above to begin the bloodthirsty Battle of Camlan. Names on the Ordnance Survey map are most significant, for Cadlan Uchaf means Upper Battlefield and Cadlan Isaf means Lower Battlefield, suggesting indeed that some gruesome happening took place here in ancient times. A twisting stream issues from the upper field and flows down a narrow valley to plunge over the cliffs and fall onto the beach below. This is the water course which is remembered as Camlan.

Local place-names provided us with further confirmation that we had discovered the location of the Battle of Camlan, thus solving one of the biggest riddles in history. Cynwyl, who is mentioned in the *Mabinogion* as one of the survivors of the battle, is the patron saint of Penrhos near Llanor, which is but a few miles away. Being very powerfully built, he is said to have escaped from the battle because the enemy were afraid to tackle him.

The family connections of Medraut are of particular significance. Not only did his father, Cawrdaf, establish a church at Abererch, but also his uncle St. Cadfarch, the brother of Cawrdaf, is remembered at Fynnon Gadfarch, which is near the site of the now-extinct capella called Llangedwydd, at the northern end of Abererch parish.

Also, it is important to remember that, when the family of Emyr Llydaw came to Wales, his sons, grandsons, and their followers comprised a band of experienced soldiers. One of his sons was Alan Fyrgan ("White Ankle"), who is mentioned in the *Mabinogion* as the leader of the "Three Faithless War-Bands of the Island of Britain," who turned away from him by night and

*Figure 55. Porth Cadlan (Battle Place Harbor), to the east of Aberdaron, near the tip of the Lleyn Peninsula, is where Arthur landed his army, prior to the Battle of Camlan.*

*Figure 56. Above Porth Cadlan, Medraut was waiting with his followers and the engagement that took place here is remembered as the Battle of Camlan. The gently sloping fields are known as Cadlan Uchaf (Upper Battlefield) and Cadlan Isaf (Lower Battlefield). Cadgamlan = Camlan = Cadlan.*

*Figure 57. Dominating Porth Cadlan is a detached rock named Maen Gwenonwy which appears to have been named after the sister of King Arthur, who came to Aberdaron to visit her son Henwyn and was perhaps a witness to the Battle of Camlan.*

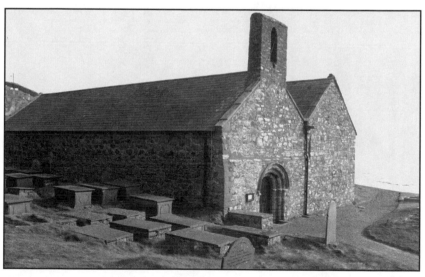

*Figure 58. St. Henwyn's Church, Aberdaron, on the Lleyn Peninsula, was founded in the sixth century by Henwyn, the son of Gwyndaf Hen. He was a cousin of St. Cadfan, the abbot of the monastery on Bardsey Island to which Arthur was taken after the Battle of Camlan.*

let him go with his servants to Camlan where he was slain. Another of Emyr's sons was Gwyndaf Hen ("the Aged"), who married Gwenonwy, the sister of Arthur. We have already mentioned the rock named after her at Porth Cadlan.

Contrary to popular belief, Arthur survived the Battle of Camlan and lived to fight another day, as we shall show in due course. Geoffrey of Monmouth made the statement that, after the Battle of Camlan, Arthur was taken to the Isle of Avalon and the true location of this magical island will be revealed in the next chapter.

> Thus fell King Arthur, and his fall was a main cause of accelerating the overthrow of the ancient Britons, or Cymry, as an independent nation. The power of the Saxons appears from this period gradually to have increased, until the Britons were, at length, deprived of their ancient dominion, which was ultimately contracted within the mountain barriers of Wales.[4]

---

[4]John H. Parry, *The Cambrian Plutarch* (London: W. Simpkin and R. Marshall, 1824), p. 14.

# 15

## ACROSS THE SEA
## TO AVALON

THE TRADITIONAL STORY relates how the wounded King Arthur was taken away by boat immediately after the Battle of Camlan to the mysterious Isle of Avalon to receive medical attention. It is reasonable to suppose that, if Arthur was badly wounded, then he could only survive a short journey. This means that the island of Avalon must be fairly close to the site of the Battle of Camlan.

Geoffrey of Monmouth, in his writings, referred to the island as "Insula Afallonis" and this name has been shortened to Avalon. However, it is significant that all the Welsh versions of the manuscript render the name as "Ynys Afallach" (the Island of Afallach).

Many centuries ago, Avalon was mistakenly identified with Glastonbury, no doubt to suit the placing of the Battle of Camlan at Camelford in Cornwall. This amazing error has created the biggest red herring of all time, although it has done much to encourage the development of a major tourist industry in the West Country.

An important clue to the identification of the mysterious island of Avalon is contained in a book called *Irish Druids and Old Irish Religions*, which was written by James Bonwick in 1894. Bonwick makes a remarkable statement: "The Welsh Avalon, or the Island of Apples, the everlasting source of the Elixir of Life, the home of Arthur and other mythological heroes, lay beyond Cardigan Bay, the Annwn of the old sun, in the direction of Ireland."[1] This statement is also substantiated by the

---

[1] James Bonwick, *Irish Druids and Old Irish Religions* (1894); republished (New York: Dorset, 1986), p. 294.

Archdruid Owen "Morien" Morgan, in *The Royal Winged Son of Stonehenge and Avebury*. He states that the Celtic Elysium was between Borth on Cardigan Bay and Arklow in Ireland.[2] When one looks at a map of the British Isles, it quickly becomes apparent that there is only one possible location for such an island and that is Bardsey, which lies off the tip of the Lleyn Peninsula.

The island of Bardsey sits in the sea like a huge mouse, with a gentle dome-shaped hump at one end and a long tail of flat land stretching out behind it. Just 3 kilometers long and 0.8 kilometers wide at its broadest point, it measures 177 hectares. Behind the 200 meter hump of Mynydd Enlli, on the leeward side of the island, is a small harbor where boats have landed saints, pilgrims, and visitors through the passing centuries.

Bardsey has often been described as Britain's most romantic island and its holiness once made it the "Insula Sanctorum," or Iona of Wales. Pilgrims used to travel here from all directions and one ancient document states that this island was once regarded as the "second Rome" in view of its concentration of sanctity. In the Vatican library, there is even a list of indulgences specially granted to pilgrims making the journey to Bardsey.

More than likely it was the Saxons who named it Bardseye after the bards who retired there, or alternatively it was perhaps named after Bardr, a Viking leader. One of the Welsh names for it is Ynys Enlli—"the isle of the current"—which is a reference to the strength of the tideway between the island and the mainland. This comparatively narrow strip of sea is one of the most dangerous stretches of water around the British Isles, for the current is always very rapid.

In order to discover why the island was once known as Ynys Afallach, we decided to compare some of the romantic traditions with ancient Welsh manuscripts. Geoffrey of Monmouth, in his *Vita Merlini*, describes how Merlin and Taliesin took the wounded Arthur by boat to *Insula pomorum que Fortunata* (the Island of Apples which is called Fortunate), so named because it

---

[2] Archdruid Owen "Morien" Morgan, *The Royal Winged Son of Stonehenge and Avebury* (London: Whittaker & Co., 1900), p. 1. Revised title is *Mabin of the Mabinogion* (London: Research into Lost Knowledge Organisation, 1984).

*Figure 59. The mysterious Island of Bardsey, which lies off the tip of the Lleyn Peninsula, has been described as Britain's most romantic island. It was once known as Ynys Afallach, and is in fact the true site of Avalon. After the Battle of Camlan, a brief but hazardous boat journey from Porth Cadlan enabled King Arthur to receive sanctuary and medical assistance in the island monastery of his cousin St. Cadfan.*

produces all things without toil. They were received by the Lady Morgan, who placed the king on a golden bed and uncovered the wound and said that she would be able to heal it and bring him back to good health.

The relationship between the evil Queen Morgan and the renowned King Arthur has always been a matter of particular fascination which has been debated by many Arthurian scholars. But the question still remains—who was this mysterious lady?

Geoffrey of Monmouth's description of Morgan and her island kingdom corresponds to a passage in the *Gesta Regum Britanniae*, written ca. 1235 by Guillaume de Rennes. It describes a mighty princess attended by nine maidens in a miraculously fertile island kingdom called Avallon and it is implied that she is the daughter of the king of Avallon. Wounded beyond measure, Arthur is brought to the court of the king of Avallon, where the Royal Virgin, who is the guardian of this place, attends to his wounds and becomes his mistress.[3]

Sir Thomas Malory, in his *Le Morte d'Arthur*, brings Morgan Le Fay into his story and tells us that she married Urien of Gorre. Now this is interesting, for, according to the *Welsh Triads*, Urien of Gorre married Modron, the daughter of Afallach, and Urien was the father of Yvaine, known in Welsh tradi-

---

[3]Roger Sherman Loomis, in *The Grail from Celtic Myth to Christian Symbol*, casts Morgan Le Fay in the part of the Grail Bearer, and Lady Charlotte Guest, in her notes for the *Mabinogion*, points out that the Welsh counterpart of Morgan is Modron. All the linguistic experts agree that the name Modron is a regular Welsh development of the great Celtic All-Mother Goddess, Matriona, worshiped by the Celts from Cisalpine Gaul to the Lower Rhine. Ulrich von Zatzikhofen, a Swiss priest, in his *Lanzelet* (c. 1195), describes a fay, having the beauty, learning, and healing powers of Geoffrey's Morgan, presiding over an island kingdom, and being the mother of Mabuz, the Anglo-Norman form of Mabon, who in Welsh tradition is the son of Modron. Lancelot is brought up in seclusion by this water-fay on an island where he is taught skill at arms. The island on which Lancelot is fostered is clearly Avalon, where Modron rules as queen with her nine attendant maidens. It is easily recognizable, like Morgan's Avalon, as a Celtic Elysium, such as the Island of Sena in the western sea, and Lancelot may be identified with Llwch Llawinawg, Lord of the Lakes, who features prominently in Taliesin's poem "Preiddiau Annwfn" (The Spoils of Annwn). See Thomas Stephens, *Literature of the Kymry*, p. 192 ff.

tion as Owain. The Welsh Triad No. 70, which is contained in the Peniarth Manuscript No. 47, states that Owain and his sister Morfudd were carried in the womb of Modron, the daughter of Afallach and the wife of Urien of Gorre.[4]

It is also significant that, according to the early Welsh genealogies, Rhun was the son of Maelgwyn Hir ("the Tall") of Gwynedd by his concubine Gwalltwen, the daughter of Afallach. This confirms that there was a royal prince named Afallach flourishing in Lleyn during the time of King Arthur.

By comparing numerous references to the Arthurian romance character of Morgan Le Fay with her Welsh counterpart Modron, it becomes evident that this daughter of Afallach was the same lady who cured Arthur of his wounds. The name of Modron is derived from that of Matriona—the mother goddess of Celtic mythology. By unraveling a highly complex web of folklore and ancient beliefs, it becomes an exciting probability that Arthur was brought to Ynys Afallach (Bardsey Island) by Merlin and Taliesin to be cured of his wounds by Modron (Morgan Le Fay) and her nine sisters, who were Druidesses skilled in the art of healing.

## BARINTHUS THE FERRYMAN

In his poem "The Spoils of Annwn," Taliesin describes how "thither after the Battle of Camlan we took the wounded Arthur, guided by Barinthus to whom the waters and the stars of heaven were well known."[5] Geoffrey's *Vita Merlini* also mentions the

---

[4]According to P. C. Bartram, *Early Welsh Genealogical Tracts* (pp. 43-91), the Afallach who was the father of Gwalltwen, the concubine of Maelgwyn Hir of Gwynedd and mother of his son Rhun, is the same man who appears in *Troedd Ynys Prydein* ( No. 70) as the father of Modron, who was the wife of Urien of Gorre and the mother of Owain and Morfudd. In certain texts of the *Achau'r Mamu*, contained in the *Peniarth Manuscript* (No. 75), Rhun appears as the son of Maelgwyn and Gwalltwen, the daughter of Afallach.

[5]Taliesin, "The Spoils of Annwn," in *The Book of Taliesin*, John Gwenogvryn Evans, trans. (Wales: Llanbedrog, 1910).

Abbot Barinthus, who appears as a Celtic Charon (ferryman) who guides Myrddin and Taliesin on their voyage to Avalon with the wounded Arthur. Barinthus was known as the "Navigator" because he was an accomplished sailor who could find his way by the stars.

According to the *Navigation Sancti Brendani*, St. Brendan was inspired to take his wondrous voyage to the Promised Land of Saints, a Christianized version of the Isle of the Blessed in the West, by St. Barrind (Barinthus), who had just returned from a journey there.[6] Brendan found a crystal tower in the sea and came to an island of giant smiths. This is an interesting statement, for it should be remembered that, according to Geoffrey of Monmouth, Arthur's sword Caliburn was forged on Ynys Afallach!

## THE CASTLE OF GLASS

It is relevant that we should try to interpret the meaning behind the well-known legend that Merlin was confined on Bardsey Island in a glass castle with the thirteen treasures of Britain. He apparently lies there in an enchanted sleep awaiting the return of Arthur.[7]

Legends, in most cases, are based on folk memories and, even though they may appear to be nothing more than fairy stories, they sometimes contain an element of truth. We found the idea of a glass castle particularly interesting and it deserved further investigation.

In the bard Taliesin's *Preiddiau Annwfn* ("The Spoils of Annwn"), we found that Annwn is depicted as a four-cornered

---

[6]*Saint Brendan*, Iain MacDonald, ed. (Edinburgh: Floris Books, 1992), p. 45.

[7]Lewis Morris in his *Celtic Remains* (p. 170), published by the Cambrian Archaeological Association in 1878, localizes the Ty Wydr (Glass House) on Ynys Enlli and rationalizes the story with an explanation that the Ty Wydr was a museum and that Myrddin Wyllt was its keeper. The connection of Myrddin with Bardsey appears earlier in Hiraethog's expanded version of Enweu Ynys Prydein contained in the *Peniarth Manuscript No. 163* (see Part 2, p. 8; Rep. I, p. 950), which states that he was buried there.

glass fortress standing on an island. Lewis Morris, in his *Celtic Remains* (1878), locates the Ty Gwydr (House of Glass) of Merlin the Wild on Bardsey Island and, according to the 16th-century Peniarth Manuscript (No. 147), he went there, accompanied by nine bards, and took with him the thirteen treasures of Britain. The Oxford Manuscript of *La Folie Tristan* informed us that Morgan, the Queen of Avalon, lived in a chamber of glass on which all the rays of the sun converged. We were consistently finding statements in Welsh and Irish tradition which referred to Annwn as Caer Wydr (Glass Castle). Gradually, we began to consider the possibility that such a building might have been the equivalent of a modern glass house. In other words, a chamber with glass windows which might conceivably be used as a solarium where illness was treated by therapeutic light. The "Castle of Glass" was clearly a solar paradise.

This glass castle, crystal palace, chamber of glass or, in modern terms, greenhouse—call it what you will—was a temple in which the sun itself appeared to live. In this solar paradise, apples were grown, and Morgan, the Queen of Avalon, was the mistress of an indoor apple orchard. It was a sort of Garden of Eden where the fruits of summer could be picked throughout the year. Hence Bardsey was known as the Island of Apples. Crops grow well on the island, but no trees survive there, being wiped out in infancy by the powerful southwest winds. However, they would, of course, have grown well in a greenhouse. In ancient religions, the apple was highly prized and accepted as an emblem of the renewal of youth. Both Roman and Celtic laws featured stiff penalties for cutting down an apple tree. The Celtic word for apple was "aval" and this word occurs in the names Avallach, Emain Ablach, and Abalum, which are the names of three islands. The name Avalon means apple orchard.

But did the people in those far-off times know how to make glass? Well, the Romans certainly did, for we know that they made it from silica (sand) blended with lime and soda. A blue-green tint in their glass was caused by iron impurities in the sand. Glass blowing was also a known skill, for it was invented in Syria during the beginning of the Christian era. So the idea of Celts in Arthur's time manufacturing glass is not as unlikely as one might think.

## THE MONASTERY OF ST. CADFAN

King Arthur was obviously very badly wounded and in urgent need of medical attention. There were, of course, no hospitals in those times, but monasteries certainly existed and the nearest one where he could be certain of receiving sanctuary and medical help was on Bardsey Island, just a short boat journey away from Porth Cadlan.

In the middle of the fifth century, King Einion, whose memorial stone can be seen on the mainland at Llanengan Church, caused the first monastery to be founded on this island. He was a great-grandson of Cunedda Wledig and the ruler of Lleyn at this time. The foundation was made in conjunction with Emyr Llydaw, whose grandson Cadfan became the first abbot.

St. Cadfan came over to Wales from Armorica (Brittany), having been driven from his homeland by the Franks. He was accompanied by numerous companions who all gave their names to various churches in North Wales and on the Lleyn Peninsula in particular. After founding churches at Towyn and Llangadfan, St. Cadfan then moved on to the island of Bardsey, where he established a brotherhood and became the first abbot of a monastery during the period 516–542, which means that he would have been there at the time of Camlan.

In 522, St. Dubricius (Dyfrig), the Archbishop of Wales, retired to Bardsey, having resigned his see, owing to old age and infirmity. So he too would have been on the island when Arthur was brought there after being wounded at Camlan. Dubricius died in 546 and was buried on the island. Six centuries later, in 1172, on the orders of Bishop Urban, his bones were removed and installed with much ceremony in Llandaff Cathedral, near Cardiff in South Glamorgan.

## SOME RELEVANT CONNECTIONS WITH LLEYN

It is of interest to look at the place names on the Ordnance Survey map which occur on the Lleyn Peninsula and examine their connections with the various personalities involved in the story of

*Figure 60. The tomb of St. Dyfrig (Dubricius) can be seen in Llandaff Cathedral, Cardiff, South Glamorgan. Geoffrey of Monmouth claimed that Dyfrig crowned the 15-year-old Arthur at Caer Vudei, a place that he misidentified as Silchester. The ceremony more likely took place at Woodchester in Gloucestershire in 497, which was the year when Ambrosius died.*

*St. Dyfrig himself died in retirement on Bardsey Island on 14 November 546. Nearly six centuries later, his bones were dug up and brought to Llandaff for reburial, on the orders of Bishop Urban, who was rebuilding Llandaff Cathedral at the time.*

*The tomb of St. Dyfrig used to be considered so holy that it was customary to take the most solemn oaths upon it. His effigy is of Early Decorated workmanship and it is carved to depict a bishop in mass vestments and wearing a miter. It was probably placed here in his honor when the presbytery was built. In 1850, the tomb was opened and the following inscription was found inside:*

*September the 8th 1736*

*On the south side of the Chansell nare the door is a tumbe whin (within) a neach (niche) now wall'd up. When I opened the tumbe the parson buried apar'd to be a bishop by his pastorall staffe and crocher. The staffe when we came to touch it dropped to peacis but the crocher being puter (pewter) but almost perished but would hold together. But within there was a large cup by his side but almost perished. The most of puter was rapt in leather and the upper part was very sound.*

*[signed]*
*John Wood, Architect of Queen Square, Bath.*
*Thomas Omar, Joyner and Carpenter of Queen Square, Bath.*

King Arthur. It is thus possible to substantiate further the placing of the Battle of Camlan and the identity of the Isle of Avalon.

When St. Cadfan came to this locality from Brittany, his companions included Cynon, Padarn, Tydecho, Trinio, Gwyndaf, Mael, Sulien, Tanwg, Sadwrn, Lleuddad, Tecwyn, and Maelrys. Let us now examine the fascinating connections between these particular personalities:

Cynon, who was of the family of Emyr Llydaw, was related to Cadfan and he became chancelor of the island monastery.

Padarn was the son of Pedwrn, the son of Emyr Llydaw. His uncles were Amwn Ddu, Umbrafel, and Gwyndaf Hen. These three brothers married three sisters, who were daughters of Meurig ap Tewdrig. Hence they became the brothers-in-law of Arthur.

Tydecho was a son of Amwn Ddu, the son of Emyr Llydaw by Anna, daughter of Meurig (Arthur's father). Tydecho's brother was St. Samson, who was a nephew of Arthur and the first cousin of St. Cadfan.

Gwyndaf Hen (the Aged) was a son of Emyr Llydaw (the Armorican). He is said to have been the confessor of his great-uncle St. Garmon and he came to Britain in the time of Vortigern. He married Gwenonwy, the daughter of Meurig ap Tewdrig, King of Morgannwg. She was the sister of Arthur. At one period in his life, Gwyndaf was the principal of Cor Dyfrig at Caerleon-upon-Usk in Gwent. In his old age he went to Bardsey, where he lies buried.

Henwyn was a son of Gwyndaf Hen by Gwenonwy, the sister of Arthur. He trained at Llanilltyd Fawr in Glamorgan and later became the confessor of his cousin St. Cadfan on Bardsey Island. He is the patron of Aberdaron Church and he eventually became abbot of Cadfan's monastery on Bardsey Island.

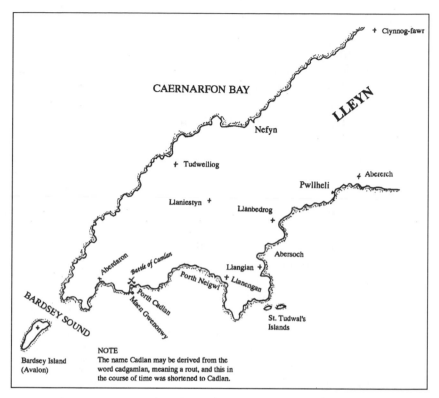

*Figure 61. Battle of Camlan and the Isle of Avalon.*

Meugant, a brother of Henwyn, also became a monk at Llanilltyd Fawr and then followed in his father's footsteps by going to Cor Dyfrig at Caerleon-upon-Usk. Geoffrey of Monmouth tells us that a certain Meugant (Maugannius) was made Bishop of Caer Vudei by King Arthur, but he wrongly identifies Caer Vudei with Silchester, when it should in fact be Woodchester. It was here that Arthur was crowned by Dubricius, who finished his days on Bardsey Island. Meugant, also in his old age, retired to the Isle of Bardsey, where he is buried.

Mael was a son of Riwal Mawr and he became the companion of his cousin St. Cadfan on Bardsey Island. In conjunction with his brother Sulien, he also founded the churches of Corwen in old Merionethshire and Cwm in the old county of Flintshire. Sulien also later settled on Bardsey Island. Mael was also known as Arthmael and he is celebrated in a fourteenth-century French prose romance concerning Artus (who is not Arthur, but named after him), the son of the Duke of Brittany.[8] He must have gained some fame in his own right and was eventually buried on Bardsey Island. This could explain the mistaken belief that King Arthur was buried on the Isle of Avalon. There were two Arthmaels living at the same time and one of them (who was also named Athrwys) was the King Arthur of legend and history. But it was his namesake, Arthmael, the son of Hywel Mawr who was buried on Bardsey Island = Ynys Afallach = Avalon.

Sadwrn was the brother of Illtyd and he married Canna, the daughter of Tewdwr Mawr, son of Emyr Llydaw. They came to Wales with Cadfan and their son was St. Crallo. Sadwrn is commemorated at Llansadwrn on Anglesey, where an inscribed memorial stone bears his Latin name, Saturninus. He died here in 530.

Sulien is, jointly with Mael, the patron of Corwen and of Cwm in Clwyd. Ffynnon Sulien is about one kilometer from Corwen Church near Rug Chapel. There is also a church in Dyfed dedicated to him.

Tanwg was a son of Ithael Hael of Armorica, another Breton refugee who came to Wales with Cadfan. He is patron of Llandonwg on the coast in Gwynedd, which became a

---

[8]Arthur of Brittany is the hero of the 16th-century prose translated by Sir John Bourchier, second Baron Berners, from the 14th-century French romance *Artus de la Petite Bretagne*. He is the son of the Duke of Brittany, and the best knight in the world, demonstrating his prowess in feats of arms and encounters with marvelous creatures. He ends the enchantment of the Port Noire and wins the hand of the fair Florence, daughter of King Emendus.

Chapel of Rest for corpses being transported to Bardsey Island.

Lleuddad was a son of Alan Fyrgan and, with his brother Llynab, became a member of the college of St. Illtyd in Glamorgan. He was later appointed abbot of the monastery on Bardsey following the death of St. Cadfan. His name survives on the island in Gerddi Lleuddad (Lleuddad's Gardens) and also near Aberdaron in Ogof Lleuddad (Cave of Lleuddad). He also founded a church on the mainland at Bryn Croes, where there is a holy well associated with him (Ffynnon Lleuddad).

Tecwyn is patron of Llandecwyn in Merionethshire. Here a stone is inscribed: "(The Cross) of St. Tegwyn, priest: to the honour of God and the most illustrious servant of God; Heli, deacon, made me." This stone was found in the north wall of the old church when it was pulled down in 1879 and the present building erected.

Maelrys was a son of Gwyddno ab Emyr Llydaw and a cousin of St. Cadfan. His name is usually coupled with his cousin Sulien. On the mainland opposite Bardsey is the church of St. Maelrys. His holy well, Ffynnon Faelrys, is some distance from the church. It is interesting that there is no other church in Britain dedicated to him.

Llynab, a son of Alan Fyrgan, was a cousin of St. Cadfan and he became a member of the college of St. Illtyd in Glamorgan. In his old age, he retired to Bardsey.

St. Cybi, a son of Selyf and Gwen (sister of St. Non, the mother of St. David) established a church near Pwllheli. He then moved on to Caer Gybi in Anglesey, where he established a church in the ruins of a Roman fort. When he died in 555, his body was brought to Bardsey for burial.

St. Padarn, the son of Pedrwn ap Emyr Llydaw, was born in Brittany. He came to Wales in 516 and subsequently founded the monastery of Llanbadarn Fawr near Aberyst-wyth, Dyfed. His death occurred in 550 and he was buried on Bardsey Island.

St. Petroc (Petrog), a son of King Glywys of Glamorgan and Gwent founded Llanbedrog on the Lleyn Peninsula.

St. Trillo and his brothers, Lleched, Tegai, and Twrog, were sons of Ithael Hael, who all had church dedications in North Wales. Trillo was also buried on Bardsey Island.

St. Tudno, the son of King Seithenyn, founded a church at Llandudno and was buried on Bardsey Island.

St. Tudwal, a son of King Riwal Mawr of Armorican Dom-nonia, lived as a hermit on Ynys Tudwal (St. Tudwal's Island East off Lleyn), where he founded a monastery. Tudweiliog in Lleyn is also named after him.

The following connections with Lleyn can be made for Medraut, the adversary of Arthur at the Battle of Camlan:

St. Cawrdaf, the father of Medraut was, according to the *Welsh Triads*, one of the three counselors of Arthur. He founded a church at Abererch, which was at one time known as Llan Gawrda. Here he lies buried. On a small em-inence about a mile from the church is Cadair Cawrdaf (Cawrdaf's Seat), a large stone boulder with a flat piece cut out of it.

St. Cadfarch was a brother of Cawrdaf and uncle of Medraut. There is a Ffynnon Gadfarch near the site of the now-extinct capella called Llangedwydd, at the northern end of Abererch parish. His name means warhorse or charger.

# 16

# ARTHUR—DUKE OF BRITTANY

IN THE TRADITIONAL STORY of King Arthur, nothing is heard of him after he is taken away in a boat to the Isle of Avalon, and the general assumption is that he did not recover from his wounds. However, our research into the life of St. Arthmael has revealed that this was not the end of the story and Arthur actually lived on to fight one more battle.[1]

Geoffrey of Monmouth tells us that, after the Battle of Camlan, Arthur abdicated and handed the crown of Britain over to his cousin Constantine in the year 542. Such a person certainly existed and he was the son of Arthur's ally, Cadwy. He was not a particularly memorable or successful king, but, late in his life, he became a Christian and founded several churches in his homeland of Cornwall (see page 79).

Arthur, having recovered from his terrible injuries, turned his back on Britain and sailed across the sea to Armorica (Brittany), where he still retained territory from his former empire. Many of his contemporaries had made similar decisions in the autumn of their lives, so there was nothing unusual in his taking this step. It was Arthur's intention, just like other soldiers and Celtic kings in retirement, to spend the remainder of his life serving his maker. During these final years, he was no longer Arthur, King of the Britons, but a highly respected man of God, who became known to the Bretons as St. Armel. The name Armel is

---

[1]The principal Breton authorities for the *Life of St. Armel* (pp. 383–387) are the *Breviaries* of Rennes (1492), Léon (1516), St. Malo (1537), Vannes (1589), and Folgoet (date unknown). The apparent gaps in the "Life" can be filled by material gathered from the "lives" of his kinsmen Paul Aurelian and Samson. Albert Le Grand, who is usually very reliable, gives the "Life" from the Breviaries of Léon and Folgoet, and the Legendarium of Plouarzel.

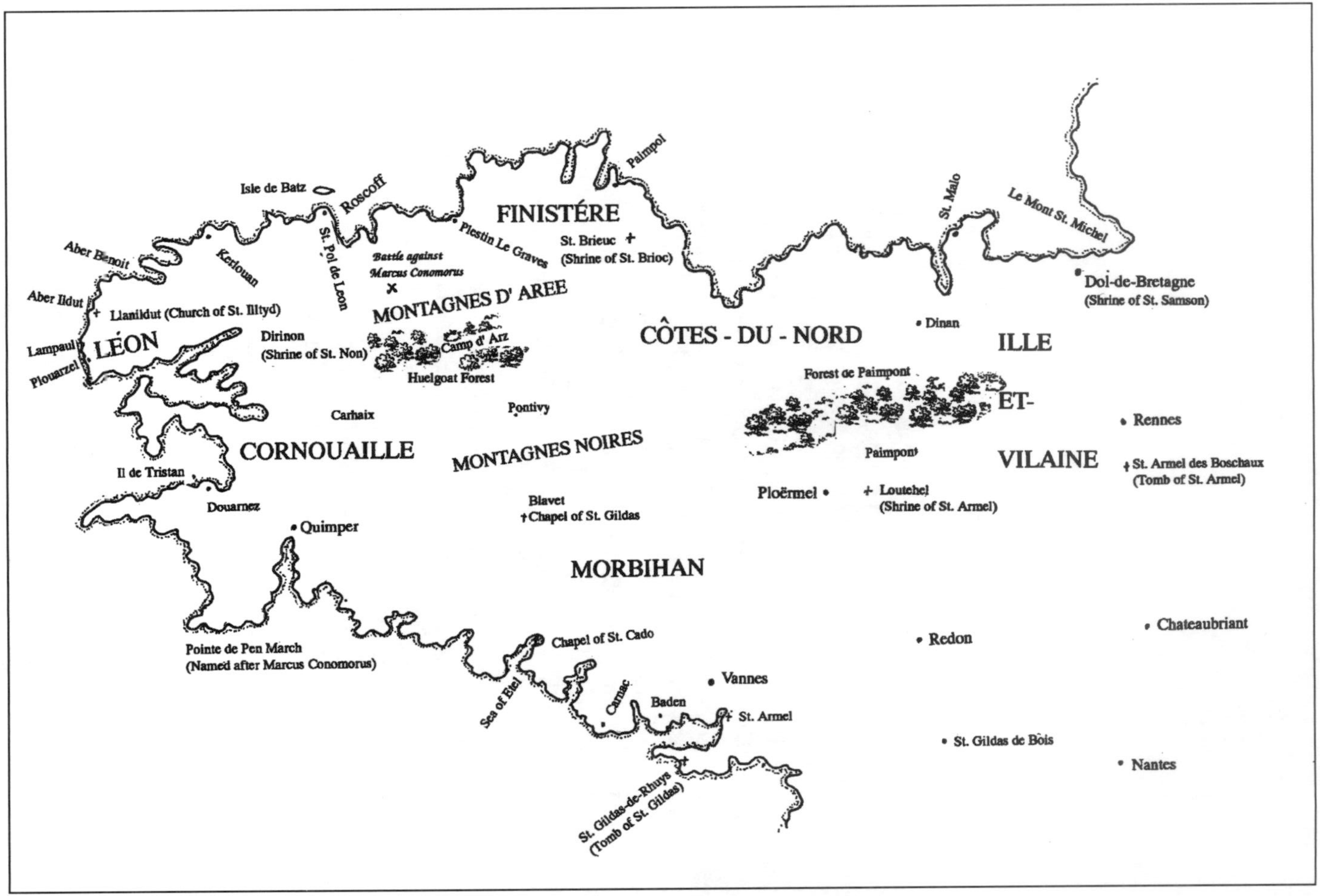

*Figure 62. Armorica.*

Breton for Arthmael, or Arzmael, meaning "Bear Prince," which is undoubtedly connected with the Celtic bear deity, for he was also known as Artor or Arzur the Bear.

To uphold and confirm the traditions of Arthur's final years spent in Brittany, we shall now refer to him by his Breton name. In most dioceses in Brittany, the feast of St. Armel is kept on August 16, and the Bollandists date his lifespan between 482–562.

Many of the Britons who emigrated in large numbers to Armorica during the fifth and sixth centuries came from the Devon-Cornwall peninsula; but it is evident that the immigrants from South Wales were not only more numerous, but also the leaders of the expeditions. A particularly large contingent came from Gwent, where the Britons felt much threatened by the Saxons. This colony planted itself in the northwest part of the Armorican peninsula. They called their territory Léon or Lyonesse, after the Caerleon which they had left behind. Later, this Léon was annexed to Domnonia in the northeast to form a single kingdom.

It was largely the princely families of Wales who led the immigration and the original settlement of Domnonia in northern Brittany was made by Riwal Mawr ("the Great"), a prince of Archenfield in southeastern Wales. Accompanied by a large party of colonists, he established himself at Champ de Rouire on the northeast coast of Armorica and set up his court at Lidhelion.

One of the recurring features in the life of King Arthur is his friendship and military involvement with his nephew Riwal Mawr. This was no doubt because Riwal (or Howel, to give him his traditional Welsh name) was the son of Emyr Llydaw, the benefactor of Ambrosius, who was descended from Magnus Maximus. Arthur had fought for his kinsman Riwal in Armorica during the early years of the sixth century, when he took a force to the continent to help him deal with an invasion of the Visigoths. In order to enable him to secure his possessions in Domnonia, Arthur left Riwal with part of his army and, in due course, Riwal was able to exercise sovereign jurisdiction over the kingdom of Armorican Domnonia. Riwal continued to rule this domain jointly with King Arthur as Dux Britannorum until his death in 524.

Riwal was succeeded by his son Deroch, who was followed by his son Jonas. The latter died suddenly and mysteriously,

*Figure 63. Inside the church of St. Armel-des-Boschaux can be seen this statue of St. Armel trampling on a dragon. This is a symbolic way of remembering how he overthrew the tyrant Marcus Conomorus.*

leaving as his successor a young son named Judwal. The widow of Jonas married Count Conomorus, who thus became the natural regent of Domnonia during the minority of Judwal.[2]

Count Conomorus was the King March of legend who can be identified as Marcus Conomorus, an exiled prince from South Glamorgan who had emigrated to Armorica from British Domnonia (the West Country). He was now Count of Poher, the rich agricultural plateau between two ranges of hills. His seat was at Cairhaix, the old Roman capital of the west, which was known as Vorgium or Vorganium.

Conomorus also made claim to a large part of Léon and took the title of Count of Léon. He is represented as a patron of the church at the beginning of his career, but he had a violent quarrel with St. Paul Aurelian, and this no doubt contributed to his evil reputation with ecclesiastics. Also, he had been in conflict with Deroch, the second king of Domnonia, and was suspected of the assassination of Deroch's son and successor, Jonas. His next move was to plot the death of Judwal, for whom he was acting as regent. Realizing his stepfather's intentions, Judwal fled to the court of the Frankish King Childebert (511–558), who was probably reluctant to have the royal heir of Domnonia under his surveillance, for Brittany was always chafing under Frankish rule.

Armel also got on bad terms with the usurper, Conomorus, and was obliged to leave the area and go to Paris, where he did his utmost to induce Childebert to displace Conomorus and restore Judwal. His efforts were unavailing until the arrival of his nephew St. Samson, whose energy and persistance in the same cause finally broke down Childebert's opposition.

---

[2]Wrmonoc's *Life of St. Pol de Léon* identifies Marcus Conomorus with Marcus, son of Marcianus, or in Welsh, March ap Meirchion. He was the exiled son of the Glamorgan prince Meirchion Vesanus (Marcianus the Mad). "March" means horse and "marchog," horseman. Chinmarchocus (Marchocus) has a name similar to the Cornish placename of Chenmark found in the *Exchequer Domesday Book I* (page 124b), which may be identical to the Cheinmerc found in the *Exeter Domesday Book* (page 263b). This has been identified with Kilmarch (Mark's Retreat), near Fowey in Cornwall, in the *Domesday Gazeteer*, by H. C. Darby and G. R. Versey (Cambridge University Press, 1975).

*Figure 64. Le Camp D'Artus (Arthur's Camp) is an Iron Age hill-fort situated in the Huelgoat Forest, about 21 kilometers northwest of Carhaix Plouguer in Finistère. It is a large fort surrounded by two embankments. The outer one is 3 kilometers in circumference and the inner one is nearly 17 meters high in places. There is a local tradition that it was utilized by King Arthur and his followers.*

St. Samson, the founder of the great abbey of Dol in Domnonia, took it upon himself to go on a diplomatic mission to the court of Childebert to enlist his help on behalf of Judwal. Samson succeeded in persuading the Frankish king to allow him to take Judwal back to Armorica to participate in a military campaign to overthrow the tyrant Conomorus and regain his kingdom.[3]

Armel (Arthur) was now living at Plou-Arzel, which is named after him and situated in the diocese of Léon. He was leading a quiet life in the service of God and had no doubt put all the memories of his fighting days behind him. But, as in the

---

[3]According to the *Life of St. Pol de Léon* (pp. 98–115), Samson was the cousin of Judwal, which helps to explain why he was so keen to give the young prince assistance in overthrowing Marcus Conomorus.

case of his kinsman St. Illtyd, the old fighting spirit could still be called upon if the occasion arose. It should be remembered that as late as the 16th century, Pope Julius II donned his armor to lead his troops into battle. In those times, there was certainly no stigma attached to a holy man who could also take military action. So no doubt Armel agreed without hesitation when his nephew Samson asked him to take up arms once more and join forces with Judwal and himself to overthrow Conomorus, the usurper, and restore the rightful heir to the throne of Domnonia.

Assisted by reinforcements provided by King Childebert, this formidable army was led by the two soldier-saints. They met the army of Conomorus near a place called Brank Aleg at the foot of the Montagnes d'Aree. Here they fought three fiercely contested battles over a period of as many days and, on the evening of the third day, Judwal ran the usurper through with a javelin. Conomorus fell from his horse and was trampled to death in the press of the charge.[4]

At the village of Mengluez, not far from Brank Aleg, is a large slab of slate called Menbeg Konmor, which was erected to mark the tyrant's grave and can be seen to this day.

Judwal, now King of Breton Domnonia, rewarded Armel for his services by granting him land beside the River Seiche, in the district now called Ille et Vilaine and here he established a monastery. The village is today known as St. Armel-des-Boschaux. It is significant that the entire region of Ille et Villaine, which was granted to St. Armel by King Judwal for services rendered, is the part of Brittany which is most associated with the legends of King Arthur and his knights of the Round Table.

St. Armel is represented in a late 16-century stained glass window in the church of St. Sauveur, Dinan. He is depicted

---

[4]In his book, *The Age of Arthur* (p. 258), Dr. John Morris mentions this battle, but he fails to identify St. Armel as the abdicated King Arthur. He mentions that the body of Marcus Conomorus was recovered from the battlefield and buried at Castle Dore. However, tradition is strong in Brittany that the defeated tyrant was laid to rest at the spot where he fell, which is marked by a large stone. According to Sabine Baring-Gould, Marcus Conomorus fell in battle on the slopes of Mont d'Aree in 555. The nearby Abbey du Relecq (of the Bones) was erected by Judwal and St. Paul Aurelian to commemorate the victory.

wearing the habit of an ecclesiastic with an armice over his shoulder and a cap on his head. A green dragon lies at his feet, bound by a stole. At Ploërmel, he is represented in a similar way, with a brown habit, but at Languedias and St. Armel-des-Boschaux can be seen 17th-century statues showing him as an abbot trampling on a dragon. This is a symbolic way of remembering how St. Armel vanquished the tyrant Marcus Conomorus.

Close to the church founded by St. Armel at Ploërmel is the Forest of Paimpont, once part of the vast Forest of Brocéliande, which extended over much of central Brittany. This, even more than our own West Country, is the center of the surviving traditions of King Arthur and his knights. Many of the place-names in this area have associations with Arthur, since Brocéliande was one of the places where he is said to have held sway and where his memory still lingers.

## CONTEMPORARIES OF ST. ARMEL WHO SETTLED IN ARMORICA

Armorica was certainly a place of sanctuary for the Britons who fled from the Saxon menace and the threat of the "Yellow Pestilence," which was a form of bubonic plague. However, many noblemen also came here for religious reasons, as demonstrated by the fact that, just as in Wales and Cornwall, most of the Breton place-names have originated from the missionary saints of the Arthurian period.

One of the most famous contemporaries of King Arthur who came to Armorica was St. Gildas, the son of Caw. He is best known for his writings describing events which occurred in the sixth century. His reprobation of the five rulers of Britannia is so severe, and his comments on the sins of these named kings so scathing, that it is evident that he must have been living in Brittany when he completed his epistle. The fact that Gildas failed to mention Arthur is easily explained, because at the time Arthur was no longer a king of Britain and was now living but a short distance from him.

*Figure 65. St. Gildas ended his days in a form of exile, for there was no way that he could return to his mother country after having poured such scorn on the ruling kings. He died in his monastery at Rhuys and his tomb can be seen inside the church.*

There was no way that Gildas could return to his mother country after having poured such scorn on the ruling kings, so he had no choice but to end his days in exile. It is significant that neither a church nor a holy well is dedicated to him in Britain, while in Brittany there are several. He died in his monastery of Rhuys and there his tomb can be seen.

St. Illtyd also had strong connections with Brittany. On the mouth of Aber Ildut is situated the parish of Lanildut, which is almost certainly a daughter house of Llanilltyd Fawr in South Glamorgan. In the same deanery is St. Tudwal's church, which contains the chapel of St. Illtyd. Loc-Ildut in the parish of Sigun has a chapel containing a statue of St. Illtyd.

*Figure 66. In the valley of the River Blavet can be seen this ancient chapel known as La Roche sur Blavet. An earlier chapel on this site was often frequented by St. Gildas and his disciple St. Bieuzi when seeking solitude.*

St. Paul Aurelian was just five years younger than St. Armel and he also was born at Boverton in Glamorgan. After spending most of his life in Wales, where he founded churches at Llanddeusant and Llangorse, he sailed to Armorica with a group of disciples. He first built a monastery at Lampol on the island of Ouessant and subsequently established a settlement on the mainland at Lampoul Ploudalmezou. From there, he went to the island of Batz, where he visited his cousin Gwythyr from Gwent, who now ruled that area. After building a monastery on the island, Paul moved on to the ruined town of Ocsimor, where he set up a monastic center which eventually developed into the city of St. Pol-de-Léon. According to his biographer, St. Paul died in 573 at age 86. His bones are kept in a gilded bronze shrine inside the great cathedral.

At Dirinon in Finistère can be seen a beautiful 16th-century shrine and effigy commemorating St. Non, the mother of David, the patron saint of Wales. She also retired to Armorica and founded a church here.

Another Welsh saint was St. Brioc who, after spending time in Cornwall where he founded St. Breoke, near Wadebridge, then came to Armorica. He established an important monastery which was the foundation of the present-day cathedral town of Saint-Brieuc. He died here in 530 at age 90.

St. Mewan (Meen) was a disciple of St. Samson who established St. Mewan Church in Cornwall. He later came to Brittany and founded a monastery in the forest of Brocéliande. From there, he moved on to a site near Rennes where he served as abbot of his church of St. Meen. Here he died in the middle of the sixth century. Another disciple of St. Samson who joined him here was St. Austol (Austell), who also originated from Cornwall and ended his days here.

## The Importance of the Armorican Connection

There was a very important union formed between two powerful families of Welsh princes who originated from Arfon (in North Wales) when Elen, the widow of Magnus Maximus, married Rhedyw, the prince of the West Welsh establishments in

Armorica. Their son was Aldwr, who was thus the step-brother of Constantine the Blessed. Aldwr was the brother of St. Garmon, the soldier-saint who helped Ambrosius defeat Vortigern. On becoming ruler of the West Welsh settlements, Aldwr set up his headquarters at Castelaudren to the east of La Meaugon in the County of Vannes, which had been occupied by the Britons from an early period.

Emyr Llydaw, his son, who is also known as Budic of Armorica, gave asylum to Ambrosius and Uthyr after the assassination of their brother, Constantine the Younger, by the usurper Vortigern in 446.

Vannes was usurped by Weroc I, who named the area Bro Weroc, after himself, and Emyr Llydaw, the son of Aldwr, was forced to flee with his family to Wales. The name Llydaw is Welsh for Armorica and it originates from Llyn Llydaw, a lake below Snowdon in North Wales. The large family of Emyr and his wife, Anaumed, are of considerable importance to the story of Arthur and a great deal may be explained by restating the following connections:

> Gwen Teirbron, their daughter, married Eneas Ledewig and their son was St. Cadfan, who established the monastery on Bardsey Island.

> One of Emyr's sons was Riwal Mawr, who was also known as Hywel Farchog, and is referred to in the *Welsh Triads* as one of "The Three Royal Knights in the Court of King Arthur."

> Alan Fyrgan, another son, was forced to flee with his father from Armorica to Wales, where he entered the college of St. Illtyd. He became a soldier-saint and his army is described in the *Welsh Triads* as one of "The Three Disloyal Hosts of the Island of Britain" who turned back from King Arthur on the night before the Battle of Camlan.

> Another son was Gwyndaf Hen, who married Gwenonwy (King Arthur's sister) and their children were Saints Meugant and Henwyn.

It is of particular significance that, during the time which he spent in South Wales, some of Emyr Llydaw's sons married daughters of Meurig ap Tewdrig, King of Morgannwg, and strengthened the family ties which were obviously upheld by Arthur when he became king.

> We know for certain, that a legend of Arthur, which included a belief in his "return," had taken root in Brittany by the twelfth century. There is, therefore, no difficulty in assuming that it was from the Bretons, rather than from the Welsh, that the Normans derived their first knowledge of Arthur, and so came to construct out of the stories connected with him the romantic cycle known as the Matiere de Bretagne.[5]

## THE TOMB OF ST. ARMEL

St. Armel, otherwise known as Arthmael, whom we have identified with Arthur, King of the Silures, died in 562 and was buried in a tomb at St. Armel-des-Boschaux where his now-empty stone sarcophagus can still be seen. In 1645, Pierre Hamon, rector of Loutehel, obviously recognized the importance of this highly venerated saint, for he obtained from M. Tyart, rector of Ploërmel, the relics and insignia of St. Armel. They were placed, in 1685, with assistance from the rector Pierre Barre, in a new shrine at Loutehel.

It is important to understand how the confusion of the stories of King Arthur operating in Brittany as well as Wales and Cornwall has occurred. When the Britons emigrated to Armorica from Wales and Cornwall, particularly in the late sixth century, to escape the Saxon threat, they brought their history and their culture with them. So many Britons settled there that, in time, Armorica became known as "Little Britain" (Brittany). Memories of their homeland must have been very important to them,

---

[5]W. Lewis Jones, *King Arthur in History and Legend* (Cambridge: Cambridge University Press, 1911).

*Figure 67. Inside the Church of St. Armel-des-Boschaux in a recess behind the altar can be seen the now-empty stone sarcophagus of St. Armel. It is typical of a sixth-century coffin, fashioned from a single large block of stone. Above the decorated archway is written in French "The Tomb of St. Armel." It is quite amazing that the Bretons, who greatly venerate both St. Armel and King Arthur, seem completely unaware that they are in fact one and the same person.*

*Figure 68. This inscribed stone, which can be seen in St. Illtyd's Church at Llantwit Major in South Glamorgan, bears a Latin inscription which has been correctly translated, but until now has never been properly understood. It is only through our investigations into the story of St. Arthmael that we have been able to piece together the truth of this matter. It would seem that, after the battle against Marcus Conomorus, St. Samson returned to Glamorgan and commemorated the victory by erecting this stone at Llanilltyd Fawr.*

*The inscription testifies that St. Samson made the cross for his own soul and for those of Iuthael (Judwal), the King, and Arthmael (Armel=Arthur). This is confirmation of a successful campaign organized by the soldier-saints or knights of King Arthur. It was the last battle he fought, several years after Camlan, and it took place in Brittany, where he became a living legend.*

*Figure 69. Close to Loutehel Church can be seen this fountain displaying an effigy of St. Armel. It was here that his relics were brought in 1685, having been obtained by the local rector M. Tyart, who recognized their importance.*

for the traditions of their hero, Arthur, were preserved and became strongly associated with the land which they had now adopted.

The legend of Arthur and the belief in his eventual return had taken firm root in Brittany by the 12th century. Thus we may assume that it was from the Bretons, rather than the Welsh, that the Normans first derived their knowledge of Arthur. In due course, a whole series of romantic stories based on his life were constructed and the truth of his life became obscured.

*Figure 70. Locked away in the church of St. Armel-des-Boschaux is a gilded casket containing the jawbone of St. Armel (St. Arthmael), who is none other than King Arthur.*

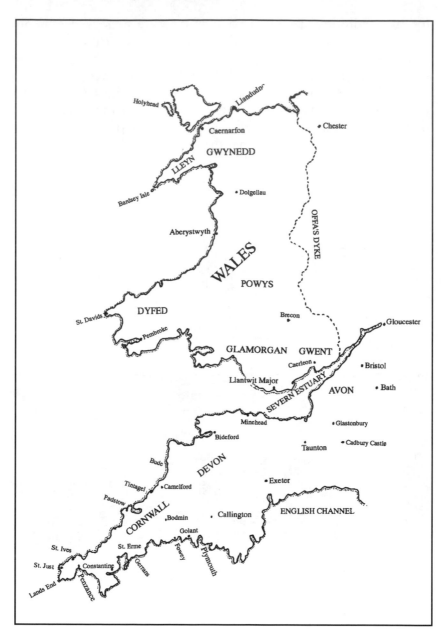

*Figure 71. Wales and the West Country.*

# 17

# The Glastonbury Grave

ONE OF THE BIGGEST RED HERRINGS in the quest for Arthur has been created at Glastonbury in Somerset. The suggestion that Arthur and his Queen, Guinevere, were buried here seems to have originated at Cilgerran Castle in Dyfed. Lord Rhys (Rhys ap Gruffydd) seized this fortress in 1165 and in the same year, when he was entertaining King Henry II there, one of his bards prophesied that the bodies of Arthur and Guinevere would be discovered at Glastonbury.

Nearly twenty years later, on the feast of St. Urban (May 25) in 1184, Glastonbury Abbey caught fire and the old church was destroyed, leaving the monks with a smoldering ruin and a financial crisis on their hands. In 1189, Henry II told the monks to search for the grave of King Arthur. He had no doubt thought long and hard about the story he had heard at Cilgerran and wished to put an end to the old Celtic prophecies that Arthur would one day return to his people. This second coming was eagerly awaited by the Celts of Wales, Cornwall, and Brittany. Obviously by "discovering" the grave of Arthur at Glastonbury, Henry could extinguish such rumors and hopes once and for all, but the monks for some reason seemed reluctant to carry out Henry's instructions and, before the year was out, the king fell sick and died. The monks' financial difficulties soon increased, for Henry's successor, Richard I, cut off their supply of money.

So, in 1191, they finally decided to look for the grave and hopefully reveal an attraction which would bring fame and fortune to their abbey. On digging a hole 5 meters deep, they found an oak coffin containing two skeletons which they

*Figure 72. In 1191, the reputed relics of Arthur and Guinevere were found 5 meters down, buried within an oak tree trunk in the cemetery at Glastonbury Abbey. A leaden cross was also "discovered," bearing a Latin inscription which, translated, reads:* Here lies Arthur, the famous king in the Isle of Avalon.

declared to be the remains of King Arthur and Queen Guinevere.[1] In addition, they claimed to have discovered a leaden
cross bearing the inscription: HIC JACET SEPULTUS INCLI-
TUS REX ARTHURIUS CUM WENNEVERIA UXORE SUA
SECUNDA IN INSULA AVALLONIA. Translated from the
Latin, this reads: "Here lies buried the renowned King Arthur
with Guinevere, his second wife, in the Isle of Avalon."[2]

Unfortunately, the lead cross was lost, but an engraving of it
appeared in William Camden's *Britannia,* published in 1607. All
that can be said is that the lettering on it is certainly not of sixth
century style!

At the time of their discovery, the reputed mortal remains of
King Arthur and his Queen were widely accepted as authentic,
but in later years, the matter became the subject of considerable
controversy. Most historians now agree that the excavation was
part of a publicity campaign, undertaken by the monks to raise
urgently needed funds for the restoration of their abbey. There is
little doubt that the monks added the leaden cross with its fake
inscription to make their discovery more convincing and perhaps
to help persuade themselves that they had indeed found the grave
of Arthur and Guinevere.

The oak coffin in which the skeletons were found was apparently shaped like a dug-out canoe, which suggests that it was
more likely to have been a pagan burial, for in Arthur's time a
stone sarcophagus would have been used. Subsequently, the

---

[1]The statement that the monks discovered the bones of Arthur and his queen at
a depth of 16 feet is explained by the fact that, in the time of St. Dunstan, the
abbot of Glastonbury, the graveyard was so full that he had it covered with a
substantial layer of earth, which was enclosed by a retaining wall. The slab that
was discovered by the monks 7 feet down would have thus been at the old
ground level and presumably marked the grave.

[2]According to Radford and Alcock, the lettering on the cross is of 10th or
11th-century style, which indicates that it may have been made during the time
of St. Dunstan. Alternatively, it may be a clever fake made when the monks carried out their excavation. The wording on it refers to "Insula Avalonia," which
seems to indicate the influence of the writings of Geoffrey of Monmouth. In
particular, the word "inclitus" (renowned) appeared on the cross and it is particularly significant that Geoffrey also used this term.

bones were enshrined in a magnificent tomb of black marble, which years later was placed before the high altar in the rebuilt abbey. It was opened for inspection in 1278 when King Edward I and Queen Eleanor came to spend Easter at Glastonbury. An eye witness, Adam of Damerham, watched the royal couple remove and examine the bones and he later wrote:

> In two caskets, painted with their pictures and arms, were found separately the bones of the said king, which were of great size, and those of Queen Guinevere, which were of marvellous beauty. On the following day the lord king replaced the bones of the king and those of the queen, each in their own casket, having wrapped them in costly silks.[3]

It seems that the bones were replaced in the caskets, with the exception of the skulls and the knee joints, which were kept outside "for the people's devotion."

John Leland was the last writer to mention the tomb. In fact, he described three tombs in the choir. On the north side lay King Edward the Elder, on the south side was King Edmund Ironside, and in the center was the tomb of "Arcturus." According to Leland, there was an inscription on the side of Arthur's tomb which, when translated from the Latin, read: "Here lies Arthur, the flower of kings, the glory of the kingdom, whom custom and learning commend by constant praise." Guinevere was also mentioned with the inscription: "Here lies buried the fortunate wife of Arthur whose virtues merit the promise of heaven."

The tomb remained inside the abbey until 1536, when Henry VIII dissolved the monasteries of Britain, and all that they contained. No doubt the reputed double tomb of Arthur and Guinevere was smashed open and their bones removed and probably destroyed. Today, a black marble stone marks the spot where the tomb once stood in front of the High Altar. The site

---

[3]Adam of Damerham, *History of Glastonbury*, c. 1290.

*Figure 73. Glastonbury Abbey in Somerset, where the monks, in 1191, claimed to discover the grave of King Arthur and Queen Guinevere.*

of the grave dug by the monks is, in fact, 15 meters from the south door of the Lady Chapel, but it has not been marked.[4]

One of the questions which remains to be answered concerns the identity of the obviously important man who was buried here with his wife in a hollowed-out log. Such a method of burial belongs to a much earlier time than that of Arthur. A possible candidate is Arviragus, who is sometimes confused with Arthur. His Gaelic-Pictish name appears to be Arc-wyr-auc meaning "the Bear-folk Chief." The Gaelic "c" would become "t" in Pictish and in Welsh it would become Arthwyr, meaning "the Bear Exalted." As we have stated previously, in times of national crisis, the Britons elected a leader whom they called Arthwyr ("the Bear Exalted"), after the Celtic bear deity.

We have already shown how Arviragus can be linked with Cadbury Castle, but it is also of considerable significance that he figures in the famous legend of the founding of Glastonbury by St. Joseph of Arimathea. In A.D. 63, Arviragus is said to have been reigning in Britain and to have granted twelve hides of land, the site of the future monastery, to St. Joseph and his companions. The British king was ruling over central Somerset and was therefore in a position to give the wandering missionaries a haven. South Cadbury was under full British control long after the Roman conquest of this part of Britain and Arviragus would have maintained his shadowy independence in the hills and marshes of Somerset at the time when St. Joseph is said to have arrived. It is possible that Joseph may have been known to Arviragus as a metal trader some time before his mission. King Arviragus himself remained unconverted, but he is said to have been kind to the missionaries.

The destruction of South Cadbury hill-fort took place after A.D. 70 as part of a Roman police action. Excavation of the site by Leslie Alcock during 1966–1970, revealed evidence of a Roman massacre. The remains of some thirty dismembered

---

[4]In 1962, the archaeologist Raleigh Radford proved by excavation that a hole had indeed been dug and refilled in the location where the monks claimed to have found the grave of Arthur and Guinevere.

skeletons of men, women, and children, possibly pulled to pieces by wild animals after slaughter, were found strewn under the burnt remains of the southwest gateway. It is possible that the British King Arviragus perished in this massacre and was buried with his wife here at Glastonbury near the site of the church founded by Joseph of Arimathea.

Having decided that the discovery of King Arthur's grave at Glastonbury was perhaps a genuine case of mistaken identity, it is now relevant to endeavor to explain why it was believed that he should have been buried there in the first place. To start with, Arthur has obviously been confused with Arviragus, who lived four centuries before his time. But an additional reason for the confusion may have arisen from the tradition that Arthur was buried at Avalon, so it is first necessary to discover why Glastonbury has become identified with this mysterious place.

To be fair to Geoffrey of Monmouth, he did not bring Glastonbury into his story. He in fact referred to the island where Arthur was taken after the Battle of Camlan as "Insula Avallonis." We have already revealed the true identity of the Isle of Avalon as Bardsey Island, so we now know that it certainly wasn't Glastonbury.

The name Glastonbury has its origins in the sixth century and means "the fort of the descendants of Glast." Glast was a great-grandson of Cunedda Wledig. He fought with Arthur at the Battle of Bassas near Lichfield (see page 191). After routing the heathen Middle Angles, Arthur instructed Glast to travel south to protect the home of his ancestors and the holy sanctuary established by St. Joseph of Arimathea. So Glast and his followers traveled via the Icknield Way and the Fosse Way to Bath, from where they continued through Wells and on to the place we now call Glastonbury. Here Glast remained and ruled over his ancestral estates. His name was still remembered a hundred years later when the Saxons captured the Celtic settlement in 658 and called it Glaston.

It was the 12th-century historian William of Malmesbury who provided one of the oldest recorded names for Glastonbury. He referred to the place as Ynys Witherin. Because the word witrin means glass and due to Glastonbury's former marshy situation the place-name was misinterpreted as "the island of Glass" when in actual fact the name stems from a Dark Age personality. He was St. Gwytherin (Victorinus), a great-great-grandson of Cunedda Wledig who founded a community here which became known as Ynys Witherin.[5]

The Norman historian William of Malmesbury spent some time looking through the abbey archives specifically for any possible mention of King Arthur, and, in his notes, he actually stated that he had failed to find any reference which connected Arthur with Glastonbury. Furthermore, in his *History of the Kings of England*, he stated that "the tomb of Arthur is nowhere to be seen, wherefore the ancient songs fable that he is yet to come."[6] A three-line stanza contained in *The Songs of the Graves* emphasizes that the location of Arthur's grave is very much a mystery. Three heroes' graves are evidently known to the writer, but the grave of Arthur is another matter.

> A grave for March, a grave for Gwythyr
> A grave for Gwrgan of the Red Sword;
> The world's wonder a grave for Arthur.

In its untranslated form, the text of the last line is: "Anoeth byd bet y Arthur," which has been interpreted in various ways, but the most important word is *anoeth* which means an "eternal

---

[5]The genealogy of the descendants of Cunedda Wledig shows a series of great political and religious leaders, who always reverted to their ancestral possessions in Glastonbury. St. Gwytherin (Victorinus) founded a community house there which became known as Ynys Witherin, which in the passage of time was reduced to Ynys Witrin.

    Cunedda
    Dunaudd
    Ebiaun
    Dinacat
    Gwytherin

[6]William of Malmesbury, *History of the Kings of England*. See *The Kings Before the Norman Conquest,* Joseph Stephenson, trans. (Felinfach, Lampeter, Wales: Llanerch, 1989).

wonder" or "unknown," suggesting that the grave of Arthur is the most difficult thing in the world to find. The use of such a word seems to suggest that Arthur is a hero who cannot die and will one day return to come to the aid of his people. Hence, the well-known legend of this "once and future king" who is not dead but merely sleeps in a secret place.

> Arthur became the embodiment of all the conscious and subconscious desires of the Britons, their longing for revenge, their love of liberty. He came to personify the whole Celtic heritage which had lived through the Roman Empire and the introduction of Christianity. Traditions clung to the memory and came back to life when needed. From the grave of a dead hero they flowed out across the whole world.[7]

---

[7]Jean Markale, *King Arthur: King of Kings* (London: Gordon & Cremonesi, 1977).

18 ❧

# ÐIÐ KING HENRY VII
# KNOW THE TRUTH?

THE EVIDENCE THAT KING ARTHUR is synonymous with the sixth-century St. Arthmael (known by the Bretons as Armel) is considerable, and we are confident that we have at last revealed the truth of this matter. Yet it seemed surprising that no one else during the passing centuries had come to the same conclusion and was aware of King Arthur's true identity.

We decided to turn our attention to examining the backgrounds of certain historical celebrities who were known to be fascinated by the life of King Arthur. For example, his identity would surely be of particular interest to a royal prince, born in Wales, who was laying claim to the throne of England and wished to convince his countrymen that he represented the return of King Arthur. Ideally, it would be a Welsh prince who had become familiar with the ancient tales related by the bards, and, if in his youth he had also spent some years in Brittany, then he would be familiar with the Breton version of the tradition. It might then become apparent to him that this warrior-king of the Dark Ages was none other than St. Armel, one of Brittany's most venerated saints.

The obvious candidate with such a background was King Henry VII, and when we came to examine his life in detail the final pieces of our jigsaw puzzle quickly began to slip into place.

Prince Henry was the son of Edmund Tudor and Lady Margaret Beaufort, the heiress of John of Gaunt. While fighting for the Lancastrian cause, Edmund Tudor died in his twenties of some epidemic disease at Carmarthen Castle three months before the birth of his son. His pregnant wife, Margaret, was just 13 years old and she sought the protection of her brother-in-law,

Jasper Tudor, who was constable of Pembroke Castle for the Lancastrians. She gave birth to Henry, the future King of England, in one of the rooms above the castle portcullis chamber on January 28, 1457. Henry spent his first years here, but when Pembroke Castle was captured by Lord William Herbert, a Yorkist, on September 30, 1460, he was taken to live at Raglan Castle in Gwent, which held a famous library of ancient manuscripts. The young prince was brought up as a member of the Herbert family. After the death of Sir William Herbert, first Earl of Pembroke, at the battle of Edgecote in 1469, his widow Anne Devereux, the sister of Sir Walter Devereux, first Baron Ferrers of Chartley, took Henry Tudor to the Devereux family home at Weobley, perhaps for greater security, for in late August 1471 her son, Sir William Herbert II, second Earl of Pembroke, and her brother, Sir Walter Devereux, were despatched to deal with Henry's uncle, Jasper. Anne Devereux kept Henry Tudor's affections even after the death of her brother, fighting for the Yorkists at the Battle of Bosworth in 1485.

At the age of 14, it became necessary for Henry to escape from the threat of imprisonment or possible death. Accompanied by his Uncle Jasper, he boarded a ship at Tenby and, like many other royal persons seeking sanctuary in earlier times, they sailed to Brittany. Here they lived in exile under the protection of Duke Francis II, who gave them political asylum for nearly fifteen years.

By now, the English throne was occupied by Richard III, and the Duke of Buckingham, Lord Marcher of Brecknock, made plans to overthrow him. As a cover for his intentions, he made use of Henry's name and also the prince's friends, but they failed to give him the support which he needed, so his plan failed. Sir John Bourchier, second Baron Berners, was also involved in this premature attempt to make Henry Tudor king, but he was forced to flee to Brittany.

When Prince Henry was about 28 years old, he decided that the time had come to make a determined attempt to overthrow Richard and seize his crown. He came to the conclusion that the only way to obtain the support which he needed was to take full advantage of his Welsh ancestry. On Christmas day in 1483, Henry swore an oath in Rennes Cathedral that, when he became king of England, he would marry Princess Elizabeth, heiress of the House of York (eldest daughter of Edward IV). Through the Mortimers, she was descended from a daughter of Llewellyn the Great, and was truly a Celtic princess admirably suited to be his queen.

Residing at the Court of Brittany for fourteen years, Henry had no doubt avidly read and listened to the Breton versions of the story of King Arthur and he would also have remembered his childhood days in Wales, when he used to listen to the old bards regularly proclaiming the ancient prophecies that a Welshman should yet again wear the crown of Britain.

Stealthily, the prince boarded a ship and came to Wales to seek assistance from his countrymen, in the hope that he could persuade them to rise once more under the standard of the Red Dragon to fulfill the old dream and place him on the English throne.

He arrived at the home of Richard ap Howell of Mostyn and pleaded his cause. However, his intentions had already been leaked to King Richard, whose soldiers marched from Flint Castle to Mostyn Hall. Hammering on the door, they demanded that Henry be handed over to them in the name of the king. Meanwhile, the young prince was being assisted out of a window at the rear of the building and he fled on horseback to a safe place in the Welsh mountains.

Henry returned to France, where he succeeded in mustering an army, leaving Sir John Bourchier, second Baron Berners, and the Marquis of Dorset as security for the money he had borrowed. Henry and his army embarked at Honfleur and the flotilla emerged slowly from the shelter of the Seine. On August 7, 1485, he landed at Milford Haven in West Wales with two thousand men. They consisted largely of criminals, but in addition he brought over two thousand exiles; men who, like himself, had fled to France for fear of death at the hands of King Richard. One observer apparently described them as "the worst rabble one could find." Henry's uncle, Earl Jasper, had also come with him with the intention of persuading the men of his earldom to join them in their fight against the king.

Henry was also relying on his countrymen to give assistance and this was the very reason why he landed in Wales. It was his hope that the Cymry would rally to his standard in sufficient numbers for them to overthrow Richard. Owain Glyndwr had raised the Red Dragon, about 85 years previously, when he proclaimed himself Prince of Wales, and Henry now marched under the same banner. He was convinced in his own mind that his destiny was not only to free Wales from English domination, but also to seize for himself, as one of the descendants of the great Cunedda Wledig, the crown of England which the Normans had wrested from the English at Hastings in 1066. Henry's slender claim to the English throne was through his mother, Margaret, who married Edmund Tudor, Earl of Richmond, a half-brother of Henry VI. On this Welsh side of his family, Henry VII's great-grandfather, Mareddud ap Tudor, was a first cousin of the great Welsh hero Owain Glyndwr, who had made a bid for Welsh independence in 1400. It can be said that Henry VII, the first Tudor Monarch, was one-quarter Welsh, one-quarter French, and half English.

Since Owain Glyndwr had broken their power, the Norman Lords Marcher had nearly disappeared and had been replaced by Welsh Chieftains who still listened to the songs of the bards and believed in the ancient prophecies. They had grown up under the spell of the old beliefs and their bards never ceased to sing of the times when the Crown of Britain had belonged to the Cymry. Word quickly spread that Henry, a prince born in Wales, had arrived on the scene and every bard was acclaiming him Mab y Darogan—"Son of Prophecy." So with very little persuasion, the men of Wales took up arms and rallied to Henry's cause.

The subsequent battle was fought to the southwest of Market Bosworth, virtually in the center of England and it resulted in the death of King Richard III, the last Norman king. Once he had fallen, all his men fled from the scene and the Battle of Bosworth was over. The dead king's crown was picked out of a hawthorn bush and solemnly placed on the head of Henry Tudor. At last the old prophecy was fulfilled, for the Crown of Britain had now returned to a Welshman.

A stone marks the spot where the crowning took place and the location is still called "Crown Hill," in memory of the only occasion that a King of England was crowned on the field of battle. This crown had been lost in battle many centuries previously,

*Figure 74. Henry Tudor ready for the Battle of Bosworth.*

but it had now been regained and the dream of Henry Tudor had ended in victory.

Richard III was buried in Grey Friars, a Franciscan Priory at Leicester, but during the Reformation, his grave was broken into and the bones removed, to be thrown into the River Soar. There is a memorial to him in Leicester Cathedral and also an inscription near the bridge over the River Soar. Richard was just 32 years of age when he died, and he is the only English king since the Norman Conquest to have no known grave.

To the Welsh, Henry Tudor was the combination of a new Owain Glyndwr and the return of their ancient hero, King Arthur. The Welshmen who assisted him to regain his crown were well rewarded. His uncle, Jasper, became Duke of Bedford and Justicar of South Wales, and was later made Lord of Glamorgan. Rhys ap Thomas was knighted and appointed Constable of Brecknock, Chamberlain of Carmarthen and Cardigan, and

*Figure 75. Henry VII; the Great Seal of Henry VII.*

Steward of the Lordship of Builth. William Gruffydd was made Chamberlain of North Wales.

Through his Welsh grandfather, Henry traced his descent from the ancient British kings and proudly saw himself as the successor of King Arthur.[1] Although only part Welsh, Henry was Celtic in appearance and temperament. He was born in Wales and spent his early years both there and in Brittany, thus enabling him to become immersed in the ancient traditions of the Celtic people. When he went to battle, he marched under the standard of the Red Dragon, which he saw as the emblem of Arthur's Britain. It is perhaps more than coincidence that Sir Thomas Malory's book *Le Morte d'Arthur* was published in the same year that Henry Tudor won the Battle of Bosworth and became Henry VII.

---

[1]The Denbighshire historian David Powell, in his *History of Cambria* (1584), states that Henry appointed a commission to chronicle his descent from the Welsh princes and British kings. It is significant that Henry adopted the Red Dragon of Cadwaladr as one of the supporters of his arms to stress his claimed descent from the ancient kings of Britain. A history of Henry VII's reign was written by Bernard André, a cleric-historian, detailing Henry's descent from Cadwaladr on his father's side and from John of Gaunt on his mother's side of the family.

Henry became so obsessed with the traditions of King Arthur that he even decided that his first son should be named Arthur, so that he would one day fulfill the ancient prophecy by becoming King Arthur the Second. In late August 1486, King Henry and Queen Elizabeth set off with a large entourage to Winchester, where he intended his heir to be born. On September 20, Elizabeth gave birth to a son whom they named Arthur, "in honour of the British race." The infant prince was christened in Winchester Cathedral a few days later.

Arthur was given the dormant title of Prince of Wales in November 1489 and twelve years later he married the Spanish Princess Catherine of Aragon. The young couple were sent to Ludlow Castle to set up court and to govern Wales with the assistance of a body of counselors. In times past, the Council of the Marches had been set up at Ludlow under Edward IV to administer Wales.

However, the dream was not to be fulfilled, for Prince Arthur only lived to be sixteen and died of influenza at Ludlow Castle on April 2, 1502.

On St. George's Day, his body was taken from the castle to Worcester Cathedral and laid in a tomb within a chantry chapel which King Henry had constructed for his son on the south side of the high altar. His death at such an early age changed the course of history, for it meant that his brother Henry was now heir to the throne. Ten months later, young Henry was created Prince of Wales, a title which obviously meant little to him, for it would seem that he never actually set foot in Wales. Henry, in due course, married his brother's widow, Catherine of Aragon, who became the first of his famous six wives.

Margaret, the daughter of Henry VII, became the wife of James IV of Scotland and, in 1509, she named her second son Arthur, but he died within a year. It is interesting that the name Arthur was also popular with royalty in later times. For example, in 1850, Queen Victoria's third son was christened Arthur and he became Duke of Connaught. King George VI had Arthur as one of his names and his grandson Charles, the present Prince of Wales, was also given the name Arthur when he was christened in 1948.

Henry VII made the Welsh Dragon one of the supporters of the royal arms and this was upheld through the Tudor period. Later, the dragon was replaced by the Unicorn of the Stuarts. Henry VII also established the office of Rouge Dragon Pursuivant in the College of Heralds to commemorate the triumph of the Red Dragon of Cadwaladr.

He set up the famous Yeoman of the Guard, who are perhaps better known as Beefeaters, as his personal bodyguard. The men who were selected as the first members of this unique body had shared Henry's years of exile in Brittany and they also fought with him on Bosworth field. Today, this is the oldest existing body of such a band of men, with an unbroken record which dates from 1485.

Henry's mother, Margaret of Richmond, was the patroness of the Universities of Oxford and Cambridge and she employed Sir Thomas Malory, at her own expense, to write a book about King Arthur. Malory was told to collect, sift, and garner material from Welsh manuscripts then extant, traditions and legends in Wales and Cornwall, and historical data wherever he could find it, concerning the British King Arthur, from whom she firmly believed her son, Henry Tudor, to be lineally descended. Thomas Malory was at that time an obscure Warwickshire knight and his *Le Morte d'Arthur* was a cycle of Arthurian romances, coordinated and welded into a book of literature which he described as "The whole book of King Arthur and his knights of the Round Table." Unfortunately, Malory did not live long enough to see his 383,000 word masterpiece in print, for he died at Newgate and was buried at Greyfriars Church in 1471, some fourteen years before it was published. This happened in the year 1485, when William Caxton brought the art of printing to England and set up his printing press in the Almonry of Westminster Abbey.

Henry VII died at his new palace at Richmond on April 21, 1509, aged 52, having suffered for some time from gout, asthma, and general respiratory problems. He left behind him a prosperous kingdom with nearly 2,000,000 pounds in the treasury.

Our search for further confirmation of the identification of St. Arthmael (Armel) as the historical King Arthur led us to Westminster Abbey and the Chapel of King Henry VII. For some time, we had suspected that Henry Tudor knew that King Arthur was synonymous with the great soldier-saint Arthmael. We had discovered through our research, for example, that Henry firmly believed that he had been saved from a shipwreck off the coast of Brittany through the intervention of the spirit of St. Arthmael. In Brittany, St. Armel (Arthmael) is highly venerated and Henry, during his fourteen years there, must have become well acquainted with details of this saint's life. He actually lived with his uncle, Jasper, for some years at the Chateau de Suscinio on the Rhuys Peninsula at or near to the site of the military headquarters of the mighty warrior-prince Arzur, who was none other than the great soldier-saint Arthmael. It is of great significance that Henry's companion-in-arms at this time was Sir John Bourchier, second Baron Berners, who translated *The History of the Most Noble and Valiant Knight Arthur of Little Britain.* Also, it is particularly relevant that Henry is said to have ascribed his successful military campaign, which ended in his being crowned King of England, to the prayers of St. Armel.

The magnificent chapel where Henry and his wife, Elizabeth of York, lie entombed is situated behind the altar. In the third bay of the south triforium is the statuette of a bearded man vested in a chasuble. His hands are enclosed in plated gauntlets and with one he holds a stole in which a dragon is bound. It is a representation of St. Arthmael (Bear Prince). He is also depicted in a statuette positioned at the east end of the north aisle. He is shown as mailed beneath his habit, confirming that he was a soldier-saint, and is trampling on a dragon, symbolically destroying evil forces. Undoubtedly, this explains the reference to Arthmael's designation as *Miles Fortissimus* ("Mighty Warrior") in the legend as given in the *Breviary of Léon* (1516) and the *Rennes Prose* (1492), in which he is invoked as the *armigere* (armor-bearer) against the enemies of our salvation.

In Latin, Arthmael's name is Armigillus, which must be derived from *armigere*. Nennius' *Historia Brittonum* refers to Arthur as *Arturus Miles* and, in the *Life of St. Efflam,* he is called *Arturus Fortissimus.* All this would seem to indicate that the great soldier-saint Arthmael was the national messiah who delivered his people from tyranny and that he is synonymous with King Arthur. Henry Tudor believed that, in freeing his

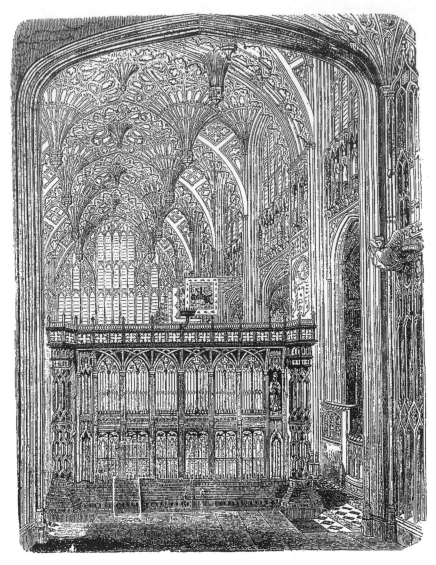

*Figure 76. The magnificent brass screen enclosing the altar tomb of King Henry VII and his queen in his chapel at Westminster.*

*Figure 77. This representation of St. Arthmael can be seen in King Henry VII's chapel in Westminster Abbey. He is depicted as a bearded man vested in a chasuble. His hands are enclosed in plated gauntlets and with one hand he holds a stole in which a dragon is bound. He is shown as mailed beneath his habit, confirming that he was a soldier-saint and is shown trampling on a dragon, symbolically destroying evil forces.*

country from the tyranny of Richard III, he was fulfilling the prophecy of Merlin which foretold the return of King Arthur.

Our relentless research in due course revealed several examples of the veneration of St. Armel in England and it would appear that the height of his popularity was during the reign of King Henry VII, for the name and pictures of St. Armel can often be found in prayer books of this period.

Further evidence for the obsession of King Henry VII with the cult of St. Arthmael is provided by the name of St. Ermyn's Hotel, Westminster, which stands on St. Ermyn's Hill. This is first mentioned in 1496 as St. Armill's and, later on, the name is found as Armell, Armen, Armet, and Ermyne. A chapel existed there in the 17th century which is now represented by the modern parish of Christchurch Westminster. St. Armel is represented on a painted wooden reredos which can be seen at Romsey in Hampshire. He has long hair and a beard and his green chasuble is lined with red. In his right hand, he carries a book; his arms are bare. His legs and feet, which appear at first sight to be bare, are really enclosed in armor, the overlapping plates of the broadtoed sabbatons being plainly visible. At his feet is a dragon, colored in light red, with a stole wrapped around its neck.[2]

At Stoneyhurst College, St. Armel is represented in medieval alabaster work, in the center of which can be seen the saint, bearded and clad in plate armor, kneeling on a mountain before a crucifix. The plates of his broad-toed sabbatons and on his arms and hands are clearly visible. He is vested in a chasuble with a tippet over it. In his left hand is a book in a red forel and in his right hand he holds his stole, which is fastened around the neck of a dragon. Behind him is a building and in the foreground is the River Seiche, into which he cast the dragon whose dead

---

[2]According to Webster's Dictionary, an armill is an ecclesiastical stole used in the British coronation ceremony. With the purpose of signifying the quasi-priestly character of the anointed king, it was placed on his shoulders by the Dean of Westminster, as one of the "garments of salvation." It seems likely that the word armill is derived from Armel and, thanks to the influence of King Henry VII and his involvement with Westminster, it preserves a memory of the illustrious King Arthur, the Defender of the Faith! (Armel = Arthmael = Arthur).

body is seen floating on the water, a symbolic representation of the overthrow of the usurper Marcus Conomorus.

In St. Mary's Brookfield Church, London, is an alabaster figure of St. Armel which, apart from being unpainted, is identical to the one at Stoneyhurst College. The Rev. Phillip H. Rogers has stated that it came into his possession on the death of his father and, in order to preserve it, he set it into a pillar near the font. The figure was discovered years ago with another fragment depicting the bound Christ, concealed under the attic floor of an old farmhouse in the Vale of Llangollen, North Wales. The building belonged to his grandfather, Thomas Rogers of Oswestry. It is possible that this alabaster figure was brought from Valle Crucis Abbey at the time of the dissolution of the monasteries and it may have been taken to form part of some mural decoration at the old farmhouse (Plas yn Pentre) before being hidden to escape the attention of Thomas Cromwell's soldiers, who are known to have fought in the neighborhood.

On Cardinal Morton's cenotaph in the crypt of Canterbury Cathedral are a series of figures of saints. They are all headless and mutilated, but the lowest figure on the east side has been identified by Dr. M. R. James as St. Armel. John Morton, in his younger days, was imprisoned by Richard of Gloucester, but he escaped and joined Henry Tudor in Brittany. After the Battle of Bosworth, he continued to enjoy the confidence of Henry VII and was his Lord Chancellor for thirteen years, until his death in 1500. His cenotaph was constructed during his lifetime.

The figure in question is that of an ecclesiastic. On the front of his right shoulder is the infula, the fringe of a tassel, such as that hanging on the back of a miter. The T-shaped pallium is clearly seen in front over the vestments. Although the hands are now missing, the left one appears to have been raised in blessing, and from below the right hand, a fold which may perhaps represent his stole descends to the dragon at his feet. In front of the lower part of the figure is a much-damaged dragon, but a wing on the right side appears almost perfect. Below is one of the saint's feet, but it cannot be ascertained if it was ever encased in plate armor for no overlapping plates are visible.

No more likely situation for a statue of St. Armel could possibly be found than on the tomb of Cardinal Morton, Henry

Tudor's companion in exile, who became his chancellor and confidant in the years after coming to the throne.

## THE ANCIENT ORDER OF PRINCE ARTHUR

In his preface to Sir Thomas Malory's *Le Morte d'Arthur*, William Caxton writes: "In the Abbey of Westminster, at St. Edward's Shrine, remaineth the print of his seal in red wax closed in beryl, in which is written 'Patricius Arthurus, Britannie, Gallie, Germanie, Dacie, Imperator'."[3] The name Arthur is given to St. Edward in the same way as William of Malmesbury, speaking of Ambrosius Aurelianus, calls this man, having quite another name, "Arthurus." It is significant that Latin writers always refer to Arthur as Arthurus, never as Artorius. The name is used as a synonym for a certain type of hero. It was a title given to those who honored and fought for the continuity of the evolution of the island kingdom in such a way that the progress and evolution of other nations were included. Many years after his death, St. Edward received the title "Patricius Arthurus" and it was sealed on his tomb. Those who did this must have had powerful authority behind them to have obtained the necessary permission. This shows that a Society of Knights must have existed, closely connected with the royal house. The name of Arthur was used by this society because they worked for the historical continuity of the best traditions of Britain.

The description of the founding of such a secret knightly society in England, using the name of Arthur, may belong to a time a hundred years earlier than its publication in book form. In the British Museum, there is a book titled *The Ancient Order, Society and Unity Laudable of Prince Arthur and Knightly Armoury of the Round Table*, by Richard Robertson, printed by John Wolf, and published in London in 1583. It is dedicated to the chief custom official of the Port of London and to the Society of Archers. The book demonstrates that the Tudors established some kind of society which, centered in England, included in its

---

[3]Sir Thomas Malory, *Le Morte d'Arthur* (London: Penguin, 1969).

membership men of other countries, some of them having been rulers of importance in Europe as, for example, the Holy Roman Emperor Maximilian I, who, one year after the publication of *Le Morte d'Arthur,* was elected Holy Roman Emperor. On his monument in the Royal Chapel of Innsbruck, the design of which had been made during his lifetime, we find twenty-eight figures as torch bearers, one of whom is King Arthur of Britain. This great monument was begun in 1509 and finished in 1583, the same year as the publication of Robertson's book. Maximilian was counted as the last knight, and there is no doubt that he was fully acquainted with the knowledge of the Arthurian traditions. It was no accident that Maximilian I erected a statue of King Arthur in the Innsbruck court chapel. On the contrary, it is evident that the attempt to revive the Arthurian legend was not only in line with the dynastic interests of the English royal family but, beyond that, was of concern to members of the nobility in general.

Sir Thomas Malory's *Le Morte d'Arthur* was completed by 1469, but lay unpublished for sixteen years, until William Caxton printed it. Caxton claimed to have done so because "many noble and divers gentlemen of this realm of England came and demanded me, many and oft-times." Thus, the book appeared at the behest of a group of English nobles who had close links with the House of Tudor, which was about to begin its rule. The Tudors had good reason to revive the Arthurian legend, for they counted Arthur among their forebears and it was therefore in their interests to re-establish the Arthurian legend.

## THE MEREVALE WINDOW

At Merevale Church in Warwickshire can be seen a very fine 16th-century stained glass window which long ago was transferred from the Cistercian abbey of Strata Florida. Founded in 1148 by Robert, the second Earl Ferrers, who died ca. 1160, Merevale Abbey is believed to have gone into dissolution voluntarily in 1538.

It is fairly certain that a figure in this stained glass window is that of St. Armel. He is shown wearing a large cape fastened by a morse at the neck and open in front, disclosing a complete suit of armor consisting of a breastplate and taces, beneath which a skirt of mail appears. The legs are in plate armor and the feet are enclosed in broad-toed sabbatons. The left hand holds a crozier; and on the head is a miter. He holds a book in his right hand, suspended from which is a stole which is wrapped around the dragon like a halter. The armor is that in vogue ca. 1500–1525 and the window glass, which is not English work, is of a corresponding period.

We examined the background of the Ferrers family, who originated from Ferrières–St. Hilaire in Normandy and came to this country with William the Conqueror, who granted Henry Ferrers Tutbury Castle and also lands in other counties. Robert Ferrers was created Earl of Derby by King Stephen in 1138 and he died the following year. His son Robert, the second Earl Ferrers, founded the abbeys of Merevale in Warwickshire and Darley in Derbyshire.

Having a reverend esteem for the Cistercian monks, who in his time began to multiply in England, Robert also founded Abbey Dore in Herefordshire and made over extensive land to the Church. He died in 1162 and was wrapped in an oxhide at Merevale Abbey. William, the seventh Earl Ferrers, was also buried at Merevale Abbey in 1254.

On the death of William Ferrers, sixth Baron, in 1460, the barony passed with his daughter Anne to the Devereux family when she married Sir Walter Devereux, who was killed at the Battle of Bosworth Field in 1485. Later, in 1532, his grandson, also Sir Walter Devereux, purchased Merevale from the crown. In the 16th century, the Manor of Merevale passed to Robert Devereux, second Earl of Essex, who was High Steward of Tamworth but was executed by the order of Queen Elizabeth I in 1601. Robert Devereux, third Earl of Essex, whose title was restored in 1604, died in 1646, and his sister, Dorothy, married Sir Henry Shirley of Staunton Harold, near Ashby-de-la-Zouch. In 1649, the Manor of Merevale was sold to Edward Stratford, a rich London merchant, and from him it passed to his eldest son, Francis. His daughter and co-heir, Penelope Bate Stratford, married Richard Geast, who in 1799 took the surname of his uncle, John Dugdale. The Dugdales are the present owners of Merevale and one of their ancestors was Sir William Dugdale, a celebrated antiquary and genealogist, who was the author of the *Monasticon Anglicanum*, a collection of records relating to monastic foundations. It was compiled by Sir William Dugdale in collaboration with Roger Dodsworth and subsequently published under Dugdale's name in three separate volumes in 1655, 1661, and 1673.

In *Monasticon Anglicanum,* volume III, page 190, from the ancient register of the Cathedral Church of Llandaff, is the only instance which occurs, in that register, of the name ARTHUR, so spelled, as the king of Gwent, son of Mouric, king of Morgannwg, and father of Morcant. Elsewhere, he is uniformly called Athruis, who was a contemporary of Comergwynus, a bishop of the See of Llandaff. It would seem that Sir William Dugdale (1605–1686) knew the true identity of King Arthur and it is a remarkable coincidence that St. Arthmael is portrayed in a stained glass window in the Church of St. Mary at Merevale, the seat of the Dugdales.

The story of the origin of this window had to be connected with the Ferrers or the Devereux family and, as we continued our research, a clearer picture of a remarkable sequence of events began to emerge, for we discovered that there was a logical connection with Strata Florida Abbey in Mid Wales.

A certain duke of Arabia known as Stedman, who was a Knight of the Sepulchre, came to this country with Richard Coeur de Lion in 1191. He brought with him from the Holy Land the famous Nanteos Cup, believed by some to be the Holy Grail, and gave it into the safe-keeping of the monks of Strata Florida Abbey.

Moving on to a time just before the Dissolution in 1539, we found that Strata Florida Abbey and its lands were under the ownership of the Devereux family. Their agent and bailiff was John Stedman, remarkably a direct descendant of the Stedman who came over from the Holy Land. In due course, Stedman purchased the abbey and its lands for himself and he claimed in a legal case that Richard Talley had leased lands to him there as early as 1533. He even lived in a part of the abbey before building a house of his own nearby.

Now the member of the Devereux family who held the first lease on Strata Florida Abbey would have been Sir Walter Devereux, third Baron Ferrers of Chartley. Merevale went into voluntary dissolution in 1538 and Strata Florida in 1539. There is a distinct possibility that the stained glass window portraying St. Arthmael came originally from Strata Florida Abbey. It is now preserved in the Church of St. Mary at Merevale and dates from ca. 1500–1525. It would seem that John Stedman took over the lease of Strata Florida in 1533, after Sir Walter Devereux had moved to Merevale in 1532, taking with him the stained glass window portraying St. Arthmael.[4]

## An Unbroken Thread through the Devereux Connection

The Devereux family traced their descent from Robert d'Evereux, a companion of William I of Normandy. Richard, third Count of Evreux in Eure, Normandy, who died in 1067, first

---

[4]When Sir Walter Devereux was created First Baron Ferrers of Chartley in 1461, Chartley Castle passed to him in that year. It had been built by Ranulph II, Earl of Chester, in 1153, who also founded Basingwerk Monastery in Clwyd, twenty-two years earlier. Originally, Basingwerk was affiliated with the Order of Savigny, but joined the Cistercians in 1147. It is of interest that the *Black Book of Basingwerk* contains *Ystoria Dared*, an early version of the *Historia Regum Britanniae*. The Cistercian monks were interested in all matters relating to King Arthur and the Holy Grail. The *Brut y Twysogyon*, the *White Book of Rhydderch,* and the *Red Book of Hergest* were all compiled at Strata Florida Abbey. The last of these two books contains the stories which make up the *Mabinogion* and the earliest Welsh traditions relating to King Arthur. It is, therefore, appropriate that both the Nanteos Cup (reputed to be the Holy Grail) and a stained glass window portraying St. Arthmael should have been kept at Strata Florida Abbey. Sir Walter Devereux, Third Baron Ferrers of Chartley, who held the first lease on Strata Florida Abbey, decided to preserve the stained glass window before the dissolution of the monasteries brought about its destruction.

We are indebted to Fred Stedman-Jones, himself a direct descendant of Stedman, the Knight of the Sepulchre, for supplying us with information regarding the Nanteos Cup and the Devereux Family connection with Strata Florida Abbey.

married Helena, a princess of the House of Léon, the same house into which St. Arthmael had married over five hundred years before. Robert d'Evreux, the head of the branch of the family who settled in Herefordshire at the time of the Norman Conquest, came into the possession of Weobley Castle, built by William Fitzosbern, Earl of Hereford, who was related to Robert by his marriage to Adelisa, the daughter of Roger I de Toeni and Godehildis. Walter Devereux of Weobley, a direct descendant of Robert d'Evreux, married Agnes Crophill, daughter of Thomas Crophill and cousin and co-heir of Sir John Crophill of the Lordship of Ludlow Castle in Shropshire. Agnes died in 1439, and her grandson, also named Walter, married Elizabeth, daughter and heiress of Sir John Merbury by his first marriage; the alternate advowson of Ludlow then descended through the Devereux family until 1601. Therefore, a member of the Devereux family would have been present at Ludlow Castle during the residence of Prince Arthur of Wales, the son of King Henry VII, from 1501 to 1502. In 1461, Sir Walter Devereux, who married Anne, the heiress of William Ferrers, sixth Baron of Chartley, became first Baron Ferrers of Chartley. After the death of her husband, Sir William Herbert, at the battle of Edgecote in 1469, Anne Devereux, the sister of Sir Walter Devereux, took the young Henry Tudor with her to the Devereux family home at Weobley for safe-keeping during the Wars of the Roses. Sir Walter Devereux, first Baron Ferrers of Chartley, met his death while fighting for Richard III at the Battle of Bosworth Field on August 22, 1485.

A grandson of Sir Walter Devereux, who bore the same name, was born in 1490 and, upon the death of his father (John Devereux) in 1501, he was created third Baron Ferrers of Chartley. In 1510, he was appointed high steward of Tamworth and joint constable of Warwick Castle with Sir Edward Belknap in February 1511. On August 1, 1513, he was appointed a member of the Council of Wales and the Marches, which had its headquarters in Ludlow Castle. Two years later, he was made a Knight of the Garter and in 1525 he became steward of the household of Mary Tudor, who was in residence at Ludlow Castle during this period. She had been sent to this seat of the Welsh government by her father King Henry VIII to supervise the administration of law in Wales. A large retinue of courtiers was

bestowed upon the 9-year-old princess, and a council was consti-
tuted for her under the presidency of Sir John Vorsey. Mary was
not formally created Princess of Wales, but she was clearly en-
dowed with all the rights attached to that title in preparation for
her future role as heiress to the throne of England. An inscription
in the chapel at Ludlow in fact stated that John Vorsey was sent
to be President of the Council of Wales and the Welsh Marches
in the time of Lady Mary, Princess of Wales. It is also significant
that Linacre, when dedicating his *Rudiments* (1523) to Mary, ad-
dressed her as Princess of Wales and Cornwall.

In the same year that Sir John Vorsey was appointed president of the Council, Sir Walter Devereux was made steward of
the household of Mary Tudor at Ludlow and Chief Justice of
South Wales. Looking deeper into the lives of these two men, we
discovered that they were both members of the Court and Council of Wales and the Welsh Marches, Knights of St. George, and
attended the Field of the Cloth of Gold. There is a strong probability that they were also members of the Ancient Order of
Prince Arthur. In 1532, Sir Walter Devereux purchased Merevale
Manor from the Crown.

Another member of the Ancient Order of Prince Arthur may
well have been Sir John Bourchier, second Baron Berners, who
died in 1533. He was the cousin of Cecily, who married Sir John
Devereux, second Baron Ferrers of Chartley, and was thus related
to their son, Sir Walter Devereux, third Baron Ferrers of Chartley.
Sir John Bourchier was fascinated by history and he devoted all
his spare time to literary pursuits. In 1523, he published the first
volume of his famous translation of Jean Froissart's *Chronicles;*
the second volume followed in 1525. He also translated from the
French *The History of the Most Noble and Valiant Knight,
Arthur of Little Britain* by Jean de la Fontaine, which was first
published in Lyon in 1493, the year following the publication of
the *Rennes Prose* (1492), in which St. Arthmael is invoked as the
"armigere" (armor-bearer) against the enemies of our salvation.
The 14th-century French prose romance *Artus de la Petite Bretagne* was published under the title *Arthur of Little Britain*. It tells
of a quest undertaken by Artus, who is not Arthur, but named
after him, to liberate an enchanted castle and win the love of
Princess Florence, daughter of King Emendus. Arthur is shown to

be the son of the Duke of Brittany and, described as the best knight in the world, he demonstrates his prowess in feats of arms and encounters with marvelous creatures.

The young Sir John Bourchier was the comrade-in-arms of Henry Tudor and he was involved in the premature attempt to make him king. The outcome was that they were forced to flee to Brittany, where they stayed with Duke Francois II at Chateau de Suscinio which had been built at or near to the site of the military headquarters of the mighty warrior Arzur in the Sarzeau Forest south of Vannes. The authority for the *Life of St. Arthmael* was taken from the *Rennes Prose* (1492); *Le Livre du Vaillant et preux chevalier Artus, fils du duc Bretagne* by Jean de la Fontaine was published in Lyon in 1493. It is, therefore, highly probable that Sir John Bourchier knew the true significance of the stained glass window portraying St. Arthmael and passed this information on to his cousin Sir Walter Devereux, whose ancestor Richard, third Count of Evreux, just like King Arthur, had married into the House of Léon. This undoubtedly explains the reason for the representation of St. Arthmael in a stained glass window in the Church of St. Mary the Virgin at Merevale. In 1550, Sir Walter Devereux was created first Viscount of Hereford. He died in 1558 and was buried in the Parish Church of Stowe-by-Chartley in Staffordshire.

It is significant that Sir William Dugdale (1605–1686), whose descendants subsequently resided at Merevale, also knew the true identity of King Arthur. Sir William Dugdale was a celebrated antiquary and genealogist who compiled the *Monasticon Anglicanum* in collaboration with Roger Dodsworth. He draws attention to the record of a grant in the ancient register of the Cathedral Church of Llandaff to the effect that ARTHUR, so spelled, was the king of Gwent, son of Mouric, king of Morgannwg, and father of Morcant. Furthermore, he states that Morcant, a king in Wales, having treacherously killed his uncle Frioc, after he had in a most solemn manner sworn an inviolable peace with him before the altar, was by Oudoceus, Bishop of Llandaff and nephew of St. Teilo, excommunicated. This statement positively dates Morgan Mwynfawr and in so doing also dates his father, Athrwys ap Meurig, who is, of course, none other than King Arthur.

# Appendix 1

## The Literary Sources

*De Excidio et Conquesta Britanniae*, "Concerning the Ruin and Conquest of Britain," by St. Gildas ap Caw (ca. 495–570).

The writings of Gildas are of considerable importance to anyone studying the Dark Ages, for his work is the only known surviving narrative of the sixth century. He was born at Alcluyd (Dumbarton) in Strathclyde and was the son of Caw. Although a northerner by birth, he received his education at the monastery of Llanilltyd Fawr in South Wales. One of his brothers was Aneurin the Bard, who was the author of the war poem "Y Gododin." Worried by the Saxon threat, Gildas left Britain and retired to his monastery at Rhuys in Armorica.

It would appear that Gildas wrote *De Excidio et Conquesta Britanniae* in about 540. It is not so much a history as a ranting diatribe in which he rebukes his countrymen for their sins and lack of unity. He describes the work as his *Book of Lamentations* and his comments are directed at the petty kings of his time who ruled various parts of Britain. Living far away across the water, Gildas was able to look back at his homeland objectively, and he no doubt felt free to speak his mind. He obviously felt angry and frustrated, for he wrote with heavy and bitter sarcasm. His document is compiled as a sermon and he wrote it because he was greatly troubled and concerned about the future of Britain. ". . . it is not so much my purpose to narrate the dangers of savage warfare incurred by brave soldiers, as to tell of the dangers caused by indolent men . . ." (p. 262). He went on to describe the sad way in which the rulers of the petty kingdoms in Wales and Cornwall were running the country. In particular, he denounced five rulers and spoke of their constant warfare against each other. "Britain has kings, but they are tyrants; judges, but they are impious men . . ." (p. 29). These contemporary kings were Constantine of Domnonia, Aurelius Caninus, Vortiporix of Dyfed, Cuneglassus (Cynlas) of Rhos, and Maglocanus (Maelgwyn of Gwynedd).

King Arthur was not mentioned in *De Excidio* and, as a result, bearing in mind that he would have been a contemporary of Gildas, his very existence has been questioned by some historians. However, there would have been no need for Gildas to mention Arthur, for he wrote his epistle at a time when Arthur was no longer a ruler in Britain. In other words, Gildas completed this work after the Battle of Camlan, at a time when Arthur had resigned his crown and was in fact also residing in Armorica, virtually as a neighbor of Gildas.

It is possible that there is a vague reference to Arthur in the manuscript for Gildas tells how "Cuneglassus—the yellow butcher—once drove the chariot of the man known as the Bear" (p. 31). This simple statement may refer to Arthwyr, the title given to Arthur, which of course means the "bear exalted," and the fact was so well known at the time that Gildas did not feel the need to explain what he meant.

The *Annales Cambriae* record the death of Gildas at his monastery of St. Gildas de Rhuys in Morbihan on 29 January 570. It is of interest that his death is also mentioned in Irish records (the *Annals of Tigernach* and the *Annals of Ulster*), for he was highly regarded in that country as a man of the Church.

*Ecclesiastical History of the English Nation,* by the Venerable St. Bede (ca. 673–735).

St. Bede was born a Saxon and spent his entire life from the age of seven in the monasteries of Wearmouth and Jarrow. He was ordained a deacon at age 19 and became a priest at 30. He was undoubtedly the foremost scholar of his time and the five books of his *Ecclesiastical History* are the priceless heritage of British Christians.

Most of the information for his work, which earned him the title "Father of English History," was taken from Orosius, who wrote in 400–450. He also made use of the writings of Gildas. Drawing his material solely from Saxon tradition and Latin records, Bede was probably ignorant of the Celtic or British stories concerning Arthur and consequently, like Gildas, he failed to mention him. However, he did confirm that there was a period of peace after the Battle of Badon.

The earliest record of Bede's *History* is dated 737, and is preserved at Cambridge. His reputed chair is still kept at Jarrow and, at one time, chips of its wood were believed to have the power to relieve a woman's pangs in childbirth.

The Venerable Bede died at Jarrow monastery, where he was buried in 685. In 1104, a Durham monk stole his bones and carried them to Durham Cathedral, above the River Wear. The tomb of Bede in the Galilee Chapel stands empty, for the bones were again stolen at the time of the Reformation. It is constructed of slate covered with stone and the uppermost slab is carved with a rhyming epitaph: "Hac Sant In Fossa Beda Venerablis Ossa." There is a local tradition that the craftsman carved the first five words and then left a space before the final word because he could not think of a suitable adjective to complete the rhyme in the second line. Tradition has it that, during the night, an angel came to the cathedral and added the word "Venerablis."

*Historia Brittonum,* attributed to Nennius (c. 822).

The Nennius manuscript was discovered in the Vatican archives by the Rev. William Gunn in a volume containing a large number of miscellaneous manuscripts. It was a very exciting find, for it provided the earliest known statements concerning King Arthur.

It would seem that Nennius was a disciple of Elfod, Bishop of Bangor, and Penlan the Presbyter. He lived in the early part of the ninth century and his Celtic name would have been Nynniaw. From a statement in the preface to his work, "Nennius, humble minister and servant of the servants of God, disciple of Elfod," we may conclude that the writer was a Welsh cleric. He apologizes for producing "a heap of all that I have found," but is obviously anxious to preserve from oblivion the traditions of ancient Britain. Others before him had undertaken a similar task but, he says, "somehow or other, have abandoned it from its difficulty, either on account of frequent deaths, or the oft recurring calamities of war."

This manuscript gives a cursory account of the history of Britain from the earliest times down to the eighth century. Nennius is the first writer whose work has survived, as far as is known, who mentions Arthur and provides a brief account of his military exploits. Very special efforts are obviously made to record the exciting story of this hero of the Britons, and we must bear in mind that the author was writing some three centuries after the time of Arthur.

The following passage, in which he describes the sources of his work, gives us some idea of the literature to which, as a priest, he had access: "I have presumed to deliver these things in the Latin tongue, not trusting to my own learning, which is little or none at all, but partly from the traditions of our ancestors, partly from the writings and monuments of the ancient inhabitants of Britain, partly from the annals of the Romans and the chronicles of the sacred fathers, Isidore, Jerome, Prosper, Eusebius and from the histories of the Scots and Saxons, although our enemies."

Nennius refers to Arthur as Dux Bellorum, which implies that Arthur held, after the departure of the Romans, a military title similar to the one established in the island during the latter years of the Roman administration. This statement by Nennius has resulted in doubt being cast on Arthur's position as a king and some writers have down-graded him to the role of a mere battle leader. "Then Arthur fought them in those days with the kings of Britain, but he himself was leader (Dux) of battles." However, after giving this statement careful consideration, it becomes clear that, when Nennius states that Arthur "led the other kings," he does not definitely say that he was NOT a king himself. The words Dux Bellorum may have been intended as a descriptive term meaning "Commander in Battle."

As leader of the British resistance against the Saxons, Arthur's role was to protect Britannia and this he did alongside the kings of the Britons, he himself being Dux Bellorum, the generalissimo of the Romano-Britons of the west. In this capacity, he commanded a formidable cavalry force whose mobility enabled them to move rapidly from one area of Britain to another, opposing external invaders wherever the need was greatest. Arthur subsequently appointed himself Comes Britanniarum (Count of Britain), the position held by his illustrious ancestor Macsen Wledig (Maximus the Imperator).

In addition, Nennius describes Arthur as Miles (Warrior), which signifies a knight and indicates that he was a cavalry leader at the head of mobile troops. The Latin version of Arthmael (to use his other name) is Armagillus, which is derived from armigere, meaning armor-bearer or squire. In his role as Miles Fortissimus (Mighty Warrior), Arthmael is invoked as armigere against the enemies of our salvation. The fact that Arthmael was a religious as well as a military leader coincides extremely well with Nennius's description of one of Arthur's victories in which he "carries the portrait of Saint Mary, ever virgin, on his shoulders, and the pagans were routed on that day, and there was great slaughter of them through the power of our Lord Jesus Christ and the strength of the holy Virgin Mary, His Mother." The word shoulder must be a mistake in the copying of the translation, for the words in Welsh for shoulder and shield are very similar. Ysgwyd means shoulder and Ysguit means shield.

It seems that much of the Nennius text is compiled from other documents which have long since been lost. The author (or authors) endeavored to place the events of the fifth and sixth centuries into chronological order. There are thirty-five manuscripts of the work in existence. Five of them made in the 13th/14th centuries are prefaced by a short piece which is said to have been written by Nennius. It is titled *The Apologia of Nennius, Historian of the British people.*

*The Anglo-Saxon Chronicle,* by Plegmund, et. al.
Plegmund, the Archbishop of Canterbury, began writing this chronicle on the request of King Alfred and the original is at Corpus Christi College, Cambridge. It is a chronological record of British history from the time when Christ lived up to the death of Plegmund in A.D. 924. He made substantial use of Bede's *History* and then added a record of his own times. After him, other people took up the work, including Dunstan the Archbishop, who was born shortly after Plegmund died. Successive hands continued adding to the chronicle until fifty years after the Norman Conquest.

The *Chronicle* relates history from the Saxon viewpoint, for its compilers were not interested in recording the British victories and they cared even less about the British chieftains or kings who won them. It was, of course, like the work of Nennius, written centuries after the events took place, with the result that the accuracy of the dating is rather dubious. No mention is made of Arthur, but the fact that this work contains no record of a battle, successful or otherwise, against the Britons for a long period after 520 seems to confirm Nennius's account of the decisive check to the advance of the Saxons which he attributed to the battles associated with Arthur. The Britons obviously won a great victory at Badon, for the Saxons made no significant advance for at least thirty-five years after this battle occurred.

*The Annals Cambriae.*
These are the ancient annals of Wales which were compiled from the eighth century onward at St. David's. There are three copies in existence and the

earliest, which is known as Manuscript A, is in the Harleian Collection in the British Museum. It is written on parchment and the script is of 10th- or early 11th-century style. Commencing in 444, it continues to 954, followed by a gap of twenty-three years, to conclude at 977 .

The entries, which are all written in Latin, are very brief, with one sentence often describing the events of one whole year. Against many of the years there are no entries at all. Generally, the content deals with the deeds and battles of kings and the deaths of saints and bishops.

One of the longest entries is for the year 517 concerning the Battle of Badon:

> The Battle of Badon in which Arthur carried the cross of our Lord Jesus Christ for three days and three nights on his shoulders and the Britons were the victors.

This entry is of special interest, for it gives the name of Arthur as the victor of the battle while, by contrast, Gildas does not mention Arthur at all. Also, the entry shows Arthur to be a Christian. He is given a second mention in the *Annals* with reference to another important event:

> 537 Strife of Camlan in which Arthur and Medraut fell and there was a plague in Britain and Ireland.

In the following entry we have a reference to the death of King Maglocunnus (Maelgwyn) of Gwynedd. It refers to the plague which spread from western Asia during the period 543–546 and hit Britain in 547:

> 547 The great mortality in which died Mailcus King of Guenedota.

*History of the Kings of Britain*, by Geoffrey of Monmouth (c. 1135–1148).
The most important source book for the matter of Arthur is undoubtedly the work written in 1132 by Geoffrey of Monmouth, titled in Latin *Historia Regum Britanniae*. Known in his time as Gruffydd ap Arthur, but today referred to as Geoffrey of Monmouth, the author was really a poet posing as a historian. Born in the vicinity of Monmouth, Gwent, in about 1090, he was the nephew of Bishop Uchtryd of Llandaff and was appointed Archdeacon of Monmouth.

Geoffrey's famous book was written between 1135–1148. In the dedication to the work, he claimed the patronage of Robert, Earl of Gloucester, who was lord of a tract of Welsh country, the northwest boundary of which extended almost to Monmouth, where he was certainly living at the time he wrote the book.

Early in the 12th century, Robert also acquired the lordship of Glamorgan by marrying Mabel, the daughter and heiress of Robert-Fitzhamon. Robert of Gloucester was an eminent statesman and soldier, but, like his father Henry

Beauclerc, he was also a student of letters and a generous friend of literary men. His enlightened patronage of scholars and poets is shown by the fact that William of Malmesbury, probably the most distinguished scholar of his day, dedicated to him his *History of the Kings of England*. Robert, Earl of Gloucester, also founded the abbey of Margam, whose chronicle is an important account of the history of medieval Wales. In his manuscript, dated 1591, Sir Edward Mansel of Margam mentions "one Morgan, a prince who lived in the time of King Arthur and was his son, as some would have it." By 1634, the *Red Book of Hergest* was back in Glamorgan with Sir Lewis Mansel of Margam. In addition, Robert, Earl of Gloucester, was one of the chief benefactors of Tewkesbury Abbey, where another valuable chronicle was compiled. On his estate at Torigini in Normandy was born Robert of the Mount who became the abbot of Mont St. Michel and gained eminence as a chronicler who compiled accounts of the legends of the Britons. It is of interest that the *Chronicon Montis Michaelis in Periculo Meris* (Chronicle of St. Michael's Mount, 1110) was Breton in origin and predated Geoffrey's *Historia*. The *Chronicle*, which records in its initial entry that Arthur was king of Britain, is part of the remains of the library of Mont St. Michel and is preserved in Avranches MS 213.

Thus, it is evident that Robert of Gloucester's close connections with both South Wales and Normandy resulted in his taking a considerable interest in the legendary tales of Wales and Brittany. It is possible that it was on his request that Walter, Archdeacon of Oxford, and Geoffrey of Monmouth embarked upon the quest for source material relating to Arthur, and the final result was Geoffrey's *Historia*. In the first chapter, he tells us that "Walter, Archdeacon of Oxford, a man learned in foreign histories, offered me a very ancient book in the Brittanic tongue, which in a continued regular story and elegant style related the actions of them all, from Brutus down to Cadwallader. At his request, therefore, I undertook the translation of that book into Latin."

It has always been puzzling where this sourcebook used by Geoffrey of Monmouth originated and whether it can in fact be identified. Arthur de la Borderie, a learned historian of Brittany, may possibly have found traces of the Breton sourcebook utilized by Geoffrey, or at least a document derived from it. The late 14th-century *Chronique de Saint Brieuc* cites a "Legenda Sancti Goeznovii" and such a legend was seen by Albert Le Grand in the 17th century. He describes it as written by William, chaplain of Bishop Eudo of Léon in 1019. The legend tells (1) how the Bretons and the insular British lived for such a long time on friendly terms; (2) of the usurpation of Vortigern; (3) the coming of the Saxons; (4) the victories of Arthur both in Britain and in Gaul; and (5) the final Saxon conquest, which led to further emigration from Britain to Brittany.

Geoffrey again refers to his mysterious sourcebook at the end of his history when he makes the following observation:

> I leave the history of the later kings of Wales to Caradoc of Llancarfan, my contemporary, as I do also the kings of the Saxons to William of

Malmesbury and Henry of Huntingdon, but I advise them to be silent concerning the kings of the Britons, since they do not have that book written in the Britannic tongue, which Walter, Archdeacon of Oxford, brought out of Britannia.

Walter de Mapes, who became Archdeacon of Oxford, was the son of Blondel de Mapes and Tiflur, the daughter of Gweirydd ap Seisyllt Hen, Lord of Llancarfan. Walter is remembered for having built the village of Trewalter and restoring the greater part of his lands to the rightful owners. He was ordained a priest and chosen by Henry II for his chaplain when he passed through Wales on his way to Ireland. It is Walter's connection with Llancarfan that is of particular significance, for it is probable that, as a priest, he had access to a Latin manuscript which was formerly kept at the monastery of Llancarfan. He translated this manuscript into Welsh and it was his translation which Geoffrey used for his *Historia*. Unfortunately, a great deal may have been lost in the translation.

Seventeenth-century antiquaries were certain that Walter de Mapes's book was a more important document than Geoffrey of Monmouth's rendering of it in the *Historia Regum Britanniae*. The Peniarth MS45 refers to a Welsh book which both Walter and Geoffrey had put into Latin, whereas the Havod MS2 and the *Red Book of Hergest* call the ancient book *Llyfyr Brwtwn*, which Walter translated into Welsh, and his rendering was Geoffrey's source.

Geoffrey's statement that the book was "written in the Britannic tongue" could mean that it was written in either Welsh or Breton. He claims that his own work is a direct translation into Latin from his sourcebook, but he no doubt gathered together several old manuscripts which covered the history of the earliest days of the Cymry and set out to rewrite them in one complete work. But Geoffrey made one serious mistake. He apparently did not understand the old way of setting things down. Assuming that all the kings mentioned reigned one after another, instead of side by side, he drew the story out in one long line, thus creating a minefield of confusion for later historians. As a result, many writers have declared that Geoffrey was a complete liar—a fabricator who invented the whole story. However, it is our opinion that, by careful analysis, one can still get at the truth of the matter and straighten out much of his material. To Geoffrey's credit, the most important point to remember is that, but for his *Historia Regum Britanniae,* the world might have completely forgotten about King Arthur.

Even in the 12th century, Geoffrey was accused of lying and the severest of his critics was William of Newburgh who, in 1190, observed that ". . . everything that this person (Geoffrey) wrote about Arthur and his successors and his predecessors after Vortigern, was made up partly by himself and partly by others, whether from an inordinate love of lying or for the sake of pleasing the Britons."

It is quite possible that Geoffrey's motive in compiling his *Historia* was patriotic and the book would certainly have gained the approval of his patron,

Robert of Gloucester, and other Norman lords. No doubt Geoffrey manipulated his material to make the story of King Arthur attractive to his Norman masters and it would also appeal to the romantic tastes of less exalted readers. The popularity of the work was immediate and immense and it is difficult to find any equivalent before the age of printed books. Its importance may be gauged by the fact that there are still so many contemporary copies of the work in existence. For example, in the British Museum alone there are no less than thirty-five copies.

Geoffrey seems to have become very confused by his muddled source material, but it is open to conjecture whether it was by accident or design that he wove a series of major errors into his entangled story. For a start, we need to explain why Geoffrey told us that Arthur was born from the union of Uther Pendragon and the wife of Gorlois. There must have been a reason for this seemingly incorrect statement and we found an important clue when we examined a 14th-century Welsh text entitled *The Birth of Arthur,* for it gave us a valuable insight into the workings of the Gwentian-Cornish-Armorican alliance. The text had been edited and translated by J. H. Davies and it appeared in Y *Cymmroder* Vol. 24 (1900) pp. 249–264. The following extract is of particular interest:

> After the death of Gwrleis (Gorlois), Uther caused a feast to be prepared for the nobles of the island of Britain, and at the feast he married Eigyr, the widow of Gwrleis, and made peace with the kinsman of Gwrleis and all his allies. Gwrleis had two daughters, Gwyar and Dioneta, by his wife Eigyr. Uther caused Dioneta to be sent to the Isle of Afallach, and of all her age she was most skilled in the Seven Arts. Gwyar married Emyr Llydaw (the Armorican) and after the death of her husband she dwelt at Gwrleis's court with her son Riwal Mawr. Now Uther caused Lleu ap Cynfarch to marry her, and they had two sons, Gwalchmai and Medraut, and three daughters, Gracia, Graeria and Dioneta.

If we identify Uther Pendragon (this being a title rather than a name) with Meurig ap Tewdrig, then it all becomes clear. Meurig had already cemented an alliance with Armorica by marrying his daughters to the sons of Emyr Llydaw (the Armorican). He then defeated and killed Gwrleis (Gorlois) and married his widow, Eigyr, thus gaining a foothold in Cornwall. Then he extended the alliance by appointing Tewdrig Mawr ("the Great"), the son of Emyr Llydaw by his first wife, Anaumed, as king of Cornwall. Athrwys (Arthmael/Arthur) may have been the son of his second marriage, to Eigyr, the previous wife of Gwrleis (Gorlois) whom he had killed. This would explain why Geoffrey of Monmouth told us that Arthur was born from the union of Uther Pendragon and the wife of Gorlois. It must be emphasized that Uther Pendragon is a title and not a name and in this instance, refers to Meurig.

Gwyar, one of the daughters of Gorlois and Eigyr, was married to Emyr Llydaw and their son was Riwal Mawr ("the Great"). When Emyr Llydaw died, she married Lleu ap Cynfarch and they had two sons, Gwalchmai and Medraut (not the one who fought Arthur at Camlan, but his namesake and a contemporary). It should also be noted that Riwal Mawr had a son called Arthmael, who became a member of the Cor of his cousin St. Cadfan on Bardsey Island. St. Cadfan was the son of Aeneas Ledewig and Gwen Teirbron, another daughter of Emyr Llydaw. The monastery of St. Cadfan was established on Bardsey Island at the joint instigation of Einion Frenhin, prince of Lleyn, and Emyr Llydaw. It is a complex and confusing web of very significant personalities who, through their family connections, are an essential part of the solution to the mystery of King Arthur's identity and life-story.

The section relating to King Arthur is, for the majority of readers, the most important part of Geoffrey's book. We are provided with an account of Arthur's career from his birth to his accession to the throne at the age of fifteen, to his campaigns against the Saxons, Picts, and Scots—in Ireland, Iceland, the Orkneys, Norway, Denmark, and Gaul—to the final Battle of Camlan. Here Arthur's rival, Mordred, is killed and Arthur, himself mortally wounded, is carried from the battlefield and taken to the Isle of Avalon to be healed.

Arthur's exploits in all these countries obviously suggests a series of major errors by the author, or perhaps a case of deliberate exaggeration, intended to make Arthur appear an even greater hero that he actually was. For example, Geoffrey's account of Arthur marching across Europe to fight the Romans, when Lucius, Emperor of Rome, demanded Arthur's submission, is probably a confused memory of Magnus Maximus (Macsen Wledig), who did exactly this. Maximus was a Celt from Spain who arrived in Britain in about 368. He held high office in western Britain and was known in Welsh tradition as Macsen Wledig. On being declared Emperor by his loyal Roman troops in Britain, Maximus crossed the sea to Gaul to establish his court at Trèves. The Emperor Gratian was assassinated and then Maximus, pursuing even greater ambitions, in 387 marched his legions into Italy and threatened Rome itself, causing the Roman Emperor Valentinian II to flee to safety. However, Maximus was betrayed at Aquileia, captured, and put to death on July 28, 388. It appears that Geoffrey of Monmouth took this story and attributed it to Arthur, either by intention or in error, when he was endeavoring to sort out his confused source material.

When Arthur vanishes from the scene after the Battle of Camlan, Geoffrey makes out that Britain is ruled successively by Constantine, Aurelius, Cynlas, Vortipor, and Maelgwyn Gwynedd. However, Gildas, who was actually around at this time and would have known best, tells us that these five kings were living and ruling side by side. They were in fact contemporary rulers of various principalities in Britain.

It can be said that Geoffrey of Monmouth's book had two results—one literary and the other political. In less than half a century, the romances of King Arthur gained an extraordinary popularity in France, Germany, and Italy. For six centuries after it was written, *Historia Regum Britanniae* was accepted by the majority of readers as accurate history, while the medieval poets found in its content a wealth of material which they utilized as a basis for writing some fascinating poetry.

*The Brut Dingestow.*

This 13th-century manuscript was found at Dingestow Court near Monmouth and is regarded as a Welsh version of Geoffrey of Monmouth's *Historia Regum Britanniae*. It is now held by the National Library of Wales. Even a superficial examination of the manuscript is enough to show that it cannot in its entirety have been taken straight from the work of Geoffrey of Monmouth, so whatever its relationship may be to the *Historia*, that of mere translation is precluded.

This raises an interesting question. Could the original of this manuscript, which is known as the *Brut Tysilio,* be the ancient sourcebook used by Geoffrey of Monmouth? He alleged that his *Historia* was translated from a certain very ancient book written in the British tongue which was acquired in Brittany by Walter, the Archdeacon of Oxford. Such a book may well have been the *Brut Tysilio*, compiled by St. Tysilio, son of Brochwel Ysgythrog, king of Powys. It would not, however, have been possible for this *Brut* to have been compiled by St. Tysilio in its entirety, for it ends with the death of Cadwaladr Fendigaid ("the Blessed") who died in 664, some fourteen years after the death of Tysilio.

In 1811, the Rev. Peter Roberts, a patriotic Welshman, translated the *Brut Tysilio* into English. From his study of the ancient Welsh manuscript, he became convinced that the *Brut Tysilio* was in fact the "vetustissimus liber" which Geoffrey of Monmouth used for his *Historia Regum Britanniae*.

The various editions of Nennius's *Historia Brittonum* are compilations from conflicting sources, which cannot be reconciled. Both Geoffrey of Monmouth and the Welsh *Brut Tysilio* give evidence of knowing Nennius and another source dealing with the same material. It appears that Geoffrey of Monmouth, Nennius, and the Welsh writers all used a common source, each working up the material independently. Nennius utilized some native sources; unquestionably for Arthur, he used a native British or Welsh source. Geoffrey of Monmouth claims to have possessed one also. They both supply traditional stories and names which are not in the Roman histories, thus each author supplements and adds to the other.

The conclusion which we draw is that, although Geoffrey of Monmouth knew the work of Nennius and occasionally borrowed a convenient phrase from him, he did not depend on him. He obviously had another source and additional material. Even if he attempted to reconcile known sources, or to combine them, there are still numerous statements and a host of names for which to account in his *Historia*. The probability is that he had a relatively complete account of the Trojan legend or Story of the Britons, which once had its roots in actual history and reached him already cast in literary form.

A vast number of priceless and highly relevant manuscripts have, of course, been destroyed during the passing centuries, so it is quite likely that Geoffrey's sourcebook has not survived. Leland, for example, when visiting

Glastonbury Abbey shortly before its dissolution, was amazed at its marvelous library and specifically mentions a Celtic history, or rather a portion of one, written by Melchin of Avalon.

*Historia Regum Anglorum* (History of the English Kings), by William of Malmesbury (c. 1125).
This work, written by William of Malmesbury in about 1125, is a serious work which was compiled three centuries after the *History* of Nennius. William wrote of Arthur before Geoffrey of Monmouth, following a visit to Glastonbury where the Benedictine monks told him tales of this great hero who had crushed the Saxons. He had already heard of the Welsh legends and came to the conclusion that this must be the same person. He wrote: "This is that Arthur of whom modern Welsh fancy raves. Yet he plainly deserves to be remembered in genuine history; for he long preserved his dying country" (p. 11).

William of Malmesbury was born in 1090 in Somerset and he became a monk at Malmesbury Abbey, which today is still famous for its library of medieval manuscripts. He later became librarian there and this position obviously gave him access to some useful sources. He wrote of Arthur:

> Arthur about whom, even today, there is so much nonsense in the absurd fables of the Britons [it is also possible to read "from Brittany"]; undeniably a man, who deserves better than to figure in deceptive fabrications and should be praised in truthful accounts as someone who rallied his shaken country for a long time and roused the confused minds of his fellow countrymen to action (p. 11).

*Brut y Twysogion* (The Chronicle of the Princes), by Caradoc, of Llancarfan.
This is a history of the kings of Britain from the time of Cadwaladr and it was written by Caradoc, who was a learned monk born at Llancarfan. The very fact that he began with Cadwaladr is an indication that there already existed some historical records of the British kings prior to that period. Caradoc died in 1157 and his chronicle was added to in subsequent years by other writers.

*The Llancarfan Charters* (1056–1099).
Bishop Herewald of Llandaff judiciously enriched his See by extorting estates from the powerful. The following three charters are all witnessed by him as bishop, and therefore date from between 1056, when he was consecrated, and 1099, when he was suspended.

The first charter is for an estate given by Iestin filius Gurcant, the last Welsh ruler of Morgannwg, from 1081. The second charter is of Caratocus rex Morcannuc, his predessor as king, who fell in 1081. It is witnessed by Caratauc filius Riugallaun, who died in 1081, and by the above-mentioned Iestin filius Gurcant. The third charter is of the above Caratauc filius Riuguallaun, and approved by Roger fitz William fitz Osbern, Earl of Hereford and Lord of Gwent, offices held by Roger, the son of William Fitz Osbern, only from 1071 to 1075.

Lifris, the son of Bishop Herewald and the author of *Vita Cadoci*, was magister of Llancarfan between 1071 and 1075, as well as earlier and later, in circumstances to make compiling a *Life* of its founder, St. Cadoc, appropriate. The probability is therefore strong that *Vita Cadoci* was written between 1073 and 1086. It seems certain that it predates Geoffrey of Monmouth's *Historia* by nearly two generations.

*Liber Landavensis* (The Book of Llandaff, ca. 1150).

Alternatively named *Teilo's Book*, this is a chronicle dealing with the early history of the diocese of Llandaff in Cardiff, South Glamorgan. It is a 12th-century work, written in about 1150, and covers the previous 500 years. It is sometimes referred to as *The Ancient Register of the Cathedral Church of Llandaff* and is a substantial volume of 336 columns (two to a page), bound between oak boards.

It contains accounts of the lives of some of the early occupants of the See, records of Celtic Saints, Charters, legends etc. In particular, it contains a *Life of St. Teilo*, whose stated author is Galfrid, brother of Urban, Bishop of Llandaff. Also, it contains the *Life of Dubricius* and two of his successors, Teilo and Oudoceus. It provides a record of the donations made to the See of Llandaff down to the time of Bishop Herewaldus, who flourished in about 1104. The last entry is by Bishop Field, who added his name to the list of Bishops in 1619.

The manuscript of the *Liber Landavensis* passed from the bishopric of Llandaff into private hands in the 17th century and came into the possession of the family of Robert Davies of Llanerch in the late 17th century. It remained there until it was acquired by the National Library of Wales.

Historians have questioned the credibility of these charters and they have been described as "a clever forgery produced to support the claims of the diocese."

Of vital importance to our research was a genealogy contained in this work which is the pedigree of the kings of Gwent and Erging. Most of the kings mentioned in the Llandaff Charters belong to the dynasties of Gwent and Morgannwg, while the kings of the dynasties of Dyfed and Brycheiniog make occasional appearances.

Sir William Dugdale, in his *Monasticon Anglicanum* (vol. III, p. 190) observed that, in one instance in the grant of Lann Cinmarch, near Chepstow, occurs the name ARTHUR, so spelled, as the king of Gwent, son of Mouric, king of Morgannwg, and father of Morcant. Elsewhere in the manuscript, he is uniformly called Athruis and is contemporary with Comergwynus (Comereg), Bishop of Erging. Sir John Whitaker, in his *History of Manchester*, vol. II (1775), utilized the registers of donations to Llandaff Church in the days of the first three bishops—Saints Dyfrig, Teilo, and Oudoceus—and writes "Arthur was the Arth-uir, great man or sovereign of the proper Silures, and therefore the denominated king of Gwent, the Venta Silurum of the Romans and the British metropolis of the nation" (p. 34).

WELSH: Athrwys ap Meurig LATIN: Athruis filius Mouric

*Llyfr Du Caerfyrddin* (Black Book of Carmarthen, early 13th century).
This is the oldest existing manuscript written in the Welsh language. It dates from the beginning of the thirteenth century and the poetry which it contains was transcribed from older material by the black-robed monks of Carmarthen Priory. The manuscript contains ancient Welsh poems such as "Hoianau, Afall-enau," and "Enlynion y Beddau."

The "Hoianau" and "Afallenau" are poems which were composed to predict the future glory of the Britons and they were attributed to Myrddin Sylvester (Merlin), who was bard to Arthur. It is quite possible, however, that they are really the work of later bards who used Merlin's name in order to fire the hopes of their countrymen.

*The Black Book of Basingwerk.*
This manuscript was written at Basingwerk Abbey and contains *Ystoria Dared*, a version of *Historia Regum Britanniae,* and *Brut y Saeson* down to 1461. Founded by Ranulph II de Gernon, Earl of Chester, in 1131, the monastery of Basingwerk was originally affiliated with the Order of Savigny, but joined the Cistercians in 1147. Ranulph II also built the first Chartley Castle in ca.1153. In 1232, on the death of his grandson Ranulph de Blundeville, sixth Earl Palatine of Chester, Chartley Castle passed to William, sixth Earl Ferrers and fourth Earl of Derby, who had married Ranulph's sister, Agnes de Blundeville. In 1461, the castle passed to Sir Walter Devereux by his marriage to Anne, the heiress of William Ferrers, sixth Baron of Chartley. Sir Walter Devereux was created first Baron Ferrers of Chartley in the same year. With the connection of Ranulph II de Gernon with the monastery of Basingwerk and the association of the Mansel family with Chester, there may well have been a continuity of knowledge which was carried on down to Sir Walter Devereux, third Baron Ferrers of Chartley (see page 281). It is also interesting to note that Thomas ap Dafydd Pennant, the abbot of Basingwerk, was the brother of Sir Huw Pennant (Fl. 1465–1514), poet and priest, who translated a *Life of St. Ursula* from Latin into Welsh. In the Welsh *Life of St. Ursula*, contained in *The Book of Sir Huw Pennant* (Peniarth Ms 182, ca. 1514), reference is made to a time when Constantine, son of Maximus, reigned in Britain, Elen, daughter of Eudaf Hen of Arfon being his mother, and Owain Finddu and St. Peblig his brothers.

*Trioedd Ynys Prydain* (The Triads of the Island of Britain).
The text of *Trioedd Ynys Prydain* has been edited with a translation, introduction, and commentary by Dr. Rachel Bromwich. The first edition was published in 1961 and the second in 1978. Dr. Bromwich's translation is the definitive one and it is an invaluable work of reference for anyone interested in the early Welsh traditions relating to the Arthurian period. The *Welsh Triads* provided us with vital clues to the true locations of Arthur's principal court and the Battle of Llongborth. Thirteen of the surviving triads mention Arthur and another ten feature his court, while two relate to his wife, Gwenhwyfar.

A collection of *Welsh Triads* was compiled by the Welsh poet and antiquary Iolo Morganwg (Edward Williams, 1747–1826). His collection is contemporary with the compilation of folktales made by T. Crofton Croker and was first published as the *Third Series of Triads* in the *Myvyrian Archaeology of Wales* (1801). Iolo's collection predates by almost a century the better-known Celtic studies of Sir John Rhys, W. B. Yeats, and Lady Augusta Gregory.

*The Lives of the Saints.*
The fifth and sixth centuries are known collectively as the Age of the Saints. This was a period when the great pioneers of the Celtic Church flourished. Many of their names are familiar today due to the innumerable commemorative names of towns, villages, and church dedications in Wales, Cornwall, and Brittany. The ancient churches and chapels which bear the names of these Celtic saints owe their foundation, in the first instance, to the fact that the saint in question actually visited the site and established there a monastic community which became the forerunner of the modern church.

During our research into the matter of King Arthur, we found the *Lives* of the Celtic Saints indispensable, and the voluminous works of the prolific writer Sabine Baring-Gould were of particular interest. His *Lives of the Saints* are of considerable importance, for he collected all the genuinely early Breton manuscripts which had survived the fires of ca. 900 and 1789. He also drew heavily on the works of the Breton historians, Arthur de la Borderie and Albert Le Grand. *Les Vies des Saints de la Bretagne* were compiled by Albert Le Grand in 1636 (reprinted in Brest in 1837 and Quimper in 1901) and contain the *Life of St. Arthmael* taken from the *Breviaries of Léon* (1516) and those of Folgoet, and also the *Legendarium of Plouarzel.*

The *Vita Sancti Samsonis*, an early Life of St. Samson (490–565), is an extremely important source, for it was written by Bishop Tigernomail at the beginning of the seventh century and it is therefore contemporary with the events which it describes. The information afforded by this early *Life* is especially valuable, for Samson was the nephew of Athrwys, king of Gwent. It is of interest that St. Samson attended the third Council of Paris in 557 and signed his name among the bishops. This recorded fact positively dates St. Samson and also his uncle, Athrwys.

The *Life of St. Pol de Léon*, or Paul Aurelian (487–573), was written by Wrmonoc in 884, but was compiled from an earlier *Life*. It also contains very useful information owing to the fact that Paul Aurelian was a cousin of Athrwys (Arthmael = Arthur).

The *Life of St. Cadog* was compiled between 1095 and 1104 by Lifris or Lifricus, who was the son of Bishop Herewald. The *Life* describes an encounter between St. Cadoc and King Arthur on the banks of the River Usk and also mentions a grant of land, now known as Cadoxton-juxta-Neath, to St. Cadoc by a certain King Arthmael ca. 530. It should be noted that, according to the early Welsh genealogies, the king reigning over Glamorgan and Gwent at that time was none other than Athrwys ap Meurig ap Tewdrig, the all-powerful King Arthur of the Silures.

The part played by the Celtic saints in spreading Eastern lore, and much that was connected with the Arthurian romances, is often overlooked. It was they who helped to spread the Arthurian stories throughout the Celtic lands, linking Cornwall with Wales and Brittany. The importance of St. Paul Aurelian in this respect deserves further appreciation. There is in existence an early *Life* of this well-known Breton saint, written by a monk named Wrmonoc before the destruction of the Breton monasteries by the Northmen in the tenth century. When the monasteries around the coast of Brittany were in danger, some of their treasures were taken inland, and a *Life of St. Pol de Léon* was taken in this way to the great Abbey of Fleury, a few miles from Orleans. It is in the handwriting of the ninth century and is now preserved in the public library at Orleans.

What is very significant is the fact that Wrmonoc definitely states that he received information directly from people arriving in Brittany from over the seas, from Cornwall and South Wales in particular, and that St. Paul Aurelian took with him from this part of Wales a party of Twelve Presbyters to the Court of King Mark (Marcus Conomorus) in Cornwall. We have already referred to this king and his family as being among those playing a very important part in the Arthurian romances. Wrmonoc states that, after visiting the court of King Mark, Paul Aurelian and his presbyters proceeded to Brittany. In that country he settled at Kastell Paol (now St. Pol de Léon), from which his cult spread to many parts of northwestern Brittany. As the late Canon Gilbert Doble pointed out, the coincidences between Wrmonoc's statements and the information derived from Welsh, Cornish, and Breton topography and archaeology are most striking and cannot be coincidental. In the story of St. Pol de Léon, we have evidence of direct contact between early Christianity and some of the leading Arthurian characters. The subsequent transference of much of this background to Brittany is the basis on which the French Arthurian romances of the Middle Ages rest. It is important that we look to this area therefore for the origins of the historical Arthur.

*Llyma Enwau Hiliogaeth Brenhinoedd Morgannwg*, by Llywelyn Sion of Llangewydd.

This manuscript was compiled by the bard-antiquary Llywelyn Sion of Llangewydd (1540–1615). He was an usher in the Glamorgan court of great sessions, but made his living transcribing manuscripts for Glamorgan gentlemen (one of whom was Sir Edward Mansel of Margam). He had access to the libraries at St. Donat's, Raglan and Y Vann. In about 1575, he is mentioned under the name Llywelyn John by Sir Edward Mansel in his *History of the Norman Conquest of Glamorgan* as a learned and diligent collector of Welsh manuscripts. The *Iolo Manuscripts* contain a Welsh document, with English translation, titled *Llyma Emwau Hiliogaeth Brenhinoedd Morgannwg*, which was copied by Iolo Morganwg (Edward Williams) from a manuscript of Llywelyn Sion of Llangewydd. It was evidently derived from the same source as a manuscript by Sir Edward Mansel titled *Another account of the coming of the Normans in a shorter story than before*. In this manuscript is the significant statement: "Now the country of Glamorgan came to be first a royal lordship from one Morgan, a prince who lived at the time of King Arthur and was his son as some would have it" (p. 23).

An antiquary of the 17th century who claimed to have a copy of the original manuscript was John Lewis (1548–1616), who wrote *The History of Great Britain 'til the Death of Cadwaladr*, which was edited by the genealogist Hugh Thomas (1673–1720) and finally published in 1729.

Sir Edward Mansel, Llywelyn Sion of Llangewydd, and John Lewis were all contemporaries and had access to the same manuscript or at least a copy of it. The original may well have been kept in the famous library at St. Donat's or that at Raglan Castle. This invaluable collection of books and manuscripts was tragically destroyed during the Civil War.

### The Monasticon Anglicanum.

*The Monasticon Anglicanum*, a collection of records relating to monastic foundations, was compiled by Sir William Dugdale in collaboration with Roger Dodsworth. It was subsequently published under Dugdale's name in three separate volumes in 1655, 1661, and 1673. Sir William Dugdale apparently used as his source the register of donations to Llandaff Church in the days of the first three bishops—Saints, Dyfrig, Teilo, and Oudoceus.

### The Mabinogion.

Lady Charlotte Guest used the title the *Mabinogion* for her translation (between 1838 and 1848) of eleven medieval Welsh tales extracted from a transcript of the *Red Book of Hergest*, contained in the library of Jesus College, Cambridge.

The definitive translation of the *Mabinogion* by Gwyn and Thomas Jones appeared in 1948, the centenary year of the completion of the first translation by Lady Charlotte Guest. Mabinogion is a word derived from Mabinog, which was a term belonging to the bardic system. A mabinog was a sort of literary apprentice, a young man who was receiving instruction from a qualified bard. The lowest description of a mabinog was one who had not acquired the art of making verse.

Arthur's final victory is recounted in a tale entitled "The Dream of Rhonabwy," in which his encampment is described as being on an island in the River Severn, where he is accompanied by Bishop Bedwin. It is surely ore than just a coincidence that Gildas locates Mons Badonicus near to the mouth of the Severn and that the Bedwin Sands are also there. Both "Culhwch and Olwen" and "The Dream of Rhonabwy" feature Osla Gyllellfawr ("of the Great Knife"), who is portrayed as Arthur's principal enemy at Caer Badon.

### Northern Poetry.

Following the departure of King Arthur, the sixth-century bard Taliesin traveled north to join the court of Urien Rheged. Several poems attributed to him are of interest. They feature Urien and his son Owen in battles with the Picts and the

Saxons. In particular, Taliesin praised Urien and Owen for their good hospitality and skill in war. Urien was victorious at Argoed, Gwen Ystrad, and other battles.

Contemporary with Taliesin was the bard Aneurin, to whom is attributed the oldest poem in the Welsh language. It is called "Y Gododin" and is a description of a gruesome battle fought in 570 at a place called Catraeth, where the Cymry confederacy suffered a disastrous defeat. This remarkable epic poem has survived in a 13th-century manuscript. Aneurin was a son of Caw, the Lord of Cawm Cawlwyd in North Britain. His brother was Gildas, another important sixth-century writer.

"Y Gododin" is a heroic song of defeat which tells us a great deal about the British warriors of the sixth century. It is named after an area on the north side of the Firth of Forth. Here the tribe of the Votadini, whose name became corrupted to Gododin, had their stronghold, and the territory became known as Manau Guotodin (roughly Midlothian). It was called Manau Guotodin to distinguish it from Ynys Manau (The Isle of Man or Monnau). In the poem, Aneurin compares some of the warriors with past heroes. For example, he speaks of Eithinyn whose "courage was enchanted like Elfin." Referring to Gwawrddur, he tells us that "he glutted black ravens on the rampart of the stronghold, though he was no Arthur." This suggests that they were fighting at a hill-fort and the reference to Arthur is, in fact, the oldest one known. It makes it appear that the writer considered it to be quite obvious who Arthur was—for surely everyone had heard of him.

Aneurin's epic poem tells us that a cavalry force was assembled by Mynyddawg, Lord of Din Eiddyn or Ysgor Eiddyn, which is the area occupied by the Edinburgh of today. The warriors were young noblemen who had come to the court of Mynyddawg to learn the skills of war and they were known as the Guard of Gododin. Many of them had traveled from Gwynedd, Elfed, and South Wales to be there. Their purpose was to attack the "men of Lloegr," recapture a place known as Catraeth, and stop the northern advance of the Saxons. The name Catraeth is derived from cad and traeth—the Battle Strand—and it was more than likely the former Roman Station of Cataractornium, which stood near a road junction now called Scotch Corner (SE 220990). Today, the name has become Catterick, which is located in North Yorkshire.

It is relevant that Cunedda Wledig started out from Manau Guotodin 150 years earlier to free Wales from the Goidels (Irish). The battle of Gododin also appears to be an imitation of one of Arthur's cavalry exploits.

We are told by Aneurin that the young men feasted for a year, after which the three hundred and sixty-three "golden-torqued warriors" set off to attack Catraeth. The detailed descriptions tell us much about their dress and weapons, for we learn that they were clad in mantles and tunics of silk, with torques around their necks, brooches in their hair, and adorned with amber beads. These men were Christians who went to church before setting off to battle. They carried shields (broad and round), spears, and swords. Mounted on horses, they rode south to Catraeth:

> Speedy steeds and dark armour and shields
> Spear shafts held high and spear points sharp-edged
> And glittering coats-of-mail and swords.

On the eve of the battle, the young warriors drank too freely of mead and then, incapacitated and hopelessly outnumbered, they fought for a week. Although they fought with desperate valor, only three out of the three hundred and sixty-three chieftains who had fought at the head of their clans survived. Aneurin was one of these fortunate three.

> None from Catraeth's vale return
> Save Aeron brave and Conan strong,
> Bursting through the bloody throng:
> And I the meanest of them all,
> That live to weep and sing their fall.

Aneurin was taken prisoner, loaded with chains, and flung into a dungeon from which he was subsequently released by Ceneu, a son of Llywarch Hen.

> From the power of the sword, (noble the succour)
> From the cruel prison house of death he released me
> From the place of death, from the cheerless region
> He, Cenau, son of Llywarch, magnanimous and brave.

It would seem that Aneurin then went south and sought refuge at the college of St. Cadoc at Llancarfan in South Glamorgan. Here, according to the *Welsh Triads*, Aneurin the Bard was treacherously slain by Eiddyn ap Einygan, who dealt him on the head one of *"the three atrocious axe-strokes of the Isle of Britain."*

The defeat at Catraeth was a blow from which the Welsh did not recover until years later when they rallied once more for a desperate fight under the command of Cadwallon. The scattered Britons of the north united their forces to maintain an obstinate struggle to defend the areas which, in later times, became the counties of Cumberland, Westmorland, Yorkshire, Lancashire, and Cheshire. It was then that they began to call each other "Kymry" (comrades or fellow countrymen) and this name has been used ever since to designate Welshmen collectively.

*Llywarch Hen* ("the Aged").
Another important bard was Llywarch Hen, who was a prince of Argoed and a cousin of Urien Rheged. A fighting man himself, he could handle the long spear with as much vigor and skill as he could write heroic verse. His father, Elidyr Lydonwyn was fourth in descent from Coel and the family lived in an area known as Argoed, which is part of the old county of Cumberland, bordered by

the great forest of Celyddon or Caledonia. Argoed is a Welsh word meaning "on or above the wood."

Llywarch probably spent a part of his early life in the court of King Arthur, where he was a respected bard. His poetry spans a considerable period and indicates that he was a contemporary of both Arthur and Cadwallon. Surprisingly, he outlived them both.

One of his poems tells of his sons fighting on the Llawen when "Arthur did not retreat." Llawen was a river in northern Britain—probably the Leven. Llywarch Hen was the father of twenty-four sons who were all military chieftains entitled to wear the golden torque. This ornament was worn around the neck as a sign of nobility and only princes and noble dames were entitled to wear it. The old bards frequently alluded to the custom of wearing this necklet of gold and we learn from Dio Cassius that such an ornament was worn by Queen Boadicea. Examples of gold torques have been discovered from time to time in different parts of Wales and they are worth a considerable amount of money. Llywarch Hen wrote:

> Four and twenty sons I had
> Wearing the golden wreath,
> Leaders of armies.

Most of his sons died defending their native land under the leadership of Urien Rheged, but Llywarch mentions at least four sons who were buried in North Wales:

> Gwell, Sawyl, Llyngedwy and Cynlliug who died at Rhiw Felin, Llangollen; Ammarch and Llug met their death in the wars of Cynyddylan.

After the battle of Gododin in 570, Llywarch Hen had to seek asylum further south and he traveled to Pengwern (near Shrewsbury), where he was warmly received by Cynddylan who ruled that area. The Princes of Powys had their seat in an ancient fortress here before the menace of the advancing Saxons drove them further west to Mathrafal.

When the Court of Cynddylan was attacked and destroyed by the Saxons, Llywarch later described the event in a poem lamenting the death of Cynddylan.

> The hall of Cynddylan is silent tonight
> After having lost its Lord:
> Great God of mercy, what shall I do?

> The hall of Cynddylan, how gloomy seems its roof!
> Since the Loegrins have destroyed
> Cynddylan and Elvon of Powys.

Cynddylan, King of Powys, was killed in this battle and Powys lost its fertile lands in the Severn Valley to the Angle kingdom of Mercia.

In the same poem, Llywarch Hen reveals that Cynddylan was buried at Bassa, which may possibly be identified with Basschurch in Shropshire and could also be the site of the Arthurian Battle of Bassas, mentioned by Nennius.

> The churches of Bassa are near tonight
> To the heir of Cyndrwyn
> The grave house of fair Cynddylan.

Llywarch Hen makes an interesting reference to the Roman fort of Wroxeter in this elegy to Cynddylan:

> Have I not gazed on the lofty city of Wrecon
> In the verdant valley of Frewer
> With grief for the destruction of my social friends.

This mention of Wrecon seems to be a reference to the Roman fort of Uriconium, which became known as Wroxeter. Alternatively, it may refer to the Wrekin, which was also an occupied hill-fortress during this period. His grief for "the destruction of my social friends" is probably a reference to the death of some of his children, who died in the massacre at the hands of the Saxons.

There is a tradition that Llywarch Hen spent his last days near Bala in North Wales and a secluded spot there still bears the name of Pabell Llywarch Hen—"Old Llywarch's Cot." Years ago, it was claimed that nearby, in the parish church of Llanvor, there was a stone with an inscription on it commemorating Llywarch, but sadly it is no longer in evidence. Another tradition claims that he died in the middle of the seventh century at the incredible age of one hundred and fifty years, (certainly living up to his epithet—Hen, "the Aged"), having outlived his children and his friends. The elegy on Cadwallon attributed to Llywarch Hen would certainly require him to have lived to this remarkable age in order to have written it!

Leland's *Itinerary.*
John Leland was librarian, chaplain, and later antiquary to Henry VIII. In 1536, the king commissioned him to travel through England and Wales with the purpose of making inquiries into the antiquities of the two countries. He finished his labors in 1542 and returned to London with the extensive records of his researches. He began writing up his work from his extensive notes in 1545. However, five weeks later he was certified insane and he died in 1552, with his work far from finished. His notes were taken over by the Bodleian Library at Oxford and, in 1710, his *Itinerary* was finally published under the editorship of Thomas Hearne.

•  •  •

We cannot conclude our remarks without a few words on the obligations of our literature and that of all Western Europe to a writer whom it has been greatly the fashion to abuse—Geoffrey of Monmouth. We leave entirely out of question the truth or falsehood of his narrative. The merit of Geoffrey consists in having collected a body of legends highly susceptible of poetic embellishment, which, without his intervention, might have utterly perished, and interwoven them in a narrative calculated to exercise a wonderful influence on national feelings and national literature.

Rev. Richard Garnett, 1840

# appendix ii

## Chronology: Events in the Life of King Arthur

King Arthur, as a war-leader and defender of his country, was undoubtedly the right man in the right place at the right time. When he departed from the scene, he must have been sorely missed. From that time, the subsequent history of the Britons was a succession of defeats, until finally all that remained in their possession was the land that we know today as Wales.

| | |
|---|---|
| 482 | Birth of Arthur at Boverton in South Glamorgan. |
| 497 | Ambrosius (Emrys Wledig) nominates Arthur as his successor and appoints his brother Uthyr and his nephew Geraint Llyngesog ("the Fleet Owner") as Pendragons to head the British forces against the Saxons. The death of Ambrosius coincides with the appearance of a comet which is described by Geoffrey of Monmouth. Arthur is crowned leader of the Britons at Caer Vudei "the Camp in the Wood," by St. Dyfrig (Dubricius). Geoffrey of Monmouth identifies this place with Silchester but it is, in fact, Woodchester in Gloucestershire, where, significantly, Ambrosius had his headquarters. |
| 501 | A war-band of Jutes from Kent and Gewissei from southeast Hampshire land at Portsmouth Harbor and pillage Portus Adurni (Portchester). |
| 508 | The Gewissei and their Jutish allies make a piratical raid up the Severn Sea, but their advance is checked by the western Britons led by Geraint Llyngesog. In the Battle of Llongborth (War-ship port), Geraint is slain. He is buried at Merthyr Gerein (Martyrium of Geraint) on the Gwent shore of the Severn Estuary. |

## CHRONOLOGY: EVENTS IN THE LIFE OF KING ARTHUR

| | |
|---|---|
| 510 | Arthur gives assistance to his kinsman Riwal Mawr, king of Armorican Domnonia (509–524) against an invasion of the Visigoths. The united armies of Riwal and Arthur succeed in repelling a seaborne attack by the Visigoths at Baden, situated southwest of Vannes. The Venetians of Vannes appoint Arthur (Arthmael) as their Dux. Armel (Arzel) is Breton for Arth (Arz) mael, meaning "Bear Prince." Arzon and the Ille de Arz, south of Vannes, are both named after a mighty warrior prince called Arzur, who utilized a fortress in the Sarzeau Forest, near to which stands St. Gildas's monastery of Rhuys. There are dedications to St. Armel at Ploermel and St. Armel, situated west and south of Vannes respectively and near to the site of Arthur's victory over the Visigoths. |
| 512 | Uthyr Pendragon comes out of retirement to fight a battle against the Teutonic alliance and avenge the death of his nephew Geraint at the Battle of Llongborth. The *Saxon Chronicle* tells us that a British Pendragon is killed at Dragon Hill (near Uffington) with five thousand of his men. Uthyr Pendragon is buried at Caer Caradoc in Mid Glamorgan. |
| | Arthur takes over as battle commander and fights a series of twelve important battles. Five of them are fought to subjugate the settlements of the Middle and East Angles. Another is fought against the northern Angles followed by one against the Picts. The remaining five battles are fought in southwest Britain against the Gewissei and their allies. |
| 517 | The final battle is fought at Mount Badon, just outside Bath, and Arthur's decisive victory results in a fifty-year period of peace for the Britons which enables them to become a united nation. But sadly, on Arthur's abdication in 537, the unity quickly disintegrates. |
| 522 | St. Dubricius (Dyfrig), Archbishop of Wales, resigns his See and retires to Bardsey Island. |
| 524 | Riwal Mawr, the nephew of Arthur dies. He is reputed to be buried at Llanilltyd Fawr (Llantwit Major) in South Glamorgan. |
| 530 | Count Gwythyr, (Victor) the father of Gwenhwyfar (Guinevere), dies and she inherits his estates. Her husband, Arthur, thus gains control of the principality of Léon in Armorica (Brittany). Léon is absorbed into the Armorican kingdom of Domnonia under the joint rule of Arthur and Riwal Mawr's son and successor, Deroch (King of Armorican Domnonia 524–535). |

## CHRONOLOGY: EVENTS IN THE LIFE OF KING ARTHUR

| | |
|---|---|
| 533 | Deroch requests help against an invasion of the Visigoths, and Arthur, as a result, is away from his own kingdom for four years. Medraut seizes Arthur's realm and Queen. |
| 537 | News of the uprising reaches Arthur, who has now moved on to Ireland to defeat Llwch Llawinawg. He returns with all that survives of his army. He lands at the little harbor (now called Cadlan—"Place of Battle") on the Lleyn Peninsula, where the family of Medraut have territory. During the ensuing Battle of Camlan, Medraut is slain and Arthur is critically injured. He is taken to Ynys Afallach (Bardsey Island) to have his wounds tended. After recovering from his injuries, he abdicates, handing over his crown to Constantine, the son of Cadwy. Following the fall of Arthur, the great confederacy of British kingdoms, which has been so effective in keeping the Saxon invaders at bay, disintegrates into its component parts. |
| 544 | St. David dies, aged 82, in his monastery at Mynyw (Menevia), where the impressive Cathedral of St. David now stands. His bones are kept in a casket. |
| 546 | Death of St. Dubricius (Dyfrig) in retirement on Bardsey Island (Isle of Avalon). |
| 547 | Maelgwyn Gwynedd dies of the bubonic plague. |
| 549 | Marcus Conomorus (King Mark), who has by now settled in Armorica, assassinates Jonas, the son of Deroch. In order to obtain the regency, Conomorus marries Jonas's widow, and Judwal, the rightful heir, is forced to flee for his life to the court of the Frankish King Childebert in Paris. |
| 554 | Arthur quarrels with the usurper Conomorus and goes to Paris, where he does his best to persuade Childebert to displace Conomorus and restore Judwal. Arthur's nephew Samson arrives and together they manage to break down Childebert's opposition. They then return to Armorica to organize an insurrection on behalf of Judwal. |
| 555 | The combined forces of Samson, Judwal, and Arthur, together with reinforcements provided by King Childebert, meet the forces of Conomorus near Brank Aleg at the foot of Montagnes d'Aree. They fight three fierce battles over three days. Finally, Judwal runs the usurper through with a javelin. Conomorus falls wounded from his horse and is trampled to death in the press of the charge. |

## CHRONOLOGY: EVENTS IN THE LIFE OF KING ARTHUR

| | |
|---|---|
| 555 | Judwal, now King of Armorican Domnonia, rewards Arthur for his services by granting him land on the River Seiche, where today stands the village of St. Armel des Boschaux. Here he establishes a monastery. It is significant that the whole region of the Ille et Villaine, which was granted to St. Armel (Arthur) by Judwal for services rendered, is the area in Brittany most associated with the legends of King Arthur and his Knights of the Round Table and that here their memory still lingers. |
| 562 | Death of Arthur (St. Armel) at St. Armel des Boschaux, where he is buried in a stone sarcophagus. He lived to be 80 years of age. The true identity of this highly venerated soldier-saint from Glamorgan was previously unknown to the Bretons. At last, with the publication of this book, the truth has finally been revealed! |
| 565 | During the next eleven years, three of King Arthur's most important contemporaries die and it is significant that they also spent their final years in Armorica.<br><br>Death of St. Samson, the nephew of Arthur, at his monastery in Dol, Armorica, where his shrine used to attract large numbers of pilgrims. |
| 570 | Death of St. Gildas, aged 94, at St. Gildas du Rhuys, where his tomb and bones can be seen in a casket. |
| 573 | Death of St. Paul Aurelian, (a contemporary of Arthur who was also born at Boverton in South Glamorgan) at his monastery, St. Pol de Léon in Armorica. He was 86. |

# Appendix III

## Why has the Identity of King Arthur not been Revealed Before?

The identification of Arthmael (Athrwys ap Meurig ap Tewdrig) as the King Arthur of legend and history, which we have put forward in this book, seems amazingly obvious, and the majority of readers should by now be wondering why historians have not come to the same conclusion before. In actual fact, the identification was made by other writers in the 18th and 19th centuries and in 1986 by the authors B. Blackett and A. Wilson, in their book *Artorius Rex Discovered*. However, their findings have been rejected by the established academics, who faithfully continue to plough the same old furrow and repeatedly claim that such an identification is not correct.

At this point, let us turn to *The Cambrian Plutarch* (pp. 1–3), written in 1834 by John H. Parry, who sums up the problems facing the Arthurian sleuth and also reveals the true identity of the renowned King Arthur.

> To rescue truth from the embraces of fiction, and to erect on the ruins of fable the fair edifice of genuine history, must be, at all times, a work of no little hazard. The visions of childhood are not easily dissipated; for, whatever may be the influence of a maturer experience, it is not without reluctance that the mind emancipates itself from the spell of its former illusions.
>
> There can be no case more strongly illustrative of the justice of these observations than the history of the renowned Arthur; enveloped, as it has been, in the splendid disguises of chivalry, and in the extravagant decorations of romantic or mythological lore. To strip our hero of these delusive ornaments, and to present him to the world in his real character—not as the triumphant invader of distant countries—not as the conqueror of giants and kingdoms—not as the possessor of every human excellence, and even of supernatural powers, but merely as a warrior, distinguished indeed by his valour and his successes, but not otherwise exalted above his contemporaries—is an undertaking of no common risk.
>
> Yet at last we may say that "when all fictions" in the life of Arthur are removed, and when these incidents only are retained, which the sober criticism of history sanctions with its approbation, a fame, simple enough

to interest the judicious and to perpetuate his honourable memory, will still continue to bloom.

Arthur was the son of Meurig ap Tewdrig, a prince of the Silurian Britons at the commencement of the sixth century, and who is, in all probability, Uthyr or Uther of legendary celebrity.[1]

An earlier book, which makes the same identification, is Lewis's *Dictionary of Wales*, published in 1759:

Meurig ap Tewdrig, a man of great valour and wisdom, was the father of that Arthur who is now regarded by Welsh writers as that hero whose exploits form so distinguished a feature of the British Annals and who succeeded Meurig in his dominion.[2]

In 1801, William Coxe published his *Coxe's Tours of Monmouthshire*, in which he observed:

A church is said to have been erected on its present site (Mathern) by Meurig, or Maurice, who is supposed to be the father of the Arthur so renowned in British history.[3]

Authorities Cited for the Identification of Athrwys, King of Gwent, with King Arthur.

1073–1086:  Lifris: *Vita Cadoci* [Life of St. Cadog].
            The Llancarfan Charters.
1120–1140:  The Registers of Donations to Llandaff Church in the day of the first three bishops—St. Dyfrig (c. 500–512), St. Teilo (c. 512–563), and St. Euddogwy (c. 563–570).
15th century: Dafydd Ddu ("Black David"), Abbot of Neath Abbey, *Y Cwta Cyfarwydd o Morgannwg* [Short Guide to Glamorgan).
            The register of Neath Abbey, containing an early history of Morgannwg.
            The register of Brecon Priory, containing an early history of Brecon.
1502–1555:  Sir John Price of Brecon, *Historia Britannicae Defensio* (1573), pp. 120–123.
1520–1565:  Lewys Morgannwg (Llywelyn ap Rhisiart) in his elegy to St. Illtyd.

---

[1]John H. Parry, *The Cambrian Plutarch* (London: W. Simpkin and R. Marshall, 1834), pp. 1–3.
[2]*The Cambrian Plutarch*, pp. 1–3.
[3]William Coxe, *An Historical Tour of Monmouthshire*, 1801 (Reprint: T. Cadell Juriar and W. Davies, eds. Cardiff, Wales: Merton Press, 1995), vol. I, p. 10.

1572:     Sir Edward Stradling of St. Donat's Castle (1529–1609), *The Winning of the Lordship of Glamorgan Out of the Welshmen's Hands.*

1572–1591:     Llywelyn Sion of Llangewydd (1540–1615), *Llyma Enwau a Hiliogaeth Brenhinoedd Morgannwg* ["These be the Names and Genealogies of the Kings of Glamorgan"], p. 45.

1591:     Sir Edward Mansel of Margam (d. 1595), *The Winning of Glamorgan: Another Account of the Coming in of the Normans in a Shorter Story than Before,* p. 23.

1606:     Thomas ap John (d. 1616), *The History of Brecon* (Harleian MS 6108).

1673:     Sir William Dugdale, *Monasticon Anglicanum,* vol. III, p. 190.

1729:     The Rev. Dr. David Nicholl, *The Antiquities of Llantwit Major,* pp. 45–53.

1747:     Thomas Carte, *A General History of England,* vol. 1, Book III, p. 202.

1759:     Lewis' *Dictionary of Wales.*

1775:     The Rev. John Whitaker, *The History of Manchester,* vol. 2, p. 34.

1777:     The Rev. N. Owen, *Yr Hynafion Cymraeg.*

1796:     David Williams, *The History of Monmouthshire,* p. 75.

1801:     William Coxe, *An Historical Tour of Monmouthshire.*

1803:     William Owen Pughe, *The Cambrian Biography,* p. 14.

1804:     John Duncumbe, *Collections towards the History and Antiquities of the County of Herefordshire,* vol. 1, page 31.

1807:     Sharon Turner, *The History of the Anglo Saxons,* vol. 1, pp. 101–102.

1819:     John Hughes, *Horae Britannicae,* vol. 2, pp. 193–195.

1824:     John H. Parry, *The Cambrian Plutarch,* p. 3.

1829:     Joseph Ritson, *The Life of King Arthur from Ancient Historians and Authentic Documents,* p. 88.

1836:     Rice Rees, *An Essay on the Welsh Saints,* pp. 185–186.

1858:     Thomas Bulfinch, *The Age of Chivalry,* p. 394.

1860:     Joseph Stephenson, in his translation of William of Malmesbury's, *History of the Kings of England,* p. 11.

1870:     Ebenezer Cobham Brewer, *The Dictionary of Phrase and Fable,* p. 66.

1891:     Robert Owen, *The Kymry, their Origin, History and International Relations.*

1911:     Owen "Morien" Morgan, *A History of Wales,* p. 118.

Modern day historians, however, have refused to recognize Athrwys, the son of Meurig, as the King Arthur of legend and history for, according to their interpretation of the early Welsh genealogies, he lived in the wrong century.

It became apparent to us that a serious error had been made by one or several respected academics, which has resulted in the true identity of King

Arthur being rejected. It is not our intention to deride the work of these out-standing scholars, but we wish to demonstrate that some serious mistakes have been made and, until these have been recognized, the truth of the matter will continue to be ignored.

Professor Hector Munro Chadwick constructed his genealogy of the dy-nasty of Gwent by basing it upon the *Bonedd y Saint* (Pedigrees of the Saints), and the *Liber Landavensis*, the ancient register of the Cathedral Church of Llandaff in Cardiff. In doing so, he misplaced Meurig ap Tewdrig, king of Glamorgan and Gwent. This created an anomaly which post-dated his son Athrwys by more than a hundred years, so disassociating him from the events of the sixth century when the real King Arthur flourished. See *Studies in Early British History* (Cambridge: Cambridge University Press, 1954), p. 51.

The situation was further confused by the late John Morris, who had Athrwys's son Morgan Mwynfawr ("the Courteous"), after whom Morgannwg (later Glamorgan) is named, fighting at a second Battle of Mount Badon in 665. However, the same author states that the most important emigrant leader of the sixth century was probably Arthmael, but that little is known of him. Arthmael is an alternative name for Arthwyr (both being titles: Arthmael = the Bear Prince; Arthwyr = the Bear Exalted). Thus, without realizing it, John Morris re-ferred to the real King Arthur.

The *Book of Llandaff* contains a genealogy which is of vital importance. It is the pedigree of the kings of Gwent and Erging, and it is of great significance that most of the kings mentioned in the Llandaff Charters belong to this dynasty.

Dr. Wendy Davies, *The Llandaff Charters* (The National Library of Wales, Aberystwyth, 1979, p.75), suggests the approximate dates for the Floruit of Peibio, king of Erging, as ca. 555–585, and, working on this compu-tation, further suggests the dates for Athrwys, son of Meurig, as ca. 625–655. This is virtually impossible, for Peibio married a daughter of the Romano-British Emperor Custennin Fendigaid (Constantine "the Blessed"), who reigned from 433 to 443, and Peibio was the grandfather of St. Dyfrig (Dubricius), who died in 546. The correct dating for the Floruit of Peibio should therefore be 100 years earlier, i.e. 455–485. Working on this basis, Athrwys (Arthur) flourished ca. 525–555, which is about right when one considers that St. Arth-mael (the "Bear Prince") was born in 482 and died in 562.

According to Dr. Davies (pp. 75–76), the occurrence of St. Dyfrig in wit-ness lists, though not in all of Peibio's charters, might just suggest dates in the mid-sixth century for the two kings of Erging named Erb and Pcibio. This is also impossible, for these two kings were the great-grandfather and grandfather of St. Dyfrig and therefore flourished in the mid-fifth century.

Dr. Davies also states that there is no straightforward father-son progres-sion of kings in the early part of this series, but this is definitely not the case. There is a natural continuity in Athrwys ap Meurig ap Tewdrig, but it must be remembered that it was the custom in those days for a king to retire to a monastery when his fighting days were over. This was certainly the case as far as Tewdrig and Meurig were concerned, and Athrwys may well have retired to his monastery in Brittany, leaving his son Morgan to rule in his stead.

It is intimated by Dr. Davies that Meurig's reign was exceptionally long and that his son Athrwys died rather early in his reign. Meurig may have lived a long time, but his son Athrwys did not die young. He was engaged in Brittany while Caradog Freichfras ruled Gwent during Meurig's semi-retirement. Meurig, however was still the nominal king of Gwent and he was still making grants. Judging by the continuity of the grants in the *Book of Llandaff*, Meurig was succeeded by his grandson, Morgan. This is quite probable, for Athrwys would not have been able to return from Brittany to reclaim his patrimony because, in the words of Alfred Lord Tennyson, the old order had changed.

Furthermore, Dr. Davies mentions an intrusive king of Erging named Gwrfoddw, who does not belong to the main dynasty but who fights against the Saxons. According to the evidence of the Llandaff charters, Meurig, the father of Athrwys, married Onbrawst, the daughter of Gwrgant Mawr ("the Great"), king of Erging. This marriage brought about the union of the kingdoms of Gwent and Erging. According to the Rev. Arthur Wade-Evans, Gwrfoddw was none other than Gwyndaf Hen ("the Aged"), the son-in-law of Meurig. Gwyndaf was the son of Emyr Llydaw ("the Armorican") and he married Meurig's daughter Gwenonwy, thus succeeding to the Kingdom of Erging.

Another son of Emyr Llydaw was Amwn Ddu (Annun "the Black") and he married Anna, the daughter of Meurig ap Tewdrig. Their son was none other than St. Samson, Bishop of Dol, who was consecrated bishop by St. Dyfrig in 521. He attended the third Council of Paris in 557, and died in 565. He was the nephew of Athrwys ap Meurig. Thus Athrwys may be positively dated.

Dr. Davies goes on to suggest that the reign of Iddon II, king of Gwent, was ca. 595–600. This computation is also incorrect, for Iddon II was a contemporary of St. Teilo, who succeeded St. Dyfrig as Bishop of Llandaff before the death of the latter in 546 (bearing in mind that St. Dyfrig spent a number of years in retirement on Bardsey Island before his death). Iddon II was the son of Ynyr II and the grandson of Caradog Freichfras ("of the Strong Arm"). Thus, Iddon was the first cousin of Medraut ap Cawrdaf ap Caradog Freichfras, who was killed at the Battle of Camlan in 537.

It would appear that Dr. Davies has drawn heavily on the works of the genealogist P. C. Bartrum (see *Early Welsh Genealogical Tracts*, Cardiff: University of Wales Press, 1966), who was in turn confused by Professor Hector Munro Chadwick. In his genealogy of the Dynasty of Gwent taken from *The Foundation of the Early British Kingdoms*, contained in *Studies in Early British History* (Cambridge University Press, 1954, p. 51), Professor Chadwick confounds two kings of Gwent named Ynyr. As a result, he makes the second instead of the first Ynyr the husband of Madryn, the daughter of Gwrthefyr Fendigaid (Vortimer "the Blessed") and grand-daughter of Gwrtheyrn Gwrtheneu (Vortigern "the Thin"), thus back-dating his father, Caradog Freichfras, into the fifth century. Ynyr I was the son of Dyfnwal Hen ("the Aged") and he was the father of Caradog I and Iddon I of Gwent. Ynyr II was the son of Caradog II Freichfras and he was the father of Iddon II.

The correct pedigree of Dyfnwal Hen, the father of Ynyr I of Gwent, is given in *Harleian Genealogy No. 5* as Ednuyed ap Antoni and corresponds with Eidinet (Eidniuet) map Anthun of *Harleian Genealogy No. 4* and Edneuet map Dunawt of *Jesus College Genealogy No. 19*. However, most later versions of the pedigree of Dyfnwal Hen incorrectly make him son of Ednyfed ap Macsen Wledig (Maximus "the Imperator"). The correct lineage of Dyfnwal Hen should therefore read:

> Macsen Wledig (Maximus "the Imperator")
> Anhun Dunawd (Antonius Donatus)
> Ednyfed
> Dyfnwal Hen ("the Aged")

It also becomes apparent from the *Bonedd y Saint Pedigrees 44 and 45* that Dyfnwal Hen established his son Ynyr I as King of Gwent Is Coed (Gwent below the Wood). Ynyr I married Madryn, the daughter of Gwrthefyr Fendigaid (Vortimer "the Blessed"), and they had as sons Caradog I, Iddon I of Gwent, and Ceidio. This important dynasty was extended thus:

> Dyfnwal Hen ("the Aged")
> Ynyr I of Gwent, who married Madryn,
>     the daughter of Gwrthefyr Fendigaid
> Caradog I and Iddon I of Gwent

Professor Chadwick further confuses the issue by taking the lineage of the kings of Erging and Gwent from the *Book of Llandaff* and, by wrongly making Erb ap Erbig ap Meurig the great-grandson of Caradog II Freichfras, projects the pedigree of the kings of Erging forward by 100 years into the next century. The ultimate result of this confusion is the post-dating of Athrwys ap Meurig by over a hundred years, thus disassociating him completely from Arthur and his contemporaries. The pedigree taken from the *Book of Llandaff* is as follows:

> Erb
> Pebiaw
> Cynfyn
> Gwrgant Mawr ("the Great")
> Onbrawst
> Athrwys
> Morgan

Caradog Freichfras belongs to the *Bonedd y Saint Pedigree 51* and not the *Jesus College Pedigree 9,* to which Erb ap Erbig ap Meurig belongs.

> Meurig
> Erbig
> Erb

The Caradog who was the father of Meurig may well be the same Caradog who was the father of Eudaf Hen (Octavius "the Aged") and belongs to the *Jesus*

*College Pedigree 4*. It should be remembered that Eudaf Hen and his family were long associated with the kingdom of Erging. The revised lineage should therefore read:

> Caradog
> Meurig
> Erbig
> Erb
> Pebiaw
> Cynfyn
> Gwrgant Mawr ("the Great")
> Onbrawst = Meurig ap Tewdrig
> Athrwys
> Morgan

Both H. M. Chadwick and P. C. Bartrum have confused two Tewdrigs and two Meurigs. P. C. Bartrum (notes on p. 132 in *Early Welsh Genealogical Tracts*), is quite correct when he states that Tewdrig ap Teithfallt, king of Garth Madryn, was the father of Marchell, the mother of Brychan Brycheiniog (*De Situ Brecheniauc Pedigree 10* ), but completely wrong in his assumption that Tewdrig ap Llywarch ap Nynniaw ap Erb (*Jesus College Pedigree 9*) was the martyr of Merthyr Tewdrig (Mathern). H. M. Chadwick further confuses the issue by making Nynniaw's father, Erb, son of Erbig, son of Meurig, son of Caradog Freichfras. It is because of H. M. Chadwick's miscalculation and P. C. Bartrum's misidentification that Dr. Wendy Davies has placed Athrwys ap Meurig ap Tewdrig in the seventh instead of the sixth century.

*Jesus College Pedigree 9*.
> Erbig
> Erb
> Nynniaw
> Llywarch
> Tewdrig
> Meurig

*De Situ Brecheniauc Pedigree 10*.
> Anhun Dunawd (Antonius Donatus)
> Teudfal (Tathal)
> Teuder (Teithrin)
> Teudfall (Teithfallt)
> Teuderic (Tewdrig)
> Marchell
> Brachan (Brychan)

The situation regarding the lineage of Athrwys ap Meurig ap Tewdrig may be rectified by adopting the *De Situ Brecheniauc Genealogy No. 10* thus:

The Lineage of Athrwys ap Meurig taken from *De Situ Brecheniauc 10.*
 Macsen Wledig (Maximus "the Imperator")
 Anhun Dunawd (Antonius Donatus)
 Tathal
 Teithrin
 Telthfallt
 Tewdrig
 Meurig
 Athrwys

According to the *Book of Llandaff,* Pepiau, or Peibio, was the son of Erb, king of Erging, and he married the daughter of Custennin Fendigaid (Constantine "the Blessed"). They had a daughter named Efrddyl, who became the mother of St. Dyfrig (Dubricius). Pepiau was succeeded by his son Cynfyn, who was in turn succeeded by his son Gwrgant Mawr ("the Great"), whose daughter Onbrawst married Meurig ap Tewdrig, king of Gwent. The son of Meurig and Onbrawst was Athrwys. We can rectify the lineage of Athrwys ap Meurig even further by adopting the pedigree of the kings of Erging and Gwent taken from the *Book of Llandaff* thus:

The Lineage of Athrwys ap Meurig taken from the *Book of Llandaff.*
 Macsen Wledig (Maximus "the Imperator")
 Custennin Fendigaid (Constantine "the Blessed")
 Daughter of Custennin Fendigaid
 Pepiau Clavorauc ("the Dravellor")
 Cynfyn
 Gwrgant Mawr ("the Great")
 Onbrawst = Meurig ap Tewdrig
 Athrwys

Dr. Davies also claims that Morgan ap Athrwys was alive ca. 635–710 and active ca. 665–710. This again is impossible. One is inclined to suspect that during the sixth and seventh centuries, there were two kings of Morgannwg and Gwent by the name of Morgan, and that the compiler of the *Book of Llandaff* has confounded them. The first was Morgan Mwynfawr ("the Courteous") ap Athrwys and the second was Morgan Morgannwg, who re-united the kingdom and died fighting the second Battle of Mons Badonicus, which is recorded in the *Welsh Annals* as having taken place in 665.

 According to the Triads contained in *The Myvyrian Archaeology of Wales* (1801), Morgan Mwynfawr, the son of Athrwys, was one of the royal knights at the court of King Arthur. The same Triads represent his adopted son Rhyhawd as Eil Morgan, the successor of Morgan Mwynfawr. Rhyhawd was presumably succeeded by his son, Einydd who was in turn succeeded by Morgan Morgannwa, who died in 665.

 The confusion of the two Morgans led the compiler of the *Book of Llandaff* to post-date the early kings of Erging and Gwent. This error caused the genealogists to stretch the pedigrees in order to accommodate Morgan Morgannwg, who died in 665, and consequently they now come down to us in a corrupt form.

J. W. James, in "The Chronology in the Book of Llandaff 500–900" (*The National Library of Wales Journal*, Vol. XVI, Aberystwyth, 1969–1970), determined that there is a gap of approximately a hundred years in the charters of Llandaff. This anomaly had not been recognized by the compiler of the *Book of Llandaff*, and he consequently made one "King Morgan" out of two men bearing the same name—Morgan ap Athrwys and Morgan the father of Ithael. The gap between the two kings Morgan may be due to the loss of a document, possibly a book of the Gospels, which contained memoranda covering the entire seventh century, and which disappeared in a series of calamities, such as are hinted at by the *Book of Llandaff* on page 192. As soon as the two Morgans are separated by a century, the chronological difficulty disappears.

**The Lineal Descent of Iestyn ap Gwrgan from Macsen Wledig.**

Macsen Wledig (Maximus "the Imperator" d. 388)

Anhun Dunawd (Antonius Donatus)

Tathal

Teithrin

Teithfallt

Tewdrig Fendigaid ("the Blessed")

Meurig

Athrwys

Morgan Mwynfawr (Morcant "the Most Courteous")

Rhyhawd (Eil Morgan)

Einydd

Morgan Morgannwg d.665

Ithel

Rhys

Arthmael

Meurig

Brochfael

Gwriad

Arthfael

Rhys

Arthmael

Meurig

Hywel d.885

Owain d.931

Morgan Mawr ("the Great"), also known as Morgan Hen ("the Aged")
    d. 974

Idwallon

Ithel

Gwrgan d. 1042

Iestyn d. 1092/3

Geoffrey Ashe, the renowned Arthurian scholar, in one of his more recent books, identifies King Arthur with Riothamus, another emigrant leader who flourished in the fifth and not the sixth century. Mr. Ashe's theory depends to a great extent upon a passage in Geoffrey of Monmouth's *Historia Regum Britanniae*, which portrays Arthur as a British king campaigning in Gaul during the reign of the Eastern Emperor Leo I (r. 457–474). This was indeed Riothamus, but certainly not Arthur, the victor of the Battle of Mount Badon in 518.

The author who comes closest to identifying the historical King Arthur and the location of his last resting place is Ronald Millar in *Will the Real King Arthur Please Stand Up?* But he chooses a light-hearted approach to the subject and does not reach a satisfactory conclusion. He does, however, mention a great warrior named Arzur, who once lived in a fortress in the Sarzeau forest at the time of Gildas, though he fails to identify this Arzur with Arthmael.

### King Arthur of the Silures—the Documentary Evidence.

The territory of the Roman Republic of the Silures, which was displaced by a monarchy early in the fifth century, included without doubt large parts of Gwent and Herefordshire, and extended east into the Forest of Dean, Gloucestershire, and west into Glamorgan.

After the Roman period, the name Silures is not found, for the independent kingdom of Gwent took its name from their capital, Venta Silurum (later Caerwent), which may be regarded as the civil counterpart of the Roman military fortress Isca Silurum (Caerleon-upon-Usk).

Thomas Malory, in *Le Morte d'Arthur* (1485), identifies Camelot with Winchester. It would seem rather doubtful, however, that King Arthur would have kept his court at Winchester in view of the fact that, during his time, Venta Belgarum (Winchester) was a canton of the Gewissei, his enemies. However, Caerwent, in Gwent, the ruins of which are still visible, may have in later times been confounded with Caer Wynt, now Winchester. We now have this plausible hypothesis:

Venta Silurum = Caer Wynt = Winchester
Venta Silurum = Caerwent = Camelot

In *Monasticon Anglicanum*, III, 190 (1673), compiled by Sir William Dugdale from the ancient register of the Cathedral Church of Llandaff, we found the only instance of the name of Arthur, so spelled, as the king of Gwent, son of Mouric, king of Morgannwg, and father of Morcant. Elsewhere, he is uniformly called Athruis, who was a contemporary of Comergwynus, a bishop of the See of Llandaff. Further investigation reveals that Comergwynus is identical with Athruis's brother Comereg, Bishop of Erging, to whom he granted Llan Cinmarch, near Chepstow in Gwent.

The *Vita Cadoci*, compiled between 1073 and 1086 by Lifris or Lifricus, who was the son of Bishop Herewald of Llandaff and master of St. Cadoc of Llancarfan, preceded Geoffrey of Monmouth's *Historia Regum Britanniae* (ca.

1136) by two generations. It shows Arthur to have been ruling in southeast Wales and as one of the prominent kings of his time. It also mentions a grant of land known as Cadoxton-juxta-Neath to St. Cadoc by a certain King Arthmael. According to the genealogy contained in the *Book of Llandaff*, the king reigning over Morgannwg and Gwent at this time was Athrwys ap Meurig ap Tewdrig. It therefore follows that Athrwys and Arthmael are one and the same person.

In the Llanover collection are two thick volumes of transcripts by Llywelyn Sion of Llangewydd, a noted Glamorgan poet and antiquary. One of his transcripts contains the following statement:

> Morgannwg extends from the River Usk, a little above Caerleon, as far as the River Tawe. This country took its name from Morgan Mwynfawr ("the Most Courteous"), who was the cousin of King Arthur. He obtained his choice of the part he might desire of Wales, in the principalities of his cousin King Arthur, and chose the twelve hundreds of Gwent Essyllt (Silurian Gwent = Venta Silurum) and called them Morgannwg. (Llyma Enwau a Hiliogaeth Brenhinoedd Morgannwg, contained in Sir Edward Mansel of Margam, *The Winning of Glamorgan*, 1591, pp. 23–47.)

It appears that Llewellyn Sion transcribed a manuscript which was in the library of Sir Edward Stradling at St. Donat's Castle, South Glamorgan. A renowned scholar and antiquary, Sir Edward Stradling was a friend of William Camden, and was described by Thomas Williams as the chief cherisher of our Welsh language in South Wales. He is also mentioned by Lewis Dwnn as among those who had written on the history and genealogies of the whole of Britain, and his name is placed first among the aristocracy by whom he was permitted to see old records and books from religious houses which had been compiled and written by abbots and priors. These must have included the register of Neath Abbey, which was in Stradling's possession in 1574, but is now lost. It contained an early history of Morgannwg (Glamorgan).

Sir Edward Mansel of Margan (d. 1595), in *The Winning of Glamorgan—Another account of the coming in of the Normans in a shorter story than before* (1591), says, "now the Country of Glamorgan came to be first a Royal Lordship from one Morgan, a prince who lived in the time of King Arthur and was his son as some have it; others say he was the cousin of Arthur" (page 23).

Sir Edward Mansel would appear to be in slight disagreement with Llywelyn Sion of Llangewydd (1540–1615), who, in *Llyma Enwau a Hiliogaeth Brenhinoedd Morgannwg* ["These be the Names and Genealogy of the Kings of Morgannwg"] (1572–1591, p. 45), says, "Morgannwg extends from the river Usk, a little above Caerleon, as far as the river Tawe; and this country took its name from Morgan 'the Most Courteous.' He was a cousin to King Arthur, and obtained his choice of the part he might desire of Wales, in the principalities of his cousin Arthur; and he chose the twelve hundreds of Gwent Essyllt (Silurian Gwent, Venta Silurum), and called them Morgannwg."

# THE ORIGINS OF THE ARTHMAEL/ARTHUR THEORY

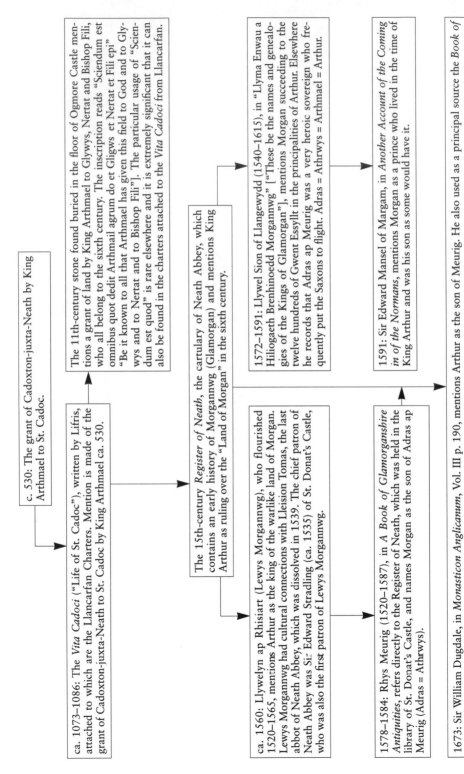

c. 530: The grant of Cadoxton-juxta-Neath by King Arthmael to St. Cadoc.

ca. 1073–1086: The *Vita Cadoci* ("Life of St. Cadoc"), written by Lifris, attached to which are the Llancarfan Charters. Mention is made of the grant of Cadoxton-juxta-Neath to St. Cadoc by King Arthmael ca. 530.

The 11th-century stone found buried in the floor of Ogmore Castle mentions a grant of land by King Arthmael to Glywys, Nertat and Bishop Fili, who all belong to the sixth century. The inscription reads "Sciendum est omnibus quot dedit Arthmail agrum do et Gligws et Nertat et Fili epi" ["Be it known to all that Arthmail has given this field to God and to Glywys and to Nertat and to Bishop Fili"]. The particular usage of "Sciendum est quod" is rare elsewhere and it is extremely significant that it can also be found in the charters attached to the *Vita Cadoci* from Llancarfan.

The 15th-century *Register of Neath*, the cartulary of Neath Abbey, which contains an early history of Morgannwg (Glamorgan) and mentions King Arthur as ruling over the "Land of Morgan" in the sixth century.

ca. 1560: Llywelyn ap Rhisiart (Lewys Morgannwg), who flourished 1520–1565, mentions Arthur as the king of the warlike land of Morgan. Lewys Morgannwg had cultural connections with Lleision Tomas, the last abbot of Neath Abbey, which was dissolved in 1539. The chief patron of Neath Abbey was Sir Edward Stradling (ca. 1535) of St. Donat's Castle, who was also the first patron of Lewys Morgannwg.

1572–1591: Llywel Sion of Llangewydd (1540–1615), in "Llyma Enwau a Hiliogaeth Brenhinoedd Morgannwg" ["These be the names and genealogies of the Kings of Glamorgan"], mentions Morgan succeeding to the twelve hundreds of Gwent Essyllt in the principalities of Arthur. Elsewhere he records that Adras ap Meurig was a very heroic sovereign who frequently put the Saxons to flight. Adras = Athrwys = Arthmael = Arthur.

1578–1584: Rhys Meurig (1520–1587), in *A Book of Glamorganshire Antiquities*, refers directly to the Register of Neath, which was held in the library of St. Donat's Castle, and names Morgan as the son of Adras ap Meurig (Adras = Athrwys).

1591: Sir Edward Mansel of Margam, in *Another Account of the Coming in of the Normans*, mentions Morgan as a prince who lived in the time of King Arthur and was his son.

1673: Sir William Dugdale, in *Monasticon Anglicanum*, Vol. III p. 190, mentions Arthur as the son of Meurig. He also used as a principal source the *Book of Llandaff*.

Calling Arthur a cousin of Morgan is undoubtedly a clerical error on the part of Llywelyn Sion of Llangewydd, for, according to lists XXVIII and XXIX in Harleian MS 3859, printed in *Genealogies and Texts: Vol. 5 of Arthurian Period Sources* (London: Phillimore, 1995), the king reigning over Gwent at the time was Arthmael or Athrwys, the son of Meurig and the *father* of Morgan.

Thomas Carte, in *A General History of England* (Vol. 1, Book III, page 202, 1747), would appear to follow Sir William Dugdale when he says that there is little room to doubt but that the Arthruis, king of Gwent, who granted the land of St. Kinmark to Bishop Comereg, was the Arthur in question. It is significant that Thomas Carte names Arthur as Arthruis and not Athruis. Geoffrey of Monmouth, who very likely lent a hand in compiling the *Book of Llandaff* during his residence there, may have seen this charter naming the granter as Arthruis or Arthurus as King of Gwent.

The Rev. John Whitaker, the foremost historian of Lancashire, in his *History of Manchester* (1775), names Arthur as king of Gwent with his court at Caerwent. In the second volume (p. 34), Whitaker writes: "Arthur was the Arth-uir, great man, or sovereign of the Proper Silures and therefore the denominated king of Gwent, the Venta Silurum of the Romans, and the British metropolis of the nation." (N.B. Arth-uir is a variation of Arthwyr, the Bear Exalted). The historians who positively identify Arthur with Athrwys ap Meurig ap Tewdrig, king of Morgannwg and Gwent, are David Williams, in *The History of Monmouthshire* (1796); Dr. William Owen Pughe, in *The Cambrian Biography* (1803); John H. Parry, in *The Cambrian Plutarch* (1834); and Owen 'Morien' Morgan, in *A History of Wales* (1911). Other writers who refer to the identification but do not necessarily agree with it are Joseph Ritson, in *The Life of King Arthur from Ancient Historians and Authentic Documents* (1825), and Rice Rees, in *An Essay on the Welsh Saints* (1836). John Duncumbe, in his *Collection towards the History and Antiquities of the County of Hereford* (1804), refers to Arthur as the king of the Silures, as does Ebenezer Cobham Brewer, in his *Dictionary of Phrase and Fable* (1870).

The reliable historian Sharon Turner, in *The History of the Anglo-Saxons* (Vol. 1, pp. 101–102, 1807), says "Arthur was a chieftain in some part of South Wales, and as a Mouric, king of Glamorganshire, had a son named Arthur at this period; and many of Arthur's actions are placed about that district, it has been thought probably that the celebrated Arthur was the son of Mouric: but he is usually deemed the son of Uther."

We will give the final word to Leslie Alcock the eminent Arthurian scholar and archaeologist who, in his book *Arthur's Britain* (1971), prophetically observed that:

A new appreciation of some of our fifth and sixth century texts is developing and it seems likely that over the next decade many of our current interpretations will be revolutionized.[4]

---

[4]Leslie Alcock, *Arthur's Britain* (London: Penguin, 1971), p. 1.

# Appendix IV

## Alternative Theories

**Geoffrey Ashe**

In *The Discovery of King Arthur* (1985), the well-known Arthurian scholar Geoffrey Ashe identifies King Arthur with Riothamus, an important immigrant leader who flourished in the fifth, and not the sixth, century as did Arthur. Mr. Ashe's theory depends to a great extent upon a passage in Geoffrey of Monmouth's *Historia Regum Britanniae*, which portrays Arthur as a British king campaigning in Gaul during the reign of the Eastern Roman Emperor Leo I (r. 457–474). The British king who was campaigning in Gaul at this time was indeed Riothamus, but he certainly was not Arthur, the victor of the Battle of Mount Badon in 517.

Paul Karlsson Johnstone, a consultant archaeologist who is well known for his *Consular Chronology of Dark Age Britain*, disputes Geoffrey Ashe's identification and asserts that Riothamus, also known as Ian Reith, and St. Rhedyw (Ridicus), the father of St. Garmon, are one and the same person. This is chronologically difficult, but certainly not impossible. He would have fathered St. Garmon when he was a very young man, lived to be a great veteran fighter, and possibly survived his illustrious son. There is no doubt that St. Rhedyw was the founder-father of a family of soldier-saints who flourished in both Wales and Brittany, and he is certainly a more likely candidate for Riothamus than the historical King Arthur.

Geoffrey Ashe utilizes the *Legend of Goeznovius* as source material for his identification of Arthur with Riothamus and places Arthur/Riothamus's Gallic War in the 460s. However, if he had consulted *The History of England* by Rapin de Thoyras (1732), he would no doubt have discovered that the true King Arthur fought his own Gallic war ca. 510.

One of the recurring features of Arthur's life is the help he received from and gave to his nephew Riwal Mawr ("the Great"), king of Armorican Domnonia. Riwal was the son of Emyr Llydaw ("the Armorican"), the benefactor of Emrys Wledig (Ambrosius "the Imperator"), who sprang from the line of Macsen Wledig (Maximus "the Imperator"). King Arthur was fighting for his kinsman Riwal in Brittany during the reign of the Frankish King Clovis I (482–511), whose wife was a Christian from Burgundy. He had taken a force over to the Continent to help Riwal against an invasion of the Visigoths. The

combined forces of Arthur and Riwal gained an overwhelming victory over the
Visigoths at Baden (another Battle of Baden!), situated southwest of Vannes.
The Venetians of Vannes, unconquered by the barbarians, took a Dux. Arthur
was that Dux.

### Baram Blackett and Alan Wilson

In *Artorius Rex Discovered* (1985), Baram Blackett and Alan Wilson claim that
the Western Roman Emperor Magnus Clemens Maximus, the Macsen Wledig
of Welsh tradition, had a son who became Arthur I, king of Greece. Macsen did
not have a son named Arthur, but one of his sons, Anhun Dunawd (Antonius
Donatus), is called Anhun Rex Grecorum (Antonius, king of Greece) in *De Situ
Brecheniauc* No. 10 Genealogy. Blackett and Wilson failed to notice, however,
that this Anhun, whom they claim as Arthur I, was in fact the direct ancestor of
Athrwys ap Meurig, to whom they refer as Arthur II. They state that Arthur II
was the son of Meurig, son of Tewdrig, son of Teithfallt, son of Nynniaw, when
in fact Teithfallt was the son of Teithrin, son of Tathal, son of Anhun Rex
Grecorum. They also confuse Nynniaw with St. Ninian of Whithorn in Galloway, at whose monastery St. Peblig (Publicius), the son of Macsen Wledig,
studied. Nynniaw was in actual fact the brother of Peibiaw and they co-ruled
Erging and Gwent.

Anhun Dunawd was appointed king of Strathclyde and Galloway by his
father, Macsen (Maximus), and Galloway was for a long time named Annwn
after him. This led Blackett and Wilson mistakenly to identify Galloway first
with Annwn, the Celtic Otherworld, and then with Ynys Afallach, the Island of
Apples or Avalon. They even go so far as to say that Ynys Wydrin was St. Ninian's White House at Galloway. The truth is that Annwn, Ynys Afallach, and
Ynys Wydrin are all alternative names for Bardsey, the Celtic Isle of the Blessed.

It is a significant fact that Bretons from Brittany ruled the ancient kingdom of Strathclyde before Anglo-Saxon times. It would seem obvious, therefore, that the descendants of Anhun sought help in preserving their independence with an army of Bretons who subsequently colonized Strathclyde. It
should be observed that Arthur, a direct descendant of Anhun, sought the assistance of Riwal Mawr ("the Great"), king of Armorican Domnonia, in preserving his realm, which included Strathclyde.

Messrs. Blackett and Wilson identify Emrys Wledig (Ambrosius "the Imperator") with Emyr Llydaw ("the Armorican"). This is certainly not the case.
Emrys Wledig was the son of Custennin Fendigaid (Constantine "the Blessed"),
the son of Macsen Wledig, whereas Emyr Llydaw was the son of Aldwr (Aldroen), the ruler of the West Welsh settlements in Armorica.

They correctly identify the location of Cernyw and stress the importance
of the fort on Lodge Hill above Caerleon-upon-Usk. They too derive the name
of Camelot from Caer Melyn, but surprisingly locate it at a somewhat obscure
site between Newport and Cardiff at the end of a spur leading to the Cefn Onn
ridge. This is certainly in the land of Cernyw, but the main fort of Arthur as
King of the Silures was Caer Melyn (Llanmelin) to the north of Caerwent.

Initially, they place the Battle of Badon on Bouden Hill in Scotland, but subsequently give preference to Mynydd Baedan in Mid Glamorgan. On examining the *Mabinogion* story titled "The Dream of Rhonabwy," they suggest that, prior to the battle, Arthur gathered his army at a location near Ogmore Castle about 11 kilometers from Mynydd Baedan.

The Battle of Llongborth is placed on the Cardigan coast and described as a prelude to the Battle of Camlan, resulting in the death of Geraint more than thirty years later than is generally supposed. Camlan itself is pinpointed just south of Dolgellau at a location where the name conveniently appears on the Ordnance Survey map. The wounded Arthur is then taken on a long journey across land and then by boat to the Isle of Whithorn in Galloway, which the two authors claim to be the Isle of Valentia.

Athrwys ap Meurig, king of Morgannwg and Gwent, is correctly identified with the soldier-saint Arthmael, but these authors claim his burial place to be Cor Emrys, now the church of St. Peter-Super-Montem at Caer Caradoc on Mynydd y Gaer in Mid Glamorgan. They seem to be unaware of the fact that St. Arthmael was buried in a tomb in the church of St. Armel-des-Boschaux in Brittany. They also claim that St. Illtyd was responsible for Arthur's burial. St. Illtyd was ordained priest by his great-uncle, St. Garmon, who died in 474. It is highly unlikely, therefore, that he would have been around at the time of the burial of Arthur in 562. Blackett and Wilson describe a memorial stone inscribed "Rex Artorius fili Mauricius," which they claim to have found at the ruined church of St. Peter-Super-Montem. If genuine, one would expect the stone to read "Athruis filius Mauricii," and its discovery here does not necessarily mean that Arthur was buried at this location.

Blackett and Wilson name Arthur's principal enemy, Medraut, as the son of Llew ap Cynfarch, a northern prince, whereas he was in fact the Medraut who was the son of Cawrdaf ap Caradog, a prince of South Wales. They also identify Arthur's other principal foe, Marcus Conomorus, with March ap Meirchion Gul, another northern prince, instead of March ap Meirchion Vesanus ap Glywys, a prince of South Wales. They thus transfer Arthur's campaign against his enemies to northern Britain.

Their book, *Artorius Rex Discovered*, certainly breaks new ground, but it is difficult to follow, for the authors frequently contradict themselves and stretch both chronology and genealogy to their breaking points in an attempt to prove their theories, which have not been accepted by historians.

### Dr. Norma Goodrich

Dr. Norma Goodrich graduated from the University of Vermont and is currently Professor Emeritus of French and Comparative literature at Scripps College and the Claremont Graduate School in California.

In her book titled *King Arthur* (1986), she claimed that Arthur was not only a Scottish king, but also the founder of the clan Campbell, and that he was born near Carlisle. She also believed that the Isle of Man was Avalon and that Arthur was buried on St. Patrick's Isle. She has since changed her mind and now claims that Arthur lies buried under the church of St. Michael and All Angels at Arthuret, near Gretna Green.

The statement that Arthur was the founder of a Scottish clan is most certainly incorrect, for the kingdom of the Dalriadan Scots was founded ca. 500 by Fergus Mac Erca and the Scottish clans could not have been established by Arthur's time. When Dr. Goodrich named St. Patrick's Isle as the burial place of King Arthur, she was obviously confusing him with Antonius Donatus, the son of the Roman Emperor Magnus Clemens Maximus. Antonius, as we have stated previously, was appointed king of Strathclyde and Galloway by his father and he later retired to the Isle of Man, where he was anointed King of Man by the bishop and king-maker, St. Garmon. He indeed lies buried on St. Patrick's Isle. However, Dr. Goodrich has revised her ideas and now claims that Arthur was buried at Arthuret, which she believes means Arthur's Head. This is certainly not the case, for Arthuret is derived from Arderydd and does not mean Arthur's Head. It is the site of a famous battle fought after the passing of Arthur.

Dr. Goodrich names Arthur's principal court as Carlisle. Carlisle was indeed the court of the kings of Rheged and there was certainly a king of Rheged named Arthwys, who was the great-grandson of Coel Hen ("the Old"), the founder-father of the Men of the North. Arthwys fought an ongoing border war with the Picts a generation before Arthur's time, but his genealogy bears no comparison with that of King Arthur.

It is relevant that Dr. Goodrich uses the works of W. F. Skene to great effect in order to establish her King Arthur in Scotland. William Forbes Skene (1809-1892) was a patriotic Scotsman and it is therefore not surprising that he passionately wanted his hero, Arthur, to be a Scotsman. However, doubt has since been cast on Skene's material, and he cannot now be considered a reliable source. Dr. Goodrich also utilizes the literary rather than the historical sources in order to arrive at her unsatisfactory conclusions.

### Martin Keatman and Graham Phillips

In *King Arthur—the True Story* (1992), Martin Keatman and Graham Phillips identify King Arthur with Owain Danwyn ("the White-toothed"), a petty prince of Rhos, and claim that he ruled Gwynedd and Powys simultaneously from 488 until his death at the Battle of Camlan in 519.

On the face of it, this is an extremely unlikely theory and would seem to indicate a distinct lack of knowledge of both the geography and genealogy of the period in question.

Owain Danwyn, the son of Einion Yrth ("the Impetuous") and grandson of Cunedda Wledig ("the Imperator"), was prince of Rhos only while his elder brother, Cadwallon Lawhir ("the Long-handed"), ruled Gwynedd and Cyngen Glodrydd ("the Renowned") ruled Powys. Owain Danwyn was killed ca. 517 by Cadwallon's famous son, Maelgwyn Hir ("the Tall"), apparently in a dispute over the succession to the kingdom of Gwynedd. There is absolutely no historical evidence to support the authors' theory that either Owain Danwyn or his son Cynlas ever ruled Powys.

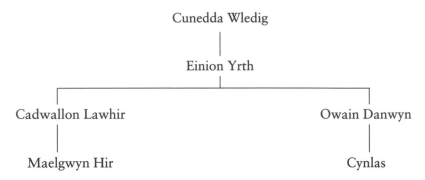

The authors base their claim on the fact that Owain Danwyn's son Cynlas was, according to Gildas, the driver of the chariot of the Bear's stronghold (Dinarth) in the old principality of Rhos, but they have jumped to the wrong conclusion when they assume that the "Bear" in question was Owain Danwyn. The latest translation from the Latin by Michael Winterbottom is as follows: "you Bear, rider of many and driver of the chariot of the Bear's stronghold."[1] Therefore, Gildas is calling Cynlas the Bear and not his father, Owain Danwyn. The epithet "Bear," after the Celtic bear deity, is applied to a strong leader of men, and does not necessarily mean that either Owain or his son Cynlas is a candidate for King Arthur.

The authors also claim that Owain Danwyn ruled Powys from Viroconium (Wroxeter). However, the genealogy of Powys was very different from that of Gwynedd. The first king of Powys was Cadell Ddyrnllug ("of the Gleaming Hilt"), the son of Cateyrn and grandson of Gwrtheyrn Gwrtheneu (Vortigern "the Thin"). Therefore, the kings of Powys claimed descent from the infamous Vortigern, as the Pillar of Eliseg denotes, and the kings of Gwynedd claimed descent from the mighty Cunedda Wledig. Cadell was succeeded by his son Cyngen Glodrydd ("the Renowned"), who did indeed rule from Viroconium, as did his son and successor, Brochwel Ysgythrog ("of the Tusks"). All the available historical evidence suggests that it was not until after the death of Rhun Hir ("the Tall"), the bastard son of Maelgwyn, in 586, that Powys replaced Gwynedd as the paramount state of Wales. Cynan Garwyn ("of the White Shank"), the son of Brochwel, became the paramount king. There is no historical evidence to support the author's theory that Owain Danwyn or his son and successor, Cynlas, both petty princes of Rhos, were ever over-kings of Powys or that they ruled from Viroconium.

---

[1]Gildas ap Caw, *De Excidio et Conquesta Britanniae*. Republished as *Gildas— The Ruin of Britain and Other Works*, Michael Winterbottom, trans. and ed. (London: Phillimore, 1978), passage 32.1, p. 31.

The authors further claim that Owain Danwyn was buried at the Berth, near Baschurch in Shropshire. The man most likely to have been buried there would have been the mighty Cynddylan the Fair, prince of Powys and lord of Dogfeiling, who ruled Powys from Pengwern near Baschurch and was killed in 656.

In two instances, the authors refer to Erging as a district in the kingdom of Powys. This is definitely not the case. Erging was a part of modern day Herefordshire and it was later annexed by Meurig, king of Morgannwg and Gwent, the father of the real King Arthur. They also suggest that Marcus Conomorus belonged to the dynasty of Gwynedd when it has already been established that he was a Glamorgan prince, the son of Meirchion Vesanus (Marcianus "the Mad"). They also present a case for this Marcus Conomorus as a candidate for Arthur's arch-enemy, Medraut. This is also impossible. We have established that Medraut was the son of Cawrdaf and grandson of Caradog Freichfras ("of the Strong Arm") and all belonged to Gwent.

The authors call their book *King Arthur—the True Story*, but the overuse of the words possible, probable, perhaps, may, might and could, seem to indicate that they are not sure of their facts.


# IN CONCLUSION

In our *Journey to Avalon,* we have shown that the key to the identity and realm of King Arthur is the simple fact that the Glamorgan and Gwentian princes of the sixth century held territory not only in South Wales, but also in Cornwall and Brittany. These lands became the main field of Arthur's influence and are accordingly the very places where he is best remembered.

Most people today are sadly unaware of the historical connections between Brittany and Wales, for they have been largely forgotten. It is particularly significant that large numbers of immigrants from Gwent and Glamorgan settled in Brittany during the fifth and sixth centuries and that they named their territory Léon after the Caerleon in Gwent which they had left behind. The simple fact that Caerleon, Cernyw, and Gelliwig in Gwent all have their counterparts in Cornwall and Brittany, has caused much confusion in the age-old quest for a solution to the mystery of King Arthur.

Numerous contemporaries of King Arthur, anxious to escape the threat of the invading Saxons and the peril of an infectious plague, also settled in Brittany, so it is hardly surprising that he also ended up there. These were people of royal and noble families who founded churches and monasteries in locations where their personal names and places of origin are still remembered.

By the 12th century, a legend of Arthur, which included a belief in his "return" had taken root in Brittany. It seems apparent that it was from the Bretons rather than the Welsh that the Normans derived their knowledge of Arthur. But it must be remembered that these Breton traditions originally came from Wales. They were brought by settlers who carried with them their own history and culture, which they transplanted into Armorica. Arthur was undoubtedly a folk hero on both sides of the channel, and for good reason, for not only was he a remarkable historical character, but also a great defender of Christian civilization whose name will never be forgotten.

> Who is there, I ask who does not speak of Arthur the Briton, since he is less little known to the peoples of Asia than to the Britons as we are informed by pilgrims who return from Eastern lands? The peoples of the East speak of him as do the West, though separated by the breadth of the whole earth. Egypt speaks of him, nor is Bosporous silent. Rome, Queen of cities sings his deeds and his wars are known to her former rival Carthage. Antioch, Armenia and Palestine celebrate his feats.[2]

---

[2]Alanus de Insulis, c. 1170.

# BIBLIOGRAPHY

Alcock, Leslie. *Dinas Powys—An Iron Age, Dark Age and Early Medieval Settlement in Glamorgan*. Cardiff, Wales: University of Wales Press, 1963.

———. *Arthur's Britain*. London: Penguin, 1971.

Ashe, Geoffrey. *From Caesar to Arthur*. London: Collins, 1960.

———. *Camelot and the Vision of Albion*. London: Heinemann, 1971.

———. *Avalonian Quest*. London: Methuen, 1982.

———. *Kings and Queens of Early Britain*. London: Methuen, 1982.

———. *A Guidebook to Arthurian Britain*. London: Aquarian Press, 1983.

———. *The Discovery of King Arthur*. London: Debrett's Peerage Ltd., 1985.

Barb, A. A. "Mensa Sacra: The Round Table and the Holy Grail," in *The Journal of the Warburg and Courtauld Institutes*. London: 1956.

Barber, Chris. *Mysterious Wales*. Newton Abott: David & Charles, 1982.

———. *More Mysterious Wales*. Newton Abbot: David & Charles, 1986.

Barber, Richard. *The Figure of King Arthur*. London: Longman, 1975.

Baring-Gould, Sabine. *Curious Myths of the Middle Ages*. London: Rivingtons, 1867.

———. *The Lives of the Saints*. 16 vols. London: John C. Nimmo, 1898.

———. *A Book of the West—Cornwall*. London: Methuen, 1899.

———. *A Book of Brittany*. London: Methuen, 1901.

———. *Brittany*. London: Methuen, 1929.

Baring-Gould, Sabine and John Fisher. *The Lives of the British Saints*. 4 vols. London: The Honourable Society of Cymmrodorion, 1907–1913.

Barley, M. W. and Hanson, R. P. C. *Christianity in Britain a.d. 300–700*. Leicester: Leicester University Press, 1968.

Bartrum, P. C. *Early Welsh Genealogical Tracts*. Cardiff, Wales: University of Wales Press, 1966.

Bede, Venerable St. *A History of the English Church and People*. London: Penguin Books, 1968. Originally published as *Ecclesiastical History of the English Nation*, or *Historia Ecclesiastica*.

Beecham, Kenneth J. *The History of Cirencester*. Cirencester: A. J. Sutton, 1978.

Benedictine Monks of St. Augustine's Abbey, Ramsgate. *The Book of Saints*. London: Adam & Charles Black, 1966.

Blackett, A. T. and Alan Wilson. *Arthur, King of Glamorgan and Gwent*. Cardiff, Wales: M. T. Byrd, 1980.

———. *Arthur and the Charters of the King*. Cardiff, Wales: M. T. Byrd, 1980.

———. *Artorius Rex Discovered*. Cardiff, Wales: M. T. Byrd, 1986.

Blair, Peter Hunter. *An Introduction to Anglo-Saxon England*. Cambridge: Cambridge University Press, 1970.

Bonwick, James. *Irish Druids and Old Irish Religions*. 1894. New York: Dorset, 1986.

Bowen, Emrys George. *The Travels of St. Samson of Dol*. Aberystwyth, Dyfed, Wales: Aberystwyth Studies XIII, 1934.

————. *The Settlements of the Celtic Saints in Wales*. Cardiff, Wales: University of Wales Press, 1956.

————. *The Glastonbury Region: The Geographical and Archaeological Background*. London: Research into Lost Knowledge Organisation, 1969.

————. *Britain and the Western Seaways*. London: Thames & Hudson, 1972.

————. *Dewi Sant* [St. David]. Cardiff, Wales: University of Wales Press, 1983.

Brandon, Peter. *The South Saxons*. London & Chichester: Phillimore, 1978.

Bromwich, Rachel. *Troedd Ynys Prydein* [The Welsh Triads]. Cardiff, Wales: University of Wales Press, 1978.

————. *The Arthur of the Welsh*. Cardiff, Wales: University of Wales Press, 1991.

*Brut Breninoedd* [The Chronicle of the Kings]. A 13th- 15th-century Welsh manuscript.

Bryce, Derek. *Arthur and the Britons in History and Ancient Poetry*. Felinfach, Lampeter, Dyfed, Wales: Llanerch, 1987.

————. *Arthur and the Britons in Wales and Scotland*. Felinfach, Lampeter, Dyfed, Wales: Llanerch, 1988.

Bu'lock, J. D. *Pre-Conquest Cheshire 383–1066*. Chester: Cheshire Community Council, 1972.

Butler, Alban. *Lives of the Saints*. Tunbridge Wells: Burns, Oates & Washbourne, 1936.

Cambrensis, Giraldus. *Gerald of Wales—The Journey through Wales* and *The Description of Wales*. London: Penguin, 1978.

Camden, William. *Britannia*. 1695. London: John Stockdale, 1806.

————. *Remains Concerning Britain*. London: John Russell Smith, 1870.

Carley, James P. *Glastonbury Abbey*. London: Guild Publishing, 1988.

Chadwick, Nora Kershaw. *Studies in Early British History*. Cambridge: Cambridge University Press, 1954.

————. *Studies in the Early British Church*. Cambridge: Cambridge University Press, 1958.

————. *Celt and Saxon: Studies in the Early British Border*. Cambridge: Cambridge University Press, 1963.

————. *Early Brittany*. Cardiff, Wales: University of Wales Press, 1969.

————. *The British Heroic Age: The Welsh and the Men of the North*. Cardiff, Wales: University of Wales Press, 1976.

Chambers, E. K. *Arthur of Britain*. London: Sidgwick & Jackson, 1947.

Childe, V. Gordon. *Prehistoric Communities of the British Isles*. Edinburgh: W. & R. Chambers, 1940.

Clayton, Peter. *A Companion to Roman Britain*. Oxford: Phaidon Press, 1980.

Clifford, Elsie M. *Bagendon: A Belgic Oppidum*. Cambridge: Cambridge University Press, 1961.

Clinch, Rosemary and Michael Williams. *King Arthur in Somerset*. Bodmin, Cornwall: Bossiney Books, 1987.

Coxe, William. *An Historical Tour of Monmouthshire*. 1801. Reprint: T. Cadell Juriar and W. Davies, eds. Cardiff, Wales: Merton Press, 1995.

Cross, F. L. *The Oxford Dictionary of the Christian Church.* Oxford: Oxford University Press, 1958.

Cunliffe, Barry. *Iron Age Communities in Britain.* London: Routledge & Kegan Paul, 1974.

Darby, H.C. and G.R. Versey. *The Domesday Gazeteer.* Cambridge: Cambridge University Press, 1975.

D'Arcy, Mary Ryan. *The Saints of Ireland.* Cork: The Mercier Press, 1985.

Darrah, John. *The Real Camelot: Paganism and the Arthurian Romances.* London: Thames & Hudson, 1981.

Davies, Edward. *The Mythology and Rites of the British Druids.* London: J. Booth, 1809.

Davies, Wendy. *The Llandaff Charters.* Aberystwyth, Dyfed, Wales: The National Library of Wales, 1979.

———. *Wales in the Early Middle Ages.* Leicester: Leicester University Press, 1982.

De Breffny, Brian. *In the Steps of St. Patrick.* London: Thames & Hudson, 1982.

De La Borderie, Arthur. *Histoire de Bretagne.* Paris, 1891.

———. *Annales de Bretagne.* Rennes, 1892.

De Thoyras, Rapin. *The History of England.* Translated from the French by N. Tindal-James. London: John and Paul Knapton, 1732.

Dicks, Brian. *Portrait of Cardiff and its Valleys.* London: Robert Hale, 1984.

Doble, Gilbert H. *The Saints of Cornwall.* Oxford: The Holywell Press, 1964–1970.

———. *The Lives of the Welsh Saints.* Cardiff, Wales: University of Wales Press, 1971.

Dugdale, William. *Monasticon Anglicanum,* 3 vols. 1655–1673.

———. *The Antiquities of Warwickshire.* Coventry: John Jones, 1765.

Duncumbe, John. *Collections towards the History and Antiquities of the County of Hereford.* Hereford: E.G. Wright, 1804.

Dunning, Robert. *Arthur: The King in the West.* Glouster: Alan Sutton, 1988.

Dyer, James. *The Penguin Guide to Prehistoric England and Wales.* London: Penguin, 1982.

Edwards, Alfred George. *Landmarks in the History of the Welsh Church.* London: John Murray, 1913.

Ekwall, Eilert. *The Concise Oxford Dictionary of English Place-Names.* Oxford: Clarendon Press, 1960.

Ellis, Peter Berresford. *Celtic Inheritance.* London: Fredric Muller, 1985.

Evans, Gwynfor. *Land of My Fathers.* Swansea: John Penry Press, 1978.

———. *Magnus Maximus and the Birth of Wales the Nation.* Swansea: John Penry Press, 1983.

Evans, J. Gwenogvryn and John Rhys. *The Text of the Book of Llan Dav.* Oxford: Clarendon Press, 1893.

Farmer, David Hugh. *The Oxford Dictionary of Saints.* Oxford: Oxford University Press, 1978.

Fleuriot, Leon. *Les Origines de la Bretagne.* Paris: Payot, 1980.

Foakes-Jackson, F. J. *The History of the Christian Church from the Earliest Times to A.D. 461*. London: George Allen & Unwin, 1914.

Fox, David Scott. *St George: The Saint with the Three Faces*. Windsor Forest: The Kenal Press, 1983.

Frere, Sheppard. *Britannia*. London: Routledge, 1967.

Gantz, Jeffrey. *The Mabinogion*. New York: Dorset Press, 1985.

Garmondsway, G. N. *The Anglo-Saxon Chronicle*. London: J. M. Dent & Sons, 1972.

Geoffrey of Monmouth. *The History of the Kings of Britain*. London: Penguin, 1966.

Gerald of Wales. *The Journey through Wales* and *The Description of Wales*. In one volume. London: Penguin, 1978.

Gies, Frances Carney. *The Knight in History*. London: Harper & Row, 1984.

Gilbert, Edward. *Deerhurst and Armorica*. Bristol: Transaction of the Bristol and Gloucestershire Archaeological Society, 1972.

Gildas ap Caw. *De Excidio et Conquesta Britanniae*. Republished as *Gildas— The Ruin of Britain and Other Works*. Michael Winterbottom, trans. and ed. London & Chichester: Phillimore, 1978.

Giles, J. A. *Six Old English Chronicles*. London: Henry G. Bohn's Antiquarian Library, 1848.

Goodrich, Norma Lorre. *King Arthur*. New York: Franklin Watts, 1986.

Gordon, E. O. *Prehistoric London: Its Mounds and Circles*. London: The Covenant Publishing Co., 1946.

Green, A. R. "The Romsey Painted Wooden Reredos with a short account of St. Armel," in *Archaeological Journal* XC, 1933.

Griffiths, R. A. and Roger S. Thomas. *The Making of the Tudor Dynasty*. Gloucester: Alan Sutton, 1987.

Griscom, Acton. *The Historia Regum Britanniae of Geoffrey of Monmouth*. London: Longmans, Green, 1929.

Guest, Lady Charlotte. *The Mabinogion*. London: J. M. Dent & Sons, 1906.

Harrison, David. *England before the Norman Conquest*. Ipswich, Suffolk, England: Haddon Best & Co., n.d.

Hasted, Edward. *The History and Topographical Survey of the County of Kent*. Canterbury: W. Bristow, 1797.

Henderson, Charles. *Essays in Cornish History*. Oxford: Clarendon Press, 1935.

———. *Cornish Church Guide and Parochial History of Cornwall*. Truro, Cornwall, England: D. Bradford Barton, 1964.

Hewins, W. A. S. *The Royal Saints of Britain from the Latter Days of the Roman Empire*. London: Chiswick Press, 1929.

Hoare, F. H. *The Western Fathers*. London: Sheed & Ward, 1954.

Hogg, A. H. A. *Hill Forts of Britain*. London: Hart-Davis, MacGibbon, 1975.

Homes-Dudden, F. *The Life and Times of St. Ambrose*. Oxford: Clarendon Press, 1935.

Hooke, Della. *The Landscape of Anglo-Saxon Staffordshire: The Charter Evidence*. Leicestershire, England: University of Keele, 1983.

Ireland, S. *Roman Britain: A Source Book*. London: Croom Helm, 1986.

Issac, David Lloyd. *Siluriana*. Newport: W. Christopher, 1859.

Jenkins, Elizabeth. *The Mystery of King Arthur*. London: Michael O' Mara, 1975.

Johnstone, Paul Karlsson. "The Riothamus Riot" in *Pendragon*, Journal of the Pendragon Society, Vol. XVI No. 2, Spring 1983.

Jones, T. Thornley. *Saints Knights and Llannau*. Llandysul, Wales: J. D. Lewis/Gomer Press, 1975.

Juvenal. *The Satires of Juvenal*. Rev. Lewis Evans, trans. Bohn's Classical Library. London: George Bell & Sons, 1880.

Kenawell, William W. *The Quest at Glastonbury*. New York: Helix Press, 1965.

Kightly, Charles. *Folk Heroes of Britain*. London: Thames & Hudson, 1982.

Kinvig, R. H. *A History of the Isle of Man*. Liverpool: Liverpool University Press, 1975.

Krappe, Alexander Haggerty. *The Science of Folklore*. London: Methuen, 1930.

Lacy, Norris. *The Arthurian Encyclopedia*. Woodbridge: The Boydell Press, 1986.

Layard, John. *A Celtic Quest*. Dallas, TX: Spring Publications, 1985.

Le Braz, Anatole. *Annales de Bretagne*. 1895.

Le Grand, Albert. *Les Vies des Saints de la Bretagne Armorique*. Quimper, Brittany, France: J. Salaun, 1901.

Leland, John. *Itinerary*. Lucy Toulmin Smith, ed. Arundel: Centaur Press, 1964.

Lempriere, J. *Classical Dictionary of Proper Names mentioned by Ancient Authors*. London: Routledge & Kegan Paul, 1978.

Lempriere, Raoul. *Buildings and Memorials of the Channel Islands*. London: Robert Hale, 1980.

Lewis, Henry, ed. *Brut Dingestow*. Cardiff, Wales: University of Wales Press, 1942.

Lewis, Lionel Smithett. *Glastonbury, "Mother of Saints": Her Saints a.d. 37–1539*. London: A. R. Mowbray, 1925.

———. *St. Joseph of Arimathea at Glastonbury or The Apostolic Church of Britain*. London: A. R. Mowbray, 1937.

Lindsay, Jack. *Arthur and His Times: Britain in the Dark Ages*. London: Frederick Muller, 1958.

Lloyd, John Edward. *A History of Wales from the Earliest Times to the Edwardian Conquest*, vol. I. London: Longmans, Green, 1911.

Llywelyn Sion of Llangewydd. *Llyma Enwau a Hiliogaeth Brenhinoedd Morgannwg* (1572–1591) contained in Cardiff Records Vols. III, IV.

Loomis, Roger Sherman. *The Grail from Celtic Myth to Christian Symbol*.

———. *Wales and the Arthurian Legend*. Cardiff, Wales: University of Wales Press, 1956.

MacDonald, Iain, ed. *Saint Brendan*. Edinburgh: Floris Books, 1992.

MacManus, Seamus. *The Story of the Irish Race*. Old Greenwich, CT: Devin-Adair, 1981.

Maitre, Leon and Paul de Berthou. *Cartulaire de l'Abbaye de Saint-Croix de Quimperle*. Paris, 1896.

Malory, Sir Thomas. *Le Morte d'Arthur*. Caxton's Text, 2 vols. London: Penguin, 1969.

Mansel, Sir Edward of Margam. *The Winning of Glamorgan*. Cardiff Records Vol. III, IV, 1591.

Markale, Jean. *Women of the Celts*. London: Gordon & Cremonesi, 1975.

———. *King Arthur: King of Kings*. Christine Hauch, trans. London: Gordon & Cremonesi, 1977.

———. *Celtic Civilization*. London: Gordon & Cremonesi, London, 1977.

Matthews, Caitlin. *Arthur and the Sovereignty of Britain*. London: Arkana, 1978.

———. *Mabon and the Mysteries of Britain*. London: Arkana, 1987.

Matthews, John. *An Arthurian Reader*. London: Aquarian Press, 1988.

———. *Gawain: Knight of the Goddess*. London: Aquarian Press, 1990.

———. *A Celtic Reader*. London: Aquarian Press, 1991.

———. *A Glastonbury Reader*. London: Aquarian Press, 1991.

Matthews, John and Caitlin. *The Aquarian Guide to British and Irish Mythology*. London: Aquarian Press, 1988.

Millar, Ronald. *Will the Real King Arthur Please Stand Up?* London: Cassell, 1978.

Miller, Molly. *The Saints of Gwynedd*. Woodbridge, Suffolk, England: Boydell Press, 1979.

Millward, Roy and Adrian Robinson. *The Welsh Borders*. London: Eyre Methuen, 1978.

Moore W. J. *Britain in the Middle Ages*. London: G. Bell & Sons, 1963.

Morgan Owen ("Morien" of Pontypridd). *The Royal Winged Son of Stonehenge and Avebury*. London: Whittaker & Co., 1900.

———. *A History of Wales from the Earliest Times including hitherto unrecorded Antiquarian Lore*. Liverpool: Edward Howell, 1911.

Morganwg, Iolo (Edward Williams). *The Iolo Manuscripts*. The Welsh Manuscript Society. Llandovery & London: Longman & Co., 1848.

Morris, John. *The Age of Arthur*. London: Weidenfeld & Nicholson, 1973.

———. *Nennius' British History and the Welsh Annals*. London & Chichester: Phillimore, 1980.

———. *Londinium: London in the Roman Empire*. London: Weidenfeld & Nicholson, 1982.

Morris, Lewis. *Celtic Remains*. Cambrian Archaeological Association, 1878.

Mountney, Michael. *The Saints of Herefordshire*. Hereford: Express Logic, 1976.

Nichols, Ross. *The Book of Druidry*. London: Aquarian Press, 1990.

Nutt, Alfred. *Studies on the Legend of the Holy Grail*. New York: Cooper Square Publishers, 1965.

O'Rahilly, T. F. *Early Irish History and Mythology*. Dublin: Institute of Advanced Studies, 1946.

Parry, John H. *The Cambrian Plutarch*. London: W. Simpkin and R. Marshall, 1834.

Parry, J.J. trans. and ed. *The Mita Merlini* [The Life of Merlin] Champaign, IL: University of Illinois Press, 1925.

Pennick, Nigel. *Lost Lands and Sunken Cities.* London: Fortean Tomes, 1987.

Powicke, F. Maurice and E. B. Fryde. *Handbook of British Chronology.* London: Offices of Royal Historical Society, 1961.

Probert, W. *The Triads of Britain.* London: Wildwood House, 1977.

Pughe, William Owen. *The Cambrian Biography.* London: Edward Williams, 1803.

Radford, C. A. *The Pillar of Eliseg.* Edinburgh: H. M. Stationery Office, 1980.

Randers-Pehrson, Justine Davis. *Barbarians and Romans: The Birth Struggle of Europe A.D. 400–700.* London: Croom Helm, 1983.

Raven, Michael. *Staffordshire and the Black Country.* Stafford: Privately published, 1988.

Reed, Trelawney Dayrell. *The Battle for Britain in the Fifth Century.* London: Methuen, 1944.

Rees, Alwyn and Brinley Rees. *Celtic Heritage.* London: Thames & Hudson, 1961.

Rees, David. *The Son of Prophecy: Henry Tudor's Road to Bosworth.* London: Black Raven Press, 1985.

Rees, Rice. *An Essay on the Welsh Saints.* Llandovery, Wales: Longman & Co., 1836.

Rees, William. *A Note on the History of Llanmelin in the Medieval Period.* Cardiff, Wales: Archaeologia Cambrensis, 1933.

———. *An Historical Atlas of Wales from Early to Modern Times.* London: Faber & Faber, 1972.

Rees, William Jenkins. *The Liber Landavensis: The Ancient Register of the Cathedral Church of Llandaff.* Llandovery, Wales: Longman & Co., 1839.

———. *Lives of the Cambro-British Saints.* London: Longman & Co., 1853.

Renouard, Michel. *A New Guide to Brittany.* Rennes: Ouest France, 1984.

Rhoscomyl, Owen. *Flame-Bearers of Welsh History.* Merthyr Tydfil, Wales: Welsh Educational Publishing Co., 1905.

Rhys, John. *Celtic Britain.* London: Society for Promoting Christian Knowledge, 1884.

———. *Celtic Folklore.* Oxford: Clarendon Press, 1891.

———. *Studies in the Arthurian Legend.* Oxford: Clarendon Press, 1891.

Ritson, Joseph. *The Life of King Arthur from Ancient Historians and Authentic Documents.* London: William Nicol, St. James, 1825.

Roberts, Brynley F. *Brut y Brenhinedd* [The Chronicle of the Kings]. Dublin: Dublin Institute of Advanced Studies, 1971.

Roberts, Peter. *Sketch on the Early History of the Cymry or Ancient Britons from 700 B.C. to A.D. 400.* London: Edward Williams, 1803.

———. *The Chronicle of the Kings of Britain.* London: Edward Williams, 1811.

Ross, Anne and Don Robins. *The Life and Death of a Druid Prince.* London: Guild Publishing, 1989.

Rutherford, Ward. *The Druids: Magicians of the West.* London: Aquarian Press, 1983.

Salway, Peter. *Roman Britain*. Oxford: Oxford University Press, 1981.

Seaby, Peter and P. Frank Purvey. *Seaby's Standard Catalogue of British Coins*. London: Seaby Publicaations, 1981.

Shaw. Stebbing. *The History and Antiquities of Staffordshire*, 1798.

Skene, W. F. *Four Ancient Books of Wales*. Edinburgh: Edmonton & Douglas, 1868.

Smith, Malcolm. *The Triads of Britain*. London: Wildwood House, 1977.

Smurthwaite, David. *The Ordnance Survey Complete Guide to the Battlefields of Britain*. Exeter: Webb & Bower, 1984.

Snailham, Richard. *Normandy and Brittany*. London: Weidenfeld & Nicolson, 1986.

Spence, Keith. *Nicholson's Guide to Brittany*. London: Robert Nicholson Publications, 1985.

Spence, Lewis. *The Legends and Romances of Brittany*. New York: Frederick A. Stokes Co., n.d.

———. *The Mysteries of Britain*. Philadelphia: David McKay, 1946.

Squire, Charles. *Celtic Myth and Legend*. Van Nuys, CA: Newcastle, 1975.

Stanford, S. C. *The Archaeology of the Welsh Marches*. London: Collins, 1980.

Stedman-Jones, Fred. "The Nanteos Cup," in *Pendragon*. Bristol: Journal of the Pendragon Society, vol. xviii. No.3, 1987.

Stein, Walter Johannes. *The Death of Merlin: Arthurian Myth and Alchemy*. Edinburgh: Floris Books, 1990.

Stenton, Frank. *Anglo-Saxon England*. Oxford: Oxford University Press, 1943.

Stephens, Meic. *The Oxford Companion to the Literature of Wales*. Oxford: Oxford University Press, 1986.

Stephens, Thomas. *The Literature of the Kymry*. 1849.

———. *Welshmen: A Sketch in their History from the Earliest Times to the Death of Llywelin the Last*. Cardiff, Wales: Western Mail, 1901.

Sterling, William. *The Canon*. London: Research into Lost Knowledge Organisation, 1981.

Stevens, C. E. *Sidonius Apollinaris and His Age*. Oxford: Clarendon Press, 1933.

———. *Magnus Maximus in British History*. Etudes Celtiques, vol. III, 1938.

Stevenson, William Henry. *Asser's Life of King Alfred*. Oxford: Clarendon Press, 1959.

Stoker, Robert B. *The Legacy of Arthur's Chester*. London: Covenant Publishing Co., 1965.

Stone, Gilbert. *Wales*. London: George G. Harrap, 1915.

Stone, T. W. *History of Hampshire*. London: Elliot Stock, 1892; republished Wakefield: E. P. Publishing, 1976.

Stubbs, Norman. *A History of Alrewas*. Alrewas, Staffordshire: R. N. Stubbs, 1987.

Sylvester, Myrddin. "Yr Afallenau Myrddin," in Thomas Stephens. *The Literature of the Kymry*. London: Longmans, Green, 1849.

Tacitus. *The Annals of Imperial Rome* A.D. 14–16. Michael Grant, trans. New York: Dorset, 1984.

Taliesin. *The Book of Taliesin.* John Gwenogvryn Evans, trans. Llanbedrog, 1910.

Tatlock, John Strong Perry. *The Dates of the Arthurian Saints' Legends.* Speculum, XIV. MA: Medieval Academy of America, 1939.

――――. *The Legendary History of Britain: Geoffrey of Monmouth's "Historia Regum Britanniae" and its Early Vernacular Versions.* Berkeley: University of California Press, 1950.

Taylor, Thomas. *The Life of St. Samson of Dol.* London: Society for Promoting Christian Knowledge, 1925.

Tennyson, Alfred, Lord. *Idylls of the King.* New York: Airmont, 1969.

Thomas, Charles. *Exploration of a Drowned Landscape.* London: Batsford, 1985.

Thorpe, Lewis. *Geoffrey of Monmouth's History of the Kings of Britain.* London: Penguin, 1966.

――――. *Gregory of Tour's History of the Franks.* London: Penguin, 1974.

Todd, Malcolm. *Roman Britain 55 b.c.–a.d. 400.* London: Fontana, 1981.

Tolkein, J. R. R. and E. V. Gordon. *Sir Gawain and the Green Knight.* Oxford: Clarendon Press, 1925.

Tolstoy, Nikolai. *The Quest for Merlin.* London: Hamish Hamilton, 1985.

Toulson, Shirley. *Celtic Journeys: Scotland and the North of England.* London: Hutchinson, 1985.

Wace, Robert. *Li Romans de Brut.* 1155. London: J.M. Dent & Sons, 1912.

Wace, Robert and Layamon. *Arthurian Chronicles.* Eugene Mason, trans. London: J. M. Dent & Sons, 1912.

Waddel, L. A. *The Phoenician Origin of Britons, Scots and Anglo-Saxons.* London: Williams & Norgate, 1924.

Wade-Evans, Arthur W. *The Life of St. David.* London: Society for Promoting Christian Knowledge, 1923.

――――. *The Emergence of England and Wales.* Cambridge: W. Heffer & Sons, 1959.

――――. *Welsh Christian Origins.* Oxford: Alden Press, 1934.

――――. *Nennius' History of the Britons.* London: Society for Promoting Christian Knowledge, 1938.

――――. *Vitae Sanctorum Britanniae et Genealogie.* Cardiff, Wales: University of Wales Press, 1944.

――――. *The Emergence of England and Wales.* Cambridge: W. Heffer & Sons, 1959.

Waite, A. E. *The Holy Grail: Its Legends and Symbolism.* London: Rider & Co., 1933.

Wheeler, R. E. M. *Prehistoric and Roman Wales.* Oxford: Clarendon Press, 1925.

――――. *Segontium and the Roman Occupation of Wales.* London: The Honourable Society of Cymmrodorion, 1923.

Whitehead, John. *Guardian of the Grail.* London: Jarrolds Publishers, 1959.

Whitlock, Dorothy. *Asser's Life of King Alfred.* Oxford: Clarendon Press, 1959.

Whitlock, Ralph. *Here Be Dragons.* London: George Allen & Unwin, 1983.

Whittaker, John. *History of Manchester.* London: Joseph Johnson, 1775.

William of Malmesbury. *The Acts of the English Kings.* Translated as *William of Malmesbury's Chronicle* by John Sharpe; revised by J. A. Giles. London: Bohn, 1947.

———. *The Kings Before the Norman Conquest.* Joseph Stephenson, trans. Felinfach, Lampeter, Wales: Llanerch, 1989.

Williams, A. H. *An Introduction to the History of Wales, vol. I: Prehistoric Times to a.d. 1063.* Cardiff, Wales: University of Wales Press Board, 1941.

Williams, David. *The History of Monmouthshire.* Monmouth: Tudor & Hall, 1796.

Williams, Gwyn. *When was Wales?* London: Penguin, 1985.

Williams, Ifor. *Breuddwyd Maxen.* Bangor, Wales: Jarvis & Foster, 1908.

———. *The Poems of Taliesin.* Dublin: Dublin Institute for Advanced Studies, 1975.

Williams, Robert. *History and Antiquities of the Town of Aber Conwy.* Denbigh, Clwyd, Wales, 1835.

Williams, Stewart. *Glamorgan Historian,* vol. I. Cowbridge, Glamorgan, Wales: D. Brown & Sons, 1963.

Williams-Nash, V. E. *The Early Christian Monuments of Wales.* Cardiff, Wales: University of Wales Press, 1950.

Williamson, David. *Debrett's Kings and Queens of Britain.* Exeter, Devon, England: Webb & Bower, 1986.

Winterbottom, Michael. *Gildas' "The Ruin of Britain and Other Documents."* London & Chichester: Phillimore, 1978.

Witney, K. P. *The Kingdom of Kent.* London & Chichester: Phillimore, 1982.

Wood, Eric S. *Collins' Field Guide to Archaeology in Britain.* London: Collins, 1982.

# GLOSSARY

## Personal Names

**Alan Fyrgan** ("White Ankle"): son of Emyr Llydaw and father of Lleuddad and Lynab.

**Aldwr** (Aldroen): king of the West Welsh settlements in Armorica 434–460, son of Rhedyw.

**Amwn Ddu** (Annun "the Black"): king of Graweg, son of Emyr Llydaw and father of St. Samson.

**Anhun Dunawd** (Antonius Donatus): king of Strathclyde and Galloway, son of Macsen Wledig.

**Anna**: daughter of Meurig, the sister of Athrwys, and the mother of St. Samson.

**Arthmael, St.**: identified with Arthur below.

**Arthur**: British Emperor 497–537.

**Athrwys**: King of Gwent, son of Meurig and father of Morgan Mwynfawr, as Arthur above.

**Bedwin**: Bishop of Gelliwig during the time of Arthur.

**Bedwyr ap** (son of) **Bedrawc**: identified with Bedivere.

**Benlli Gawr** ("the Giant"): king of Ial (Clwyd), the chief protagonist against Garmon.

**Bicanys**: son of Aldwr and the father of St. Illtyd.

**Brychan Brycheiniog** ("of the Speckled Tartan"): king of Brycheiniog, son of Anlach.

**Cadell Ddyrnllug** ("of the Gleaming Hilt"): founder king of Powys, son of Cateyrn.

**Cadfan, St.**: grandson of Emyr Llydaw and first abbot of the monastery on Ynys Enlli (Bardsey).

**Cadfarch, St.**: son of Caradog Freichfras ("of the Strong Arm"), king of Gwent.

**Cadoc, St.**: son of Gwynllyw Filwr ("the Warrior"), king of Gwynllywg (Went-looge).

**Cadwallon Lawhir** ("the Long Handed"): king of Gwynedd, son of Einion Yrth.

**Cadwy** (Cato): king of British Domnonia, son of Geraint Llyngesog ("the Fleet-owner").

**Cai ap Cynyr Ceinfarfog**: identified with Sir Kay.

**Caradog Freichfras** ("of the Strong Arm"): king of Gwent and Chief Elder of Gelliwig.

**Cawrdaf, St.**: Chief Officer of Britain, son of Caradog Freichfras and father of Medrod.

**Ceindrech**: daughter of Rheiden and the first wife of Macsen Wledig.

**Cerdic**: Earldorman of the Gewissei, the son of Elesa.

**Comereg** (Comergwynus): Bishop of Erging, the son of Meurig and brother of Athrwys.

**Cunedda Wledig** ("the Ruler"): ruler of Manau Guotodin, and founder of the kingdom of Gwynedd.

**Custennin Fendigaid** (Constantine "the Blessed"): British Emperor 433–443, son of Macsen Wledig.

**Custennin Gorneu** ("the Cornishman"): king of British Domnonia, son of Cadwy (Cato).

**Custennin Vychan** (Constans "the Younger"): British Emperor 443–446.

**Derfel Gadarn** ("the Mighty"): son of Riwal Mawr ("the Great").

**Deroch:** king of Armorican Domnonia 524–535, the son of Riwal Mawr ("the Great").

**Dyfrig** (Dubricius), St.: son of Efrddyl and grandson of Pepiau Clavorauc.

**Efflam, St.:** son of the Irish king of Dyfed and associate of Arthur in Armorica.

**Efrddyl** (Ebrdil), St.: daughter of Pepiau Clavorauc and mother of St. Dyfrig.

**Einion Yrth** ("the Impetuous"): king of Gwynedd, the son of Cunedda Wledig.

**Elen Luyddog** (Helen "of the Hosts"): daughter of Eudaf Hen and second wife of Macsen.

**Elesa:** son of Esla and the father of Cerdic, Earldorman of the Gewissei.

**Emrys Wledig** (Ambrosius "the Imperator"): British Emperor 465–497.

**Emyr Llydaw** (the "Armorican"): ruler of the West Welsh settlements in Armorica 460–509.

**Erbin:** king of British Domnonia, son of Custennin Fendigaid and father of Geraint.

**Eudaf Hen** (Octavius "the Aged"): prince of Arfon, Gwent, Erging and Ewyas.

**Garmon, St.:** Bishop of Aleth and Man, the son of St. Rhedyw (Ridicus).

**Geraint Llyngesog** (Gerontius "the Fleet-owner"): king of British Domnonia, son of Erbin.

**Germanus, St.:** Bishop of Auxerre.

**Glast:** great-grandson of Cunedda Wledig, founder of Glastonbury.

**Glywys:** king of Glywysing, son of Solor and father of Gwynllyw Filwr.

**Glywys Cernyw** ("the Cornishman"): son of Gwynllyw Filwr ("the Warrior").

**Gwalchaved** ("Hawk of Summer"): identified with Sir Galahad.

**Gwalchmai** ("Hawk of May"): identified with Sir Gawain.

**Gwenhwyfach:** daughter of Count Gwythyr and sister of Gwenhwyfar.

**Gwenhwyfar:** daughter of Count Gwythyr and Arthur's queen.

**Gwenonwy:** daughter of Meurig and sister of Athrwys.

**Gwladys:** daughter of Brychan Brycheiniog and wife of Gwynllyw Filwr.

**Gwrgant Mawr** ("the Great"): king of Erging, son of Cynfyn.

**Gwrthefyr Fendigaid** (Vortimer "the Blessed"): son and successor of Gwrtheyrn Gwrtheneu.

**Gwrtheyrn Gwrtheneu** (Vortigern "the Thin"): over-king 428–433 and 446–465.

**Gwyndaf Hen** ("the Aged"): king of Erging, the son of Emyr Llydaw and father of Henwyn.

**Gwynllyw Filwr** ("the Warrior"): king of Gwynllywg, son of Glywys of Glywysing.

**Gwythian:** Count of Gelliwig, son of Count Gwythyr of Léon.

Gwythyr: Count of Léon, father of Count Gwythian of Gelliwig and Gwen-hwyfar.

Henwyn, St.: son of Gwyndaf Hen and his wife Gwenonwy. He became abbot of Ynys Enlli (Bardsey).

Hywel Farchog ("the Knight"): son of Emyr Llydaw. Identified with Riwal Mawr.

Ian Reith: king of Armorican Cornouaille, identified with Riothamus.

Illtyd Farchog ("the Knight"): son of Bicanys and great nephew of St. Garmon.

Jonas: king of Armorican Domnonia 535–549, son of Deroch.

Judwal: king of Armorican Domnonia 555–580, son of Jonas.

Llacheu ("the Gleaming or Glittering One"): son of the Emperor Arthur.

Llwch Wyddel ("the Irishman") or Llwch Llawinawg (Lord of the Lakes): Sir Lancelot.

Macsen Wledig (Maximus "the Imperator"): Western Roman Emperor 383–388.

Madryn (Matriona), St.: daughter of Gwrthefyr Fendigaid and wife of Ynyr I of Gwent.

Maelgwyn Hir ("the Tall White Prince"): king of Gwynedd 517–547, son of Cadwallon Lawhir.

March ap Meirchion (Marcus son of Marcianus): identified with Marcus Conomorus.

Marcus Conomorus: Count of Poher and Léon and ruler of Armorican Dom-nonia 549–555.

Medrod or Medraut (Mordred): son of Cawrdaf and Arthur's chief adversary.

Meirchion Vesanus (Marcianus "the Mad"): son of Glywys and father of March.

Meurig: king of Gwent, son of Tewdric and father of Athrwys.

Modron: daughter of Afallach and wife of Urien of Gorre. Identified with Mor-gan Le Fay.

Morgan Mwynfawr (Morcant "the Most Courteous"): king of Gwent and Morgannwg.

Myrddin Emrys (Merlin Ambrosius).

Myrddin Wyllt (Merlin "the Wild").

Octha I (Hengist).

Octha II (Osla Gyllellfawr).

Onbrawst: daughter of Gwrgant Mawr, the wife of Meurig and the mother of Athrwys.

Osla Gyllellfawr ("of the Long Knife"): enemy of Arthur. Identified with Octha II.

Owain Danwyn ("the White-toothed"): prince of Rhos, son of Einion Yrth ("the Impetuous").

Owain Finddu ("the Black-lipped"): Pendragon 388–394, son of Macsen Wledig and Ceindrech.

Paul Aurelian, St.: son of Count Porphyrius Aurelianus and companion of St. Arthmael.

Pepiau Clavorauc ("the Dravellor"): king of Erging, son of Erb.

**Porphyrius Aurelianus** ("the Red Dragon"): Count, father of St. Paul Aurelian.

**Riothamus** (Ian Reith): king of Armorican Cornouaille.

**Riwal Mawr** ("the Great"): king of Armorican Domnonia 509–524, son of Emyr Llydaw.

**Samson, St.:** son of Amwn-Ddu and his wife Anna, daughter of Meurig.

**Selyf:** son of Geraint Llyngesog.

**Sevira:** daughter of Macsen Wledig and Elen Luyddog, and wife of Gwrtheyrn (Vortigern).

**Teithfallt:** king of Gwent, son of Teithrin.

**Tewdrig Fendigaid** (Theodosius "the Blessed"): king of Gwent, son of Teith-fallt.

**Tristan:** son of Marcus Conomorus.

**Urien of Gorre:** Identified with Gwrgant Mawr.

**Uthyr Pendragon:** Pendragon 497–512, the son of Custennin Fendigaid.

**Yvain** (Owain): Knight of Léon, son of Urien of Gorre and Modron.

## Welsh Place-Names

| Welsh Name .. | English Translation ..... | Example from Text |
| --- | --- | --- |
| aber ........ | river mouth .......... | Abertwggi (Mouth of the Troggy) |
| allt ......... | wooded hillside ........ | Allt Gwynllyw (Gwynllyw's Wooded Hillside) |
| afon ........ | river | |
| arth........ | bear | |
| bangor ...... | great choir or college .... | Bangor Illtyd (Illtyd's Great Choir) |
| bedd ........ | grave ............... | Bedd Illtyd (Illtyd's Grave) |
| betws ....... | house of prayer ....... | Betws Garmon (Garmon's House of Prayer) |
| blaen........ | source of river | |
| borth........ | harbor .............. | Llongborth (Harbor of Boats) |
| bryn ........ | hill | |
| cadair ....... | seat ................ | Cadair Cawrdaf (Cawrdaf's Seat) |
| caer......... | fortress, city or camp.... | Caer Caradoc (Caradoc's Fortress) |
| capel........ | chapel .............. | Capel Curig (Curig's Chapel) |
| carn ........ | cairn ............... | Carn Fadrun (Madryn's Cairn) |
| carreg ....... | rock | |
| castell ....... | castle ............... | Castell Gwalchmai (Gawain's Castle) |
| cefn ........ | ridge ............... | Cefn Ceidio (Ceidio's Ridge) |
| cerrig........ | stones | |

| | | |
|---|---|---|
| coed . . . . . . . . | wood . . . . . . . . . . . . . . . | Gwent-is-Coed (Gwent below the Wood) |
| cor . . . . . . . . . | choir or college . . . . . . . | Cor Emrys (Choir of Ambrosius) |
| craig . . . . . . . . | rock . . . . . . . . . . . . . . . . | Craig Gwrtheyrn (Vortigern's Rock) |
| croes . . . . . . . . | cross | |
| cwm . . . . . . . . | valley . . . . . . . . . . . . . . . | Cwm Cattwg (Cadoc's Valley) |
| dinas . . . . . . . . | hill-fortress or citadel . . . . | Dinas Emrys (Fortress of Ambrosius) |
| dyffryn . . . . . . | valley of a river | |
| eglwys . . . . . . . | church | |
| ffynnon . . . . . . | well or spring | |
| gaer . . . . . . . . . | fort or camp . . . . . . . . . . | Mynydd-y-Gaer (Mountain of the Fortress) |
| gallt . . . . . . . . | wood or hillside | |
| garth . . . . . . . . | headland of enclosure . . . | Garth Madryn (Madryn's Enclosure) |
| gelli . . . . . . . . . | grove . . . . . . . . . . . . . . . | Llan-y-Gelli (Church of the Grove) |
| glan . . . . . . . . . | river bank | |
| glas . . . . . . . . . | green | |
| glyn . . . . . . . . . | glen | |
| gors . . . . . . . . . | marsh | |
| hafod . . . . . . . | summer dwelling | |
| hen . . . . . . . . . | old | |
| hir . . . . . . . . . . | long or tall | |
| llan . . . . . . . . . | church or sacred enclosure | Llangystennin (Constantine's Church) |
| llech . . . . . . . . | flat stone . . . . . . . . . . . . | Llech Gwrtheyrn (Vortigern's Stone) |
| llwyn . . . . . . . . | bush or grove | |
| llygad . . . . . . . | smooth stream . . . . . . . . | Llygad Amir (Amir's Stream) |
| llyn . . . . . . . . . | lake . . . . . . . . . . . . . . . . | Llyn Llydaw (Lake of the Armorican) |
| llys . . . . . . . . . | court . . . . . . . . . . . . . . . | Llys Brychan (Brychan's Court) |
| maes . . . . . . . . | field or plain . . . . . . . . . . | Maes Garmon (Garmon's Field) |
| melin . . . . . . . . | mill . . . . . . . . . . . . . . . . | Llanmelin (Church of the Mill) |
| merthyr . . . . . . | martyrium . . . . . . . . . . . | Merthyr Tewdrig (Tewdrig's Martyrium) |
| moel . . . . . . . . | bare hill . . . . . . . . . . . . . | Moel Fenlli (Benlli's Bare Hill) |
| mynydd . . . . . . | mountain . . . . . . . . . . . . | Mynydd-y-Gaer (Mountain of the Fortress) |
| nant . . . . . . . . | small valley . . . . . . . . . . | Nant Gwrtheyrn (Vortigern's Valley) |
| pant . . . . . . . . | hollow | |
| pen . . . . . . . . . | head . . . . . . . . . . . . . . . . | Penmark (Mark's Head) |

plas . . . . . . . . mansion or hall
pont . . . . . . . . bridge
porth. . . . . . . gateway or harbor . . . . . . Porth-is-Coed (Harbor below the
                                                Wood)
pwll . . . . . . . . pool . . . . . . . . . . . . . . . . Pwll Meurig (Meurig's Pool)
rhos . . . . . . . . moorland
sarn. . . . . . . . . causeway . . . . . . . . . . . . Sarn Elen (Elen's Causeway)
tir . . . . . . . . . . land
traeth . . . . . . . beach . . . . . . . . . . . . . . . Traeth Troit (Beach of the Pig)
ty . . . . . . . . . . house . . . . . . . . . . . . . . . Ty Gwydr (House of Glass)
ynys . . . . . . . . island . . . . . . . . . . . . . . . Ynys Afallach (Afallach's Island)

# INDEX

# the authors

Chris Barber FRGS lives in Llanfoist, Abergavenny, Gwent, and has worked as an industrial research technician, Chief Instructor at an outdoor education center and from 1976–1996 was responsible for the organization of the Gwent County Council Countryside Service. On taking early retirement he has been writing, lecturing and publishing. During the last twenty years, he has written seventeen books, with particular emphasis on the mysteries and legends of Wales. His beautifully illustrated lectures, based on his books are very popular and his skills as a photographer and writer are widely acknowledged.

David Pykitt lives in Burton-on-Trent and worked in Derby as an administrator with East Midlands Electricity until 1993, when he took early retirement. Since an early age, he has been fascinated by the mystery of King Arthur and the history of Dark Age Britain. In recent years, he has had several articles published in the journal of the Research into Lost Knowledge Organisation and the Pendragon Society.

By undertaking an intensive program of research, these two authors have combined their knowledge to unravel one of the greatest mysteries of all time. Not since *The Holy Blood, Holy Grail* has such a fascinating book of historical detection been published.

*Journey to Avalon* will no doubt prove to be very controversial, for so much has been written about King Arthur and new theories are being produced by authors every few years. However, Chris Barber and David Pykitt have provided a solution to this intriguing riddle that is convincing and conclusive, throwing new light on the forgotten history of Dark Age Britain.